THE FOUNDING
OF INSTITUTIONAL
ECONOMICS

Institutional economics has been a major part of economic thought for the whole of the twentieth century, and today remains crucial to the understanding of the development of heterodox economics. The two principal publications that founded the school were Veblen's *The Theory of the Leisure Class* and Commons' *A Sociological View of Sovereignty*, both published in 1899.

As a tribute to these two seminal works, Warren Samuels has assembled an exceptionally prestigious international group of scholars to produce this landmark volume celebrating the centenary. The chapters assess the work of Veblen and Commons and their influence on the school of institutional economics from a variety of theoretical perspectives. The contributions on Veblen appraise his anthropological analysis of consumption habits of American households from sociological, linguistic and feminist points of view. Conversely, the essays on Commons' work focus on the concepts of property, power and the relationship between laws and economics.

The following have contributed: Glen Atkinson, Philippe Broda, E. Ray Canterbery, Richard Dawson, Richard Gonce, David Hamilton, Lewis E. Hill, Geoffrey Hodgson, Ann Jennings, Margaret Lewis, Anne Mayhew, Steven G. Medema, Edythe S. Miller, David Sebberson, Rick Tilman and Marc R. Tool.

Warren J. Samuels is Professor of Economics at Michigan State University, specializing in the history of economic thought, methodology, and law and economics.

ROUTLEDGE STUDIES IN
THE HISTORY OF ECONOMICS

THE FOUNDING
OF INSTITUTIONAL
ECONOMICS

The Leisure Class and Sovereignty

Edited by

Warren J. Samuels

London and New York

First published 1998
by Routledge
11 New Fetter Lane, London EC4P 4EE

Simultaneously published in the USA and Canada
by Routledge
29 West 35th Street, New York, NY 10001

Typeset in Garamond by
The Florence Group Limited, Stoodleigh, Devon
Printed and bound in Great Britain by
Biddles Ltd, Guildford and King's Lynn

British Library Cataloguing in Publication Data
A catalogue record for this book is available from the British Library

Library of Congress Cataloguing in Publication Data
The founding of institutional economics : the leisure class and
sovereignty / edited by Warren J. Samuels.
Includes bibliographical references and index.
1. Institutional economics. I. Samuels, Warren J.
HB99.5.F68 1998
330.1–dc21   98-9405

ISBN 0–415–18757–5

In tribute to John R. Commons and
Thorstein B. Veblen, for their contributions
to the demystification of economy,
polity and society.

CONTENTS

CONTRIBUTORS

Professor Glen Atkinson
Department of Economics
University of Nevada, Reno
Reno, NV 89557–0016 USA

Dr. Philippe Broda
ICN-Pole Lorrain de Gestion
13 rue Michel Ney – CO 75
54037 Nancy Cedex, France

Professor E. Ray Canterbery
Department of Economics
Florida State University
Tallahassee, FL 32306 USA

Mr. Richard Dawson
Department of Economics
University of Auckland
Private Bag
Auckland, New Zealand

Professor Richard Gonce
Department of Economics
Grand Valley State University
Allendale, MI 49401 USA

Professor David Hamilton
Department of Economics
University of New Mexico
Albuquerque, NM 87131–1101 USA

Professor Lewis E. Hill
Department of Economics
Texas Tech University
Lubbock, TX 79409–1014 USA

Professor Geoffrey M. Hodgson
Judge Institute of Management Studies
University of Cambridge
Mill Lane
Cambridge CB2 1RX United Kingdom

Professor Ann Jennings
Department of Economics and Business
Lafayette College
Easton, PA 18042–1776 USA

Professor Margaret Lewis
Department of Economics
College of Saint Benedict
St. Joseph, MN 56374 USA

Professor Anne Mayhew
Department of Economics
University of Tennessee
Knoxville, TN 37996–0550 USA

Professor Steven G. Medema
Department of Economics
University of Colorado at Denver
Denver, CO 80217–3364 USA

Professor Edythe S. Miller
580 Front Range Road
Littleton, CO 80120 USA

Professor David Sebberson
Department of English
St. Cloud State University
St. Cloud, MN 56301–4498 USA

Professor Rick Tilman
809 W. Murray Road
Flagstaff, AZ 86001 USA

Professor Marc R. Tool
5708 McAdoo Avenue
Sacramento, CA 95819–2516 USA

INTRODUCTION

Warren J. Samuels

In 1899 Thorstein Veblen published *The Theory of the Leisure Class* and in
1899–1900 John R. Commons published in *The American Journal of Sociology*
the series *A Sociological View of Sovereignty* (subsequently edited by Joseph
Dorfman and published as a book in 1965 by Augustus Kelley). This volume
commemorates the centenary of these publications. It particularly commemorates them as founding, or at least foreshadowing, the school of thought
which eventually became known as Institutional Economics. Although both
writers, perhaps especially Commons, were intellectually ambitious, it is
probably the case that neither of them intended or expected to found such
a school.[1]

The choice of these two publications is admittedly somewhat arbitrary.
By 1899 (when he turned 42) Veblen had published several relatively
conventional articles and essays on the barbaric status of women, the instinct
of workmanship and the beginnings of ownership. In 1898 he published
his brilliant and now famous essay on why economics is not an evolutionary
science. In 1898–1899 he published his equally brilliant and now almost-
as-famous three-part series on the preconceptions of economic science. Surely
those essays were monumental; they established central methodological
themes for institutional economics. But *The Theory of the Leisure Class* went
beyond criticism and programmatic prescription. It conducted institutional
analysis, providing empirically grounded theoretical, if interpretive, analyses
of certain habits and their place in economic and cultural life. The book is
one of the greatest and most original works published by an American.

By 1899 (when he turned 37) Commons had published his books *The
Distribution of Wealth* (1893), *Social Reform and the Church* (1894), and
Proportional Representation (1896) as well as close to two dozen articles in
economics, religious and other journals. Taken together this earlier work
indicates his breadth and catholicity of interest, social activism and incipient
theoretical interest. *A Sociological View of Sovereignty* demonstrated the combination of (1) his concern with deep structural problems and processes, (2)
his interest in theorizing about those problems and processes, and (3) his
practice of trying to stay close to the actual world of affairs. In particular

we see here the beginnings of Commons's analyses of the legal foundations of the economic system and of wherein those legal foundations fit into a larger analysis of the economic system as a whole. The former culminated in his *Legal Foundations of Capitalism* (1924) and the latter, in his *Institutional Economics* (1934).

Accordingly, this volume celebrates the centenary of Institutional Economics, without putting too fine a point on it, by focusing on *Leisure Class* and *Sovereignty*. The individual authors, each in their own way, appraise and interpret these works and their contribution, as well as other aspects of the intellectual careers of Veblen and Commons.

The essays were commissioned for this volume. The authors were given complete discretion consistent with the rationale of the volume; they could write on either or both of the centenary writings. They have responded with an imposing variety of topics and insights. Two essays, by David Hamilton and Edythe E. Miller, deal, respectively, with a source common to both Veblen and Commons and with the concept of community relevant to them. Four further essays relate to Commons's work and nine to Veblen's. This distribution was not designed; it developed from the interests of their authors. In addition, I have contributed a short piece which reproduces and comments upon a short newspaper piece by Commons which antedates *A Sociological View of Sovereignty* but prefigures his research program, of which *Sovereignty* is an early major result.

The essays on Commons's work not surprisingly deal with property, power, and the legal basis of the economic system. Those on Veblen's work treat the leisure class phenomenon itself; the relevant theory of demand; his contributions to normative instrumentalism and to evolutionary economics; his treatment of feminist and anthropological subjects; the rhetoricality of Veblen's book; Veblen in relation to Georg Simmel; and Veblen's theory of social change.

I am indebted to the authors of the contributions to this collection and to the staff of Routledge.

NOTE

1 I have some doubts about that: Both men wanted to advance the development of an economics broader and less mechanistic than the developing mainstream practice; and probably both, certainly Commons, had in mind a "movement," which is pretty close to a "school."

Part I

VEBLEN AND COMMONS

1

VEBLEN, COMMONS, AND THE INDUSTRIAL COMMISSION

David Hamilton

At the opening of the nineteenth century the American economy was by every measure an agrarian one; by its close it was an industrial economy (Adams, 1961 [1889]; US Industrial Commission, 1902–3). That does not mean that the agrarian dimension diminished; it most certainly had not done so at any time during the transformation from agrarianism to industrialism. Even today, when the agrarian dimension is a relatively small fraction of the total economy, American agricultural products provide a significant part of the world's food supply. But the growth in industrialism was so startling following the Civil War that it permanently surpassed the agrarian dimension in relative importance.

While the new industrialism was accepted with a certain amount of delight, as testified by the public response to the industrial wonders of the Philadelphia Exposition of 1876, the new forms of business organization that accompanied the technological change were troubling to the American economic mind. In fact, even today, that economic mind is troubled by an attempt to accommodate these new forms of organization to an economic model that came to the shores of the western Atlantic two and even three hundred years ago. The dominant economic collective representations at the close of the nineteenth century were still those that prevailed at its opening. As Joseph Dorfman contended in *The Economic Mind in American Civilization*, that mind was largely imbedded in the notions of Adam Smith concerning the virtues of a competitive market (Dorfman, 1946).

Much of the social discontent that prevailed in the agrarian sector in the second half of the nineteenth century was generated by contact between the still competitively organized agrarian economy and the industrial economy, which was rather rapidly diverging from the competitive ideal. The farmer met the new dispensation daily as cash crop agriculture as well as ranching opened along the routes of the newly created rail net. It cut two ways.

3

Everything needed for this type of agriculture came in by rail; everything produced left by rail. And there usually was but one railroad dominant in any region, which was most certainly organized in the corporate form in contrast to the sole proprietorship that still characterized the agrarian dimension. The family farm faced daily the impersonal corporation at the railroad depot, coming and going. The railroad was the symbol for this alien intrusion into what, according to folk memory, had been a simpler and more natural way of life.

However, the railroad was merely the most visible means by which the industrial discipline made its presence known to the relatively declining agrarian economy. The rancher and farmer who raised cattle, sheep, or hogs found that meat packing, once a function of a local slaughter house, had been mechanized and centralized. The development of the reefer car meant that meat could be slaughtered in Chicago, Cincinnati, Omaha, and Fort Worth and shipped to the rest of the nation, once dependent upon local slaughter houses for fresh killed meat. But, with such nationalization, control of the price seemed to pass from the farmer and rancher to rather impersonal stockyard and packing companies far from the open range on which the product was raised.

A similar change affected grain production. Flour producers and cereal processors were found in central cities processing the grains from the farms not just for domestic use, but for an international market as well. Grain prices seemed to be determined by speculators in impersonal markets far removed from the site of production. And although farmers were still large in numbers, they were selling to a diminishing number of buyers. The market was national and international; any personal relationship between seller and buyer in a local market as envisioned in Adam Smith's economics had long vanished. The farmer was a price taker; those to whom he sold his product seemed to be price makers.

And so it went with the items that farmers bought. The industrial discipline was impinging upon the farmers, still largely horse-dependent for power, by the development of planting, cultivating, and harvesting machinery. The later twentieth-century displacement of horsepower by gasoline- and diesel-driven prime movers was foreshadowed by the development of steam-powered harvesting and threshing machinery. Awkward as those innovations seem today, they correctly forecast the mechanization that even agriculture was bound to take up. Although mechanical cotton pickers were still a long way off, the direction was clear. Here, too, the farmer ran into impersonal corporations that manufactured the machinery in central locations and sold the machinery through local agents, who had the same kind of limited autonomy over sales conditions as do automobile dealers today. International Harvester and McCormick seemed heartless entities in corporate form (Singer, *et al.*, Vol. 5, Chs 1, 2).

One of the consequences of the 1862 Morrill Act was to hasten the contact of the American farmer with the new industrial discipline. The Act provided for a system of land grant colleges to make the latest in agricultural knowledge available through both university education and an extension system disseminating the latest research in methods and crops to farmers on the farm. But this set up a demand for new seed and fertilizers, as well as farm machinery, from central producers, thus making one more contact linking the farmer to the industrial economy and its impersonalities.

If these were the major points of contact between the farmer and the new industrial discipline, the consumer became aware of it by a flow of new products the cultural incidence of which was to change the "American way of life." Gas lighting systems in the growing cities was one of the by-products of the petroleum industry in the mid-century, but was soon to be displaced by the development of central station electricity by the 1880s. A new entity, the public utility for gas and electricity, entered the American way of life to join the railroad. But these services were delivered by monopolies that did not conform to the classic competitive model.

The same entities to which the farmer's fate seemed increasingly attached also impinged on the urban dweller and consumer through the food chain. As menacingly portrayed by the cartoonist Nast in *Harper's*, the consumer was confronted by the meat packing, sugar, whiskey, flour, cereal, and other "trusts" delivering much of what the farmer produced to the consumer, seemingly infinite in numbers, facing a finite number of processors. And at the top of them all was the new oil trust in a civilization becoming rapidly dependent upon petroleum products. And, of course, each trust had their strings to powerful senators of the day as Nast portrayed in one of his almost immortal cartoons.

To the economic mind of the public this was all rather troubling and perplexing. At least at the end of the century the trick of accommodating awkward facts to a long-held ideology by verbally redefining the awkward facts to fit the ideology had not yet been accomplished. "Contestable markets" were still a long time off. The large-scale corporate organizations that made feasible the private ownership of large-scale technology were commonly referred to as "trusts," although the Sherman Act had eliminated the use of the actual legal form of a trust. The nimble minds of attorneys and corporate promoters rapidly developed other devices to achieve the same end. The term "trust" became a generic one that referred, with a certain degree of largely unhidden animosity, to that which was viewed as contrary to the natural order outlined by Smith. And hence there were the steel, the oil, the sugar, the whiskey, the meat-packing, the rail and other trusts, all raising troubling questions. Just what was their origin and what was their function? Were they not somehow contrary to the historical and ancient way of economic life? Were they not pestiferous invasions of an almost divinely ordained market? While the technology over which these new trusts held ownership may have been welcomed, as it was in Philadelphia, were not these forms of business organization contrary to social well-being?

5

Unlike today, when the corporate world is perceived as benign and the governmental as detrimental to social well-being, at the turn into the twentieth century much scepticism prevailed concerning the intent and social role of the new corporate world aborning. To the conventional mind today, such an attitude seems, if not archaic, at least quaint.

Congress addressed these issues by the creation of the United States Industrial Commission to examine the form and functioning of the new industrial and business discipline. The commission members were appointed by President McKinley and the Commission did its work at the turn of the century. The research and inquiry of the United States Industrial Commission was but one of two times that there was a concerted effort to determine the actual nature and character of the American economy. The second was the work of the Temporary National Economic Committee in the late 1930s. The latter patterned its inquiry on that of the earlier Industrial Commission. Both acknowledge the fact that it takes what at least seem to be major catastrophes to force us to do what Guy Routh refers to as "look and see" (Routh, 1977). The way of conventional wisdom is to seek knowledge by deduction and redefinition. But the seeming incongruity of the "trusts" with that conventional wisdom was sufficiently apparent at the turn of the century to provoke looking and seeing. The Depression of the 1930s was sufficient to provoke another "look and see."

The Industrial Commission had subpoena power, but it was not a body intent on ascertaining criminal behavior; it was interested in economic behavior. It employed economists and other experts familiar with industry and business rather than a swarm of lawyers. And, while much of the information was secured by testimony secured from questioning witnesses, there was no inference of wrong-doing even though some of the behavior revealed might have provoked outrage on the part of those strongly imbued with the conventional wisdom of the time. Witnesses and the specialists employed by the commission submitted exhibits that were to be published in the Reports of the Commission, of which there were some nineteen long and heavy volumes.

In the course of its inquiry, the Commission probed the reasons for the combination movement that characterized the second half of the post-Civil War era. The matter that attracted attention was the combination of previously independent companies into large corporations dominating an industry. The most prominent and notable cases were, of course, the Standard Oil Company and later the United States Steel Corporation. But attention was also given to the occurrence of a "big three" or a "big four" as in meat-packing, where the participants acted in consort. These situations were the most obvious diversions from the "tried and true" competitive model. Time was taken to determine the causes of such combinations. Some insisted that it was a matter of "excess" competition that led to combination in order to defend against "cut-throat" competition. Others saw as the driving force

6

against competition what would later be referred to as the economies of scale. And there was testimony from business leaders that put the matter in this light. One might easily be led to conclude that the first cause was driven by business ambitions and the second by efforts to achieve greater engineering efficiency. This distinction, however, was not one made by either the businessmen testifying or by the Commission in its final Report.

Of course, such explanations were in conformance with the conventional notion of a competitive market. These reasons for combination were simply expressions of an attempt to maintain either order or greater efficiency. In either event the public was supposed to benefit from the more orderly market and from efficiencies of scale. No one seemed to raise the question of just how a reduction in the level of competition could benefit a public which, according to the conventional theory, thrived only in its presence. Nor was the question raised that, if combination aimed at securing economies of scale reduced the number of competitors, just how those economies of scale would be passed off to the public in the form of a reduced price.

Questions such as these were almost precluded by the nature of the inquiry. The testimony of the participants in the combination movement could hardly be expected to delve into possible deleterious consequences of their activity. They themselves were, of course, habituated to viewing their own activities in the best possible light. Private vice, was a public virtue. And after all it was St Adam himself who indicated that in the pursuit of self-interest businessmen worked an end not part of their intention as though guided by an invisible hand. Since such an attitude was a part of the received theory, who would deny its applicability to the present scene at the end of the nineteenth century? Most certainly not the major participants who were also the major witnesses, if not even among the major beneficiaries. Of course, there was testimony from aggrieved participants who had not fared well in the process of combination. This was all to the effect that the winners had been rather ruthless in pursuing what might well have been called economic manifest destiny.

But what does become quite clear in the hearings was a matter which was no part of its intention. The most startling case and one that attracted national attention far beyond the bounds of the Industrial Commission was that of the creation of the United States Steel Corporation, which exhibited every aspect of the combination period that differentiated it from the early nineteenth century.

United States Steel was a combination worked by the tycoons, the bankers, and startling personalities in the business world of the time. What made it so unusual at the time was its position as the first billion-dollar corporation in the history of the country. Its story was recounted in detail in the hearings of the Industrial Commission. It is far more helpful in understanding what was going on than are the details of the Standard Oil Company, also present in the hearings, because the latter is much more lurid and one is apt to lose sight of the ball in all the intrigue. The account is also helpful in that it illustrates that, although ostensibly the whole matter was one of controlling competition and of realizing economies of scale, these were incidental to the major drama.

In the case of United States Steel the major participants in the steel industry prior to its creation were concerned over the alleged efforts of Andrew Carnegie to introduce by several means greater competition in the already fairly concentrated steel industry: threatening to build a railroad from Pittsburgh paralleling the eastward course of the Pennsylvania Railroad as an alternative means of getting steel to the East Coast; building a new rolling-mill at Conneaut, Ohio; and enlarging the open-hearth capacity of the Edgar Thompson works at Homestead, Pennsylvania. This was all interpreted as an effort to disrupt the stable "competitive" situation that was then alleged to characterize the steel industry. Whether it was the intended effect or not, the other steel barons made a plea to the investment banker most prominent in the steel industry as well as rails, J. P. Morgan, by his investment prowess, to fund a consolidation of steel companies that constituted 65 percent of steel capacity at the time.

It was contended that the aggregate pecuniary value of these assorted companies, including that of Carnegie, was in the range of $700 million. However, put together in one combine as United States Steel the same physical properties had a capitalized worth of approximately $1.4 billion. Since steel mills, unlike mushrooms, do not spring up overnight and since this fact is known even to the mentally sluggish, this case alone made clear what came to be the major revelation of the Industrial Commission: the capital value of any corporation had little or no relation to the pecuniary value of the physical properties the capitalized value had always supposedly represented. The physical assets, or physical capital, was separate and distinct from the capitalized value of the corporation. The latter was the capitalized value of the anticipated rate of return on the pecuniary investment. It meant that the capital value of a corporation was wholly dependent upon the pecuniary earning power of that corporation, not on the pecuniary value of its physical assets no matter how calculated, on the basis of original cost or at replacement cost.

Traditionally the pecuniary value of a corporation was held to have a close relationship to the real capital of that entity. The term capital had one meaning. It could be either the physical stuff called capital or it could be the pecuniary value of that physical stuff. The pecuniary meaning was the measure of the physical stuff. But if the hearings of the Industrial Commission had any meaning we had one word for two separate and distinct things. And it was not just a matter of confusion. Two things were going on at the same time; the production of steel and the creation of money. And both were designated by the same word which led to the notion that when one activity was taking place so was the other. The enhancement of pecuniary values was taken as synonymous with the production of goods and services.

So it had been in economics from the time of the ancients long before Adam Smith. In order to make money it was necessary to make goods, or at least so it was contended. Any pecuniary return was taken as evidence of having rendered some real service. If there was a seeming discrepancy between the pecuniary return and the real value presumably produced, it was taken as evidence of monopoly. And so some took the reports of the Industrial Commission to mean that just such a discrepancy did exist in the new industrial economy and that it was evidence of the dimension of the monopoly problem. It suggested that anti-monopoly measures were called for. To these individuals the revelations indicated that vigilance on behalf of competition was a perennial need and that the market was the best of all possible arrangements only in the absence of monopoly. Not many interpreted the revelations to mean that large-scale organization was a function of large-scale technology; nor that money could be made solely by the deft manipulation of the paper that represented ownership claims.

The issuance of stock was on the basis of the capitalized earning power of the corporation and hence anything that could be argued to have contributed to the earnings could be capitalized. Of course, such things as good-will, patents, trade names, brands, and even advertising to secure an advantageous position could be said to have contributed to those earnings and thereby worthy of capitalization. Some of the more fastidious witnesses before the Commission felt that there should remain some traditional relationship between preferred stock and the physical assets of the corporation, but that all the rest, now referred to as intangible capital, was fair game for capitalization. Not only was there testimony in favor of such notions, but in the world of business such practices were now accomplished fact: it was the way of the world of business.

Despite the allegations of some purists that this extension of capital to the "intangibles" was nothing short of stock watering, a heinous offense once held to be the *modus operandi* of the true robber barons, Jay Gould, Jim Fiske, and Daniel Drew, it represented the way of the future. Again United States Steel was the prime example. By securing 65 per cent of the basic steel capacity of the nation, USS was indeed able to control the price, and, in fact exercised that power, the most prominent feature of which was the annual Gary dinner at which the base price for steel was announced to all the guests. The guests were the "independent" steel barons who played follow-the-leader with USS. The game remained intact for at least five decades, and it enabled USS to maintain a break-even point at 35 percent of capacity. The value of the water, air, intangibles, or whatever had been capitalized, was sustained by the earning power of the corporation. This, of course, was merely the largest example of the new way of business life brought forth in the second half of the nineteenth century. Forty new millionaires had been created in the Carnegie Steel Company alone and their new wealth was sustained by the strategic position of USS in the American industrial economy. Microsoft, which provokes so much surprise today, should not be surprising. It is really the same song, second, or perhaps third, verse.

To the conventional economics this separation of real from financial capital was a troublesome practice and proposition. To the traditional economist land, labor, and capital were the real substances out of which came a flow of real goods and services. It was as contributors to these real goods and services that incomes in the form of rent, wages, and interest were justified. All the factors of production are equal, but, in fact, capital had always been more equal than the others. It was the life-blood and primary force of capitalism. The very name of the system was derived from this primary force. But if, in fact, it could be no more than the capitalized value of the contribution of a trade name to the ultimate vendibility of a product, it was indeed a troublesome development. On the other hand, if the goods produced represented no more than subjective feelings or utilities then the nebulousness of production joined the parallel nebulousness of consumption. The Industrial Commission was not innocent in its findings.

To some the Industrial Commission merely drew out the details of the monopoly problem in all of its ramifications. It indicated how far the economy had strayed from the classic and simplistic model of the founding Saints: Smith, Malthus, and Ricardo. In all aspects of the economy – banking, insurance, manufacturing, transportation, and even organized labor – there were threatening elements of monopoly. In the conventional view the meaning of the reports was a call for vigorous enforcement of the anti-trust laws. And the government, indeed, under Roosevelt as well as his successor, Taft, entered a period of vigorous enforcement, the culmination of which was the breakup of the Standard Oil Company at the end of the first decade of the twentieth century. To most of those who took this course and saw this meaning in the Reports, monopoly seemed to be a manifestation of conspiracies to enhance profits, evidence for Smith's admonition that businessmen never get together even for conviviality without it ending in a conspiracy against the public interest.

But if the findings of the Commission were not innocent, and were perhaps even subversive of conventional theory, so were the developments in what came to be known as institutionalism, the rudiments of which first manifested themselves in the work of Thorstein Veblen and later in that of John R. Commons. Veblen made his mark in the final decade of the nineteenth century with *The Theory of the Leisure Class*, although a dozen or so essays preceded that major work. Commons earlier spread a rather wide net in sociology as well as economics, but was an active participant in the inquiries of the Industrial Commission. He completed a study of the impact of immigration on labor. The massive immigration of the final two decades of the nineteenth century, largely from Europe in the East and mid-West and from the Orient in the West, especially in rail transportation, mining, and lumbering, provided a workforce for the new industrialism. The impact of this population influx on wage rates and labor conditions was one of the peripheral issues examined by the Commission. Commons participated on this part of the inquiry. On the other hand, Veblen had no direct participation in the work of the Commission, but was well aware of its reports and used them to analyze the business system. That analysis came out as *The Theory of Business Enterprise* in 1904.

While it would not be possible to argue that the economics of either Veblen or Commons derived solely from the Reports of the Industrial Commission, a substantial case can be made that they were both influenced by the insight into the new industrial economy the Reports did provide (Dorfman, 1934, 223; Commons, 1959 [1934], 649–77). In *Institutional Economics*, in a section largely devoted to Veblen's dichotomy of business and industry, Commons is a willing participant in so far as the distinction between real and intangible capital is concerned. He most certainly did appreciate the impact such a distinction had on the traditional notion of capital. The traditional meaning, in which the pecuniary value was the measure of the size and extent of real capital, could no longer be held. An expansion in capitalization did not necessarily mean an expansion in real productive assets. It could mean no more than a pecuniary enhancement of ownership equities.

In the distinction Veblen made between business and industry, Commons seemed to agree when he made a distinction between wealth and assets and reinforced it when he said that the populace at large had an interest in increasing wealth while business had an interest in maintaining scarcity so as to maintain the pecuniary value of assets. And when he later made a distinction between engineering efficiency and business efficiency he seemed to be in agreement with Veblen (Hamilton, 1953).

However, it must be admitted that Commons, while making these distinctions, did write in *Institutional Economics*, in an analysis of Veblen's *Theory of Business Enterprise*, that Veblen was indeed too acerbic concerning business. And when the courts interpreted business efforts to maintain scarcity, these decisions became a part of the working rules and aided in determining reasonable value (Commons 1959, 672 ff.).

Most certainly it cannot be said that Commons left evidence that he drew upon the revelations of the Industrial Commission in formulating his theory as had Veblen. In his autobiography *Myself*, however, he does admit an awareness of the use to which Veblen had put the Industrial Commission Reports. One of those seemingly ever-present financial backers of Commons' research had commissioned him to produce a summary version of the Industrial Commission Reports that would be useful and understandable to the public. In retelling this event he wrote, "Veblen had himself been

11

constructing this testimony into his brilliant book on modern business organization, published in 1904" (Commons, 1964, 79). This would certainly indicate that Commons was well aware of the content of the Reports and it may be assumed that, although he left no paper trail, it had some influence on the formulation of his own distinction between business and industry, assets and wealth, real capital and intangible capital, business efficiency and engineering efficiency.

In the case of Veblen there is no doubt about the influence of the Reports. It is all documented in numerous footnotes and references in *The Theory of Business Enterprise*. That Veblen may have been more receptive to the findings is because the basic distinction between business and industry had been made in an essay entitled "Industrial and Pecuniary Employments," published in 1901 before the Reports were available (Veblen, 1919). Although this was no doubt a factor, a larger reason can be found in Veblen's background in anthropology. As was true of *The Theory of the Leisure Class*, even though Veblen was writing about the conspicuous consumption that followed the new wealth made possible by the American post-Civil War "industrial revolution" the anthropological references and comparisons point to the cultural source of his basic distinction between technology and institutions. The distinction between business and industry was simply a special case of the more general formulation.

To those who have read substantial amounts of the anthropological and the archaeological literature of Veblen's time as well as that which is subsequent, culture has two readily apparent dimensions. It seems that at all times two things are going on simultaneously. Tools are being manipulated to achieve some readily apparent end-in-view, matter-of-fact activity the technological efficacy of which can be readily explained; simultaneously activities are taking place that involve the vestiture and divestiture of mysterious potencies in individuals and things.

The latter seems to have a one-for-one relationship to the former and this is what Veblen meant by referring to the latter as the ceremonial adequacy that authenticated the first. Actually all peoples have two accounts of all cultural activity. One is the technological process by virtue of which the tribe secures a livelihood. This is matter-of-fact, social, and is carried along as the cultural heritage of improvement, as Edwin Cannan put it. This process is not dependent upon any one individual's peculiar potency to assure success. Anyone with the adequate training and skill can accomplish the technological ends, and so it goes for the group as a whole. A recounting of this process is mundane, unexciting. But the same events can be personalized and told in terms of the acts of heroic figures who instill their mystic potencies into the process and assure success. This latter cultural phenomenon gives rise to an "instituted hierarchy," as referred to by the French anthropologist Maurice Bloch, based upon a differential holding of productive power (Bloch, 1977). The dramatic dimension of culture simulates the matter-of-fact, the latter being impersonal and the former drawn in personal terms. The first is a social process; the second is a social drama.

Anyone familiar with these aspects of culture and being familiar with production and ceremonialism in other cultures would readily interpret those activities revealed by the Industrial Commission in this light. That is what Veblen did. As he had done in the *Leisure Class* he interpreted our economic activity as but one of many cultural ways and the Industrial Commission served as his field work. He was an anthropologist in the middle of all the massive evidence. Others without this background saw the revelations as demonstrating how far the industrial economy had strayed from the eternal verities in both folk wisdom and in formal economic treatises. To Veblen these latter were the tribal keepers of the eternal verities.

Veblen, some seventy-five years before Guy Routh wrote that the economist should "identify and study the ills of society with the meticulousness of virologists, and the devotion of anthropologists studying a primitive tribe" did just that (Routh, 1977, 311). The Reports of the Industrial Commission helped make it possible.

Although the Industrial Commission had an impact at the opening of the nineteenth century on the development of what became "institutional economics," that impact is most evident in Veblen, but most certainly is not absent in Commons. No one could say the Industrial Commission was the origin of institutional economics, but it most certainly did play a significant role.

REFERENCES

Adams, Henry. 1961 (1889). *The United States in 1800*. Ithaca: Cornell University Press.

Bloch, Maurice. 1977. "The Past and the Present in the Present." In *Man* 12 (August): 278–92.

Commons, John R. 1959 (1934). *Institutional Economics*. Madison: University of Wisconsin Press.

—— 1964 (1934). *Myself*. Madison: University of Wisconsin Press.

Dorfman, Joseph. 1934. *Thorstein Veblen and his America*. New York: Viking.

—— 1946. *The Economic Mind In American Civilization*. Vols I, II. New York: Viking.

Hamilton, David. 1988 (1953). "Veblen and Commons: A Case of Theoretical Convergence." Reprinted from *The South-Western Social Science Quarterly*. In *Institutional Economics*, ed. Warren Samuels. Aldershot, England: Edward Elgar.

Routh, Guy. 1977. *The Origins of Economic Thought*. New York: Vintage Books.

Singer, Charles *et al.* (eds). 1958. *A History of Technology*. Vol. 5. New York: Oxford.

U.S. Industrial Commission. 1902. *Report of the Industrial Commission*. 19 vols. Washington: U.S. Government Printing Office.

Veblen, Thorstein. 1942 (1919, 1901). "Industrial and Pecuniary Employments." Reprinted in *The Place of Science in Modern Civilization*. New York: Viking.

—— 1935 (1904). *The Theory of Business Enterprise*. New York: Charles Scribner's Sons.

—— 1934 (1899). *The Theory of the Leisure Class*. New York: Random House.

2

VEBLEN AND COMMONS AND THE CONCEPT OF COMMUNITY

Edythe S. Miller

The institutionalist literature recently has been enlivened by a dispute about the consistency of the theoretical systems of Thorstein Veblen and John R. Commons. Specifically, the contention has been advanced, and challenged, that a disparity exists between Veblen's theory of instrumental value and Commons's theory of reasonable value (Ramstad 1989, 765–8; 1995, 999–1000; Atkinson and Reed 1990, 109; 1991, 1137–9), so basic as to render their systems not simply discordant, but competitive or substitute paradigms. One purpose of this essay is to examine, without exploring that specific question except as it touches tangentially the major topic, the question of whether, whatever the differences between Veblen and Commons, there is sufficient correspondence on major premises, and whether the concepts on which there is correspondence are sufficiently central to institutionalism, to justify their classification as part of a unified school. The concept of community, and its underlying precepts, is the major premise explored.

Community itself is an intricate abstraction, encompassing numerous strands that are themselves complex. At bottom, however, allegiance to the concept turns on such questions as whether individuals are viewed as isolated datum, co-existing within but not merged into a social whole; the extent to which humans are perceived as bound together by a sense of connectedness and mutual obligation; whether there is acknowledgment of the existence of a public interest – a common good – independent of aggregations of private interests, itself a major point of contention among contemporary institutionalists (for example, Gordon and Adams 1989, 83, 87; Samuels 1990, 700–7; Miller 1991, 998–9), and whether public policy should seek the achievement of that common good or policies of *laissez-faire* should instead be followed. The present inquiry centers on the question of whether Veblen and Commons exhibit commonality of thought when it

14

comes to this concept. Because of the complexity of the topic, it is important to explore its ancillary aspects.

INDIVIDUALS AS SOCIAL BEINGS

It is well recognized that both Veblen and Commons dispute the economic wisdom of their (and our) day that posits individuals as self-contained units of productive power and innate desire, and substitute a vision of human actors as social creatures, born into cultural complexes and shaped by communal influences that surround them from birth. Veblen points to the inconceivability of any human being, or any household, at any time maintaining an isolated, self-sufficient life, and insists that the life history of mankind has been the life history of communities (1919a, 324–5). Commons notes that at no point in time have humans started as isolated beings, that they are born into going concerns,[1] with their own working rules; that is, customs, beliefs, and habits of thought. He elaborates that custom, "the most elementary fact of living creatures" is not simply habit, it is "social habit" (1934, 44–5). Commons describes his "volitional theory of value" as a "concept of membership, citizenship, participation" as opposed to a view of society simply as a mass of individuals. That is, his volitional theory is "a concept of both individual and concerted action, governing and being governed, of . . . custom, common law, routine, ancestor-wisdom, even stupidity . . ." (1934, 242–3).

Both view production and consumption as communal. Veblen notes that technological knowledge is the joint stock of any community, that the technology in use in any society at any given time is a "product of group life and is held as a common stock" (1914, 138). "[I]nvention," he maintains, "is the mother of necessity." It is the state of the industrial arts that gives to specific natural resources their usefulness (1923, 63, 63n.11). For example, petroleum becomes a useful (a necessary) resource only after the industrial technology that employs it is developed. Prior to that, it is neither valued nor sought. Commons rejects a view of society as no more than a "population of molecules" (1934, 225–6, 323), and points to the "jointness" of both production and consumption. All that we use in our work, our domestic lives, even in our play – tools, food, clothing, luxuries, etc. – is the "joint product of all society, past and present" (Commons 1899–1900, 100). Each of us, he alleges, participates in economic activity as a member of a group, and helps in the production of a joint product, which then must be shared through the various types of transactions (1934, 422).

It is important to note that Veblen and Commons both specify that accepted myths, ceremonial beliefs, habits of thought, and working rules also are part of a common heritage and are jointly held. The pages of Veblen's *Theory of the Leisure Class* are replete with descriptions of the influence of emulation and status seeking, that is, the desire for approval and admiration of contemporaries and peers, upon consumption styles and settled beliefs, and habits of "use and wont." Commons's acceptance of the communal influence on human activity is no better illustrated than in his very definition of an institution as "collective action in control of individual action" (1934, 69), expanded to "collective action in restraint, liberation, and expansion of individual action" (1934, 73). He defines collective action as the societal customs and beliefs that specify individual rights and duties, and that are enforced by "collective sanctions" (1934, 70–3). In Commons's view, the transaction, the basic unit of economic activity within the going concern, is itself a social relationship (1934, 323). He describes the transactional relationship as one, not between man and nature, but rather between man and man (1934, 117–18). An institution, in Commons's view, is "an enduring relation" (1934, 96). Veblen defines institutions as settled habits of thought common to the generality of men, also an unambiguously interactive and social concept.

There is little question that, for both Veblen and Commons, individual life is social life. Humans are creatures of, even as their joint actions re-create, their cultures. The productive process is structured by the state of the industrial arts, which are a common heritage and reservoir. Production and consumption are communal activities. This is the basis for the rejection by both Veblen and Commons of the marginal productivity and marginal utility theorems, individualistic concepts that are basic to standard theory. The very "jointness" of production and its dependence, for structure and content, upon an evolving state of the industrial arts – a common stock – makes it impossible to determine "legitimate" relative distributive shares, or specify the "right" of any group to a specific reward. That is to say, distribution is not an economic, but a political, determination, resolved by relative power.

Commons points out that even in the case of his "bargaining transactions" – the only one of his three types of transactions[2] that takes place between relative equals – the equality specified refers to a state of legal, and not necessarily economic, equality (1934, 62–3). Economic inequality gives the more powerful partner in the transaction a bargaining advantage. Veblen, too, stresses the differential advantage that exists in all societies, and that assumes the character of intangible assets for groups so favored. He adds that differential advantage does not accrue to identical groups in different societies, but that the fact of its existence is a constant (1919a, 360–3). In like manner, marginal utility theory becomes questionable given that preferences are not innate and inherent, but rather responses to social conditions. To the extent that desires are the product of the aspiration to emulate one's "betters," or to the extent that they have been created or manipulated by advertising or other forms of salesmanship, they again bespeak a domination of the relatively less by the relatively more powerful. In either event, they cannot be accepted as innate, and seem more a matter of a "deference effect" than an expression of "consumer sovereignty."

It has been suggested that Commons accepted marginalist principles (Dorfman 1965, ii, n.3). It would appear, however, that Commons's acceptance, if such it was, of traditional tenets was not grounded in a traditional rationale. For example, in writing of the principle of diminishing utility, Commons attributes its existence, not to an increase in supply or a decrease in demand for a product, as the economic wisdom would have it, but rather: (1) in an objective sense, to depreciation, wear and tear; and (2) in a subjective sense, to changes in culture or civilization "as in the change from arrows to dynamite, from horses to automobiles" (1934, 357). He terms this "Civilization Value," or "Cultural Value." Despite the adoption of mainstream terminology, his support of the maxim seems more akin to the general Veblenian concept of technological determination, for example the technological determination of natural resource value, than to mainstream thought. Commons makes clear his view that the replacement of products and services by new products and services occurs by virtue of a general growth in understanding, that is, the growth and accrual in the community at large of new knowledge and ideas (1934, 327–8), a thought that bears strong resemblance to Veblen's thinking in regard to technology as a joint stock. The sense is of a social, and not an individualistic, process.

In like manner, Commons's acceptance of the principle of scarcity, a controlling principle of traditional theory, is not related to a perception on his part of limited resources, as in mainstream thought. It is related, rather, to the ability to withhold that is a component of intangible value (a perspective shared with Veblen), and a function of economic power. Commons's view of scarcity is related also to his distinction between use and exchange value. Commons defines use value as centered, not in scarcity, but in an abundance that increases social wealth. Exchange value, in contrast, is a creature of scarcity. Exchange value increases private wealth, rather than social wealth. Commons posits use value as a technological concept; exchange value as a pecuniary one. The use value of a good is increased by an increase in its supply, exchange value is increased by a decrease in supply (Commons 1934, 371–7).

THE THEORY OF HUMAN NATURE

A unifying feature of institutional economics in general is its portrayal of human nature as multi-faceted. Both Veblen and Commons describe individuals as diversely motivated in their economic dealings. Both take strong exception to the "rational economic man" of standard theory. Commons quotes with approval (1934, 228–9) Veblen's mocking description of the mainstream representation of the individual, as "a lightning calculator of pleasure and pain who oscillates like a homogeneous globule of desire of happiness under the impulse of stimuli that shift him about the area but leave him intact" (1919a, 73–4). Both Veblen and Commons reject the hedonistic perspective of mainstream theory with its view of humans as atomistic, passive, rational, and maximizing and substitute for it an active and often irrational social being.

Indeed, both point to the variety of motives that drive individual activity. They see behavior as influenced by the "working rules" of such going concerns as the family, the corporation, and the church (Dorfman 1965, ix; Commons 1899–1900, 62; 1934, 69); that is, as driven by custom, convention, habits of "use and wont," legal standards, the common sense of the community – all social – in addition to anticipations of pleasure and pain. Veblen points to the continuous tension that exists between the creative and caring tendencies of workmanship,[3] idle curiosity, and the parental bent, and the destructive propensities of exploit and predation. The elements in the first category relate to community; they foster sustenance and improvement in the human condition. The latter are propelled by motives of self-interest and self-regard, without care or concern for others. These conflicting tendencies are simultaneously present in human endeavor, co-existing in a state of unremitting strain. Both Veblen and Commons are at pains to point out that they do not dismiss the so-called rational tendencies, but neither do they view them as sole motivating forces.

THE INSTRUMENTAL–CEREMONIAL DISTINCTION

The instrumental–ceremonial distinction is an essential aspect of institutionalism. It also is characterized as the technological and institutional distinction: that between making goods and making money, between workmanship and ownership, between serviceability and profitability. It is most often associated with Veblen, and frequently is identified simply as the Veblenian dichotomy. The creative proclivities enumerated by Veblen of workmanship, idle curiosity, and the parental bent are illustrations of instrumental tendencies; exploit, predation, and absentee ownership, of ceremonial tendencies. However, it seems evident that, despite its common association with Veblen, Commons also utilized the so-called Veblenian dichotomy in his system of thought. For example, it has been observed, correctly in my view, that the dichotomy is central to the distinction drawn by both Veblen and Commons between tangible and intangible property[4] (Atkinson and Reed 1990, 1097; Commons 1934, 522–3; Veblen 1919a, 364–6). The distinction also is perceptible in Commons's differentiation of use and exchange value (1934, 371–7), which engendered his further separation between the two types of economics, institutional and engineering economics. He describes institutional economics as concerned with exchange values, "the activity of transactions in the relation of man to man," and engineering economics, as dealing with use values, "the activity of increasing output in the relation of man to nature" (1934, 424). It is a distinction between technology and institutions that is virtually indistinguishable from that in the Veblenian dichotomy. Traces of the Veblenian dichotomy also are evident in Commons's differentiation of the going concern and the going plant (1934, 423).

The technological–institutional distinction is behavioral, rather than structural. Institutions are not ceremonial or instrumental. All human activity, whatever its nature, occurs within institutions. The same entity serves both ceremonial and instrumental function. Our homes, our automobiles, the colleges to which we send our children, the very food we serve, provide shelter, transportation, education, nourishment, and at the same time are markers of social status. The factory, or other form of business enterprise, typically sustains both workmanship and ownership/salesmanship functions, it is both going plant and going concern. Veblen points out that the worth of the same parcel of land may be estimated from its rental value or its apprehended exchange value, and that these often will be widely divergent quantities. The first is an indication of the use or production value of the land, the second of the hopes and dreams that surround it, that is, of its speculative value (Veblen 1934, 369–70). Commons points out that the limits of transactions in business establishments, the "proprietary economics of transferable rights and liberties," are specified by the working rules of going concerns, and at the same time, the going plant operates under engineering rules of technical efficiency. Although it is possible to distinguish the going concern and the going plant conceptually, they are conjoined. They operate concurrently, as a common process. "The two," as Commons notes, "are inseparable" (1934, 423).

Veblen's distinction between tangible and intangible property follows on his differentiation of industry and ownership, of production and salesmanship. Returns on tangible property are the returns for the productive use of resources. That is, tangible property is used for making goods. Intangible property, in contrast, is used for making money. Some examples of intangible property are good will, monopoly, trade marks, and patents. But an increasingly important aspect of intangible property is the ability to withhold supply in order to maintain price, an ability which is vested by virtue of ownership, which increasingly has become separated from workmanship (Veblen 1919b, 41–4, 69–73). Veblen identifies intangible assets as vested interests, defined as "a marketable right to get something for nothing" (1919b, 100). He deems the ability to withhold supply "sabotage," defined as a "conscientious withdrawal of efficiency," an activity of which there is little doubt that Veblen disapproves. "Business" he states "is the pursuit of profits." Profits are maintained by restricting output. However, "[t]he

19

common good, so far as it is a question of material welfare, is evidently best served by an unhampered working of the industrial system at its full capacity, without interruption or dislocation" (1919b, 90–3).

Commons's analysis runs along similar lines. Commons also sees the very existence of property and ownership as granting the ability to withhold. The meaning of property, in Commons's view, includes "the right to hold, to withhold, to alienate, to acquire, to be free from interference" (1934, 523). He adds that the purchase or sale of property means the transfer of some or all of these proprietary relations, rather than of physical things. As noted above, Commons distinguishes use value, with a basis in abundance that increases social wealth, and exchange value, centered in scarcity, and amplifying only private wealth. Scarcity is a property of the ability to withhold, a major aspect of intangible property. The use value of a product is its Civilization Value; it is a function of the existing state of the industrial arts, a technological concept. The exchange value of a commodity, in contrast, is a pecuniary concept. It is measured in price, and because price increases with scarcity, it is enhanced by the ability to withhold (Commons 1934, 371–7).

REALISM AND IDEALISM

Veblen and Commons are social and economic realists. In contrast to mainstream economists, they focus attention upon real world conditions and the underlying forces that produce them – that is, upon Veblen's matter-of-fact knowledge. They perceive an evolutionary system in a process of indeterminate development. Their perspective is thus in stark contrast to that of neoclassicism, with its focus upon a static system tending toward equilibrium, and the frictions, leads, and lags that deflect it from that state. Rather than uniformly accepting market solutions, Veblen and Commons look to real world conditions and their underlying causes, and to the effect on them of policy proposals. Concepts of a first Cause and of an ultimate Truth, both outside the system, are rejected. The methodology of the mainstream that uses deductive methods to apprehend a certain and exogenous Truth is challenged. To enhance understanding, these institutional economists look to the results of experimentation in application to the real life facts of experience. Knowledge is possible, but certainty is not. Knowledge is acquired as a by-product of the human experience, rather than through reasoning from First Principles. Practice is an inseparable aspect of theory; knowing and doing are interdependent. The dualistic thinking that informs standard thought is denied (Miller 1989, 341–2; 1991, 999–1000).

Veblen and Commons are equally dismissive of the natural laws of automatic guiding tendencies, sustained by principles of natural rights, that the mainstream conceives as propelling the economy; a conception of a state of being determined at any moment in time by conditions at a prior time in combination with immutable natural laws. That is, they repudiate mechanical causation; there is a role envisioned for chance and spontaneity. At bottom, it is not underlying tendencies, but purposive human beings acting as members of communities that they posit as creators of the present through past activities, and as creating the future through current ones.

Veblen describes orthodox economists as formulating "laws of the normal or natural, according to a preconception regarding the ends to which, in the nature of things, all things tend" (1919a, 65). Moreover, not only are these laws perceived by these economists as part of a higher authority, they are conceived as working toward some beneficent goal. The automatic law that neoclassical economics views as guiding society is "a consistent propensity tending to some spiritually legitimate end" (1919a, 61); that is, it is viewed as moving the economy toward what "the instructed common sense of the time accepts as the adequate or worthy end of human effort. It is a projection of the accepted ideal of conduct" (1919a, 65).

Commons, in turn, describes his method of approach as based, not in a search for an ideal or ultimate purpose, but rather in an examination of the actual processes of the evolution of the state. He depicts his method as one of inductive, comparative inquiry, that looks not at what is potential or ideal, but at what is actual and historical. He claims to seek to uncover the "flow" of history, rather than to observe a state of being, and to use methods that are dynamic and evolutionary rather than static (1899–1900, 106–8). "[B]y recognizing the state as a process and not an entity, [the method] allows for [an understanding of] its further growth and extension . . ." (1899–1900, 108).

While Commons's analysis of the natural rights philosophy of mainstream economics is neither as extensive nor as detailed as Veblen's, his assessment of it is unmistakable. Commons criticizes classical economics for attempting to "start at the beginning of things" and attempting to arrive at an ultimate that was "in the nature of things . . . [and] had a fixity and stability for all time." It should instead, he maintained, have looked to the complex cross-section of going concerns, formed – no matter how – by past activities, and moving on to an unknowable and changeable future (1934, 213). Veblen, for his part, posits modern science, in contrast to its predecessors, as viewing its subject matter as an "unfolding process of cumulative causation" – that is, as a genetic evolutionary process, with neither beginning nor end point; without initial impetus that gives the process direction, nor a state of rest after the initial impulse is spent (1914, 326).

Commons rejects the concept of natural rights, maintaining that "such rights as we have proceed from national and other collective action, and are not 'natural'" (1934, 681). He maintains that the perceived "natural rights of man" such as the right to life, liberty, and the pursuit of happiness, are not natural at all, but rather, customary. He acknowledges that

21

customs change, but maintains that they change very slowly, resulting in individuals embracing habits and wishes that accord with customs established in early childhood. "Then they appear to be natural, unchangeable, inalienable, though they are artificial, collective, transitory, forfeitable" (1934, 703). Commons distinguishes his views from that of mainstream economists on the basis of how society and collective action are viewed. Thus, where he sees working rules of going concerns controlling individual activity, the "mechanical" school envisions society as propelled by natural law, and thus tends toward a belief in *laissez-faire* (1934, 119–20). He adduces that Adam Smith and his followers based their case on the emotions of man and God because workaday transactions and habits of thought were considered too shallow and commonplace an element upon which to base theory. In the view of these economists, he maintains, economics should be based in "something more fundamental – an ultimate essence of God, Nature, Reason, Instinct, Physics, Biology. The most familiar things are the last to be investigated." And yet, in Commons's view, it is the most familiar things that comprise the real world material of economic science. "[I]t is these familiar transactions controlled by collective action that are the wages, profits, interest, rents, employment, unemployment, welfare, misery, of nations and individuals" (1934, 216).

POLICY REFORM

Joseph Dorfman, in his Introduction to Commons's *A Sociological View of Sovereignty*, notes that reform of public policy engaged Commons early in his career. His writing and lecturing, as early as the end of the nineteenth century, covered such diverse policy domains as: the alleviation of poverty and unemployment, support of unionization, establishment of a minimum wage, tax reform, and reform of the money and banking system among others (Dorfman 1965, iv–v, viii). Dorfman points out that Commons consistently advocated experimentation, supporting such programs as compulsory arbitration in cases of arbitrary discharge, unemployment insurance to alleviate technological unemployment, and monetary reform to prevent extremes of the business cycle (Dorfman 1965, vi–vii).

Commons maintained his interest in policy reform throughout his professional life, addressing his proposals primarily to conditions of bargaining inequality and insecurity of sustenance and expectations that he viewed as impairing, not only those most immediately affected, but the nation as a whole. That is, he substitutes for the individualistic model one that stresses "solidarity of interests" (Commons 1919, 102) and mutual obligation (Commons 1919, 127). In essence, he aspires to smooth the sharp edges of the capitalist system by softening some of its harshest features, thereby increasing both individual security and economic stability.

Thus, among the innovations he calls for is compulsory universal health insurance (1919, 97), compulsory universal old-age, disability, and life insurance (1919, 90–105), a national employment office to ensure job security (1919, 81) and, that with which he is perhaps most closely identified, the control of monopoly power through the establishment of public utility commissions. The structure he primarily endorses for the agencies he recommends be established for these purposes is equal representation of the various affected interests.

While Veblen had a more detailed and explicit analysis than did Commons of the natural law and natural rights philosophy underlying mainstream economics, Commons had the more focused and detailed program for policy reform. At bottom, what most engrossed Veblen was not so much a practical political agenda, as the reform of economics itself.[5] Nevertheless, Veblen does indicate, if sometimes somewhat obliquely, conditions that he sees as requiring modification.

Examination of Veblen's work leaves little doubt that he advocates systemic change. Taken in its entirety, his work is a protest against privilege in all its forms, and the natural laws and natural rights invoked to justify it. His real world focus exposes the existence of power and powerlessness. When it comes to such issues, Veblen positions himself squarely on the side of the underdog. His realism also allows emphasis upon the interdependence and interrelatedness of individuals and reveals the importance he gives to the concept of mutual responsibility. Indeed, the concept of mutual commitment is central to Veblenian thought, evidenced in the pride of place given such propensities as the parental bent, idle curiosity, and the instinct of workmanship. Veblen defines the parental bent as not simply concern for the welfare of one's natural children, but for successive generations to come, that is, as the well-being of the community at large, and for a future "common good" (1914, 26–7, 161). Workmanship and curiosity involve stretching the bounds of human knowledge to enhance present and future productive capacity and serviceability, and are viewed as means of applying the parental bent. In fact, Veblen sees the parental bent and workmanship as so intimately related as not only to reinforce each other, but often to be indistinguishable (1914, 25).

Veblen's analysis was, in important respects, a theory of power, its sources, nature, and uses. Power inheres in groups and individuals (absentee owners, vested interests, captains of industry) who control the nation's wealth and assets. It is maintained through affirmation of the business ethic as a habit of thought, and the use of manipulation, coercion, and emulation to sustain it. Veblen points out that the natural rights philosophy, with its support of principles of individualism, private property, and free contract, furthers the appropriation by vested interests of a disproportionate share of community output. He maintains that ownership does not create the product; it is not the source of earnings, but only of legal claims by owners to earnings.

Production comes from workmanship, earnings from ownership (1923, 61). However, in an era in which business principles are dominant, efficiency comes to be measured in terms of pecuniary gain, serviceability to be assessed by pecuniary tests. Those who appropriate an appreciable share of social wealth are adjudged to be social benefactors. The differential advantages and conventional privileges that accrue as a result come to be accepted as natural (1914, 216–17, 288–94). All this occurs, in Veblen's view, at a cost of serviceability to the community at large (1919b, 117).

Veblen perceives modern industry as requiring cooperation on the part of all participants, both in regard to technological knowledge and the materials required for production. The success of industry is measured by the effective team-work of all participants, without regard to plant or industrial or even geographic boundaries (1919b, 117). It is based on shared matter-of-fact knowledge (1923, 266–9). Industrial workers are "bound in a network of give and take of such a nature that the lines of interdependence are endless" (1923, 269). But the present business system promotes competition, not coordination. It sanctions the pursuit of profits, including by restricting production, rather than the maximization of output, to the detriment of the common good (1919b, 93). "Secrecy and mystification may be 'good for trade,' but they are altogether bad for industry, sabotage may be indispensable in business, although it is invariably disastrous for production" (1923, 269–70). That is, "the businesslike manoeuvres of the vested interests . . . each managing its own affairs with an eye single to its own advantage, deranges the ordinary conditions of life for the common man . . ." (1919b, 117). It is unquestionable that Veblen perceives the business practices of the vested interests and absentee owners as explicitly at odds with the material benefits of society (1923, 10). Industrial efficiency and maximum production is achieved by cooperation between industrial entities. Salesmanship, in contrast, is carried on along lines of sharp practice and distrust (1923, 326, 326 n.11).

Moreover, Veblen believes that the legal right of sabotage conferred by ownership results not only in the restriction of output to below its potential, but also in the unemployment and partial employment of persons and industrial plant, all so as to increase price and maintain money values ("keep capitalization intact") (1923, 66–7, 218–20). The result, as he sees it, is impairment of material values, of industry, of the industrial work force, and of the consumptive needs of the population (1923, 112–13). An additional device employed to maintain money values is reduction of the wages of labor, resulting in suffering and privation (Veblen 1923, 220), and increasing distrust and hostility among employers and employees, resulting in strikes and lockouts, and the use of strikebreakers and labor spies (1923, 221–2). On the question of labor relations, Commons expresses the view that the worker displaced by technological change has "an ethical claim for compensation"; that is, when the worker, encouraged by society to acquire skills for a particular occupation, which is abolished in the interest of society, then: "[t]he employer, first, and society, ultimately, should share the loss with him" (quoted from Commons by Dorfman 1965, vi).

A common perception of Veblen is that he is morally neutral, a perception that seems confirmed by many of his own words. But, often, to read Veblen literally is to misread him. As often as not, he proceeds by way of indirection. For example, he frequently will conclude a particularly devastating commentary about contemporary practices and beliefs with an aside to the effect that: perhaps this is as it should be, or that his words are not to be taken as judgment or condemnation.[6] Nevertheless, his words clearly contain both condemnation and judgment, and frequently unambiguously contradict his posture of detachment. For example, in an uncharacteristically direct comment, Veblen notes: "The present businesslike management of the industrial system is incompetent, irrelevant, and not germane to the livelihood of the underlying population. . . . [The] concrete working out [of absentee ownership] is incompatible with the current state of the industrial arts . . ." (1923, 425). The statement does not contain the markings of moral neutrality, and nor does the overall posture taken in the body of his work. It is clear that his position involves the judgment that all is not as it should be.

I think it possible to distinguish the thinking of Veblen and Commons in one regard, although the distinction is to an extent a matter of inference. Moreover, although it seems clear initially that a distinction exists, further inquiry reveals a distinction without much of a difference. Commons's reasonable value theory involves the augmentation of the working rules of going concerns to ensure full participation of all interested parties and full expression by all participants. That is, Commons's concept of reasonable value is processual (1934, 683). It is closely related to the juridical concept of due process of law. Final resolution then inheres in tribunals with decision-making authority up to, in the case of the United States, the Supreme Court. "Reasonable Value is the evolutionary collective determination of what is reasonable in view of all the changing political, moral, and economic circumstances and the personalities that arise therefrom to the Supreme bench" (1934, 683–4). It is a theory of processual, rather than of substantive value. It specifies a process that permits the adoption of ends that are of a transitory, evolutionary, corrigible, experimental nature. Commons makes it clear that he is seeking "achievable" goals – goals that are attainable – given existing circumstances (1934, 741). He makes it clear also that goals appropriately change as societies evolve.

Veblen doubtless would agree with the stated provisional, experimental, and evolutionary nature of goals. His reservations would more likely have been in regard to two additional and inherent aspects of the theory: first, to the lack of content and standards in Commons's reasonable value theory, and next, to the implied credibility afforded interest group opinions, so

25

long as all affected groups are represented. That is, Veblen surely would contend that it is possible to specify viable standards of choice and life circumstances. Moreover, in light of his views about the manipulability and susceptibility to coercion of popular habits of thought, and his views about the control exercised by business principles and interests over the common sense of the community, including that of public officials, he undoubtedly would reject the idea that full participation by itself is sufficient to achieve reasonable conclusions.

On the other hand, Commons clearly did not reject the idea that standards are specifiable. He maintains that his method provides a means to achieve attainable goals, but also indicates that there are goals beyond those which presently are achievable. Moreover, his goals, apart from the means of their achievement, are clearly substantive. And in fact, when it comes to both goals and criteria of choice among competing goals, the ideas of Veblen and Commons appear to be compatible, if not interchangeable.

For his part, Veblen does not reject the process specified by Commons. He points out that popular acceptance of political action is necessary for successful governance, that is, that policy must have public support. "The advice and consent of the common run has . . . come to be indispensable to the conduct of affairs among civilized men. . . . [N]o line of policy can long be pursued successfully without the permissive tolerance of the common run" (1919b, 16).

CONCLUSION

The question posed at the beginning of this essay was whether there is sufficient correspondence between the thought of Veblen and Commons on matters central to institutional economics to justify grouping them together as part of a unified school. It seems undeniable that both are strong adherents of the concept of community when it comes to matters of primary relevance: that is, that individuals are social beings, that they are bound together by a sense of mutual obligation, that there is such an attribute as the public interest, and that policies should be pursued to achieve it. In light of these areas of agreement, it is difficult to accept the view that the ideas of Commons and Veblen are representative of competing paradigms. It seems equally clear that these are matters of profound concern for institutional economics, and that they should be so for economics generally.

Veblen and Commons are both suspicious of market solutions, recognizing that markets often are controlled by private power. Both condemn the abuse of power in its various manifestations, and the persistence of privilege and differential advantage. The themes that engage each of them, directly or indirectly, end in disparaging the wastefulness encountered in business and social life; for example, the failure to realize potential, the underutilization of human and other resources, the veneration of predatory business principles, conspicuous display in all its forms, invidious discrimination in its various manifestations, and so forth. As noted, Veblen did not present a detailed agenda for reform, but this is not an indication of lack of ethical engagement. And for both, ethical engagement included the recognition both of mutual responsibility among humans, and of a public interest that is more than the arithmetic summation of private interests; that is, the recognition of a common or social good that is part of the achievement of a more efficient – in the sense used by both Veblen and Commons of usefulness and workability – and a more equitable functioning of the economic and social world.

Veblen is frequently described as a pessimist (for example, Dowd 1964, 130). This, in my view, is a mischaracterization. I believe it is at least arguable that both Veblen and Commons were optimists. That case may be made on a number of grounds; for example, their belief that individuals are not simply creatures, but also architects, of their societies. That is, and as noted above, both see humans as actively engaged in shaping their futures, rather than as mere pawns in an alien grand design. This outlook is not the mark of a pessimist. Moreover, both Veblen and Commons see an industrial system that is vastly productive. Nor is this a pessimistic outlook. Indeed, so potentially productive is it in their view that the vested interests that control it are led to practice sabotage to maintain their profits.

Veblen and Commons envision the future as open-ended, indeterminate, and non-predictable. This, and their recognition of the ability of vested interests to seize control, would perhaps indicate that, when it comes to questions of the fate of humankind, they are best described as skeptics or agnostics, rather than as either pessimists or optimists. That is, it is their view that the future is unknowable. As Veblen notably maintained, technology could win out in the end, but so also could "imbecile institutions" (1914, 24–5).

NOTES

1 It is notable that the term "going concern," although primarily associated with Commons, is a term that Veblen also uses, and to the same effect (for example, 1919b, 37–9).
2 The other two, as is well known, are managerial and rationing transactions.
3 Commons also points to the attraction of work as an incentive to industry. "A free man works because he finds an interesting outlet for his energies, and because he wishes to support wife, children, preacher, government." That is, "[w]ork has an interest for its own sake" (1899–1900, 75–6). Neither Veblen nor Commons equates work solely with pain nor, for that matter, the lack of work (leisure) solely with pleasure.
4 This is an important basis of Atkinson and Reed's response to the claim that the theories of Veblen and Commons are competing, rather than complementary. See references in text.

5 Veblen notes that although the economic process is comprised of two parts, business and industry, it is the former rather than the latter to which economists have turned their attention. He contends that economists, as imbued as are others with the conventional wisdom, have focused upon business enterprise and the price system, and have virtually ignored the technological aspect of the dichotomy. Moreover, he maintains, not only have they focused solely on business, but they have become its advocates, and have centered their attention on ways and means of attaining for business price advantages and differential gain in terms of price (Veblen 1934, 10–12).

6 For example, after strongly criticizing the support and ratification he feels is invariably given by government to employer positions in employer–employee disputes, Veblen footnotes: "There is no fault to be found with all of this, of course; but it is necessary to note the fact. It is one of the substantial factors in the case" (1923, 405, n. 3). After condemning business principles (1923, 438–9) as "a means of curtailing and impairing the material conditions of life for the underlying population, and an arrangement for the increase and diffusion of ill will among men," and as a "tissue of dissension, distrust, dishonesty, servility, and bombast [with] . . . [t]he net product mutual and collective defeat and grief," he footnotes: "[T]his characterization has nothing to say as regards the moral or aesthetic excellence of these [principles, nor] . . . as to the right-eousness, goodness, or beauty [of methods of supporting them]. . . . These are questions of taste and fashion, about which there is no disputing" (1923, 439 n. 13). It seems clear that the qualifications Veblen appends to his message are at odds with the message itself.

REFERENCES

Atkinson, Glen and Mike Reed. 1990. "Institutional Adjustment, Instrumental Efficiency, and Reasonable Value." *Journal of Economic Issues* (December): 1095–107.
—— 1991. "Rejoinder." *Journal of Economic Issues* (December): 1136–40.
Commons, John R. 1899–1900. *A Sociological View of Sovereignty.* Reprint 1967. New York: Augustus M. Kelley, Publishers.
—— 1919. *Industrial Goodwill.* Reprint 1969. New York: Arno Press, Inc., and the *New York Times.*
—— 1934. *Institutional Economics.* Reprint 1961. Madison, Wis.: The University of Wisconsin Press.
Dorfman, Joseph. 1965. "John R. Commons' General Theory of Institutions." Introductory Essay to *A Sociological View of Sovereignty.* Reprint 1967. New York: Augustus M. Kelley, Publishers.
Dowd, Douglas. 1964. *Thorstein Veblen.* New York: Washington Square Press, Inc.
Gordon, Wendell and John Adams. 1989. *Economics as a Social Science: An Evolutionary Approach.* Riverdale, Md.: The Riverdale Company.
Miller, Edythe S. 1989. "Economics for What? Economic Folklore and Social Realities." *Journal of Economic Issues* (June): 339–56.
—— 1991. "Of Economic Paradigms, Puzzles, Problems, and Policies; or, Is the Economy too Important to be Entrusted to the Economists?" *Journal of Economic Issues* (December): 993–1004.
Ramstad, Yngve. 1989. "'Reasonable Value' Versus 'Instrumental Value:' Competing Paradigms in Institutional Economics." *Journal of Economic Issues* (September): 761–77.

—— 1995. "John R. Commons's Puzzling Inconsequentiality as an Economic Theorist." *Journal of Economic Issues* (December): 991–1012.

Samuels, Warren J. 1990. "The Self-Referentiability of Thorstein Veblen's Theory of the Preconceptions of Economic Science." *Journal of Economic Issues* (September): 695–718.

Veblen, Thorstein. 1899. *The Theory of the Leisure Class.* Reprint 1953. New York: The New American Library.

—— 1914. *The Instinct of Workmanship.* Reprint 1964. New York: W. W. Norton and Co.

—— 1919a. *The Place of Science in Modern Civilisation.* Reprint 1961. New York: Russell & Russell, Inc.

—— 1919b. *The Vested Interests and the Common Man.* Reprint 1969. New York: Capricorn Books.

—— 1923. *Absentee Ownership and Business Enterprise in Recent Times.* Reprint 1964. New York: Augustus M. Kelley.

—— 1934. *Essays in Our Changing Order.* Reprint 1964. New York: Augustus M. Kelley.

Part II

COMMONS,
A SOCIOLOGICAL VIEW
OF SOVEREIGNTY

3

AN EVOLUTIONARY THEORY OF THE DEVELOPMENT OF PROPERTY AND THE STATE

Glen Atkinson

It is my objective in this chapter to demonstrate that Commons was, in fact, a pioneer in applying evolutionary thinking to social systems and provided a foundation upon which we can build. *A Sociological View of Sovereignty* should be read as an attempt by the author to explain the purpose and evolution of the institutional structure of a society. Social evolution brings about a differentiation and specialization of institutions. In these essays Commons discusses the family, the church, political parties, and industrial corporations as important contemporary institutions. In earlier, more primitive times, all of these functions were performed in an undifferentiated whole (Commons 1967, 5). Commons places special emphasis on the function and evolution of private property and the state and their interaction. Private property is significant in an evolutionary sense because it was the original institution. The state is important because it limits the capriciousness of property and because "until a people become politically organized in the form of a state there is no sovereignty" (Commons 1967, 38).

It is not my intention to fully develop the relationship between this early work of Commons and his later publications. Obviously Commons developed his theoretical system throughout his academic and practical career, but I believe it would be useful to see how he understood institutional order and evolution at the close of the nineteenth century. It has often been said that Commons is difficult to understand because of his nontheoretical approach and his turgid prose. For instance, Kenneth Boulding remarked that "Commons' theoretical structure remains today exactly where he left it: a tangled jungle of profound insights, culled by an essentially nontheoretical mind from a life rich with experiences of economic realities" (Boulding 1957, 8). Even Joseph Dorfman's introduction to this volume of essays by Commons states that "Commons' formulations are generally awkwardly phrased" (Dorfman in Commons 1967, xi). A person who could continually offer profound insights without benefit of a sound theoretical structure would have to be considered a genius or a prophet. Commons was neither, but he was a scholar who struggled to understand evolving social systems at a time when the theoretical foundation for such inquiry was terribly underdeveloped. Likewise, his phrasing often seems awkward because he was attempting to explain cumulative change to an audience that held a mental model of mechanical and repetitive change rather than cumulative change. He was attempting to describe a system where the agents were not independent, passive atoms, but were, instead, interactive and interdependent. We now know that positive feedback relations in a system can drive the system away from equilibrium rather than toward it, but those concepts had not been developed yet. In addition, his interest in experiencing economic realities led him away from a search for theoretical optimums, but not away from theory.

These essays on sovereignty by John R. Commons were written at the time when scholars were first attempting to apply evolutionary theory developed in natural history and biology to social institutions. The structure of the natural and the social world had seemed to scientists, working in the classical mechanical paradigm of Newton, to be static and both the natural and social worlds were considered to be governed by a few immutable laws beyond human control. In fact the social world was thought to be governed by natural laws. A static world is not a world without change however, but the change is mechanical and repetitive rather than cumulative (Hamilton 1970). Static means a stable structure rather than the total absence of change, while dynamics refers to an evolving structure. Cumulative change will ultimately lead to structural change, but mechanical change leads to a new equilibrium position within an unchanged structural order. The concept of a natural order defined by a few natural laws had particularly dominated the study of economics (Randall 1940, 323–331 and 499–501). This approach encouraged the search for a minimal set of natural laws that would allow axioms to be expressed which could be used to explain and predict all change. Deduction from axioms would be feasible and sufficient because the structure of the system was stable, but would be insufficient to understand and explain cumulative change. The other approach to this inquiry was the naive empiricism of the German Historical School, which rejected deductive logic but offered little explanatory power. The question facing scholars such as Commons was how to explain the order of society when the structure was evolving. Commons found the natural order approach to be anti-evolutionary and the empirical approach to be anti-theory. Moreover, the natural law approach was non-empirical because all outcomes were built into the axiomatic assumptions.

The purpose of scientific theory is to identify determinants of order and the patterns of change. When we say "economic system" we imply there is an order which can be understood and explained. Science would be impossible in a world where all events were random. Scientists have an almost religious belief that meaningful order exists which can be explained. It is a much more difficult task, however, to discover the patterns of evolutionary change than nonstructural changes because they are not simply repetitive and this is the task Commons set for himself in these essays on sovereignty.

To begin to understand the contribution Commons made in these essays on sovereignty, we examine his innovative theory of institutional evolution. That section is followed by a section devoted to the origin and development of property and a section on the state. The final section on the rule of law helps us to understand why Commons concluded that the purpose of state control of power of private property is not to create a condition of moral perfection, but to insure that competition will drag our behavior down to the most selfish elements of society.

THE SOCIOLOGICAL VIEW OF INSTITUTIONAL EVOLUTION

The sociological view according to Commons is the scientific study of the emergence, evolution, and role of institutions. With respect to sovereignty it is about the role of the state relative to other institutions and to other states. The sociological view is contrasted with the philosophical and the legal approaches. The philosophical approach is concerned with the ultimate or rational end of the state. On the other hand, the lawyer focuses on particular disputes between two parties within the existing system. Neither the philosophical nor the legal approaches are conducive to the study of the evolution of the state and its relationship to other institutions. The philosopher establishes the moral end of the state deductively, while the lawyer is totally practical in approaching the question. The science of sociology approaches the issue from the historical and comparative method. When and how did the state emerge from other institutions and what different evolutionary paths have been taken in various nations? It presumes that the state will take different forms in different circumstances, but that some practices work better than others. It also presumes that the state is not simply shaped by rational processes, but by community forces as well and there is no certainty that these forces will lead to progressive improvement. Institutional development creates new circumstances that must be adapted to as an ongoing process rather than as a route to an ultimate, rational end.

Institutions provide social order, which means that limits are placed on individual discretion. Because individuals resist such constraints, institutions develop sanctions to provide the necessary discipline and get the individuals working in the same direction. These sanctions can either be persuasive or coercive. However, as we shall see later, the state has taken most of the coercive sanctions from private institutions. Questions of equity hinge to a large extent on how these coercive sanctions can be used to divide the social product without harming the incentives to produce. Extant institutions, or going concerns, are organized by a set of working rules which reflect the social beliefs of the participants and these beliefs "are the psychic foundation of each institution" (Commons 1967, 6). These beliefs, when backed by social authority, have real force.

Adam Smith stressed the importance of the division of labor among individuals as a critical determinant of the relative economic performance of nations. In fact, that is the foundation of the theory of domestic and international exchange. The title, *The Wealth of Nations*, would suggest that Smith understood that the state was an institution of fundamental importance. However, the theory of exchange has been developed with little attention to the function of institutions other than their hinderance of the attainment of the natural order. Smith and his followers said little about the beneficial aspects of institutions. Instead, it is implied that any restraint on the liberty of individuals will prevent a nation from achieving its natural or rational end-state. Commons, on the other hand, worked to provide a theory of the technical and ethical function of institutions which govern production and exchange.

As circumstances change due to improvements in technology and population growth, social beliefs will be altered which will require modifications of the institutional structure. The struggle over the institutional changes are hard-fought and are usually led by social mavericks. The genesis of the change is caused by changing relative scarcity caused in turn by the developments in technology and growth of population. For instance, population growth can make land more scarce than labor or a new technology can create a new resource that will require new rules of ownership. Each of these developments can cause a sufficient shift in social beliefs to require an institutional adjustment. As these developments and adjustments continue, we can begin to discern an evolutionary path.

Commons and Thorstein Veblen were interested in the findings of anthropologists regarding the role and evolution of institutions in primitive societies, and independently arrived at the importance of ownership in early stages of social evolution (Commons referred to the work of Veblen on page 13 of these essays). Commons' reading of this record was that in very primitive societies there were no specialized institutions for the functions of the family, church, economy, or government. Instead the clan structure was an amorphous whole. As demographic and technical conditions changed, the social beliefs changed causing a separation and specialization of institutions. Evolution in biology and society is synonymous with differentiation rather than optimality.

Even in biology "natural selection does not lead to the superlative fittest, only the tolerably fit. But even in a weaker sense, evolution is not necessarily a grand or natural road leading towards perfection" (Hodgson 1994, 209). In social evolution the question is, what institutional form will give expression to the emerging social beliefs, and will this new institution fit tolerably well with other institutions. Institutional development is not about the natural selection of institutions in some pre-ordained path toward an ultimate rational end-state of society. It is also not suggested that the institutional structure can be anything that is desired, but considerable discretion does exist. There are, however, a range of institutions which are incompatible with the existing and emerging technical circumstances. The evolutionary path a society is on is determined both by technology and previous choices.

The most significant point is that social evolution involves the continual development of specialized institutions and structure and interrelationships of the separate institutions is at least as important to the performance of the economic society as the specialization of individuals in production. Specialization does not imply independence, but the opposite. "The differentiation of institutions is not their isolation. They all continue to act organically, each upon the other, through the beliefs and desires peculiar to each" (Commons 1967, 7).

The final point to make in the general discussion of institutional evolution is that institutions are not created to remove the obstacles to happiness. Instead their ability to invoke negative sanctions on individuals and thereby constrain individual liberty of action can bring about unhappiness. The organizations of interest to Commons are created to cope and survive rather than for social recreation. "They are organized for struggle, survival, and supremacy. There is iron in them. They are based on the coercive sanctions intrinsic in private property, which is the social expression of self-consciousness and the origin of social institutions. Herein social organization is fundamentally different from physical and biological organization" (Commons 1967, 31). These statements are a fitting way to end this discussion on the general features of institutional evolution and turn to the particular institution of private property followed by an examination of Commons' view of the state.

PRIVATE PROPERTY:
THE ORIGINAL INSTITUTION

The differentiation and specialization of institutions began with private property. This is perhaps the fundamental tenet of these essays. All institutions, including the state, cannot be understood without an understanding of the origin, function, and evolution of private appropriation. This is so because property is not only the original institution, but it is also the origin of reflective self-consciousness. The highly developed level of self-consciousness, or knowledge of self, is a distinguishing feature between humans and other animals. "All social institutions originated as private property; this differentiates human from animal society; private property is the social expression of the highest unity of man, self-consciousness" (Commons 1967, 13–14). If the origin of private property has such distant roots and is so tightly linked with the development of the fundamental human attribute, self-knowledge, it is a moot point whether the drive for private appropriation is fixed in human nature or simply a cultural factor. In either case it is a deeply held social belief that cannot be simply dismissed. As a social reformer Commons might wish it were otherwise, but as a social scientist he had to deal with what he regarded as the truth.

According to Commons, those things that were useful and scarce were the first to be appropriated. Ownership probably began with appropriation of crude tools, fetishes, and animals that could be domesticated. These acts, because they were not threatening at first to the larger social order, went without retribution or sanction. Later, wife capture and wife purchase were practiced as an extension of the hunting function. As with the earlier appropriations, these practices met with little social resistance or sanction initially. But wife capture and purchase had very profound effects on social organization. Family consciousness began to complement and reinforce self-consciousness and challenge clan consciousness as the family became a specialized institution. The individuals who gained control of the fetishes were able to spin off a separate, specialized religious institution. The sociology journals of the late nineteenth century devoted considerable space to the origin and evolution of kinship structures and spiritual practices. Also, the infant discipline of anthropology made these practices the core of its inquiry (Fox 1985, 31; Bloch 1985, 698–700). This literature on the creation of specialized institutions had a strong influence on the work of Commons and Veblen and established the path of institutional economics. Veblen emphasized the exploitative and ceremonial aspects of ownership. Commons was more impressed with the functional attributes that could be used to develop human character. If a specialized institution could be more effective than an undifferentiated society in overcoming scarcity, then it had real social value. Commons remarked favorably on Veblen's distinction between economic property and that quasi personal fringe of material things distinguishing the individual's personality, but paid more attention to economic property in his work.

Gradually as people became more fixed in their territory, wife capture was extended to appropriation of males through the institution of slavery. With settlement and an adequate labor supply through wife capture and slavery, agriculture could be developed. The increased output and the need for more labor both supported and encouraged population growth. Population growth changed the relative scarcity from labor to land. Conquest of land and rules of land ownership led to the evolution of feudalism and "the establishment of feudalism completed the extension of self-consciousness through all the institutions of society" (Commons 1967, 13).

Feudalism is prior to the modern state and the concept of sovereignty. The government is still depicted as an extended household. "In settling upon a fixed territory we find a decisive step in the organization of the modern state, but it must be borne in mind that this step could be taken only by extending the principle of private property. The state originates as private property, like all other institutions" (Commons 1967, 28). The legal basis of feudalism was custom and was very binding even on the monarch. Feudal organization was more of a confederation of barons that had to be restructured on the death of each king. Even the king was tightly bound by custom and the social beliefs of the barons. However, economic forces accompanied by the rise of manufacturing, commerce, and money "broke down the rule of custom, and permitted the king to infringe more upon its precincts" (Commons 1967, 29). In the resulting absolutism the king's will could override custom which is the germ of the idea of law, but it is not the rule of law that we understand because there is no effective limit on the king's authority. The king is still a private proprietor because "the sanctions which he controls are exactly those corporeal and privative sanctions controlled by the primitive proprietor" (Commons 1967, 29). All coercive authority is held by a private proprietor outside the control of the wider community and even the community's custom could be overturned. It becomes clear that absolutism was a necessary step between the rule of custom in feudal society and the rule of law in the modern state. It was the need to limit the capricious actions of the absolute monarch acting as a private proprietor that led to the creation of the modern state.

Private appropriation preceded the right of appropriation and was resisted by the prevailing belief system. But the evolution of appropriation culti-vated self-knowledge, which transformed social organization and control. Self-knowledge reduced the role of instinct and imitation in social organiza-tion and human behavior. At this point in the story private ownership enjoys the protection of a moral right, but the machinery to provide a legal right is not yet in place. The next step is to describe how the state began to appropriate the coercive authority from the hands of the absolutist monarch acting as a private proprietor and develop the institutions to vest coercive powers in the larger community.

THE EMERGENCE OF THE MODERN STATE

The modern state was first a means to establish public order by wresting coercive sanctions from the monarch acting as a private proprietor. Therefore, a despotism is not a true state, but private property instead (Commons 1967, 42). The state emerged as the will of the king was checked by enduring constitutional processes. Order requires coercive sanctions, but the question is, in whose hands are the sanctions vested? We tend to equate the modern state with constitutional government. Though there is not complete agreement on the definition of constitutional government, Norman Cantor has suggested that the minimal elements are a viable government, a sense of community, and the rule of law (Cantor 1967, 205). First, peace and security must be established. Second, the order should not be established by an alien group. Third, the process for changing and enforcing rules should not be arbitrary or capricious. After order was established, it was possible to deal with equity and justice. However, if survival through competitive struggle is the situation facing society, then equity is of little concern relative to order. Hence, Commons dealt with the issue of sovereignty as problems of order first and right second.

With the increase in population and scarcity of land came a breakup of serfdom. This led to a wage system, an unstable price system, and population mobility. These phenomena reduced the power of custom and increased the power of the monarch and "his lawyers now introduced the fiction that custom becomes law only because 'what the sovereign allows he commands'" (Commons 1967, 41). Feudal chiefs, who had been able to exercise coercive power of property as sovereign lords under existing custom, saw their power eroded by the transfer of power to the monarch. This decline of custom and separation of property and political authority was the first step toward public sovereignty. However, this step created absolutism rather than a constitutional state. The demise of custom was not replaced by any restraint on the coercive power and capricious acts of the king. This path led to despotism in China, India, and Russia, but ultimately to constitutional government in England.

Through various phases and acts the old English feudal nobility was able to combine together and help shape the sovereign will. Magna Carta of 1215 was one of the first acts, but absolutism continued until the revolution of 1688. But Magna Carta must be understood as an act which established the path away from despotism toward constitutionalism. According to Cantor, "Article 39, the due process clause, is the basis of English constitutionalism." Further, this clause made it clear "that the legal system is not the king's, that the law of the land resides in the community" (Cantor 1967, 206–207). These two points combined, due process and community as the source of law, established law as an evolutionary process. Unlike continental law, which envisioned law as a code describing a pure ideal, the English common law evolves through resolution of disputes as judged by peers. It was a break with natural law and reliance on expert authority to interpret an act with respect to the ideal of the code. Right and wrong are judged by human experience rather than as an attempt to achieve moral perfection. Cantor suggests that English history can be told as the institutional working out of clause 39. It was the difficulties in developing those institutions that allowed absolutism to prevail for centuries.

Early community based law through due process was the law of peers and not the law of the common man. It took several more centuries to develop democracy out of these ideas. The first step on this path was ability of the feudal nobility to develop a class consciousness to challenge the will of the monarch. They were able to secure sovereignty over their own property by sharing sovereignty with the king. "The political problem which marks the genesis of order and the state begins in the attempt of social classes which have been subordinated on the basis of coercive sanctions to coerce in turn the monarch, in order to set boundaries to his coercion and to secure private property for themselves" (Commons 1967, 42). The development of sovereignty requires that self consciousness be supplemented and muffled by class consciousness (Cantor 1967, 217). "State consciousness is simply class consciousness organized for partnership in the coercive control of society" (Commons 1967, 47). When the institutions are developed to share this control through the rule of law based in the community, it can be said that the modern state has arrived. This is the beginning of combining mutuality with order. However, at this point in the evolution, this is still law as due process and not justice. It is law determined by class participation through due process, not basic human rights. At this point,

> the common law contains no idea of equity. The aim of the common law is to give every man his due, to maintain society as it exists, to preserve whatever belongs to a man in law, what he owns as the member of a group which has certain established privileges. But Roman law, which is structured around principles of abstract justice, says that law should control society in conformity with the law of nature, with some sort of abstract, higher law.
>
> (Cantor 1967, 267)

After order becomes established, the issue of equity or right can become the propelling force. Which classes can win a position in shaping the sovereign will must be decided by which group is successful in creating an effective class interest. Few are invited to share in the power structure; the position must be won. Moral rights are not effective rights, but moral arguments can be used to win popular and legal rights. Moral rights are subjective and, therefore, "they are simply a dogmatic way of asserting one's own opinion of what ought to be a legal right is above question" (Commons 1967, 57). Only legal rights are substantive rights, so the question becomes, how to consider equity when creating legal rights? As long as coercive sanctions are the domain of private proprietors, it is unlikely that equity will be considered. It is the continual flow of coercive sanctions from the proprietor to the state that allows questions of right and wrong to be addressed. It is when the state emerges as a separate institution that right gains equal footing with order.

When we realize that the division of labor is not just on an individual basis as in classical theory, but also includes institutional differentiation, we come to understand that equity cannot simply be grounded only on the natural rights of individuals. Equity considerations must be placed in an institutional context. Furthermore, if social evolution is defined as a continual increase in institutional differentiation and institutions help shape self consciousness, then equity processes must be dynamic as well. This was a fundamental dilemma for Roman-based law and early common law in attempting to govern an evolving society. Roman law looked to some code of moral perfection to determine justice. Early common law sought maintenance of the existing social order which was, itself, founded on earlier won privileges secured by property rights. Neither system supports an evolutionary view of continuous institutional differentiation.

Because there is institutional division of labor as well as individual specialization, "society is mutual service" (Commons 1967, 100). We depend on each other, but how do we distribute the output when output is dependent on individual effort and the institutional structure? To get your fair share of output, you must join with others with similar interests. "Consequently everywhere we find those with common interests are compelled to join together to gain power which united effort secures" (Commons 1967, 100). Hence, equity cannot be based solely on individual rights because distribution is largely determined by institutional effectiveness. "The political problem of the state occurs at exactly this point. It is concerned with the extent to which compulsion shall be used by private persons, by sects, or classes, in promoting their interests. It is not independent of technology and business. In fact, as shown above, it depends on these to further its ends" (Commons 1967, 101). Since society is mutual service the political question is "who shall get the advantage of social production?" (Commons 1967, 101). The political question must be addressed within the context of the technical framework for production, however.

RULE OF LAW, DUE PROCESS, AND EQUITY

Sovereignty of the modern state requires rule of law that is derived from community standards. "The state is the coercive institution of society. It is not an ideal entity, superimposed upon society, but is an accumulated series of compromises between social classes, each seeking to secure for itself control over the coercive elements which exist implicitly in society with the institution of private property" (Commons 1967, 45). It would be a mistake, then to view law as a perfectly rational endeavor. As Lawrence Friedman wrote, "Americans are naturally used to American laws. Law is an integral part of their culture. They could adjust to *very* alien laws and procedures about as easily as they could adjust to a diet of roast ants or a costume of togas" (Friedman 1973, 13). As an example Friedman noted that American law has treated corporations as persons and slaves as real estate (Friedman 1973, 19).

As explained above, English common law is a very different process than the continental legal procedure. The common law was developed as a bulwark against absolutism and authoritarianism. The emphasis was on due process rather than equity. Everyone was afforded due process, but what that process was depended on your class. Much of the responsibility for implementing the law was left to local justices of the peace for many issues at various times. This allowed local conditions to influence the process and outcome of disputes. "The whole legal system ultimately rested not on the king's will but on the legislative consent of the leaders of society and on the acquiescence and cooperation of the knightly class in law and administration" (Cantor 1967, 190). The gentry enjoyed access to local courts administered by itinerant justices, but the barons had access to the royal courts for major land disputes. This dual judicial system led to great tension in English history that has continued in American law. The gentry court reduced the power of the central government, but did not eliminate it. "The idea of equity, which is the justification for the proceedings in the king's chancery, is the principle out of which the conciliar courts will develop. The common law has no idea of equity" (Cantor 1967, 267). Friedman offers the following illustration. "It was possible for a man to have a claim which equity would enforce but common law would not, and vice versa. For example, the common law tended to treat a deed of land as valid, if it was executed in proper form. In equity, however, the deed was good only if it was free from undue influence, fraud, or deceit" (Friedman 1973, 23).

Due process and equity have had a tortured relationship throughout history in the American and English systems. The problem in England was that redress for equity tended to lead back to absolutism and away from community based law. One had to appeal to a central authority who could dispense equity. The tendency toward a paternalistic monarch was an attractive alternative for the gentry at certain times. The gentry welcomed the proceedings of Star Chamber during the sixteenth century as a means to overrule and mitigate abuses of the common law. But by the end of the century they came to resent the intervention of the crown in the operations of common law. The common law was seen as a bulwark against authoritarian tendencies of the crown (Cantor 1967, 431). The gentry, who had access to common law, preferred a haphazard, cumbersome legal system to a more rational one that would dispense justice if that required centralized authority. In essence, they rejected the more logical Roman system as they always had.

As Cantor has argued, the purpose of the early common law was to provide liberty through due process for the protected classes and, consequently, maintain the social structure. An unintended consequence of this

43

amalgam of centralization and decentralization in the quest for due process tempered with justice was social evolution rather than maintenance of the status quo. This became apparent in England with the 1628 Petition of Right without resort to the natural rights doctrine (Cantor 1967, 441). These rights are not God given nor enshrined in nature, rather they were the product of law and could be removed by the due process of law. "A democratic movement triumphs and great political reform is accomplished – but without any recourse to natural rights theory. It was an amazing process" (Cantor 1967, 448). However, England remains a rather stodgy class society continuing to be shaped by the evolution of democratic institutions. In America certain inalienable rights derived from nature were layered on top of the concept of due process. America has been able to reduce the strictures of overt class structure, but reliance on individual rights secured in nature has hampered the recognition that individual rights must actually be secured within institutions. Further, these institutions require some loss of liberty for participants in order to gain institutional power. The powerful in the United States achieved that power through institutions, but would have the less powerful believe that it can only be accomplished through individual pluck. The resolution to these conflicts between process and justice fits the culture of each country with all of the strengths and weaknesses of each culture. Social and legal fictions are perhaps necessary to create social bonds, but scholars should work to understand these fictions as potentially useful and harmful.

Commons was helping to make us aware that institutions are the result of compromises among social classes rather than ideal entities governing an ideal natural system. The state cannot simply override the technical requirements of business to produce, but it can lift the social standards. "Social coercion is necessary as against private coercion, not because the state can elevate the people to a higher level than that attained by the free exercise of their own persuasive powers, but in order to prevent the lower and selfish elements of society from dragging the several institutions down. The state sets the minimum level below which the struggle for existence shall not be permitted to force an institution" (Commons 1967, 104). A few years later in his famous shoemakers article Commons would develop this thought into the concept of the menace of competition (Commons 1909, 79–81). Institutional rules are needed to lift the standards of competition in recognition of inherited compromises of institutional structure. Because the concept of property is so deeply ingrained in our culture, this may require bringing more interests into the property system rather than directly reducing the vested rights (Atkinson 1974).

Equity as an individual, natural right achieved by appealing to authority will likely result in absolutism. Equity won through institutional strength will be more secure and has the potential of lifting society above the lowest results of competition. Equity can only be considered after an organization has survived competition. "Property is a requisite for survival, but it is not mere ownership. It is also the organization, subordination, discipline, efficiency of the human agents combined under the management of the proprietor. And until monopoly is reached the organization is never so secure that it can dispense with the equipment to fight" (Commons, 1967 59). Property provides the security to consider right and wrong in our choices.

Sovereignty is a condition of dynamic tension between the coercive authority of private property and that of the state. The state emerged from private property and is, therefore, shaped by those interests. But the state attempts to reduce the coercive powers of property institutions and leave them with persuasive powers only. A function of property is to provide the organization to overcome scarcity. Because what is scarce changes over time due to the effectiveness of institutions and the development of technology, property institutions need to be modified and created continually. In other words, since our institutional and technological structures are dynamic the rules governing property need to evolve as well. It is the duty of the state to develop property laws in order to mitigate the effects of the competitive menace even though the state is a creation of the property interests. The state and property are specialized institutions, but act organically upon each other and this interaction is a primary determinant of the evolutionary path. The historical and comparative method is better suited to uncover the dynamics of this interaction than either the philosophical or legal approaches.

REFERENCES

Atkinson, Glen W. "Property in an Evolutionary Economic System." *The Rocky Mountain Social Science Journal* (October 1974): 7–14.

Boulding, Kenneth E. "A New Look at Institutionalism." *The American Economic Review* (May 1957): 1–12.

Bloch, Maurice. "Religion and Ritual." *The Social Science Encyclopedia*, ed. Adam Kuper and Jessica Kuper. London, Boston and Henley: Routledge and Kegan Paul, 1985: 698–701.

Cantor, Norman F. *The English: A History of Politics and Society to 1760.* New York: Simon and Schuster, 1967.

Commons, John R. "American Shoemakers, 1648–1895: A Sketch of Industrial Evolution." *Quarterly Journal of Economics* (November 1909): 39–84.

Commons, John R. *A Sociological View of Sovereignty.* New York: Augustus M. Kelley, 1967.

Dorfman, Joseph. "John R. Commons' General Theory of Institutions." In John R. Commons, *A Sociological View of Sovereignty*: iii-xi.

Friedman, Lawrence M. *A History of American Law.* New York: Simon and Schuster, 1973.

Fox, Robin. "Anthropology." *The Social Science Encyclopedia*, ed. Adam Kuper and Jessica Kuper. London, Boston and Henley: Routledge and Kegan Paul, 1985: 27–32.

Hamilton, David. *Evolutionary Economics: A Study of Change in Economic Thought.* Albuquerque: University of New Mexico Press, 1970.

Hodgson, Geoffrey M. "Evolution and Optimality." In *The Elgar Companion to Institutional and Evolutionary Economics*, ed. Geoffrey M. Hodgson, Warren J. Samuels, and Marc R. Tool. Brookfield, Vermont and Aldershot, England: Edward Elgar Publishing Company, 1994: 207–212.

Randall, John Herman, Jr. *The Making of the Modern Mind.* Cambridge: Houghton-Mifflin Company, 1940.

4

SOVEREIGNTY AND WITHHOLDING IN JOHN COMMONS'S POLITICAL ECONOMY

Richard Dawson

Perhaps one of the reasons why judges do not like to discuss questions of policy, or to put a decision in terms upon their views as law-makers, is that the moment you leave the path of merely logical deduction you lose the illusion of certainty which makes legal reasoning seem like mathematics. But the certainty is only an illusion, nevertheless. Views of policy are taught by experience of the interests of life. Those interests are the field of battle. Whatever decisions are made must be against the wishes and opinion of one party, and the distinctions on which they go will be distinctions of degree.

(Justice Holmes 1894, p. 7)

INTRODUCTION

In the year 1895 the Supreme Court of Illinois decided *Ritchie v. People*. This case concerned a statute limiting the hours of labour for women and children in factories and workshops to 8 hours per day. The Illinois Legislature had acceded to petitions from various groups, including philanthropists and labour organisations, to make it unlawful for employers to require employees to work up to 16 hours per day. The long hours to which the employees were subjected contributed to, among other things, cramps, exhaustion, swollen legs, and low immunity to diseases. The owners of several factories, however, through their attorneys, contended that the statute violated the Fourteenth Amendment of the United States Constitution in that it deprived them *and their employees* their liberty to make contracts.[1] The Supreme Court agreed with this contention, and vetoed the statute.

In the same year that the *Ritchie* case was decided John Commons accepted the chair in sociology at Syracuse University. He also began a career

47

demythicising judicial decisions, commenting on the decision in an article entitled 'The Kingdom':

> It is not likely that the law deprives such women of a great amount of freedom. There are various degrees of freedom. The court would probably not permit the sweaters' victims to sell themselves by contract into absolute slavery, although many of them would doubtless better their condition by doing so. Speaking of the decision the *Chicago Times-Herald* says:
> "There is a ghastly sort of irony in the attempt of the supreme court to explain or excuse its decision upon the plea that it is protecting the rights of the weak individuals with labor to sell. Of course, a judicial tribunal cannot be expected to take cognizance of the facts that working people, insofar as they are represented by labour organizations and earnest but unofficial friends of the laboring classes, urged the enactment of the law, and that millionaire firms attacked its constitutionality. These things cannot, perhaps, be brought within the official purview of a court, but they can and shall be represented to the people. What a mockery it is to read that the supreme court has demolished this . . . law on the plea that it robs the poor on the right to sell their labor as they will. Dives demands protection. The court accedes to this demand, but pleads that it acts in the interests of Lazarus."
>
> (Quoted in Ely, 1914, p. 652)

Commons objected to the decision in the *Ritchie* case in so far as the members of the Court obfuscated their privileging of the employers' interests through the use of an individualistic conception of freedom. The issue, in his view, was *whose* freedom, that is: freedom for the employers to command employees to work 16 hours per day versus freedom for the employees from injurious commands of employers.

Commons undoubtedly considered the judiciary at the time to be, to paraphrase Karl Marx and Frederick Engels (1848, p. 69), a committee for managing the affairs of capitalists. Unlike Marx and Engels, however, Commons did not urge the propertyless to get control of the state by way of physical force. Instead, he clarified the existence of an alternative non-violent means to the same end. As he stated four years after the *Ritchie* case in *A Sociological View of Sovereignty*:

> Freedom is the command over the services of others. But in acquiring this opportunity and this freedom the lone individual is helpless against the pressure of others. Consequently everywhere we find that those with common interests are compelled to join together to gain the power which united effort secures. If their interest is

urgent enough and their demands are not granted, they will resort to compulsion. History is full of the uprisings of sects and classes, of riots and wars, brought about by this struggle to share in larger degree the freedom and opportunities which society vouchsafes. This struggle, however, is not always violent. It may be constitutional. That is, the machinery of government may be so constructed and the suffrage so extended that different sects and classes may get a share of social services by simply getting control of the constituted authorities through well-recognized channels and without resorting to violence. This . . . is the injection of order into coercion. But, in either case, whether violently or orderly, it must be noted, the resort is to compulsion. The power of compulsion, wherever it exists, is the power to put one's own opinion or desire into effect regardless of the desires and opinions of others.

(Commons, 1899–1900, pp. 100–1)

In *A Sociological View* Commons urged the conceptualisation of sovereignty as a process rather than an entity, personified as "The State." He perceived the state as a process of negotiation over the control of the sanction of physical force. For analytical and interpretive purposes Commons in effect proffered the following proposition: Sovereignty is an instrument of physical force available for the use of whomever can get into a position to control it.

This principle of the use of sovereignty is, he considered, a descriptive, non-normative proposition. Anyone's theory or conception of what the state should or should not do is, in effect, their normative approach to the use of sovereignty. An approach to sovereignty based on this principle would, he thought, tend to compel treatment of each approach to the state objectively as a use of sovereignty.[2]

Several months before the publication of *A Sociological View* officials of Syracuse University voted to discontinue the chair held by Commons. The Chancellor explained to Commons that hoped-for contributors refused to give money to the University as long as Commons held a chair in the University. He also told him that at a recent national meeting of college presidents all had agreed that no person with radical tendencies should be appointed to their faculties. The Chancellor told Commons that his prospects for another college position were poor. In his autobiography, *Myself*, Commons tells us he drew the conclusion "It was not religion, it was capitalism, that governed Christian colleges" (1934b, p. 58). In 1904, however, Commons returned to academia, accepting a teaching job from Richard Ely, professor of political economy at the University of Wisconsin.[3] Commons took with him to Wisconsin a further insight from his dismissal from Syracuse:

Afterwards I sought the fundamental reason, and included it in my historical development of Institutional Economics. The older

49

economists based their definitions of wealth on *holding* something useful for one's own use. . . . I distinguished a double meaning. The other meaning was, *withholding* from others what they need but do not own. This was something real to me and the Chancellor. . . .

When I first drafted, in my early days at Wisconsin, an article on "withholding" as a neglected economic concept, I was dissuaded by an orthodox colleague from publishing it. Eventually, after many years' investigation, I included it in my *Institutional Economics*. I figured that a "chair" in political economy was not physically pulled out from under you, it was economically pulled out by withholding the funds. This was such a customary, legal, and quiet way of doing it, under the institution of private property, that everybody, including economists, took it as part of the Natural Order not needing investigation. At least, I knew, after 1899 at Syracuse, that holding and withholding were not the same, and that the latter was more important.

(Commons 1934b, pp. 58–9)

This paper examines aspects of Commons's political economy relating to the concept of withholding. The focus is on Commons's blending of withholding with sovereignty. His work in this domain is largely in reference to the American system of judicial sovereignty, especially the constraints on the police power of national and state legislatures in the form of the Fifth and Fourteenth Amendments of the Constitution of the United States.[4] The first section below calls upon Commons's discussion of the emergence of what he calls the "economic power" of property, which is the power to withhold from others what they need but do not own. This is followed by visiting Commons's explicit rejection of a key premise underpinning the "neutral umpire" concept of the state. The second section examines a United States Supreme Court case in 1877, *Munn v. Illinois*, which Commons identified as the first occasion in which the Court explicitly identified and restrained economic power. The case facilitates consideration of the interrelations between the physical power of sovereignty and the economic power of property. The next section looks at another Supreme Court case involving economic power, *Holden v. Hardy*. Among other things, this case serves as a base for exploring Commons's model of legal concepts which he developed to aid analysis of relative economic power. The penultimate section looks at three Supreme Court decisions critiqued by Commons using his model of legal concepts. The final section provides a summary.

THE EMERGENCE OF ECONOMIC POWER

A central facet of Commons's *Legal Foundations of Capitalism* is the identification of a structural transformation which produced a change in the nature of property. The change that he pin-pointed was from holding a physical tangible thing for use and enjoyment of self to the power to withhold from others what they need. The change attended the closing of the frontier and the emergence of the widespread reliance on buying and selling for a living. Commons describes the process of change as follows:

> The transition from the notion of holding things for one's own use and enjoyment to the notion of economic power over others evidently accompanies the historical evolution of property from slavery, feudalism, colonialism and a sparse population, to marketing, business and the pressure of population on resources. Where production was isolated, or the owner held under his control all of the material things as well as the laborers necessary to the support of himself and dependants, the concept of exclusive holding for oneself was a workable definition of property. But when markets expanded, when laborers were emancipated, when people began to live by bargain and sale, when population increased and all resources became private property, then the power to *withhold* from others emerged gradually from that of exclusive *holding* for self as an economic attribute of property. The one is implied in the other, but is not unfolded until the new conditions draw it out. Just as the scales of the reptile become the feathers of the bird when the environment moves from land to air, so exclusive holding for self becomes withholding from others when environment moves from production to marketing. The transition was hardly noticeable as long as the merchant, the master, the laborer, were combined under small units of ownership, but becomes distinct when all opportunities are occupied and business is conducted by corporations on a credit system which consolidates property under the control of absentee owners.
>
> (1924, pp. 52–3)

In the above passage, as noted by Michael Carter (1985, pp. 802–3), Commons describes what Karl Marx calls the separation of labour from the means of production and Karl Polanyi studies as the destruction of the socially embedded economy. Propertyless people in such an economy are, in Amartya Sen's language, without exchange entitlements. Such people are compelled to acquire wages or else starve. This, Commons (1934a, p. 200) emphasised, places them at a disadvantageous position in bargaining with, say, wealthy employers whose alternative to employing a worker "may be only the inconsequential alternative of foregoing one out of hundreds or even thousands of laborers in filling the jobs in his concern." That is to say, there is inequality in economic power in the sense of differential capacity "to hold back until the opposite party consents to the bargain" (Commons 1924, p. 54). Propertyless people, such as women and children in the *Ritchie* case, may well "consent" to working long hours in unpleasant and dangerous conditions rather than starve.

Use of sovereignty

In situations of conflict involving economic power, Commons recognised that the state could not play the role of neutral umpire. In *Institutional Economics* Commons (1934a, pp. 33–5) drew attention to the premise underpinning the concept of the state as a self-subsistent entity, which only wields the sovereign sanction of force when rights are violated. The premise is John Locke's "earthly abundance." In Locke's view, God had given freely a bounty, and all that people need to do is take what they want. The appropriation of any parcel of land did not have a negative effect on the welfare of others "since there was still enough, and as good left; and more than the yet unprovided could use" (Locke, quoted in Commons, 1934a, p. 35). It is this starting point which underlies the doctrine of natural rights. As Commons put it:

> Locke's idea of nature's abundance is also his presupposition of the natural right of liberty as well as property. "Every man has a property in his own person: this [property] nobody has a right to but himself." Thus his idea of labor is . . . the idea of freedom and ownership. The laborer has a natural right to do as he pleases with his own body, and every other person is subject to the duty of letting him alone, while he takes his own property . . . from nature's supplies.
>
> (1934a, p. 34)

Lockean abundance, Commons emphasised, became obsolete soon after the "discovery" of America by Columbus. For under Lockean abundance, among other things, the Indian nations would have been "let-alone." But force was used to dispossess them of land to the benefit of favoured persons and corporations (see Felix Cohen, 1941, pp. 123, 420). Thus in the United States, Commons insisted, there never was a time when the theory of *laissez-faire* was the practice. As Commons stated in his presidential address to the American Economic Association, demythicising the doctrines of *laissez-faire* and natural rights, and urging his principle of the use of sovereignty:

> No, our theory of natural rights has *not* been a *laissez faire* theory of government, but a pork-barrel theory. Not a let-alone theory but a let's grab theory. And it is embedded deep in our every relation to the government, while the river and harbor bills are its picturesque outcropping.

And this theory was roughly suited to the nineteenth century of America. It was the century of conquest of Indians and Mexico, of expansion and occupation westward, of civil war that centralized power. . . . Unlike the theory of *laissez faire* that the state is a necessary evil, it is a theory that the state is the political method by which individuals unite to use the sovereign power for their own purposes. . . .

So with our natural resources and public domain. The homestead law and its many collateral timber, desert, and mining acts were a conclusion from the natural right of anybody to get anything that belonged to the government. . . .

But the theory [of *laissez-faire*] is a half truth. Nature may endow the individual with rights, but she does not seem to burden the same individual with duties. The duties are imposed on other persons. But if rights proceed, not from nature, but from the state, then the very act that grants a right imposes an equivalent duty . . .

This is the missing half of the pork-barrel theory. It was not missed particularly in the nineteenth century, when those who did not have rights of property could move west and get them. It is missed in the twentieth century when those who are short on rights are compelled to make terms with those who have them.

(1918, pp. 8–9)

When those short on rights, such as the women in the *Ritchie* case, seek to use the sovereign power to reduce their exposure to injurious commands, the issue is not one of *laissez-faire* or intervention, but the pattern of power to be *re*-created by the state. The appeal to *laissez-faire*, Commons discerned, serves to obfuscate the past uses to which the state has been put; that is to help perpetuate a pattern of privilege. As such, the effort amounts to an agenda for the use of sovereignty:

The businessmen and economists did not really mean all that they said about *laissez faire*. . . . By *laissez faire* was really meant a maxim of advice to these officials of sovereignty recommending the use of physical force against persons who interfered with ownership, but alternatively recommending the use of physical force in favor of the owners themselves.

(1950, pp. 82–3)

MUNN V. ILLINOIS

Commons (1924, p. 34) identified *Munn v. Illinois* (1877) as the first case in which the United States Supreme Court explicitly "recognized . . . the

53

economic power of property, or power to withhold, growing out of economic conditions, as distinguished from the physical power of sovereignty. . . . "[5] Ira Munn and Ian Scott were lessees and managers of a grain elevator in Chicago. Wheat shipped from the Western wheat fields to the Atlantic seaboard had to be trans-shipped at Chicago, and while waiting for trans-shipment, had to be stored in elevators located near the terminals of the western and eastern transportation systems. There were fourteen such elevators, including those of Munn and Scott, but because the area available for the purpose was very limited in extent, they had no fear of outside competition. The nine firms which controlled them had a virtual monopoly. In response to complaints from shippers of exorbitant prices, the legislature of Illinois enacted a statute fixing maximum storage rates. Munn and Scott, through their attorneys, contended that the statute violated the Fourteenth Amendment in that it deprived them of their property without due process of law. After unsuccessfully challenging the statute in the Illinois Supreme Court, Munn and Scott took the case to the United States Supreme Court. An argument was presented on the phrase "due process." They insisted it was to be interpreted in light of the common law; represented Lord Chief Justice Matthew Hale as the great authority upon that subject; cited his treatise on *The Ports of the Sea* for the rule on price regulation; declared its meaning to be a limitation of legislative action to businesses "affected with a public interest"; and denied that grain elevators were anywhere to be found within that catalogue. A commonality of the businesses identified by Hale being "affected with a public interest" was the holding of a special grant of sovereign power. And in the case of a grant of sovereign power, the power of the sovereign to regulate the charges went along with that grant. The charges must be reasonable and this was the common-law rule applying to all special grants. The warehouse company, however, had always been a private business and had never been granted any special grant of sovereign power to carry on its business. Counsel for the plaintiffs argued that the prerogative of the King, now the police power of the legislature, could not lawfully be extended to a private business.

Chief Justice Waite, for the majority of the Court, accepted the rule of law from the plaintiffs, but, ironically, affected the warehouse company with a public interest and sustained the Act. The majority perceived that many producers and consumers had become dependent upon the warehouse company and the latter should not be in a position to take advantage of this. Chief Justice Waite stated:

> Neither is it a matter of any moment that no precedent can be found for a statute like this. It is conceded that the business is one of recent origin, that its growth has been rapid, and that is already of great importance. And it must also be conceded that it is a business in which the whole public has a direct and positive interest.

... [S]omething had occurred which led the whole body of the people to suppose that remedies such as are usually employed to prevent abuses by virtual monopolies might not be inappropriate here. ... [T]he owner could make his rates at will, and compel the public to yield to his terms, or forego the use.

(*Munn v. Illinois*, pp. 132–4)

"The Munn Case", Commons (1924, p. 62) remarked, "was an innovation in that it recognized a source of power unknown to common law and unrevealed until property assumed its modern dimensions." Prior to the decision the term power had meant only the physical power of the sovereign over subjects in enforcing the laws, out of which power came the grants of special privileges or monopolies. Chief Justice Waite identified and restrained "the economic power of citizen over citizen" (Commons, 1924, p. 35).

Recognising the power of citizen over citizen, the majority of the Court held that property lost its strictly private character. On the blending of public and private Commons (1924, p. 33) directed us to the words of Chief Justice Waite, who held:

Property does become clothed with a public interest when used in a manner to make it of public consequence, and affect the community at large. When, therefore, one devotes his property to a use in which the public has an interest, he, in effect, grants to the public an interest in that use, and must submit to be controlled by the public for the common good, to the extent of the interest he has thus created.

(*Munn v. Illinois*, p. 126)

Following the *Munn* case, justification for the use of the sovereign power to restrain economic power, by regulating prices, was, wrote Commons (1924, p. 34), "but a mere showing that the citizen had engaged in business upon which other citizens depended for their liberty and property." Put differently, "the majority ... enlarged the definition of the police power ... to the control of the bargaining power of property where prejudicial to the bargaining power of others" (p. 35).

Commons directed attention to Justice Field's instructive dissent in the *Munn* case (in which Justice Strong joined). Justice Field began with an expression of concern for what the case might lead to:

If this be sound law, if there be no protection, either in the principles upon which our republican government is founded, or in the provisions of the Constitution against such invasion of private rights, all property and business in the State are held at the mercy of the

majority of its Legislature. The public has no greater interest in
the use of buildings for the storage of grain than it has in the . . .
manufacture of cotton, woollen and silken fabrics; in the construction of machinery; in the printing and publication of books . . .
indeed, there is hardly an enterprise or business engaging in the
attention and labor of any considerable portion of the community,
in which the public has not an interest in the sense in which that
term is used by the court in its opinion. . . .

(Munn v. Illinois, pp. 140–1)

Justice Field then turned to the meaning of the term "property" as used
in the Fourteenth Amendment. He attacked the meaning given to it by
the Illinois Supreme Court in its rejection of the claim by Munn and Scott
that the statute deprived them of their property. The Court had held that
property was not taken to the extent that company owners were not deprived
of the "title and possession." In this respect, as Commons remarked,

the Illinois court adhered to the primitive definition of property as
the holding of physical objects for one's own use and enjoyment.
The legislature, under the police power of the state, might reduce
the charges which a warehouse company had established for its
services, but that was not a "taking" of their property. The owners
continued to hold their physical property even though deprived of
the power to fix the prices for its use.

(1924, p. 15)

To this Justice Field answered:

All that is beneficial in property arises from its use, and the fruits
of that use; and whatever deprives a person of them deprives him
of all that is desirable or valuable in the title and possession. . . .
If the Legislature of a State . . . can determine, against the consent
of the owner . . . the prices which the owner shall receive for its
uses, it can deprive him of the property as completely as by a
special Act for its confiscation or destruction. . . . There is indeed
no protection of any value under the constitutional provision which
does not extend to the use and income of the property, as well as
to its title and possession.

(Munn v. Illinois, pp. 142–3)

Commons (1924, p. 15) agreed with Justice Field's conception of property
as "exchange value" as opposed to a tangible thing in so far as buying and
selling was relied upon for making a living: "For, of course, the title of
ownership or the possession of physical property is empty as a business asset

if the owner is deprived of his liberty to fix a price on the sale of the product of that property." But exchange value, as Commons pointed out, is not independent of the power to withhold – the issue in dispute. Munn and Scott's favourable location, which prevented competition, enabled them to increase their prices and profits, and therefore the exchange value of their business. Justice Field's blindness to the economic power of property is evident in his assertion that the decision by the Court was an unwarranted departure from precedent:

> It is only where some right or privilege is conferred by the government or municipality upon the owner, which he can use in connection with his property, or by means of which he can use of his property is rendered more valuable to him, or he thereby enjoys an advantage over others, that the compensation to be received by him becomes a legitimate matter of regulation.
>
> (*Munn v. Illinois*, p. 146)

Here Justice Field expressed the view underpinned by Locke's "earthly abundance" that in assigning and enforcing property rights the government conferred no rights or privileges on the owner "by means of which . . . . he thereby enjoys an advantage over others." In fact, however, the virtual monopoly of the nine firms who operated these warehouses was rooted precisely in their legal right to keep competitors from competing. No one could, as a practical matter, engage in the business without maintaining a warehouse in the narrow area, all the land of which was owned by these nine firms or leased by them. Maintaining such a warehouse would have been forbidden by law, since it would have involved trespass on someone else's property. The legal prohibition of trespass on this area was in effect, though not in name, a prohibition of competition. The result was the same as if the law had, in so many words, conferred on the nine corporations a legal monopoly – in which case Justice Field would have admitted the legitimacy of regulating their charges.[6] As Commons stated in a passage clarifying the link between physical and economic power:

> the two meanings of power coalesce . . . for a legal monopoly or franchise, based, as it is, on direct participation in the physical power of the sovereign preventing competition, is economically similar to the power of such private property as a grain elevator in Chicago, whose owners have power to charge for their services more than they cost, owing to superior location but without legally preventing competition. In the one case competition is physically prevented; in the other case competition is economically prevented. In the one case the monopolist is favored by the sovereign as against the equal competitive liberty of others; in the other case the owner

is favored by his economic situation while the sovereign treats his property and liberty equally with all others. Ultimately each, of course, rests upon the physical power of sovereignty to protect the holder of either the monopoly or the situation. But in the case of the legal monopoly the protection is the direct prohibition of competition, while in the case of the favorable situation the sovereign protects only the ownership of the situation. In either case, economic power emerges, since economic power is simply power to withhold from others what they need. In short, the change in the concept of property from physical things to the exchange-value of the things is a change in the concept of *holding* things for one's own use to *withholding* things from others' use, protected, in either case by the physical power of the sovereign.

(1924, p. 52)

The *Munn* case may be considered in terms of the principle of the use of sovereignty. In the absence of the statute fixing maximum storage rates, under the state law of property, which created the situation of a virtual monopoly for the owners of the grain elevators, the firms had the economic power to charge for their services significantly more than they cost. In response, shippers of grain went to the Illinois Legislature and argued for the passage of a statute protecting them from exorbitant prices. That is to say, the shippers attempted to use the physical power of sovereignty to reduce the economic power of the firms. The Legislature acceded. In response, Munn and Scott, on behalf of the nine firms, went to the lower Illinois courts, the Illinois Supreme Court and the United States Supreme Court in an effort to have the statute vetoed. That is to say, Munn and Scott attempted to use the state to defuse the shippers' efforts to use the state. But the shippers won.

The issue of the control of sovereignty was raised in the *Munn* case. Recall that Justice Field, in his dissent, expressed the concern that: "If this be sound law . . . all property and business in the state are held at the mercy of the majority of its Legislature." Chief Justice Waite, for the majority of the Court, who enlarged the police power, was not oblivious to the fact that the door was being opened for its arbitrary use:

We know that this is a power which may be abused; but that is no argument against its existence. For protection against abuses by Legislatures the people must resort to the polls, not the courts.

(*Munn v. Illinois*, p. 134)

Commons (1924, p. 36) informs us that thirteen years after the *Munn* case, in *Chicago, Milwaukee, & St. Paul Railway Co. v. Minnesota*,[7] the judicial branch of government took jurisdiction of the police power in determining how far the legislature might go in exercising it. This, ironically, followed the approval of Justice Field's definition of property as exchange value. Thereafter all property and business in the state were held at the mercy of the majority of the Supreme Court.

HOLDEN V. HARDY

Commons (1924, p. 62) identified *Holden v. Hardy*, decided in 1898 (three years after the *Ritchie* case), as the first case in which the economic power of property in the dealings of employers with employees was restrained. This case involved a statute passed in 1896 by the Utah Legislature limiting the hours of labour in underground mines to 8 per day. To work longer than this was considered detrimental to health. In 1897 the statute came before the Supreme Court of the United States. Albert Holden, an employer, had been arrested by the sheriff, Harvey Hardy, after employing one John Anderson to labour as an underground miner for 10 hours per day. Holden argued that in so far as Anderson had voluntarily engaged his services the statute violated his right of liberty to make contracts protected by the Fourteenth Amendment. However, Justice Brown, for the majority of the Court, sustained the statute as a legitimate exercise of the police power. He emphasised that the right of contract was "subject to certain limitations" (*Holden v. Hardy*, p. 391). Company employers, he argued, had acquired relative strength in bargaining power vis-à-vis employees, enabling them to induce people to work longer hours through the fear of poverty. In his words:

> The legislature has . . . recognized the fact which the experience of legislators in many states has corroborated, that the proprietors of these establishments and their operatives do not stand upon an equality and that their interests are, to a certain extent, conflicting. The former naturally desire to obtain as much labor as possible from their employees, while the latter are often induced by the fear of discharge to conform to regulations which their judgement, fairly exercised, would pronounce to be detrimental to their health or strength. In other words, the proprietors lay down the rules and the laborers are practically constrained to obey them. In such cases self-interest is often an unsafe guide, and the legislature may properly interpose its authority. . . . The fact that both parties are of full age and competent to contract does not necessarily deprive the state of the power to interfere where the parties do not stand upon an equality, or where the public health demands that one party to the contract shall be protected against himself.
>
> (*Holden v. Hardy*, pp. 391–3, 397)

The Court, in placing a limit on the liberty of the employer, thereby clothed the employee with the liberty to refuse to work more than 8 hours per day without fear of discharge. With the *Holden* case in mind, Commons said of liberty: "liberty is a matter of the degree of coercion, and the definition of liberty is a matter of the degree of the allowable amount of pressure that may be employed in order to induce action" (1924, p. 326).

In the *Holden* case the economic power of the weaker class was enlarged at the expense of the stronger class. Commons remarked on this means of doing this in relation to both the normative goal and the categories of public and private:

> The physical power of the nation is called upon to limit the economic power of one class and thus to enlarge the economic power of an opposing class as respects that particular class of transactions. But this could be done in no other way than by giving to the private purposes of a weaker class a public preference over the private purposes of the stronger class; their private purposes became public purposes to that extent.
>
> How far this preference shall go is a matter, not of equality or logic, but of opinion and valuations. The weaker class, for some reason, is valued more highly than the strong class, at that particular juncture or class of transactions. Those who exercise the determining powers of the nation make a choice between classes of human beings and resolve to employ the sovereign powers on behalf of one class by placing ... responsibilities on the other class.
>
> (1924, pp. 130–1)

As Commons suggested in his analysis of the *Munn* case, the physical power of sovereignty is fused with economic power of the individual or corporation.

A LEGAL-ECONOMIC COMPASS

Commons (1924, p. 124) developed a "compass" to facilitate analysis of relative economic power.[8] The compass is comprised of four verbs: can, cannot, may, and must. When restated into formal juristic terms, they are distinguished as right, exposure, liberty, and duty. The authority to act involves an assignment of a capability or a *right* to one party, with a correlative constraint or *duty* on the part of another party to act in accordance with the right assigned. Rights and duties are subject to limits. The limit of a duty defines where a party is at *liberty* to act. The limit of a right defines where a party stands *exposed*. Limits are subtractive in the sense that party A's degree of exposure subtracts from their rights; party B's liberty subtracts from their duties. Exposures and liberties are correlated in the same sense as rights and duties. The liberty of party B has as its correlative the exposure of party A. Liberty can be granted to B only by reducing their duties, which entails reducing the rights of A. With B granted liberties A stands exposed, that is, potentially damageable without remedy or protection to the acts of B, who is unrestrained by duty.

In the case of each pair of limits and correlatives there is an underlying or implicit structure of advantage and disadvantage, depending upon who has what right, liberty, duty, and exposure. Thus, for example, with respect to the correlatives *right* and *duty*, party A may have an affirmative claim over party B, thereby controlling their conduct, and party B is under compulsion or obligation to the benefit of the former. The parties in question are not and cannot be under symmetrical or equal bargaining conditions. There is in-built inequality and injury:

> An authorized right cannot be defined without going in the circle of defining its correlative (corresponding) and exactly equivalent duty of others. One is the "I" side, the other is the "you" side, one the beneficial, the other the burdensome side of the identical transaction. . . . The same is true of liberty and exposure. One's exposures are exactly equal to the correlative liberties of others, but one's exposure is the reciprocal of one's own liberty, and is always unequal, since no person is ever exactly equal to any other person to whose liberty he is exposed.
> (Commons, 1924, p. 131)

Application of the juristic terms to the *Holden* case runs as follows: In sustaining the statute fixing maximum hours of work in mines, the Supreme Court held that the employer, Holden had *no right* to require his employees to work more than 8 hours per day. As such, the employees had *no duty* to work more than 8 hours per day if Holden commanded. That is to say, the employees were granted the *liberty* to refuse to work more than 8 hours per day without fear of discharge. This reduced their *exposure*. The decision by the Court thus inflicted injury on Holden. Had the Court deemed the statute in question to be unconstitutional, the employees would have been exposed to the liberty of Holden to discharge them if they refused to work more than 8 hours per day.[9]

The decision in the *Holden* case, as remarked above, enlarged the economic power of the weaker class at the expense of the stronger class. The means of doing this, in the jural terminology, Commons noted, was to place "limits . . . on the liberties of the more powerful under the name of duties. . . . These duties are correlative rights on behalf of the inferiors which are equivalent to reducing the exposure of the weaker parties by reducing the liberty of the stronger" (1924, p. 130).

Commons extended his compass of legal concepts to cover interrelations between citizens and officials of government. Among other things, this facilitates a deeper analysis of economic power which, as we have seen, is blended with physical power of sovereignty. A further four juristic terms are included in the larger compass, namely: power, disability, immunity, and liability. The term *power* connotes the capacity to determine and enforce rights, duties, liberties, and exposures. The correlative of power is *liability*, the condition wherein one may have one's legal relations determined by another. The limit of liability is *immunity*, the exemption from power. The limit of power is *disability*, the condition wherein one lacks the power to determine another's legal relations. Immunity, thus, is the correlative of disability.

Application of these terms to *Holden v. Hardy* runs as follows: When Holden brought suit against the sheriff Hardy, the issue was whether the sheriff had the constitutional *power* to enforce an 8-hour law upon the mine-owners of Utah. The Supreme Court decided against Holden and in favor of the sheriff. The Court decided that Holden was under a *disability* in that particular exercise of his will, and the sheriff enjoyed therefore *immunity* from damages or imprisonment if he should enter upon Holden's premises and enforce the law. That is to say, the Court decided that the sheriff possessed the constitutional *power* and therefore Holden was under the correlative *liability* of the sheriff's forcible entrance on his premises if he violated the 8-hour law.

Commons emphasised that when the relations between citizens and officials are determined this determines the relations between citizens themselves (1924, p. 105; 1934a, pp. 689–90). Thus when Holden obtained a decision as to the powers, immunities, liabilities, and disabilities, he simultaneously obtained a decision as to the pattern of rights, liberties, duties, and exposures. In particular, Holden's *disability* was equivalent to *no-right* to require more than 8 hour's labour. This is an *exposure*. The decision also meant that the correlative *immunity* of Holden's employees from action by the sheriff in evicting them from the premises was equivalent to *no-duty* to work more than 8 hours; this no-duty constitutes their *liberty*. Thus Holden's *disability* was the sheriff's *immunity*, and this constituted Holden's *exposure* to the *liberty* of his employees. Had the Court's decision been the reverse, then Holden's *power* to call on the Supreme Court would have been the sheriff's *liability* to damages due to Holden, or imprisonment for contempt of court, if he trespassed on Holden's premises. As such, Holden would have had the *right,* of his own free will, to require his labourers to work more than 8 hours, and they, correlatively, would have been under the legal *duty* to obey the will of Holden if they entered and worked upon his premises.

Upon presenting his compass of legal concepts, Commons made some critically important remarks covering several issues, including a limitation of the compass, his conception of both the state and legal rights, and the common human tendency to avoid recognition of this conception:

A logical scheme of this kind is valuable as a compass or method of analysis and contrast, but of itself is not only open to the criticism of Justice Holmes as to the "illusion of certainty," but that very illusion gives rise to metaphysical "entities" and "substances" conceived as existing apart from and independent of the behavior of officials and citizens. Thus the "state," ... is often conceived to be a vague entity acting as a "principle," and the officials are represented as the "agents" of the state who may or may not execute the "will of the state." But the state, from the practical standpoint of politicians, lawyers, business men and workingmen without illusions, is none other than officials-in-action. Instead of bringing suit against the "state," Holden brought suit against Hardy, the sheriff. This was nominally the state of Illinois, but actually the officials of Illinois, against whom Munn brought his suit. The citizen can disregard the state – he wants to know what the court and the sheriff will do.

These illusions naturally arise from the hopes and fears of mankind which substitute wishes for behavior. We conceive that what we wish is the reality, the real thing. Thus rights and duties also, like the state, are given the illusion of a reality existing apart from the conduct of officials. ... These metaphysical notions have, indeed, a powerful influence on men's minds, simply because man lives in the future and acts in the present. Thus constituted, he projects outward into a world of ideas his hopes and fears, and gives to his expectations a local habitation and a name.

Yet these ideas are but ideals – they exist, but they exist in the mind. They exist because man craves for security of expectations. ... Let anarchy surround him, where there are no officials to bring a collective power to his aid. ... No wonder he fills the sky with deities and entities – they are his hopes.

(1924, pp. 124–5, 364)

Yellow Dog contracts

Commons employed his compass to critique three leading cases early this century involving efforts to protect labour interests, including the right to unionise and strike. A primary purpose of his critique was to expose the differential treatment of labour and business interests by the Courts. He did not seek to construct an argument as to what the Courts ought to have done or not done.

The first case concerned an Act of Congress in 1898 which made it a criminal offence, punishable with fine or imprisonment, for any interstate carrier or any of its agents to discharge or otherwise discriminate against an employee because of their membership in a union. It thus prohibited making a "yellow dog" contract a condition of employment. In the jural terminology the Act meant that the employers had *no right/power* to require employees to resign their union membership as a condition of employment. The primary purpose of the Act was to prevent a repetition of the Pullman strikes that had been of considerable agitation to various commercial interests throughout the country. As the secretary of the Interstate Commerce Commission remarked on the Act in question:

> With the corporations as employers, on one side, and the organizations of railway employees, on the other, there will be a measure of equality of power and force which will surely bring about the essential requisites of friendly relation, respect, consideration, and forbearance. It has been shown before the labor commission in England that, where the associations are strong enough to command the respect of their employers, the relations between employer and employee seem most amicable.
>
> (Quoted by Justice Mckenna, *Adair v. United States*,
> 1908, pp. 187–8)

In 1906 William Adair, an agent of the Louiseville and Nashville Railroad Company, discharged Oscar Coppage, an employee of the company, because of his membership in the Order of Locomotive firemen. Suit was brought against Adair, and he was convicted for violating the statute. Adair appealed. The Supreme Court divided. Justice Harlan, for the majority, declared the Act unconstitutional and reversed the conviction. The principal argument was that the Act interfered with the liberty of contract both of the employer and of the worker, and was thus a violation of the Fifth Amendment. In Justice Harlan's words:

> It was the right of the defendant to prescribe the terms upon which the services of Coppage would be accepted, and it was the right of Coppage to become or not, as he chose, an employee of the railroad company upon the terms offered to him. . . . The right of a person to sell his labor upon such terms as he deems proper is, in essence, the same as the right of the purchaser of labor to prescribe the conditions upon which he will accept such labor from the person offering to sell it. So the right of the employee to quit the service of the employer, for whatever reason, is the same as the right of the employer, for whatever reason, to dispense with the services of such employee. . . . In all such particulars the employer and employee have equality of right, and any legislation that disturbs that equality is an arbitrary interference with the liberty of contract, which no government can justify in a free land.
>
> (*Adair v. United States*, pp. 172–3)

It would seem that Justice Harlan's assertion that "It *was* the right of the defendant [Adair] to prescribe the terms upon which the services of Coppage would be accepted" puts him in the category of people who suffer the "illusion of certainty" which "give[s] to the notion of right and duty an eternal, heavenly, natural, or preexisting 'substance,' apart from the actual behavior of mundane courts and executives who are depended upon to recognize and enforce it" (Commons 1924, p. 109). Adair's *right/power* to govern Coppage to the extent of inducing him to give up his "right" to join a union was not "there," but rather was *granted* by Justice Harlan in his decision. It would seem that the majority of the Court were either not conscious of or candid about their role as law-*makers*.

The Court's veto of the Act, Commons argued, was placed on "John Locke's definition of the will" (1924, p. 69). Locke's concept of the will is, wrote Commons, a "will-in-vacuo," a "mere faculty of acting and not-acting" (p. 69). This concept is embodied in Justice Harlan's assertion that "the employer and employee have equality of right." The equality of right is, Commons stated, "an equal right to choose between acting and not acting" (p. 71). He elaborated:

> The working man had the right to choose between working for the corporation and not working for it. The corporation had the equal right to choose between employing the man and not employing him. The two *rights* on the two sides of the transaction are exactly equal. There was "equality of right," because each had the equal right to choose between acting and not acting, between an "act" and an "omission."
>
> (1924, p. 71)

But, as Commons points out, the "will-in-vacuo" abstracts from the structure of the interaction of wills of the employer and the employee – the precise issue in dispute. Analytically, the interaction requires attention on what Commons calls the "will in action" – one "continually overcoming resistance and choosing between different degrees of resistance, in actual space and time" (p. 69). Put differently:

> For the will is not an empty choosing between doing and not doing, but between different degrees of power in doing one thing instead of another. The will cannot choose nothing – it must choose something in this world of scarcity – and it chooses the next best alternative. . . . The will chooses between opportunities, and opportunities are held and withheld by other wills which are choosing between opportunities, and these opportunities are limited by principles of scarcity.
>
> (1924, p. 303)

The issue in the *Adair* case was, Commons argued, the pattern of relative withholding capacity. In the jural terminology, this concerned the pattern of liberty and exposure. The Act in question, as noted above, sought to clothe the employees with the liberty to join a union without fear of discharge. This would expose the employer to damage on account of the possible exercise of that liberty. The damage would consist of the greater bargaining power of employees. Without the Act, the employees were exposed to discharge if they did not forego their "right" to belong to a union. In the latter situation, the relative bargaining power could not in any sense be deemed "equal." As Commons put it: "If the corporation has 10,000 employees it loses only one ten thousandth part of its working force if it chooses to not-employ the man, and cannot find an alternative man. But the man loses 100 per cent of his job if he chooses to not-work and cannot find an alternative employer" (1924, p. 72). Later, he added:

> When the laborer and his family could escape to other employers, before the incoming of these corporations, the doctrine of equality had some leeway; but when whole economic governments controlled the opportunities for employment of specialized workmen fitted mainly for that kind of employment, then the nation by these decisions of the courts was confronted with a conflict of inequality of power between great corporations and unorganized individuals.
> (1950, pp. 268–9)

The majority of the Court in the *Adair* case, however, was blind to the necessity of choice over the pattern of relative withholding power, and, like the Illinois Court in the *Ritchie* case, enshrined the pattern of power favouring the employers.

Commons saw merit in the dissent of Justice Holmes in the *Adair* case, who diffidently held:

> I . . . think that the statute is constitutional, and, but for the decision of my brethren, I should have felt pretty clear about it. . . . The [Act] simply prohibits the more powerful party to exact certain undertakings, or to threaten dismissal or unjustly discriminate on certain grounds against those already employed. . . . Where there is, or generally is believed to be, an important ground or public policy for restraint, the Constitution does not forbid it, whether this court agrees or disagrees with the policy pursued. It cannot be doubted that to prevent strikes, and, so far as possible, to foster its scheme of arbitration, might be deemed an important point of policy, and I think it impossible to say that Congress might not reasonably think that the provision in question would help a good deal to carry its policy along.
> (*Adair v. United States*, p. 191)[10]

The status of the *Adair* case became an issue in another dispute involving a similar statute prohibiting "yellow dog" contracts. In this dispute, however, a state instead of a federal statute was involved, and this statute was somewhat broader in scope. The Kansas Legislature made it a criminal offence for any individual or member of any firm "to coerce, require, demand, or influence any person" to enter into any agreement not to join or remain a member of any union, as a condition of employment. Terence Coppage, a superintendent of a railway company, requested Robert Hedges, a switchman, to sign an agreement to withdraw from the Switchman's Union while in the company's employ and told him he would lose his job if he did not sign. Hedges, who would forego benefits in the nature of insurance to the amount of $1,500 if he ceased to be a member of the union, refused to sign, or to withdraw from the union. Coppage discharged him. Suit was brought against Coppage and he was convicted in a state court for violating the statute. The conviction was affirmed by the Kansas Supreme Court. The Court followed the line of reasoning of Justice Brown in the *Holden* case, and noted:

> employees, as a rule, are not financially able to be as independent in making contracts for the sale of their labor as are employers in making a contract of purchase thereof.
>
> (Quoted in Commons, 1924, pp. 290–1)

The Court thus sustained the statute designed to reduce inequality of economic power, by deeming employers to have no right/power to compel the employee to forego their right to join a union as a condition of employment, as a legitimate exercise of police power.

Coppage appealed. Justice Pitney, for the majority of the United States Supreme Court, declared the Kansas law unconstitutional and reversed the conviction. He deemed the statute in question to be indistinguishable from the statute involved in the *Adair* case (*Coppage v. Kansas*, p. 9). He cited Justice Harlan's opinion asserting that the employer and employees had "equality of right" and any disturbance to this equality was an unjustifiable interference (*Coppage v. Kansas*, pp. 10–11). Justice Pitney then stated:

> Unless it is to be overruled, this decision is controlling upon the present controversy; for if Congress is prevented from arbitrary interference with the liberty of contract because of the "due process" provision of the 5th Amendment it is too clear for argument that the states are prevented from the like interference by virtue of the corresponding clause of the 14th Amendment.
>
> (*Coppage v. Kansas*, p. 11)

Justice Pitney, who accepted Justice Harlan's doctrine of equality, went on to reject the definition of coercion held by the Kansas Legislature and

Court: "[A] state [cannot], by designating as 'coercion' conduct which is not such in truth, render criminal any normal and essential innocent exercise of personal liberty or of property rights" (*Coppage v. Kansas*, p. 16). He asserted that

> there is nothing to show that Hedges was subjected to the least pressure or influence, or that he was not a free agent . . . and was at liberty to choose what was best from the standpoint of his own interests. Of course, if [Coppage] was otherwise in his legal rights in insisting that Hedges should elect whether to remain in the employ of the company or to retain his membership in the union, that insistence is not rendered unlawful by the fact that the choice involved a pecuniary sacrifice by Hedges.
>
> (*Coppage v. Kansas*, p. 8–9)

And further: "Coppage insisted that Hedges should freely choose whether he would leave the employ of the company or would agree to refrain from association with the union while so employed" (p. 15).

Justice Pitney went on to distinguish the case from the *Holden* case and others in which the Court had approved the use of the police power to limit liberty. The purpose of the statute in the *Holden* case, in his view, was "preserving the public health" (*Coppage v. Kansas*, p. 18). This differed from the Kansas statute, which he considered was: "to deprive employers of a part of their liberty of contract, to the corresponding advantage of the employed and the upbuilding of the labor organizations" (p. 16). On this, Justice Pitney stated: "no attempt is made, or could reasonably be made, to sustain the purpose to strengthen these voluntary organizations" (p. 16). In response to Kansas Court's decision to sustain the statute aimed at reducing inequality, Justice Pitney stated:

> No doubt, wherever the right of private property exists, there must and will be inequalities of fortune; and it naturally happens that parties negotiating about a contract are not equally unhampered by circumstances. And, since it is self evident that, unless, all things are held in common, some persons must have more property than others, it is from the nature of things impossible to uphold freedom of contract and the right of private property without at the same time recognizing as legitimate those inequalities of fortune that are the necessary result of the exercise of those rights.
>
> (*Coppage v. Kansas*, p. 17)

Here it is recognised that the inequalities that result from the exercise of "freedom of contract" are due, in part at least, to the fact that the different contracting parties do not have equal capabilities in the sense of wherewithal. They are "not equally unhampered by circumstances." A switchman, dependent on his job for his livelihood and hampered by the "circumstance" that he had little property, had little capacity to bargain effectively so as to retain his union membership. The railroad superintendent, because of the "circumstance" that the law, in assigning to his corporation the ownership of its property, enabled him to determine who might work and who might not on his railroad, had the capacity in the exercise of his "freedom of contract" to compel withdrawal from the union. It is true that these inequalities were the result of the coexistence of "the right of private property and the right of free contract." But the "circumstances" which hamper the parties unequally are a function of law, that is, judicial choice.[11] As Commons pointed out, the "inequalities of fortune" which Justice Pitney spoke of in response to the decision by the Kansas Court "were not the inequalities of Hedges and Coppage, but of Hedges and the railway company" (1924, p. 251). The difference involves the issue of whether the Kansas Legislature could create and protect a right of association of persons as against an association of property-owners. This question, a matter for judicial choice, was not even passed upon. The reason for this, Commons suggested, "resides in the fact that, for the purposes of the Fourteenth Amendment, a corporation is deemed to be a person and not an association of persons" (p. 291). (This had become settled doctrine since a decision in 1886.[12]) The doctrine of the personhood of the corporation, as Commons noted in reference to the *Coppage* case, is not a neutral fiction: "To Hedges . . . the railway company might appear to be a Leviathan controlling ten thousand jobs, but when he gets into court it is only Coppage, a person like himself" (p. 291). (The case was not called the *Frisco Railway Corporation* case but only the *Coppage* case.)

Whilst Justice Pitney treated a corporation as a person, he treated a union to be a "conspiracy" of individuals. His position was made explicit two years after the *Coppage* case in the *Hitchman* case. In that case a union and its agents, who were attempting to unionize the mines of the Hitchman Coal & Coke Company in West Virginia, were enjoined against even persuading the employees from joining the union in pursuance of a plan to unionise the mines by means of a strike, if necessary. The employees had been taken back at the end of a lost strike some years before on condition that they should agree not to belong to a union while working for the company, and all employees taken on afterward had been required to agree to this condition. In the *Adair* and *Coppage* cases it was the Congress and state legislatures that were forbidden to prohibit employers from insisting on such conditions in the contract of employment. In the *Hitchman* case it was the labour union that was forbidden to interfere with such contracts. Justice Pitney, for the majority of the Court, held that the union had no "just cause or excuse" for inflicting damage on the corporation by means of a strike "in order to compel plaintiff, through fear of financial loss, to consent to the unionization of the mine as the lesser evil" (*Hitchman v. Mitchell*, p. 259). The lesser evil, in Justice Pitney's view, was indeed evil:

> [An] error in defendants' position consists in the assumption that all measures that may be resorted to are lawful if they are "peaceable," – that is, if they stop short of physical violence, or coercion through fear of it. In our opinion, any violation of plaintiff's legal rights contrived by defendants for the purpose of inflicting damage, or having that as its necessary effect, is as plainly inhibited by the law as if it involved a breach of the peace. . . .
>
> It was one thing for plaintiff to find, from time to time, comparatively small numbers of men to take vacant places in a going mine, another and much more difficult thing to find a complete gang of new men to start up a mine shut down by a strike, when there might be a reasonable apprehension of violence at the hands of the strikers and their sympathisers. The disordered condition of a mining town in time of strike is a matter of common knowledge. It was this kind of intimidation . . . that defendants sought to exert upon plaintiff, and it renders pertinent what was said by this court in the Gompers Case . . . immediately following the recognition of the right to form labor unions: "But the very fact that it is lawful to form these bodies, with multitudes of members, means that they have thereby acquired a vast power, in the presence of which the individual may be helpless. This power, when unlawfully used against one, cannot be met, except by his purchasing peace at the cost of submitting to the terms which involve the sacrifice of rights protected by the Constitution; or standing on such rights and appealing to the preventative powers of a court of equity. When such an appeal is made, it is the duty of government to protect the one against the many."
>
> (*Hitchman Coal & Coke Co. v. Mitchell*, p. 257–8)

Commons would have us consider two questions: (i) If it is coercion for the union to compel plaintiff, through fear of financial loss, to consent to the non-unionization of the mine as the lesser evil, then why not also the efforts of the corporation to compel defendant, through fear of financial loss (in the form of unemployment), to consent to the unionization of the mine as the lesser evil? (ii) If, in the *Coppage* case, according to Justice Pitney, Hedges was *free* to choose Coppage's terms of employment for the pecuniary sacrifice of foregoing the right to union membership, then why was the Hitchman Coal Company deemed to be *free* to accept the union terms of labour supply for the pecuniary sacrifice of foregoing the right to non-union labour (Commons, 1924, p. 297)? His answer to this is as follows:

The Hitchman Coal Company appears in court as a single individual rather than an association of individuals who have combined their property into a unit. . . . According to . . . the court, as we have already seen, a unit of property has no power; it is an inert mass, no matter how large its dimensions; but a union of persons is power, and the reason why the corporation does not have power is because it does not appear as a unit of persons but as a unit of property. The opposite of this, we have seen, was approved in the Munn Case.

This appears to be the legal doctrine of conspiracy. The essence of conspiracy is in the duress, or coercion, exercised over an individual by a combination of individuals, as evident in the fact that that which may be lawful for a single individual, such as refusal to buy or sell or work, may become unlawful when done in concert by a combination of individuals. The illegality of a conspiracy is in the concert of action, and not the act itself. . . .

But a combination of property, distinguished from a combination of human faculties, is not deemed to exercise greater coercive power than a single person, else it would be deemed unlawful for a corporation to do what the isolated individual might legally do. The corporation, by the grant of sovereign power, is looked upon as a single person like other persons and may lawfully refuse to buy or sell or lease or hire, just as other persons may lawfully refuse.

(pp. 296–7)

Commons (1924, pp. 308–9) directs us to an instructive dissent by Justice Holmes concerning the right to strike, wherein Holmes, unlike Justice Pitney, correctly identified a corporation as equivalent to a labour union in the sense of being a combination, and correctly distinguished between threats of physical force and economic loss:

[I]t is plain from the slightest consideration of practical affairs, or the most superficial reading of industrial history, that free competition means combination, and that the organization of the world, now going on so fast, means an ever increasing might and scope of combination. It seems futile to set our faces against this tendency. . . . Combination on the one side is patent and powerful. Combination on the other is the necessary and desirable counterpart, if the battle is to be carried on in a fair and equal way. . . .

If it be true that workingmen may combine with a view, among other things, to getting as much as they can for their labor, just as capital may combine with a view to getting the greatest possible return, it must be true that when combined they have the same liberty that combined capital has to support their interests by argument, persuasion, and the bestowal or refusal of those advantages which they otherwise lawfully control. I can remember when many people thought that, apart from violence or breach of contract, strikes were wicked, as organized refusals to work. I suppose that intelligent economists and legislators have given up that notion today. I feel pretty confident that they equally will abandon the idea that organized refusal by workmen of social intercourse with a man who shall enter their antagonist's employ is wrong, if it is disassociated from any threat of violence, and is made for the sole object of prevailing if possible in a contest with their employer about the rate of wages. . . . I think the more intelligent workingmen believe as fully as I do that they no more can be permitted to usurp the State's prerogative of force than can their opponents in their controversies . . . [13]

But it should not be doubted that the workingmen were permitted to try to use the prerogative of force to bolster their capacity to coerce their employers. Justice Holmes's efforts to cloth the workers with the right to strike was unavailing in the *Hitchman* case. The employers thus were successful in using the Court to enshrine their coercively advantageous position vis-à-vis their employees. The employers were assisted by a majority of the Court who, like the majority in the *Adair* case, were either not conscious of or candid about their role as law-*makers*.

Needless to say, Commons objected to the decisions in the "Yellow Dog" cases for the same reason he objected to the decision in the *Ritchie* case, namely the obfuscation of valuational decision over the determination of the pattern of relative economic power.

SUMMARY

Commons's analysis of the interrelations between economic power and the physical power of sovereignty conflicts with the dominant ideology of individualism and *laissez-faire*. In Commons's view, no person is completely autonomous. With the frontier closed (and Locke's "abundance" obsolete), each person has scarcity relationships to others. The state is an arena of power play in which individuals and groups compete to make their interests count as rights and liberties, and thereby impose duties and exposures on others. Rights and liberties are not antecedent to the state. As Commons put it: "It is the sanctions of sovereignty that make property what it is for the time being . . . by keeping people off" (1950, pp. 41, 81). Thus the issue for society confronted with conflict is the determination of *who is to be kept off what*. The issue is not whether to employ the sanction of violence, but rather the direction in which the sanction of violence is to be wielded.

Recognition of this underpins Commons's principle of the use of sovereignty. In his words:

> Sovereignty . . . is an organized instrument of physical force which individuals endevor to use in order to enforce their own wills on others, or to prevent others from using their will on the individuals.
>
> (1934a, p. 695)

The critical analytical and policy questions pursued by Commons are: Who uses sovereignty and for what purposes? With regard to the latter and the making of public policy, Commons wrote:

> The question always is, not, *What* is a private purpose over against a public purpose? but, Is the private purpose *also* a public purpose, or *merely* a private purpose?
>
> (1924, pp. 236–7)

There is an inescapable necessity of choice by the state when private interests conflict. The line between private and public, as clarified by Commons in his analysis of the *Munn* and *Holden* cases, would seem to be non-existent – save in the imagination.

Both the raising and pursuit of the questions associated with the use of sovereignty have significance at least in so far as they expose as pretence the idea that the structures of power are to be treated as natural, and that sovereignty is not an instrument available for use. This, Commons hoped, would prevent the unreflective functioning of law and economics as power play – typically in the service of the privileged. Commons held the normative judgement that normative judgements with regard to the use of sovereignty should be made explicit. That Commons had his own normative agenda for the use of sovereignty is quite a different story.

NOTES

1 Fourteenth Amendment (1868): "Nor shall any state deprive any person of life, liberty, or property, without due process of law; nor deny to any person within its jurisdiction the equal protection of the laws."
2 The foregoing paragraph is a re-statement of Warren Samuels's outline of "A principle of government", Section 1 of his article "The State, Law and Economic Organization" (1979).
3 Commons had made a positive impression on Ely when studying political economy and law under him at Johns Hopkins in 1888. Ely had experienced similar difficulties as Commons with regard to allegations of being a radical (see John Henderson 1988, 329). Ely wrote an introduction to Commons's (1894) *Social Reform and the Church*.

4 Fifth Amendment (1791) applicable to the Federal Government: No person shall be "deprived of life, liberty or property, without due process of law; nor shall private property be taken for public use without just compensation."

5 The following interpretation of the *Munn* case has not only been influenced by Commons but also Walton Hamilton (1930) and Robert Hale (1952, 402–5).

6 The foregoing paragraph is drawn from Robert Hale (1952, 407).

7 *Chicago, Milwaukee, & St. Paul Railway Co. v. Minnesota* 134 U.S. 418, 458 (1890). Managers of a railway company, through their attorneys, asked the court to review the decision in the *Munn* and similar cases and to restrain the state legislature from fixing what they considered unreasonably low prices charged for the use of the property. Justice Blatchford, for the majority, held: "If the company is deprived of the power of charging reasonable rates for the use of its property, and such deprivation takes place in the absence of an investigation by judicial machinery, it is deprived of the lawful use of its property, and thus, in substance and effect, of the property itself, without due process of law and in violation of the Constitution of the United States."

8 The following discussion of Commons's compass has been heavily influenced by Warren Samuels (1973), Richard Gonce (1976), and Vincent Ostrom (1976).

9 The foregoing is largely drawn from Commons (1934a, 689–90).

10 *Adair v. United States*, 208 U.S. 161, 191 (1908). Commons did not specifically refer to Holmes's dissent in the *Adair* case, but he did quote Holmes's identical response in the *Coppage* case, which, as we shall see, is similar. See Commons (1950, 267).

11 The foregoing paragraph is drawn from Robert Hale (1952, 392–3).

12 *Santa Clara County v. Southern Pacific Railroad*, 118 U.S. 394 (1886). For a discussion of the normative significance of the personhood of the corporation, see Warren Samuels (1987).

13 This passage is taken from Holmes's dissent in *Vegelahn v. Gunter* (105–8) – he did not write a dissent in the *Hitchman* case.

BIBLIOGRAPHY

Carter, Michael (1985), "A Wisconsin Institutionalist Perspective on Microeconomic Theory of Institutions: The Insufficiency of Pareto Efficiency." *Journal of Economic Issues* 19: 797–813.

Cohen, Felix (1941), *Handbook of Federal Indian Law*. Washington, DC: U.S. Printing Office.

Commons, John R. (1894), *Social Reform and the Church*. Reprinted. New York: Augustus Kelley (1967).

——— (1899–1900), *A Sociological View of Sovereignty*. Reprinted. New York: Augustus Kelley (1965).

——— (1918), "Economic Reconstruction: Foreign and Domestic Investments." *American Economic Review*, 8: 5–17.

——— (1924), *Legal Foundations of Capitalism*. Reprinted. Madison: University of Wisconsin Press (1968).

——— (1934a), *Institutional Economics: Its Place in Political Economy*. Reprinted. Madison: University of Wisconsin Press (1961).

——— (1934b), *Myself*. New York: Macmillan.

——— (1936), "Institutional Economics." *American Economic Review*, 26: 237–49.

——— (1950), *The Economics of Collective Action*. New York: MacMillan.

Ely, Richard T. (1914), *Property and Contract in their Relation to the Distribution of Wealth*. New York: Macmillan.

Gonce, R. A. (1976) "The New Property Rights Approach and Commons's Legal Foundations of Capitalism." *Journal of Economic Issues* 10: 765–97.

Hale, Robert (1952), *Freedom Through Law*. New York: Columbia University Press.

Hamilton, W. H. (1930), "Affectation With Public Interest." *Yale Law Journal* 8: 1089–112.

Henderson, John P. (1988), "Political Economy and the Service of the State: The University of Wisconsin." In *Breaking the Academic Mould*, edited by William J. Barber, Connecticut: Wesleyan University Press.

Holmes, O. W. (1894), "Privilege, Malice, and Intent." *Harvard Law Review* 8: 1–12.

Marx, K., and Engels, F. (1848), The Communist Manifesto. Reprinted in Karl Marx, *The Revolutions of 1848*, edited by David Fernbach. Allen Lane in association with New Left Review.

Ostrom, Vincent (1976) "John R. Commons's Foundations for Policy Analysis." *Journal of Economic Issues* 10: 839–57.

Samuels, Warren J. (1973), "The Economy as a System of Power and Its Legal Bases: The Legal Economics of Robert Lee Hale," *University of Miami Law Review* 27: 261–371. Reprinted in Warren J. Samuels, *Essays in the History of Heterodox Political Economy*. New York University Press, New York (1992).

—— (1979), "The State, Law, and Economic Organization." *Research in Law and Sociology* 2: 65–99.

—— (1987), "The Idea of the Corporation as a Person: On the Normative Significance of Judicial Language." Reprinted in Warren J. Samuels, *Essays on the Methodology and Discourse of Economics*. New York University Press, New York (1992).

—— (1989), "The Legal-Economic Nexus." *George Washington Law Review* 57: 1156–578.

CASES

Adair v. United States, 208 U.S. 161 (1908).

Chicago, Milwaukee, & St. Paul Railway Co. v. Minnesota, 134 U.S. 418, (1890).

Hitchman Coal & Coke Co. v. Hitchman, 245 U.S. 229 (1917).

Holden v. Hardy, 169 U.S. 366 (1898).

Munn v. Illinois, 94 U.S. 113, (1877).

Ritchie v. People, 155 Il. 98 (1895).

Santa Clara County v. Southern Pacific Railroad, 118 U.S. 394 (1886).

Vegelahn v. Gunter, 167 Mass. 92, (1896).

5

THE IDENTITY
AND SIGNIFICANCE OF
COMMONS'S *A SOCIOLOGICAL
VIEW OF SOVEREIGNTY*

Richard Gonce

INTRODUCTION

Around 1894 John R. Commons began two projects: one culminated in
Proportional Representation (1896), a transparent book, the other in a nearly
opaque series of articles titled *A Sociological View of Sovereignty* (1899b–
1900) – in fact a compressed outline of a massive treatise he had intended
to finish after 15 years of work (Commons 1897a). *A Sociological View of
Sovereignty* (hereafter *SVOS*) raises questions. First, what is its identity? It
spreads across topics in religion, ethics, psychology, sociology, political
science, juristic law, history, and public policy. Is it simply a sociological
theory of sovereignty[1] emphasizing economic factors (Barnes 1924, 131),
or a "general" theory of the growth and functioning of "the dominant institutions of modern society" applicable to all the social sciences (Dorfman
1965, iii, iv), or a conjectural history of the development of society (Harter
1962, 216)? Second, is it significant, foreshadowing the finished work that
Commons called his "Institutional Economics" (1934b, 44) and also his
social philosophy of trade unionism or "modern Liberalism"?[2]

This essay argues several theses. First, much of *SVOS* emanated from ideas
Commons had developed during an initial stage of his thought prior to
1894 that were partly fixed and partly changing during 1894 to 1899 while
he was working on *SVOS*, and so an awareness of this context of ideas can
help to clarify the identity of *SVOS*. Second, seen in this context the cardinal
feature giving *SVOS* its identity is a theory of political and economic history
intended to justify public policies to improve the welfare of the American
labor class. The theory is not a value-free, general theory lying in any one
partial social science, but instead reflects Commons's ethics, is relative to
Anglo-American evidence, and is multidisciplinary in the name of sociology.

Third, *SVOS* is significant because Commons used it in large part as an outline for the development during the following decades of what he called his social philosophy of trade unionism or modern liberalism.

The essay will first glance at the initial stage of his thought, and next survey the context of his ideas from 1894 to 1899. It will then critically review *SVOS* in its context, and finally consider its significance.

THE INITIAL STAGE[3]

In the early 1890s Commons was one of R. T. Ely's disciples and protégés, a professor of political economy and sociology, but foremost a member of the social gospel movement collaborating with Ely and its other protagonists. For Commons, following Ely, the social gospel interpretation of the Christian religion is a blend of one-half theology and one-half of a sociology that attributes to institutions great causal force upon individuals' physical well-being and upon their souls or moral character, and in the name of religion demands the reform of institutions to establish "righteous relations" among individuals, and so to bring to pass the Kingdom of God on earth. These principles led Commons to a set of social welfare criteria, inspired his faith in Christian socialism, roused his devotion to Christian sociology as a general social science that "co-ordinates all the special social sciences, such as ethics, politics, and religion" (*sic*) (Commons 1894c, 3), and influenced his political economy in his *The Distribution of Wealth* (1893). His thesis strewn about and buried in that volume was that a disproportional representation of social class interests in the state, or sovereignty, had resulted in a disproportional distribution of property rights, and that relative to these political and legal institutional parameters, the economic system was disproportionally distributing freedom, power, income, and wealth, enriching the few and degrading and crushing the godlike out of the many in the labor class. Based on all of the foregoing, Commons proposed that the state should enact numerous public policies and taxes to finance them. But the state did not proportionally represent social class interests and was corrupt. To enact his policies Commons, as did Ely, sought to enlist the church in the vanguard of a popular movement to reform first the political and then the economic order.

By 1894 failure was staring at him. Critics had censured his interpretation of the Christian religion. Professionals who had reviewed *The Distribution of Wealth* had accused him of covert socialism and questioned his competence as an economic theorist, and some popular journals had denounced him for presenting theories "preposterous enough to give him claim to originality" ("Economic Discords" 1894, 236), and for dreaming of a "despotic commune" (Review 1894, 242). Neither the church nor the general public would support his reform proposals. His principles were not workable. What to do?

THE CONTEXT OF *SVOS*: 1894–1899

By mid-1894 Commons decided that the solution to the social problems was "for workingmen to enter politics and secure legislation in their own behalf" (1894a, 4). What research could best help bring about this solution?

The emphasis in his field of research shifted from economics to sociology. He conceived two projects in the field of sociology, as he saw it. The first one he had had in mind for some years and it culminated in 1896 in his *Proportional Representation*, a book on sociology, for the province of that field includes efforts to discover a "just balancing of social forces which will harmonize antagonisms and make for progress" (Commons 1896, 229). The second project stemmed from his conviction in 1894 that a theory of social evolution might explain how social classes have entered into sovereignty and "gradually risen to political equality with the ruling classes, and how they may still nearer approach political and economic equality." Such a theory, he held without any explanation, was the topic of political economy (1894b, 4). He launched a study of the evolution of institutions (Commons 1895b). The outcome was *SVOS*.

He did not proceed with these projects unaided by any intellectual momentum. The ideas from his initial stage of thought partly remained unchanged and partly changed and altogether they formed the context of *SVOS*.

Social gospel principles

His beliefs remained fixed that the social gospel version of the Christian religion is true, that it is primarily concerned with this world, that it is one-half theology and one-half sociology, and that it demands the Christianizing of institutions.

The theological half tells that God has created a community of individuals who are social creatures, each being equal in God's sight, and each having an interdependent body and soul. God commands each to work for subsistence for the body, and to this end has given the earth and its fullness as a free gift to all. Such work affects the soul, for the body and soul are not separate. Inviting censure, Commons urged that one "should learn from social science that the body must be saved before the soul" (1894c, 18), for otherwise it is "not only absurd, it is cruel to expect individuals to become Christians" (38, 43). Next come God's "two greatest commandments," according to Ely and Commons. First, one must love God. Second, one must love oneself and one's neighbor as oneself, meaning that one must develop one's talents or faculties, and do this for the sake of others. So wrote Ely, and Commons agreed during the initial stage of his thought. In 1898 Commons believed that the Christian religion "makes the goal of human evolution to be the development of moral character and personality in the individual," and that while brotherhood is not the end it is "the indispensable means toward establishing the highest expression of selfhood in all individuals" (1898b, 699, 700). In effect he was alluding to the ethics of personal idealism, or self-realization, or self-development, an ethics he apparently never critically considered.[4] While at first he had imposed one prerequisite for moral behavior – that the body must first be saved – by 1899 he imposed another: because struggle for survival makes it vain to speak of right and wrong, it is only when competition is past and monopolies established that conditions are "ripe for the claims of morality" (1899a, 136, 137).

The sociological half of his social gospel presupposes that reality is evolutionary. Human beings have evolved into being and are social creatures intimately bound up in a social organism. Their self-interest, plus scarcity, set off a struggle for survival, engender conflict of interest and social classes, and lead to the formation of institutions. Individuals and institutions are reciprocally related, Commons implicitly held. A few strong-willed, ambitious individuals rise above their environment and influence institutions. Christians can and should do this, he believed. As for the many, institutions influence them, almost deterministically, and in both body and soul. Institutions control access to opportunities to obtain subsistence, working conditions, and level of material welfare, and thus influence the body of the individual who must adapt to these conditions. The influence reaches the soul, for "the soul is simply the expression and flower of the body" (1894c, 32). The institutional influence on the many as he saw it in the early 1890s was precluding self-development: it was crushing "the godlike" out of individuals (30), driving them into immorality, and affecting heredity, producing results in the soul that "will cumulate . . . from generation to generation" (74). Hence, if moral character is degraded, the cause and responsibility for it lie largely in the institutional environment. And behind that responsibility lies the responsibility of the powerful few who have influenced the institutional environment for their own benefit – a point that Commons (1898b, 703–4) scathingly made in September 1898 and that probably contributed to Syracuse University's decision to dismiss him in early 1899.

His beliefs about institutions' influence on individuals create an unresolved conflict in his thought. Evil institutions can create evil moral character. Reformed, Christianized ones presumably can create good moral character. Can then Christianized institutions be not only a necessary condition but the necessary and sufficient condition for the saving of the body and soul? Some passages in his work suggest this, but implicitly he denies it, maintaining that another condition, the preaching of the gospel, must be satisfied if the soul is to be saved.

Social welfare criteria

Policies are needed to reform the institutional environment to make it promote the moral good of individual self-development, but what specific social welfare criteria should the policies satisfy? Commons deduced them from his social gospel principles. As a first instance, "equality of opportunity, free scope for development of such gifts as we have, are the logical conclusions of Christianity" (1894c, 10). Another criterion is public education to help individuals to begin self-development. Another is social freedom to pursue one's own authentic self-development; coercion can preclude this by overriding its victim's will, and so it is a great evil. The God-given duty for individuals to work to obtain subsistence corresponds in society to a right to employment, obligating society to create stable, full employment conditions. However, excessive hours of employment doom "spiritual possibilities" (38), and so adequate leisure time is necessary. Still another criterion is not insecurity, as some economic theorists concerned to promote efficiency would have it, but security, meaning security of laborers against threats arising inside the firm, such as arbitrary and capricious employment policies and hazardous working conditions, and threats arising outside the firm, such as trade cycles causing unemployment. Next, since God has created all individuals, brotherhood or fraternity is desirable and competition is dubious. Finally, since all are equal in God's sight and equality exists in the religious realm, Commons projects equality into the political and economic realms and stands for democracy in the sense that the interests of the social classes governed should be proportionally represented in government.

Social organization

The social organization that would best satisfy these social welfare criteria would be neither pure individualism or capitalism nor pure non-Marxian socialism, but a Christianized mixture of the two called Christian socialism, thought Commons during the initial stage of his thinking. However, he "became upset as to the meaning of Christian socialism" (1934b, 51). He began to wonder about the practicality of socialism. Seemingly in response to the reviewers who had said that *The Distribution of Wealth* amounted to covert socialism, he labeled his own position "progressive individualism" (1895a).

Sociology

Social reform policies should be based on social science, the protagonists of the social gospel movement believed, and they turned to a sociology to be grounded in Christian principles. During the initial stage of his thought Commons agreed with this and professed Christian sociology as "the science that deals with society as a whole. It co-ordinates all the special social sciences, such as ethics, politics, and religion" (*sic*) (1894c, 3). Soon, however, he became "upset as to the meaning of . . . Christian sociology" (1934b, 51).

He disjoined sociology from Christian beliefs. He became "suspicious of Love as the basis of social reform" (51), and in 1898 stated: "Men are selfish and even inhuman in their economic relations, and there can be no disregard of the serious problems that confront Christianity more fatuous and cruel than the optimistic quietism which coolly assumes that love and altruism are the ruling forces in society" (1898b, 704). The ruling force, he had come to believe, is coercion.

Public policy and administration

Two different policies and administrations were needed. The first was to preach the gospel to reform individuals. The church was to administer this. Second, because the existing institutions of society were exerting an evil influence on the body and soul of the great mass of individuals, society was to be seen as "the subject of redemption" (1894c, 71). To idly wait for a divine redemption as the premillennialists were doing was unacceptable, he wrote shortly before completing *SVOS* (1898c). The task of reforming institutions would call for more than feeble idealism, for while it may be a religious duty to Christianize institutions, self-interest is "too powerful, or too ignorant, or too immoral to promote the common good without compulsion" (1893, 61). Coercion is required to overcome evil, and the state would have to administer it, thought Commons, who said that he was "never a pacifist" (1934b, 140).

Enactment of policies

During the initial stage of his thought he appealed to the public and especially religious audiences, hoping to arouse the church to lead a popular movement that would reform first political and then economic institutions. But the church criticized and rebuffed his ideas. Reacting to this shortly before completing *SVOS* he wrote that spiritual support for social reform is vibrant in the nation, but "is finding other channels than the Church. It is often running into vagaries. It needs leadership. These leaders will come. Christianity will not disappear; but the Church – which is only a name for a method of Christian work – may disappear" (1898c).

In retrospect, between 1894 and 1899 Commons was contending that the moral good is self-development, that social welfare criteria were deducible from his principles, that institutions were evilly influencing the body and soul of those in the labor class, and that first political and then economic institutions should be reformed to promote the good. While adhering to these ideas, his belief that they could be grounded in Christian principles was weakening, and his commitments to Christian socialism, Christian sociology, and the Christian church as the vanguard of a social reform movement were growing cold. His beliefs in evolution and in the necessity for workable principles had become pre-eminent. He was becoming a hard-boiled meliorist.

SVOS

From this context Commons developed *SVOS*. His objective was the one he had remarked upon in 1894: it was to develop a theory of history – of institutional evolution – showing how lower social classes have entered into sovereignty and risen toward political and economic equality with the ruling classes. His reasoning in *SVOS* falls into five parts. First, in keeping with the context of his thought he adopts an evolutionary, moral, and multi-disciplinary approach. Second, following this approach he analyzes, defines, and interrelates a set of conceptions that are fundamental relative to his objective.[5] Third, he achieves his objective by constructing a theory of history concerning the special, Anglo-American case of how lower social classes have entered into sovereignty and risen toward political and economic equality, resulting in the evolution into being of the modern state and economic system. Fourth, exploiting this theory he picks out a common feature running through the history of public policy. Finally, and almost between the lines, he proposes policies that the state should enact next.

The evolutionary, moral, and multidisciplinary approach

Belief in evolution had played a role in his earlier writings, but by the time of *SVOS* he had completely accepted it and without concern for either the metaphysical issues it raises or the question as to whether evolution as a world view is reconcilable with Christian theology. How do institutions evolve? That was the great question. For an answer he needed "laws of development" (Commons 1899b, 3). For these he drew on the work of Herbert Spencer. His own Spenceresque version of these laws assumes that human beings evolved into existence and at first lived in an original, homogeneous, indefinite social mass. Then differentiation begins. The differentiated social parts become organized and definite. A "universal law of monopoly and centralization, enforced by necessity and the struggle for existence" takes hold (72). Then monopoly and centralization give way to decentralization. "Socialization" and "democratization" may occur. Will evolution bring cycles of centralization and decentralization? Commons gives no answer. He implicitly holds that evolution is not a teleological, but an aimless, endless process.

His approach is also moral. Endless, evolving self-development, now called "self-perfection" (1899b, 54) is the moral good. To facilitate its pursuit by all requires the satisfying of social welfare criteria, and the criteria evident in *SVOS* are those he set up during his initial stage of thought, plus a new one.

The criteria include freedom; absence of coercion, a great evil that overrides the victim's will and interferes with self-development; power, for it will be seen that in *SVOS* Commons makes freedom contingent upon power; equalization of power that will discourage resort to coercion and encourage recourse to "mutual persuasion" that in turn will inspire feelings of brotherhood; security; and democracy, to be attained by the "democratization" or "socialization" of private ownership over property. A new, momentous criterion coming out of the context appears in *SVOS*: monopoly must supersede competition. Competition means hellish struggle for survival, which makes ethical dictates unaffordable. Monopoly, however, makes such dictates affordable. "Only in the lulls of competition, or in the final victory of perfected and centralized organization, is it possible to introduce the ethical purpose" (109). However, monopoly in a labor market in the form of monopsony or collusive oligopsony would spell employers' power of coercion over labor. In response to this Commons's criteria call not for breaking up monopoly, which would yield the hell of competition, but for the equalization of power, to be achieved by allowing the creation of labor unions, yielding counterbalancing power, and thereby encouraging recourse to mutual persuasion.

His approach is also multidisciplinary, but titled sociological. In *SVOS* he continues to regard sociology as a science that underlies and unifies "all the social sciences" (1899b, 10), a stand taken by some sociologists that representatives of already-established special social sciences including orthodox political economy had criticized heatedly.[6] In *SVOS*, under the heading of sociology, he treats topics in a wide array of disciplines.

Analysis, definition, and interrelation of fundamental conceptions

Following this approach he analyzes, defines, and interrelates a set of fundamental conceptions ranging from human nature as it now is, to society, social freedom, power, coercion, persuasion, private ownership over property, institutions, sovereignty, order, right, and the state.

Human beings have evolved "from the animal" (1899b, 11). Each individual has a self, is prompted by self-interest, and has various "psychic elements," and throughout *SVOS* Commons grounds his discussions in these elements. The foremost one is not rationality, but voluntarism: individuals "are, first of all, creatures of desire" (102). Desires are the basis of beliefs (1899b, 5), and desires and beliefs underlie the will (53). The will seeks power and the "will unchecked is capricious, self-seeking, oppressive" (60). It is malicious, ready to dominate, exploit, and degrade others, and it is insensitive to the miseries of the oppressed. In this fearsome world of self-interest as Commons interprets it, cannot rationality supplant voluntarism and coercion? In *SVOS* he acknowledges that it can, when equalization of power encourages recourse to persuasion.

From this sort of human nature it follows that society is not a scene of natural scarcity that prompts rational individuals to foresee that in division of labor and exchange lies a harmony of interests, and so to choose peaceful social cooperation. Instead the scene is one of natural scarcity that sets off conflict of interests, rival assertions of private ownership over property, struggle for power, coercion, the emergence of social classes, class conflict, and the formation of offensive and defensive institutions.

In such a scene social order and social freedom can only be made by art rather than nature, by conflicting social classes who realize that order and freedom are necessary for the pursuit of their individual self-development. In *SVOS* Commons defines social freedom positively, fusing freedom with power to carry choices into action that secures control over the products or services of others (1899b, 58, 100). This definition, plus the idea that individuals struggle for power and organize themselves, leads to the doctrine that freedom requires membership in an organized group. "The lone individual is helpless against the pressure of others," and is compelled to join others "to gain the power which united effort secures" (100), and which assures freedom.

Power, an element in his definition of social freedom, is a fundamental conception he fails to analyze. He does not distinguish among such economic conceptions as productive power, monopoly and monopsony power, and power of coercion, nor between any of these economic conceptions and the legal conception of power.

Coercion, not love, is the "decisive social relation" he states (1899b, 62), his days of Christian sociology gone, and he equates the evolution of coercion with the evolution of society (29, 32). He strangely ignores the relation between coercion and social freedom. He treats coercion and persuasion as contraries, not contradictories. He views each as an ethical conception, remarking that coercion is "solely in the field of ethics" (52). His analysis and definition of coercion is sophisticated but not beyond criticism. Coercion, he begins, has its psychic basis in the will (39), and involves an agent, a human person with power who acts (thus, but left unsaid, impersonal social forces cannot coerce), confronting a subject who faces only two choices and so is boxed in with no "third choice" (22). The agent has "the power to drive" the subject "to an act of service" by making "tacit or avowed threats" (22) to the effect that if noncompliance occurs, then sanctions will be imposed. The sanctions will occur relative to the normalcy the subject would otherwise experience (a point Commons does not make). The sanctions can cause (1) increased costs or reduced benefits. Thus, (1a) a pure monopolist controlling a necessity coerces when he raises the price the consumer must pay. (1b) A monopsonist who faces an employee with no "third choice" (1899b, 22) and who offers a wage that spells exploitation practices coercion. (1c) An employer who says, "Either perform work or I'll offer no job opportunity," does not coerce, for normalcy includes the need to work to obtain subsistence. (1d) An employer who offers a wage only equal to the value of the employee's contribution does not coerce, for self-interest decrees that quid pro quo is part of normalcy. (Points (1c) and (1d) are left out by Commons.) Sanctions of reprobation by individuals other than the agent represent not coercion but persuasion, as Commons notes. However, (2) promises of reduced costs or increased benefits are not "threats" that "drive" the subject and so do not represent coercion (points not made by Commons). Finally, promises of approbation by individuals other than the agent represent not coercion, but persuasion, as he notes. On the whole, the points Commons omits can allow his meaning of coercion to become overinclusive. The sanctions are strong enough relative to the subject's particular character to override the subject's will (23–4), and cause the subject to choose what otherwise would not be chosen. Coercion means that the threat alone suffices, allowing the agent to hold force in reserve (16). Finally, coercion creates evil effects: the agent "becomes haughty, intolerant, commanding," and the subject "servile, obsequious, deceptive" (24). Worst of all, the subject of coercion becomes the limb of another, is deprived of a will of his own (42), and cannot pursue his own authentic self-development.

Persuasion, the contrary of coercion, occurs when the agent possesses intellectual powers such as diplomacy, reasoning, and eloquence (1899b, 25, 99), applies the "wholly psychic" sanctions of approbation and reprobation (22, 25), and inspires a choice by the subject. Persuasion elicits rationality and good moral effects; mutual persuasion can inspire negotiation and mutual compromise, and can realize perfect partnership, or brotherhood, "the indispensable means to self-development."

Private property Commons implicitly defines as not physical custody over property but person-to-person relations with respect to property. It "springs from the very nature of man" and is a "necessity of the struggle for life" (1899b, 108). It confers private dominion, and the characteristic quality of that is caprice (39). Private ownership over property he identifies with power of coercion, but here his reasoning is fallacious, as will be shown below. Private ownership over property, he continues, is "the beginning and basis of all social institutions" (107).

By institutions he means primarily organizations, and he considers their origin, parts, viability, evolution, and influence on individuals and their social freedom. Necessity originates them: in the struggle to survive, some individuals believe that their rights have been violated and that if they are to survive, they must organize. If adequate social class consciousness, mutual confidence (1899b, 46), and a leader with both coercive and persuasive power exist, they will create an institution. An institution will have political, technical, and business (dealings with outsiders, such as by purchasing and selling) parts, and while Commons makes the political part pivotal, he does not consider the interdependencies among the three parts and fails to show the practical bearings of his analysis. The viability of institutions depends on their ability to pass the test of survival of the fittest, and so in *SVOS* he denies that the state can by fiat create viable institutions. Institutions evolve over time, and the "universal law of monopoly and centralization" will act on them. Commons was not a Pollyanna: as institutions attain monopoly power they are prone to exalt caprice above justice (61), and to exalt the interests of their hierarchy above those of the community (72). As to be expected, he contends that institutions profoundly affect individuals, but in a new way, for in *SVOS* he speaks not about their impact on body and soul, but their educational influence on individuals' desires, beliefs, and capacities (5). Institutions especially affect their individual members' social freedom. Their freedom in relation to outsiders, or their external freedom, increases. Their freedom within the institution, or their internal freedom, may decrease, for as an institution evolves and the "universal law of monopoly and centralization" takes hold, its organization will become "more and more inexorable and despotic" (31), subordinating and restricting more and more its members' freedom. Institutions can increase and decrease their members' social freedom, but as to their net influence Commons remains silent.

Sovereignty is a form of coercion, he proposes by a series of definitions. Human nature is the grounding of the will. The will is the psychic basis of coercion. Coercion is the common basis of private and public dominion (1899b, 39). In private hands coercion or private dominion has caprice as its characteristic quality (39). Private dominion is but another name for private ownership over property, which is the beginning and basis of all social institutions (107). In the hands of public officials coercion or public dominion means sovereignty, a "political term" (38, 39). "Sovereignty is not original . . . for it is derived from private dominion. It is . . . limited by so much of coercion as still remains in private hands" (51). Being derivative of private dominion, its characteristic quality is caprice.

Finally, the state emerges when "order" and "right" are forced into the coercion of sovereignty. "Order" signifies the elimination of caprice by the creation of rules of procedure or due process. "Right" means the ethically "righteous relations" Commons spoke of during the initial stage of his thought, but now, according to *SVOS*, made possible only during the lulls of competition or the attainment of monopoly. His evolutionary approach causes him to see the state "as a process and not an entity" (1899b, 108).

The evolution of the modern state and economic system

The cardinal feature of *SVOS* is an effort by Commons to construct a theory of political and economic history explaining how lower social classes have forced their way into sovereignty in quest of political and economic equality, resulting in the evolution of sovereignty and the emergence of the modern state and economic system. To accomplish this he applies his

Spenceresque laws of development, and puts his fundamental conceptions to use.

Institutions, he begins, were originally a homogeneous blend of familial, economic, religious, political, and military elements. Progressively these elements were differentiated off and underwent centralization. Stages of history went by. "History is full of uprisings of sects and classes, of riots and wars" (1899b, 100).

Passing over "minor stages" (1899b, 27), he moves straightaway to the special case of English history and begins with the feudal stage subsequent to the Norman invasion in 1066. The law of centralization took hold, and the kings in the Norman dynasty accumulated power at the expense of their subordinate feudal chiefs, bringing about absolutism. Then occurred what Commons regarded as an exemplary event. The aggrieved, the barons, sensing encroachment upon what they felt should be their property rights, organized, acquired power equivalent to the king's, and in light of this equalization of power were able to engage in mutual persuasion or collective bargaining, and come to an agreement, Magna Carta, that secured their rights. This modified in two ways the king's sovereignty. First, it injected "order" into it. The barons, suppressed by the king, forced their way into participation in sovereignty, causing the king's ownership to move from a private to a social character or for "socialization" to occur. Thus the barons entered into "partnership" in determining the king's will, meaning that the aggrieved could restrain the arbitrary and capricious will of the king, or that "order" was introduced into the coercion of sovereignty. Second, it injected "right" into sovereignty. The king, having a monopoly position, could afford to listen to ethical appeals. The barons induced him to act upon such appeals, and thus "right" was injected into the coercion of sovereignty. By Commons's definition, when order and right are injected into the coercion exercised by sovereignty, then sovereignty becomes the state. In his account this exemplary event occurred again and again over centuries in England as more and more suppressed and aggrieved social classes organized and forced their way into participation in sovereignty, converting absolutism into constitutionalism and autocracy into democracy. Consequently, by an aimless evolutionary process, the modern democratic state has come into being as "an accumulated series of compromises between social classes, each seeking to secure for itself control over the coercive elements which exist implicitly in society with the institution of private property" (45).

The origin and evolution of the modern economic system remain to be explained. Employing his ideas about evolution, Commons reasons that from an early blend of institutions gradually the institution of private ownership over "industrial" property was differentiated off, and became in some measure independent of political, military, and ecclesiastical control. "Democratization of property" occurred as more and more individuals were empowered

87

to have private ownership over property (1899b, 79). Necessity drove individuals to form institutions such as guilds and more recently corporations. In these institutions he finds illustrated his trio of political, technical, and business parts. This trio, later renamed the going firm, going plant, and going business, is suggestive, but it does not interrelate organizational, technological, and monetary considerations. By stating that in successful private business managers apparently must have "complete power of appointment and removal of subordinates" he begins to recognize efficiency as a social welfare criterion (84).

The universal law of centralization has done in competition among firms. "Pools, combines, trusts, and monopolies" have come about (1899b, 48). "The state has not only not interfered, but has contributed positively to the process of centralization by its laws creating and protecting business corporations" (81). Private ownership over industrial property has grown in "coercive control over all subordinates, over the community, and over the sovereignty in which it has acquired partnership"; it has become "capitalism or plutocracy," a form of "government by transferable property." (48).

In the context of capitalism he identifies private ownership over property with power of coercion, apparently because in a market, an owner has the power to withhold goods and services (a privative sanction in Commons's terms), or an employment opportunity, and so forth, until an adequate value is offered in return. Here his reasoning is fallacious, for private ownership over property is a necessary but not a necessary and sufficient condition for the existence of power of coercion. The case of a market for labor service of a given kind will illustrate this. First, if private ownership over property by employers and employees (who own their own human capital) exists, and if additional conditions exist, these being pure competition among employers and employees alike, financial ability to withhold equally distributed among employers and employees, zero market imperfections, and zero transaction costs, then no power of coercion will exist. Second, if some or all of these additional conditions are absent, then power of coercion will come into being, due not to private ownership over property alone, but to the additional conditions being absent. This is seemingly the case Commons has in mind, for he implicitly assumes monopsony, or oligopsony, and competition among employees who have little or no financial ability to withhold, who face serious market imperfections, and who have no "third choice," being instead "shut up to the two alternatives of accepting reward for service or going without altogether" (1899b, 22). Third, if private ownership over property exists but some of the additional conditions are absent, such that monopsony exists, then an employer will have power of coercion; but if the employees are able to organize and to acquire enough power of coercion relative to the employer's such that an equalization of power or a counterbalancing power comes about, then by Commons's own reasoning both sides will fear to exercise coercion and will resort to persuasion; and thus while private ownership over property exists, power of coercion will exist but be unused. Fourth, it is conceivable that private ownership over property as the basis for social organization may by itself alone imply that all of the additional conditions and furthermore the equalization of power of coercion will be absent, and thus by itself confer power of coercion, but Commons does not attempt to prove this. Thus, for the case of a market for labor service of a given kind his claim that private ownership over property can be identified with power of coercion is fallacious.

History was repeating itself, he thought. Just as in the political sphere centuries ago absolutism had arisen, provoking the aggrieved to organize and to attempt to secure what they took to be their rights, in the economic sphere the same problem was reappearing. "The old problem of absolutism and paternalism is on us again," as he had put it earlier (1894a, 4). He elaborated the point in *SVOS*: the new absolutism held by firms was compelling the working classes "to organize in labor unions" and attempt to acquire "partnership" or participation "in the control of industry," or, in other words, to bring about a "socialization" of the private ownership enjoyed by capitalists (1899b, 49).

The historic policies of the state

Because his ethics makes individual self-development the moral good, and because to enable that to be pursued in society requires the creation of social freedom, which in turn requires the extraction of coercion, Commons understandably saw such extraction as a common thread running through the historic policies of the state. As he develops this in *SVOS*, the state, which has been differentiated off from familial, ecclesiastical, and other institutions, has repeatedly turned upon these now subordinate institutions, acknowledged the structure they have attained by struggle for survival, but has abstracted from their structure powers of coercion, and injected into them right and order, causing these subordinate institutions to undergo socialization. By abstracting out private powers of coercion and absorbing them into its own structure, the state has expanded, but has compelled the subordinate institutions to resort to persuasion, which has liberated certain underlying psychic elements formerly suffocated by coercion. For example, the state has abstracted coercion from the family, forcing it to rely on persuasion based on the psychic element of love; it has abstracted coercion from the church, forcing it to rely on persuasion based on spiritual elements; but it has yet to abstract coercion from firms with monopoly, forcing them to rely on persuasion based on the psychic elements of "love of work," the "persuasive basis of industry" (Commons 1899b, 75). Because the state has been carrying out this policy Commons calls it the "peculiarly ethical institution" (109).

What the state should do next

The solution to the social problems, he had said in mid-1894, was "for workingmen to enter politics and secure legislation in their own behalf" (1894a, 4). His *Proportional Representation* (1896) urged a policy that would help workingmen to do that, and the argument in *SVOS* justifies another policy to the same end. In keeping with what he regarded as a long series of precedents, the suppressed working class, having organized its own institutions, labor unions, should be allowed to enter into participation in the public sovereignty of the state, and, in an idea that he would make more clear in the coming days of his five-year exile, into participation in the private dominion of firms in the economic system. Both kinds of participation would shift ownership over industrial property from a private toward a social character and eliminate coercion and oppression.

In *SVOS* Commons also favors a variant of this policy. Already begun by the state, it was to create legal rights for minority stockholders, allowing them to enter into the private dominion of corporations, thus adding to "the process of socialization of these corporations" (1899b, 82).

A policy that does not flow out of the argument in *SVOS* is one favoring public ownership over monopolies, a move that "is probable in many cases" and is in part to create security for laborers (1899b, 83).

Behind these several policies stands Commons's rejection of a procompetition policy to deal with power of coercion. His principles tell that such a policy will set off a hellish struggle for survival that will only cause monopoly to reemerge. He laments that "the public opinion controlling the state has not yet recognized the inevitable monopoly of corporations and is still busied with plans for their democratization" (1899b, 82), that is, with an antitrust policy.

The consequences of these policies would, in unspoken but faintly audible words, bring to pass the Kingdom of God on earth. With workingmen participating in the sovereignty of the state and the dominion of corporations, additional order and additional right could be introduced, eliminating arbitrary and capricious employment practices, and assuring security for workers. Removing coercion would uncover "love of work," a psychic element in human nature previously suffocated by coercion, and allow the "immense increase in production . . . producible only through methods of persuasion" (1899b, 78). With workers and employers being in partnership and engaging in mutual persuasion, laborers would acquire "increased scope of self-direction" (86), the social value of brotherhood would be realized, and workers would be more able to pursue self-development.

Conclusion

When seen in its context, the cardinal feature giving *SVOS* its identity is a theory of political and economic history intended to help the American labor class to enter into the sovereignty of the state and the private dominion of firms, to rise toward political and economic equality with the then ruling class, and then at best be able to bring about institutional reforms that would satisfy Commons's social welfare criteria. The theory is not a value-free, general theory lying in any one partial social science. It reflects Commons's ethics, is relative to Anglo-American evidence, and is multi-disciplinary in the name of sociology, a science he thought could unify and coordinate the various special social sciences including economics. In *SVOS* the direct bearings of this sociology upon economic theory are quite few.

SIGNIFICANCE

SVOS explains much of the subsequent unrolling of Commons's thought, but not all of it. It does not prophesy his exile from academia from 1899 to 1904 that put him in touch with captains of industry, great labor leaders, especially Samuel Gompers, and labor market conditions that educated him anew such that when, thanks to Ely, he re-entered academic life in 1904 he felt that he had been "born again" (1934b, 95). Nor does it prefigure his years on the trail of documentary evidence of the history of the American labor union movement, nor his becoming independent of Ely, nor his twentieth-century triumphs as a social reformer, nor much of his work as an institutional economist.

None the less *SVOS* does foretell much, for it largely served him as an outline that he would fill in here, revise there, and elaborate upon during the following decades to create what he called his social philosophy of trade unionism or modern liberalism. As a first example, as *SVOS* signals, he was beginning to shift the ground of his published work over to evolutionary rather than Christian religious doctrines, and doing so even though his own personal religious faith evidently persisted.

Individual self-development is the moral good, he continued to believe. The social welfare criteria he had set out during his initial stage of thought and again in *SVOS* stayed intact, but he refined his conception of freedom and distinguished it from liberty, and added efficiency as an explicit criterion. He also added justice as still another criterion, and because justice means fair play between not individuals, "as our legal philosophy would have it," but between social classes (1908, 764), he held that each social class should have its own institution "for expressing its will" (1899b, 50). He soon acknowledged that his ethics was utilitarian, for it would judge customs, juristic laws, and all sorts of working rules by their consequences.

Over time he began to distinguish at least two classes of people. For the great mass of individuals, voluntarism marks them, as he had indicated in *SVOS*. He elaborated: they are beings of passion, stupidity, and ignorance who resist change (1934a, II, 682, 846, 874). Away with illusions, he advised: "Capitalism, like dictatorship and party politics, thrives on the stupidity of mankind." For a social reformer it is better "to recognize in advance the foundations of capitalism, than to turn out eventually disillusioned, hopeless, reactionary, or contented with 'natural law'. ..." (846). For the few, however, who rise to positions of leadership, have power, but confront equal power forcing them to resort to persuasion, rationality marks them. During his five-year exile and afterward, he met such individuals – great captains of industry, great labor leaders, and others – admired them, probably as the paragons of his ethics of self-development, and so became attached to capitalism (1934b, 143).

Reading plus conversations with a long series of active and former socialists and Marxists cooled his sympathy for socialism. Familiarity with politics tempered his belief in what the state and public ownership could accomplish.

He carried on his multidisciplinary endeavor in social science, becoming entrenched in his beliefs about institutions' influence on individuals, the reality of social classes and class conflict, and the need for conflict resolution by way of customs, juristic laws, and working rules. His study of Anglo-American juristic law, begun before *SVOS*, he carried into depth and used it to expand upon his ideas in *SVOS* concerning the evolution into being of first the modern state and second the modern economic system. The first enabled him to see labor unions and collective bargaining in a certain historical perspective, and to see how he could controvert the Marxian materialist conception of history. The second set up some of the framework for his *The Legal Foundations of Capitalism* (1924).

He continued to regard political economy as a part of sociology. His penchant was to attribute to institutions much explanatory power over economic behavior. He launched a study of the history of economic thought, hoping to make a contribution to economic theory. He faced two problems: how could he formulate an institutional economic theory logically reconcilable with his social philosophy, and moreover, given his commitment to evolutionism, how could he develop a general theory that would hold true through place and time? He ended by analyzing, sorting out, and interrelating a host of variables under the headings of scarcity, efficiency, custom, sovereignty, and futurity, apparently proffering them as a propaedeutic for the development of special economic theories relative to place and time.

His plan to secure the enactment of his policies during his initial stage of thought was first to inspire the church to accept the social gospel interpretation of the Christian religion and have it lead a popular movement to reform the state, and then the economy. Later experience convinced him that effort to reform the church was neither possible nor necessary. The church, he believed by 1903, "has ceased to be a political factor essential to the integrity of a nation" (1903, 160).

Could the state, corrupt as it was, be reformed? The general legislature could not be expected to proportionally represent conflicting social class interests. He remained firm in his belief expressed in *Proportional Represen-tation* that the hallowed practice of electing representatives from political districts drawn not by social class lines but by geographical lines encom-passing diverse social class interests leads to rule by bosses and lobbyists, the election of incompetent compromise candidates, and the wrecking of proportional representation and justice. Economic developments had outdated the once-sensible geographical district system. If democracy were to survive, "the machinery of government needs adapting to a wholly new ground-work" (1902, 2261). To reform politics he entertained several ideas. His hope dating from his initial stage of thought to bring about propor-tional representation of social class interests in the general legislature stayed alive. But two ways to supplement general legislature and achieve propor-tional representation beckoned. *SVOS* had indicated one of them and familiarity with Gompers and field conditions during his exile made it vivid: it was to delegate policy-making to labor and management in partic-ular industries. In a representative democracy "in miniature" (1900, 87), in an industrial government remarkably like "parliamentary government in a country of its origin, England. . . ." (1901, 328) wherein equalization of power exists and both sides are equally afraid of each other, the two sides would not employ coercion, but would resort to mutual persuasion, progres-sively resolving their conflicts. Thus he developed his "trade union" viewpoint, likening it to "the social philosophy of Samuel Gompers" (1934b, 73). Later, however, he worried that "perhaps my generalizations on collec-tive bargaining in place of legislation were too sweeping" (1934b, 124). The other way to supplement the general legislature and achieve propor-tional representation featured administrative commissions, each having jurisdiction over a specific area of social class conflict. Each commission could embody proportional representation because each social class could elect its own representatives who at best would be experts. Moreover, each commission might be able to perform not only legislative but also execu-tive and judicial functions as well, being a "fourth branch of government" continuously governing its jurisdiction.

As an economic reformer he became a success story. Omitting religious arguments, using his knowledge of economics and law, and collaborating with his graduate students, he could investigate field conditions and draft politically and legally acceptable bills. At the same time, however, as an advocate of democracy he favored economic reform by collective bargaining and administrative commissions.

He added a final touch. While constructing *SVOS* he had read some of the work of William James and John Dewey.[7] Decades later he studied more of their ideas and those of others in the pragmatist movement and found it easy to reconcile his own thinking with theirs about evolution, method, meaning, truth, idealism, justice, juristic law, and social control. As he saw it, his system of thought could come to rest upon pragmatism.

During the first third of the twentieth century Commons became known as an institutional economist. He was more than that. At first a visionary member of the social gospel movement and a failure as a social reformer, he soon became a hard-boiled meliorist concerned about how to control the social order so as to widely distribute wealth and opportunities for individual self-development. Having produced SVOS, during the following decades as he rose to success as a social reformer he used it in large part to develop what he called a social philosophy of trade unionism or modern liberalism.[8]

NOTES

1 Previously others had created sociological interpretations of sovereignty. See Bullowa 1895, "Chapter VIII. – Sovereignty from the sociological standpoint – Spencer, Letourneau and Gumplowicz."

2 A difficult term to define narrowly and to distinguish from political philosophy, social philosophy proceeds on philosophical grounds to treat ethical values or social ideals, methods in social science, and the concepts involved in the study of society, social institutions, and politics. Commons was aware of social philosophy early in his career: in his 1898a, 74 he cites Mackenzie 1895. Commons 1934a, I, 93, 97, 98 gives his own definition of social philosophy. On his own position see Commons 1934a, II, 902–3, and 1934b, 73.

3 This section draws on the detailed account in Gonce 1996.

4 During these years John Dewey was critically developing his ideas about self-realization. Commons 1897b told Ely that he planned to take lectures in philosophy and ethics in "Chicago University" the summer quarter. At that time Dewey was with the University of Chicago. Later, Commons 1898a cited Dewey 1897.

5 See Commons 1899b, 3, lines 20–2. Earlier, while telling Ely about his project that became SVOS, Commons 1897a said: "The great difficulty of course will be the *terminology* – how to get scientific exactness with popular terminology."

6 While criticizing H. C. Adams, Hadley 1886, 94, 95 held it to be erroneous to deny independence to economic reasoning, and folly to reject it, which we have, for the sake of a whole, sociology, "which we have not." Discussing the historical relation of sociology to the special social sciences, Barnes 1924, 16–18 notes that the "'pretentions of sociology'" had elicited "alarm and repugnance," and "heated discussions and numerous clashes."

7 Commons 1898a, 73 cites James 1890 and 1897. Concerning Dewey, see endnote 4 above.

8 I thank J. E. Biddle, A. W. Coats, P. Isely, M. Rutherford, and W. J. Samuels for comments on an earlier draft of this essay. Any errors are mine alone.

REFERENCES

Barnes, Harry E. 1924. *Sociology and Political Theory: A Consideration of the Sociological Basis of Politics*. New York: Knopf.

Bullowa, Ezra M. 1895. *The History of the Theory of Sovereignty*. Published Ph.D. diss. New York: Columbia College.

Commons, John R. 1893. *The Distribution of Wealth*. Reprint. New York: Kelley, 1965.

—— 1894a. "Democracy vs. Paternalism." *The Kingdom* (Minneapolis) (July 27): 3, 4.

—— 1894b. "Christianity and Wages." *The Kingdom* (Minneapolis) (November 2): 3, 4.

—— 1894c. *Social Reform and the Church.* Reprint. New York: Kelley, 1967. (A collection of prior essays, one dated 1891.)

—— 1895a. "Progressive Individualism." *The American Magazine of Civics* 6 (June): 561–74.

—— 1895b. Letter to R. T. Ely. September 7. R. T. Ely Papers. Archives, Wisconsin State Historical Library, Madison.

—— 1896. *Proportional Representation.* New York: Crowell.

—— 1897a. Letter to R. T. Ely, January 17. R. T. Ely Papers.

—— 1897b. Letter to R. T. Ely, May 15. R. T. Ely Papers.

—— 1898a. "Sociology." University of the State of New York Extension Department. Subject no. 300. Syllabus 74. Albany, New York, June.

—— 1898b. "The Value of the Study of Political Economy to the Christian Minister." *Methodist Review* 14 (September): 696–711.

—— 1898c. "Social Economics and City Evangelization. Part I." *The Kingdom* (Minneapolis) (November 24): 121–3.

—— 1899a "The Right to Work." *The Arena.* 21 (February): 131–42.

—— 1899b *A Sociological View of Sovereignty.* A series of articles in *The American Journal of Sociology* 5 (July 1899) to 6 (July 1900). Reprinted as a book. New York: Kelley, 1965.

—— 1900. *Representative Democracy.* New York: Bureau of Economic Research.

—— 1901. "A New Way of Settling Labor Disputes." *American Monthly Review of Reviews* 23 (March): 328–33.

—— 1902. "Democracy in America." *The Independent* 54 (September 18): 2260–62. An unsigned editorial by Commons. See The J. R. Commons Papers, Archives, Memorial Library, University of Wisconsin–Madison, Box 3.

—— 1903. "Labor Union and Professional Classes." *The Independent* 55 (January 15): 159, 160. An unsigned editorial by Commons. See The J. R. Commons Papers, Archives, Memorial Library, University of Wisconsin–Madison, Box 3.

—— 1908. "Is Class Conflict in America Growing and is it Inevitable?" *The American Journal of Sociology* 13 (May): 756–66, 781–3.

—— 1910. "How Wisconsin Regulates Her Public Utilities." *American Monthly Review of Reviews* 42 (August): 215–17.

—— 1934a. *Institutional Economics: Its Place in Political Economy.* 2 vols. Reprint. Madison: The University of Wisconsin Press, 1961.

—— (1934b). *Myself.* Reprint. Madison: The University of Wisconsin Press, 1964.

Dewey, John. 1897. *Study of Ethics: A Syllabus.* Ann Arbor, Michigan: Wahr.

Dorfman, Joseph. 1965. "John R. Commons' General Theory of Institutions." In *A Sociological View of Sovereignty,* by John R. Commons, iii–xi. A series of articles in *The American Journal of Sociology* 5 (July 1899b) to 6 (July 1900). Reprinted as a book, New York: Kelley, 1965.

"Economic Discords" 1894. *The Nation* 58 (March 29): 236.

Gonce, Richard A. 1996. "The Social Gospel, Ely, and Commons's Initial Stage of Thought." *The Journal of Economic Issues* 30 (September): 641–65.

Hadley, Arthur T. 1886. "Economic Laws and Methods." pp. 92–7 in Henry C. Adams, Richard T. Ely, and others. *Science Economic Discussion.* New York: The Science Company.

Harter, Lafayette G., Jr. 1962. *John R. Commons: His Assault on Laissez-Faire.* Corvallis, Oregon: Oregon State University Press.

James, William. 1890. *Principles of Psychology.* New York: Holt.

——— 1897. *The Will to Believe and Other Essays in Popular Philosophy*. New York: Longmans.

Mackenzie, John S. 1895. *Introduction to Social Philosophy*. 2nd edn, enlarged. New York: Macmillan.

Review 1894. "*The Distribution of Wealth*. By John R. Commons." *The Independent*. 46 (February 22): 241–2.

6

COMMONS, SOVEREIGNTY, AND THE LEGAL BASIS OF THE ECONOMIC SYSTEM

Steven G. Medema

INTRODUCTION

In his introduction to Commons' *A Sociological View of Sovereignty*, Joseph Dorfman hails the volume because "the argument is presented as a general theory of institutions applicable to all the social sciences" (Commons, 1899–1900, p. iii).[1] The same, of course, might be said of the New Institutional Economics of Oliver Williamson, Douglass North, *et al.*[2] Indeed, the study of institutions and the development of a theory of institutions has become a rather fashionable topic of late within the field of economics. Yet, apart from the occasional obligatory reference to Commons or Veblen, this work has proceeded largely independent of the "old" institutionalism – turn of the century or contemporary. So, why is it that one should be interested in Commons' *A Sociological View of Sovereignty* a century after its publication? Is it merely an historical curiosum, or does it offer lessons for doing economics in the modern age? While *A Sociological View of Sovereignty* is useful for historians of economic thought by virtue of the light that it sheds on the development of Commons' own thinking, the focus of this paper will be on the lessons that it offers for contemporary economic thinking and understanding – in particular, for conceptualizing the role of government within the economic system, or law and economics in its broader sense.

A Sociological View of Sovereignty can be analyzed and interpreted from several perspectives. But for present purposes – that is, approaching this volume from the viewpoint of an economist – one might classify it as a study of the evolution of economic role of government, one more fully elaborated with regard to the United States capitalist system in his 1924 treatise, *Legal Foundations of Capitalism*. *A Sociological View of Sovereignty*, like *Legal Foundations of Capitalism* which followed it, sets Commons apart from both his classical forebears and his neoclassical contemporaries in the manner in which the subject of the economic role of government is treated. The classical approach, by and large, involved the discussion of how the government *should* or *should not act* within the economic realm in order to promote the general well-being, variously defined. The neoclassical view, flowing out of Alfred Marshall and A.C. Pigou, focused on how the government *could act* to improve economic well-being (again variously defined, but with a more quantitative frame of reference – for example, social versus private net products, consumer surplus, etc.) if such changes were deemed desirable by the policy-making body. The early neoclassical view has been carried forward, with some modifications,[3] into contemporary law and economics, which assesses legal rules according to the dictates of wealth maximization (for example, Posner, 1992). In *A Sociological View of Sovereignty* Commons, in contrast, approaches the subject with the goal of attempting to flesh out how the government forms and operates *within* the economic system, and, in particular, how government lays the foundation and framework for the economic system's operation. In his words, his approach involves an examination of the state's "actual qualities, and its concrete relations to other institutions," and the development of the same over time (1899–1900, pp. 2–3). If policy is a drug, the classical and neoclassical approaches offer prescription; Commons, on the other hand, is doing the chemistry.

COMMONS' CONCEPTION OF SOVEREIGNTY AND HIS EVOLUTIONARY APPROACH

Sovereignty, for Commons, is a phenomenon that reduces coercion to order through rights (1899–1900, p. 53), and, as such, replaces or supersedes religion, custom, the arbitrary authority of individuals, etc. in the institutional ordering of social relations. Sovereignty is a social, or socio-economic, institution, and its genesis and/or the form in which it manifests itself in a given society or at a particular point in time is the outcome of a process of social development or evolution. Given this, and given Commons' stated goal of describing how government forms and operates within the economic system and the development of the same, it becomes important to understand the forces underlying the development of those institutional forms that have culminated in the sovereign state.[4]

Commons (p. 13) locates the starting point for the development of social institutions in the problem of scarcity, which manifests itself in various facets of human activity.[5] From the problem of scarcity arises the desire for private appropriation – or private property – which, in his words, "is a social relation based on coercion" – the latter being "a command, expressed or tacit, issued by a determinate person with the power to enforce obedience on others by means of external material or bodily suffering" (p. 25).[6] The form, source, and manifestation of this coercive process has varied across time and place, evolving along with the organization of society and social institutions generally. The organization process, in turn, reflects the desire for order, and the organizational structure in force the attempt to bring about or maintain order in the face of the problems introduced by scarcity. And since the constraints imposed by scarcity themselves evolve (i.e., new forms or manifestations of scarcity appear) over time, the issue of the appropriate organizational structure or form is one of ongoing concern for society. Organization, then, matters – not just in its existence or not, but in the form that it takes. The organizational form affects, among other things, the degree of coercive power that can be brought to bear by one agent toward another and the ability of one agent, a group of agents, or the larger society to limit, channel, or otherwise control coercive force by the exercise of its own coercive force. By setting up institutions, be they family, church, or state, as structures or organizations that create order out of conflict, Commons is explicitly working from a conflict, rather than harmony, view of the world.

The understanding that Commons is seeking requires, in his hands at least, the adoption of an evolutionary frame of analysis. This is a perspective that pervades the greater body of his theoretical analysis and which is particularly well illustrated in his *Legal Foundations of Capitalism* (1924), where he discusses the substantial impact on economic activity of the evolution of the legal definition of "reasonable value," along with which comes the content given to terms such as "private property" and "public purpose." Taking the example of private property, the adoption of an historico-evolutionary approach allows Commons to develop an analysis of the ramifications of a particular definition of property in force at a given period of time and the degree of congruence (and changes therein) between the legal definition of property and other social-economic phenomena and forces, how the evolving social situation gave rise to pressure for change in the definition, and how the changes adopted by the courts subsequently influenced economic activity. From Commons' extensive discussions of numerous legal cases in *Legal Foundations of Capitalism* – getting into the dispute at issue and its context, and the majority and minority opinions – one gains an understanding of how law is *worked out* over time – often through a succession of challenges to the status quo which are at first rejected strongly, then rejected in the face of a strong analytical dissent, and ultimately accepted by the majority of the court.

This process is a microcosm of the process through which the sovereignty of the state emerges in *A Sociological View of Sovereignty*. Sovereignty, too, is worked out, when one institutional form replaces another due to pressures brought to bear for changes that satisfy the needs of society, somehow defined. In an earlier essay entitled "Political Economy and Law" (1896), Commons summarizes that which he elaborates in greater detail in *A Sociological View of Sovereignty*, pointing out that

Law is coercive. It is regulated by force. The direction in which it shall work is determined by compromise between the antagonistic interests of society. In primitive times there was no compromise. The strongest ruled by mere might. Pure unmixed arbitrary force reduced the masses of the people to slavery, and compelled them to cultivate the fields for warlike rulers. There was no question of law or human rights. Law first appears when certain interests antagonistic to despotism gained sufficient power to lay down rules which should check the arbitrary coercion by the monarch. These interests were the nobility and the subordinate chiefs. Coercion still kept the masses in slavery and made the land the private property of the nobles and the monarch.

(Commons, 1896, p. 225)

But while this feudal system constituted "a decisive step" (p. 28) toward the organization of the state, Commons, writing in *A Sociological View of Sovereignty*, contends that

political and industrial conditions were against the permanence of this loose organization. The anarchy of the period, resulting from the private sovereignty of the feudal lords, forced upon the people the longing for a united government with adequate coercive powers, and the rapid changes in industry following the rise of commerce and manufactures, the introduction of money, and the fluctuations of prices, broke down the rule of custom, and permitted the king to infringe more and more upon its precincts.

(Commons, 1899–1900, pp. 28–29)

Like law, organization in general is not given, but, rather, worked out. Sovereignty, as one form of organization, is thus the culmination of a process of working out what organizational form suits the needs of society in its more developed state.[7]

Let us try to further bring out the import of the foregoing set of ideas – here, at a micro level – by reference to Commons' discussion of transactions in his *Legal Foundations of Capitalism*, as his analysis of transactions very much incorporates and develops from these ideas. For Commons, the transaction constitutes "the minimum of all economic and social relations whatever, whether it be that of the family, of business or politics" (1924, p. 67), and the framework within which a transaction (or a given class of transactions) takes place determines the opportunity set of each of the parties to the transaction. These opportunity sets are in part a function of the positions of those wishing to buy and sell – in particular, the actual buyer and seller and the next best alternative for each. However, Commons notes, there are an indefinite number of possible disputes between the parties to the transaction that may arise before or after the completion of the transaction. These disputes do arise and always have arisen in the history of the race from the most primitive times, simply because man has always been subject to the principle of scarcity which limits his choice of opportunities and exercise of power.

(Commons, 1924, p. 67)

Given this,

if transactions are to go on peaceably without resort to violence between the parties, there must always have been a fifth party to the transaction, namely, a judge, priest, chieftain, paterfamilias, arbitrator, foreman, superintendent, general manager, who would be able to decide and settle the dispute, with the aid of the group to which the five parties belonged.

(Commons, 1924, p. 67)

The rules so developed create order in the face of conflict. They serve to limit or expand the opportunity sets of the agents involved in a particular transacting process or class of transactions, and, as such, facilitate a particular mode of transacting.

For Commons, the transaction is not merely an economic phenomenon; rather, it is the basic unit of analysis in (and which correlates) law, economics, and ethics (Commons, 1932). This, in turn, serves to change the frame of reference for the analysis of economic action *vis-à-vis* received economic thinking. The transaction is a *social* arrangement or relationship, predicated upon the form and interaction of legal, economic, and ethical institutions; it "is not an individual seeking his own pleasure: it is five individuals doing something to each other within the limits of the working rules laid down by those who determine how disputes shall be decided." (Commons, 1924, p. 69). And because it is social, it is also endogenous. This is not to say that there is no benefit to be gained from considering max U_A given the positions of B, C, D, and E. Indeed, in a highly competitive market situation under a given legal regime (and assuming, for the sake of argument, that individuals are more or less rational maximizers of their satisfaction), such analysis has enormous power. The point, rather – and this is particularly important for the study of law and economics – is that the positions of B, C, D, and E (and thus A's opportunity set) are not necessarily given. In particular, one must understand how it is that changes in the legal (or non-legal authoritative) regime work to redefine opportunity sets of the various agents involved and thus the scope of actions available to each.

Furthermore, and in this same vein, these positions, opportunity sets, and so forth are themselves endogenous, worked out through a process in which certain individuals or groups bring to bear pressures for change while others advocate continuity – that is, maintenance of the status quo. As such, the rules – and the interpretation thereof – governing the nature of transactions evolve over time, with those existing at any given point in time and the path of the evolution being derivative of the reconciliation of the tension between continuity and change. While the ongoing reconciliation of the forces for continuity with those for change is typically described in terms of the relative strength of the competing interests in effecting or preventing legal change, Commons' discussion in *A Sociological View of Sovereignty* brings to the fore the role of the form taken by the authority – sovereign or otherwise – within this process. The manner in which the tension between continuity and change is resolved by the authority – the relative weights given to the competing interests, the degree of enforcement power, etc. – will be impacted by whether that authority is family, church, monarchical state, democratic state, and so forth. That is, who controls (or is allowed to control) the flow of coercion is very much at the center of the determination of governance institutions, with sovereignty providing one set of potential answers to the control question. The form in which sovereignty manifests itself in a given society provides the actual answer, and this may have multiple parts, as in the US, where the executive (and especially its agencies), the legislature, and the courts each have jurisdiction over particular classes of situations and/or their own means of influencing any given situation or class of situations. And given the rather different form and make-up of each of these agents of sovereignty, their respectively different constitutionally or otherwise imposed operating procedures, and so on, the form in which sovereignty is exercised may vary accordingly.

INSTITUTIONS MATTER

As we noted above, Dorfman praises *A Sociological View of Sovereignty* as a general contribution to the analysis of institutions. Given that our purpose here is to attempt to draw implications for legal-economic thought and analysis, we shall concern ourselves with one of these institutions: law – defined broadly to encompass common law, statutes and other types of regulatory activities, and constitutions. In doing so, we remain fully consonant with Commons' focus on sovereignty, as sovereignty is, in his view, a phenomenon that reduces coercion to order through rights – that is, law.

Commons maintains that an institution consists of three parts:

> first, a body of accepted beliefs, which color and shape the individual's desires from infancy; second, a group of material products, designed to satisfy these desires; third, an organization which sets the alignment of individuals toward one another.
>
> (Commons, 1899–1990, p. 4)

As regards law, the second aspect, the "group of material products," is the set of legal rules in force at any given point in time. The legal rules, in turn, are reflective of "a body of accepted beliefs" – norms, customs, and so on – regarding the appropriate structure of rights and duties between individuals. The organization that aligns individuals is thus the courts, or, in the case of statutes and regulations, perhaps the legislature or regulatory agency.

Commons' description of institutions is obviously very general; it is amenable to various interpretations and can encompass various types of theories. As with neoclassical economics, the new institutional economics, and contemporary mainstream law and economics, Commons grounds his analysis in the problem of scarcity. However, Commons does not take the existence of scarcity for granted or as a given, but attempts to show, instead, how the problem arose, the manner in which it manifests itself at particular points in time, the evolution of the parameters of scarcity and their location, and the determinants of all of this.[8]

In his discussions of the state, Commons speaks repeatedly of the state being "differentiated out from the primitive, homogeneous blending of institutions" of family, church, and industrial property (p. 85). These institutions evolved simultaneously with (among other things) the economic system through a process of cumulative causation in response to changing (scarcity-driven) needs and circumstances, and the pressures for change that accompanied them. And each of these institutions, in its particular period of dominance and afterward – that is, when superseded by a more authoritative institutional form – interacts with the economic system in various ways, including in helping to structure or order it.

This raises the immediate question of why these institutions evolved in the manner that they did. There is no settled answer to this question, and, while there are a number of theories of institutional change and institutional dynamics, there is likely no singular answer to be given, either for a particular class of institutions (for example, firms or the law) or for institutions generally.[9] Within economics, the most widely accepted theories of institutional development have their basis in the idea of *efficient* adaptation. In developing his transaction-cost-based theory of the firm, Oliver Williamson (1975, p. 20) consciously adopts the position that "in the beginning there were markets" and posits the firm as an efficient (transaction-cost mini-mizing) response to the costliness of operating through markets. A similar frame of reference pervades the efficiency theory of the common law, which argues, if you will, that "justice" effectively translates into efficiency, with the result that the legal rules which have evolved are those which most efficiently dealt with the disputed matters. One finds in Commons a rather different and more general view: the evolution of institutions and institutional forms – family, church, and state – based on particular needs, circumstances, and pressures brought to bear. While one could adopt a

Beckerian perspective and place each of these institutions and the general course of their evolution into a market-based framework, Commons instead takes a sociological view, one that, in his words, is purely inductive. Resolution based on "particular needs and circumstances" does not, for Commons, necessarily equate to efficiency. Nor is efficiency, for Commons, a unique, self-subsistent concept.

The extent to which alternative perspectives on the development of institutions can be subsumed within the general framework that Commons lays out (especially in *A Sociological View of Sovereignty*, but also elsewhere) can be seen by considering the following set of hypotheses offered to explain the structure and/or evolution of legal rules:

1 Flowing from a body of accepted beliefs, law may be said to reflect the common will – that is, the will of a majority of the members of society.

2 If one believes that a small group of powerful interests can shape individual desires or authoritative decision making, law may be said to reflect the will of a set of small, powerful interests.

3 If individuals are reasonable, as the standard view of the common law presupposes, then law can be said to reflect the reasonable views of reasonable people.

4 If individuals are rational, as neoclassical law and economics presupposes, then law can be said to reflect the processes envisioned by the rational efficiency calculus, including, for example, the efficiency theory of the common law.

As Commons' (1924; 1934) later work reveals, he himself comes down on the side of reasonableness (which, in an economic context, translates into reasonable value) and would likely reject those theories reflecting a straightforward maximization of self-interest point of view.[10]

But the point to take note of, for present purposes (and this is particularly strongly emphasized by Commons), is that, regardless of the explanatory framework adopted, one confronts the fact that law is *set down* by those vested with such authority and in response to pressures brought to bear for legal change. It is consciously developed rather than an unintended consequence. Given this, one cannot avoid the conclusion that law matters; it matters allocatively and it matters distributionally. The very existence of the pressures brought to bear for the establishment of or changes in (and against changes in) legal rules testifies to this point. None the less, as Commons points out in "Political Economy and Law," economists

> have overlooked (and, one might add, largely continue to overlook) positive law. In seeking to trace out the workings of self-interest they have taken for granted certain laws as natural and inherent in the constitution of society, such as laws sustaining private property,

104

while other laws have been considered as an artificial and unnatural interference with beneficent self-interest.

(Commons, 1896, p. 225)

Yet, he says, "No economic problem is more important than the just estimate of the part played by customary and statutory law in social evolution" (p. 225). That is, law matters economically and thus should matter for economic analysis, and not simply in the sense of applying microeconomic theory to the law, following most of contemporary law and economics, but in the examination of the legal foundations of the economic system, or the interrelations between legal and economic processes generally.

But this point is only one part of a larger point: that institutions matter in determining the structure and evolution of the economic system and economic activity. These institutions are both numerous and heterogeneous in their import. Commons' work in *Institutional Economics* (1934) represents an attempt to bring out the extent of this influence and to provide an approach (albeit an incomplete one) through which economists might proceed to incorporate these insights into the general framework of theory and analysis. The point here is not that there must be some singular economic theory that encompasses all manner of phenomena that influence economic behavior and performance. Indeed, Commons himself was rather a "horses for courses" person, recognizing that different theoretical frameworks and tools (of varying degrees of abstraction) can be fruitfully applied to the analysis of particular economic problems. The point, rather, is that ascertaining what frameworks and tools should be applied in particular contexts or how the frameworks and tools might be modified to better serve the analysis of these problems requires that economists first attempt to come to grips with the wide range of phenomena that influence economic behavior and performance, and, from there, sift down to the components of a useful theory or theories.

THE ECONOMIC ROLE OF GOVERNMENT AND ITS PERVASIVENESS

In considering the various stages of the evolution of authoritative governance structures, it is not until the point when the sovereign state is in place that we confront the issue of the role of government, or the state, within the economic system. This is the point at which discussions of the role of government – be they scholarly or popular – usually begin, taking as given the existence of the state and a particular set of functions for it. And it is from this point of view that changes in the economic role of government are traditionally assessed, often in terms of more or less intervention by government, governmental interference in matters in which it had hitherto been absent, expanding or contracting the actions of government, government versus the market, and so on.

But one of the points that emerges quite clearly from Commons' discussion in *A Sociological View of Sovereignty* and elsewhere is that this is a wrong-headed manner in which to couch arguments about the economic role of government. The state evolves out of a struggle to create order out of conflict and, as Commons illustrates in *A Sociological View of Sovereignty*, the state is, at the most basic level, just another institution of authority – like pater familias, the church, the tribal leader, or the duke. This is not to say that these last are identical to the state (or to each other, for that matter); the state arises because of its differential capacity to carry out the authoritative function – to create and maintain order – when other authoritative institutions are no longer able to perform this task to society's satisfaction.

But, this having been said, it remains the case that the state is, in essence, an instrument of authority, and, as such, it governs all manner of social activities and relations from the moment of its inception. Put in a slightly different fashion, the state, from the moment of its inception, determines the boundaries of agent opportunity sets. It allows certain classes of actions and restricts others. "Law," in Commons' words, "is part of the environment of every individual" (1896, p. 225). Once the state is in place, "new" laws, "new" rights, and, more generally, legal change serve only to *change* the classes of actions permitted or restricted by the state. These are thus not matters of government interfering where it had hitherto been absent, of "regulation" or "deregulation," etc.; rather, they are simply changes in the class of interests which government serves to protect.

Recognition of this point gives the lie to discussions couched in terms of "government versus the market." While one can think of – and find illustrations of – markets without government, it is much more difficult to find illustrations of markets (or at least reasonably well-functioning markets) without authority, or even to conceive of such in theory when considerations of large numbers, locational dispersion, intertemporal exchange, and so on are taken into consideration.[11]

Now, the state evolves as an authoritative institution that can provide the desired degree of order when other authoritative institutions fail to do the job, and one facet of this process of order creation is the economic, which includes the establishment of the set of laws that orders market relationships and determines the range of actions available to those who participate in markets. Included here are the laws governing property and contract, those governing combination (of firms and workers), wage and price controls, and so on.[12] In each case, the form of the specific legal rules in force, or the presence or absence of a specific rule, is nothing more than the government giving effect to this set of interests or that, exposing A to the exercise of coercive force by B or conversely. Changes in legal rules, or the putting in place of formal legal rules that in some way restrict the actions of agents as they operate in markets, reflect a change in interests given effect to or the degree to which A is exposed to the exercise of B's coercion within the market process. Commons is worth quoting at length on this point:

> The growth of monopoly and centralization increases the coercive powers of the private owners of industry by strengthening the privative sanctions. ... But the grounds for private coercive authority having ceased through the cessation of the struggle, the state as the coercive instrument of society tends to absorb this side of the industrial institution. It constitutes itself the coercive frame-work of industry within which the persuasive motives operate. This framework consists in the statures and codes of the laws governing property and corporations, the factory laws, the judicial decisions, the administrative methods which determine the relations of pro-ducers to each other. The state becomes the framework of industry, just as it becomes the framework of the family and the church. The laws governing property and labor constitute the bulk of its func-tions, and the legislatures, courts, and executives have been created expressly for, and are busied mainly with, the regulation of this important institution (p. 85).

Given the existence of the state then, government is ubiquitous within the economic system. The importance of these ideas cannot be overstated and they remain to be fully (or often even partially) grasped by either contem-porary economists or the general public.

In light of the foregoing, the issue for policy, then, is not one of govern-ment versus the market, nor of more versus less government, nor of more government interference versus less, but of how the ubiquitous authority of government is to be exercised within the economic system: who is to be exposed to the coercion of whom, and to what extent. As such, the exercise of sovereignty in the legislative, judicial, and executive branches is, at its heart, the exercise of *choice*. In Commons' words, the state "is concerned only with the questions: Who shall get the advantages of social production? For whose benefit shall services be rendered, and who shall bear the burdens?" (p. 101). And because the working out of the economic role of government is an exercise in choice, it is also an exercise in *valuation* and the attendant influence of selective perception and sentiment. The role of valuation in the policy-making process is extensively discussed by Commons in *Legal Foundations of Capitalism*. For our purposes, it is sufficient to restrict ourselves to a single illustration – the role of valuation in the process of reasoning from precedent.

The process of reasoning from precedent is considered by many to give law an objective, scientific air – removing the roles of normativism, value judgments, and arbitrariness from the legal decision-making process. As

Commons points out, however, no case that comes before the court is perfectly identical to any previous case, and, as a result, the court must classify a new case within the precedential schema in order to apply precedential reasoning (Commons, 1924, p. 346). This first involves the inclusion of some facts and the exclusion of others, according to whether the facts are similar or dissimilar, respectively, to a particular precedent. And all of this, according to Commons takes place "with reference to their fitness in attaining the purpose of the one who does the classifying" (p. 347). Secondly, the facts must be weighed. And, as Commons points out,

> Weighing the facts is not a mere statistical enumeration of them. The facts, when they come before a person, do not automatically seek their own specific gravity. Weighing is not a mere intellectual process of distinguishing the various qualities or faculties of objects or persons. Nor is it a logical process of abstracting a certain class of qualities and arranging them in a system. It is also an emotional valuation of qualities and faculties of social life.
>
> (Commons, 1924, p. 348)

Both the process of classification and the process of weighing are exercises in choice – of what will be included or excluded, and, for that which is included, the weight which it will be given in the decision calculus. And throughout this process, valuation, and the influence of selective perception and sentiment, is unavoidable:

> This (fact) may be good or bad, worthy or unworthy, desired or undesired, important or unimportant. This is the ultimate feeling of value, the emotional process of valuation that tinges all definitions, the place where the feelings exercise the power of choice by including the facts which are felt to be important and excluding those deemed unimportant, thus converting truth into belief, and facts into opinions regarding facts.
>
> (Commons, 1924, p. 349)

And as Commons correctly argues, this holds with regard to economic "facts" or "values," as well as with regard to those values that are more commonly considered to be normative. Upon noting several alternative ways in which capital and property can be valued, and the non-identity of these measures, he points out that "If value were a fixed external object, having a physical existence, there could be but one value of a thing at one time and place. But if value is a *process of valuing* then the *purpose* of the valuation determines what the value shall be" (Commons, 1924, p. 211). The resolutions worked out through the choice process – the determination of how government shall act within the economic system at any given point in time – "is settled by opinion, prejudice, and preference, not by knowledge, skill, and tact" (p. 102).

In *Legal Foundations of Capitalism*, Commons contends that, within common law decision making, this valuation process involves a search for reasonable value on the part of the courts in the determination of legal rules, the content given to them, and the manner in which the relevant terms are defined. More recently, others, such as Posner (1992, Part II) have argued that, as regards the evolution of the common law, at least, the choice among alternative rules reflected the desire to achieve efficiency in the ordering of legal-economic relations. But regardless of the goal that is imputed to the legal decision makers, it remains the case that the determination of that which is "reasonable" or "efficient" or "just" requires that the decision makers engage in a process of valuing – imputing values and weights to – benefits, costs, distributions, etc. This, of course, has all manner of implications, calling into question claims to correspondence with natural law, framers' intent, adherence to precedent, and so on. For present purposes, however, we emphasize the implications for efficiency in normative and positive law and economics.[13] The point is a simple one: as all assessments of benefit and cost are filtered through a process of valuation, any putative efficient result is uniquely efficient only relative to the particular valuation made. That is, there is no singular efficient result, only results that are efficient given particular valuations.

INSTITUTIONS IN CONFLICT

As was noted above, Commons contends that sovereignty reduces coercion to order through rights, and, as such, supersedes custom, etc. in the institutional ordering of social relations. However, rights only set the boundaries for action; custom can still act within these boundaries to influence the scope of individual action within the defined opportunity set. Indeed, "The state sets the minimum level below which the struggle for existence shall not be permitted to force an institution" (p. 104). Moreover, while law is the ultimate authority, this authority is only brought to bear if invoked. And, as Commons notes, "For the mass of people actual state interference (i.e., invocation) is not needed, because of their obedience, not only to the state minimum, but also to an even higher standard of right" (pp. 104–5).

Commons (pp. 8–9) correctly recognizes that institutions will almost never, if ever reflect the unanimity that the purest concept of common will might imply, nor the sort of absolute mastery that would allow a single small group to mold social institutions such as law. Rather, the development of law reflects the interaction of bundles of interests – some coincident and some divergent – and the processes of persuasion and coercion to secure a majority view. It seems logical to assume that the expanded opportunity set boundaries granted to agents through changes in legal rules will be exploited. Indeed, it is the desire to do just this that gives rise to the pressure for legal change in the first place. At the same time, however, others will be more or less indifferent to the legal change, while still others will be overtly hostile to it – perhaps because their opportunity set boundaries are narrowed by the change.

It is in these last two cases that we can observe the fact that institutions themselves are potentially interacting, and, in some cases, in conflict – in particular, for present purposes, law and norms/customs. Consider the following recent studies. Woodbury and Spiegelman (1987) report on an experiment conducted in conjunction with Illinois Department of Employment Security in which they attempted to determine whether the payment of bonuses to workers and employers would reduce the duration of unemployment. Certain unemployed workers were offered bonuses for finding new employment within a specified period of time, while other workers were told that their new employers would be given bonuses for hiring them if they found employment within a specified period of time.[14] However, substantial numbers of workers failed to report the existence of these bonus plans to potential employers, and, as Ellickson (1989b) has suggested, this is likely due in part to the deviation of such schemes from standard employment practices and the fear of associated stigma effects. Rather than taking advantage of the opportunities granted them under the "legal rule" in force, individuals seemed to rely on what they perceived to be the norms governing the employer–employee relationship to govern their behavior.

In another recent study, Hanley and Sumner (1995) report that owners of farms and timberland in the Scottish Highlands whose crops and forests are being damaged by high red deer populations that roam from neighboring estates tend to refuse to take advantage of the free deer culling offered by the government. Instead, these individuals choose to work out the problems with the owners of neighboring estates, who derive substantial income and estate value from the presence of red deer on their estates.

Finally, consider Ellickson's (1986, 1991) study of the relationship between cattle ranchers and their neighbors in Shasta County, California. Ellickson examines, among other things, the effects of open- versus closed-range laws on cattle trespass disputes in Shasta County, California. Under open-range laws, cattlemen are not usually responsible for accidental trespass damage, whereas they are strictly liable under closed range laws. Ellickson finds that cattlemen and their neighbors cooperate to resolve their disputes regardless of who is liable at law. And, in doing so, these individuals seem to rely on community norms to determine their behavior. For example, while the one would predict that the cattleman would install a fence if he were liable (closed range), and that the neighboring farmer would do so if he were liable (open range), it is almost always the cattleman who installs the fence because both cattlemen and their neighbors believe that the cattleman is morally obligated to do so, since his cattle cause the damage. In fact, in a number of cases the citizens seem to be very ignorant of the relevant law and ignore those aspects of the law that conflict with their view of the world. As such, they do not bargain "in the shadow of the law,"[15] but beyond it; community norms seem to have much more force than the legal rule in place.[16]

Each of these situations illustrates a case in which the institutions of norms/customs and law come into conflict and in which custom supersedes, in a *de facto* sense, the law. In each instance, individuals have rights which they choose not to exercise or act in light of, basing their actions instead on the norms or customs that have evolved to govern relations in these particular contexts. While law, as Commons points out, tends to have its basis in customs and to establish customary actions in authoritative form, it remains the case that law and custom may conflict and that, in such cases, law – the opportunity set boundaries created by rights – may not, *de facto*, govern individual actions.

This fact points to the limits of law and of sovereignty generally. The ability of sovereign authority to influence behavior or structure relationships in this way or that remains, in important cases, limited, as Commons (p. 51) notes. The task for economics, then, becomes not merely one of examining the legal underpinnings of the economic system, but of uncovering their influences and the extent of these influences vis-à-vis other forces. That is, it is not sufficient to look at law and individual actions without attention to how it is that individuals do in fact respond to law and legal change, if at all. To the extent that factors such as norms and customs influence actions in a manner that may deviate from what is suggested by the legal rules per se, a simple "economic" approach to analyzing law and legal change – one that assumes that all advantages made available will be exploited and/or that all constraints imposed by the legal system will be binding in fact – is insufficient. Of course the sociological approach reflected in Commons' *A Sociological View of Sovereignty* is also insufficient. What is required is a multifaceted approach, from which one can gain an understanding of how institutions and their interaction influence economic behavior and performance, which in turn can be distilled down to a theory that can be used to predict and assess the implications of law and legal change for economic behavior and performance.

CONCLUSION

This essay began with the assertion that Commons' *A Sociological View of Sovereignty*, written a century ago and largely ignored within the subsequent development of economic thought and analysis, contains useful insights for contemporary economic thinking. The goal of this essay has been to bring out a few of these points, centering on the analysis of the legal basis of the economic system.

For Commons, sovereignty plays a fundamental role in structuring economic relationships and outcomes – channeling, restraining, and facilitating the omnipresent exercise of coercion so as to provide order within the economic system. As such, the state, through law, becomes a central player in defining agent opportunity sets, doing so through a valuational process in which choices are made between competing interests. As a result, the state exercises profound influence over individual agent choices and the resultant economic outcomes. To understand the development and/or present-day workings of a given economic system, one must understand the form and extent of sovereignty – in the modern age, how government in particular has operated and/or continues to operate in and through the economic system and how the economic sphere has continued to play a powerful role in determining the nature and direction of sovereignty. Because sovereignty is the means by which rights are established or created, rights become a matter of policy rather than something pre-existing or given. Thus, to speak of rights is to speak of policy, and to speak of policy is to speak in terms of making choices as to which interests government will support – market or otherwise.

From the present author's point of view, it is this aspect of Commons' work – evidenced earlier in "Political Economy and Law" and later in *Legal Foundations of Capitalism* and *Institutional Economics* – that constitutes his most significant contribution to economic analysis and method. *A Sociological View of Sovereignty* is an integral part of this, both in the conclusions reached and in the method employed.[17]

NOTES

1 Unless otherwise noted, all page references contained herein are to Commons (1899–1900).
2 See for example, the survey in Eggertsson (1990).
3 Pigou used the criterion of maximizing the national dividend, but tempered this with various ethical or distributional considerations – in particular, what one might call a preferential option for the poor. See Aslanbeigui and Medema (1998).
4 It is important to realize at this point that, for Commons, property is sovereignty. As such, the evolution of the state from medieval times forward has involved a diffusion of property-power-sovereignty. To frame the issue in Robert Lee Hale's (1952) terminology, we are dealing with the recognition of the simultaneous existence of public and private government and the relative scope of each. The breadth of Commons' conception notwithstanding, this essay will focus most heavily on the topic of state sovereignty (or, in Hale's term, public government).

5 Later, in his *Institutional Economics*, Commons (1934, p. 6) places the problem of scarcity at the center of the analysis, but in a manner somewhat different than that observed within neoclassical economics.

6 As such, coercion differs from persuasion "in that the latter does not depend primarily on material means for inducing compliance, but mainly on direct psychic influence" (p. 25).

7 Of course, this cuts both ways, since sovereignty allows society to reach further stages of development.

8 Again, the reader is referred particularly to *Legal Foundations of Capitalism* (1924) and *Institutional Economics* (1934) for broader and more extensive expositions. See Commons (1934, pp. 5–7) for a statement of the general perspective.

9 While the literature on this topic is far too vast to touch upon here, one can find useful readings from a variety of perspectives in Hodgson (1993), Samuels (1988), and Witt (1993).

10 This having been said, Commons did not reject the usefulness of the rational maximizing model or the role of self-interest in individual decision making. However, he did believe that a fuller and richer approach was necessary to explain the forces at work.

11 This is not to say that government is overtly present or acknowledged in such conceptions, merely that it is implicitly assumed to be present to provide the framework or order necessary for markets to function in such circumstances.

12 Various facets of each of these are discussed by Commons in his *Legal Foundations of Capitalism* (1924).

13 The reader is referred to Medema and Samuels (1998) and Mercuro and Medema (1997, Chapters 4 and 7) for more extensive discussions of this point.

14 For commentaries on this experiment in the context of law and economics, see Donohue (1989), Ellickson (1989b), and Lindgren (1990).

15 See Mnookin and Kornhauser (1979) and Cooter, Marks, and Mnookin (1982).

16 Ellickson suggests that this may be due to the fact that relations among the neighbors are both complex and continuing, because of which the transaction costs associated with acquiring information and litigating disputes are high, and reliance on norms offers a lower-cost way of resolving these disputes. Ellickson (1989a, 1991) also suggests that this norm-based behavior points to the need to revise certain of the behavioral concepts underlying law and economics. This issue goes beyond the scope of the present paper, but see Medema (1997).

17 The comments of Warren J. Samuels were very helpful in clarifying certain of the arguments made in this chapter and are gratefully acknowledged here.

REFERENCES

Aslanbeigui, Nahid and Steven G. Medema. 1998. "Beyond the Dark Clouds: Pigou and Coase on Social Cost." *History of Political Economy*, forthcoming.

Commons, John R. 1896. "Political Economy and Law." *The Kingdom* 24 (January), 225. Reprinted in Malcolm Rutherford and Warren J. Samuels, eds, *John R. Commons: Selected Essays*, Vol. 1. London: Routledge, 1996, 41–2.

—— 1899–1900. *A Sociological View of Sovereignty*. Reprint. New York: Augustus M. Kelley, 1967.

—— 1924. *Legal Foundations of Capitalism*. New York: Macmillan. Reprinted Clifton, NJ: Augustus M. Kelley Publishers, 1974.

—— 1932. "The Problem of Correlating Law Economics and Ethics." *Wisconsin Law Review* 8, 3–26.

—— 1934. *Institutional Economics*. New York: Macmillan. Reprinted Madison: University of Wisconsin Press, 1959.

Cooter, Robert D., Stephen Marks, and Robert Mnookin. 1982. "Bargaining in the Shadow of the Law: A Testable Model of Strategic Behavior." *Journal of Legal Studies* 11, 225–51.

Donohue, John J. III. 1989. "Diverting the Coasean River: Incentive Schemes to Reduce Unemployment Spells." *Yale Law Journal* 99, 549–609.

Eggertsson, Thráinn. 1990. *Economic Behavior and Institutions*. Cambridge: Cambridge University Press.

Ellickson, Robert C. 1986. "Of Coase and Cattle: Dispute Resolution among Neighbors in Shasta County." *Stanford Law Review* 38, 623–87.

—— 1989a. "Bringing Culture and Frailty to Rational Actors: A Critique of Classical Law and Economics." *Chicago-Kent Law Review* 65, 23–55.

—— 1989b. "The Case for Coase and Against 'Coaseanism.'" *Yale Law Journal* 99, 611–30.

—— 1991. *Order without Law: How Neighbors Settle Disputes*. Cambridge, MA: Harvard University Press.

Hale, Robert Lee. 1952. *Freedom Through Law: Public Control of Private Governing Power*. New York: Columbia University Press.

Hanley, Nick and Charles Sumner. 1995. "Bargaining Over Common Property Resources: Applying the Coase Theorem to Red Deer in the Scottish Highlands." *Journal of Environmental Management* 43, 87–95.

Hodgson, Geoffrey M., ed. 1993. *The Economics of Institutions*. Aldershot: Edward Elgar Publishing.

Lindgren, James. 1990. " 'Ol' Man River, . . . He Keeps On Rollin' Along': A Reply to Donohue's Diverting the Coasean River." *Georgetown Law Journal* 78, 577–91.

Medema, Steven G. 1997. "The Trial of *Homo Economicus*: What Law and Economics Tells Us About the Development of Economic Imperialism." *New Economics and Its Writing: History of Political Economy Annual Supplement*, forthcoming.

Medema, Steven G. and Warren J. Samuels. 1998. "The Economic Role of Government as, in part, a Matter of Selective Perception, Sentiment, and Valuation: The Cases of Pigovian and Paretian Welfare Economics." Mimeo.

Mercuro, Nicholas and Steven G. Medema. 1997. *Economics and the Law: From Posner to Post Modernism*. Princeton: Princeton University Press.

Mnookin, Robert and Lewis Kornhauser. 1979. "Bargaining in the Shadow of the Law: The Case of Divorce." *Yale Law Journal* 88, 950–97.

Posner, Richard A. 1992. *Economic Analysis of Law*, 4th edn. Boston: Little, Brown and Co.

Samuels, Warren J., ed. 1992. *Institutional Economics*, 3 Vols. Aldershot: Edward Elgar Publishing.

Williamson, Oliver E. 1975. *Markets and Hierarchies: Analysis and Antitrust Implications*. New York: The Free Press.

Witt, Ulrich, ed. 1993. *Evolutionary Economics*. Aldershot: Edward Elgar Publishing.

Woodbury, Stephen A. and Robert G. Spiegelman. 1987. "Bonuses to Workers and Employers to Reduce Unemployment: Randomized Trials in Illinois." *American Economic Review* 77, 513–30.

7

JOHN R. COMMONS'S "POLITICAL ECONOMY AND LAW"

Harbinger of *A Sociological View of Sovereignty* and *Legal Foundations of Capitalism*

Warren J. Samuels

INTRODUCTION

John R. Commons's *Legal Foundations of Capitalism* (1924) was his magnum opus of legal-economic theory and history. In it, Commons developed a number of themes. The economic system is a function of government action – to wit, law – which necessarily resolved both conflicting views of what the economy (and society) should be and conflicting material and other interests. Government itself is a vehicle for both the social reconstruction of economy and society, and the advancement of interests. Both government itself and the legal foundations of the economy, and perforce the economy itself, emerged out of a process constituting a legal-economic nexus. The economy was, *inter alia*, a structure of rights, exposures, immunities, and duties, all constituting a structure of liberty, power and coercion. The economic system evolved through the process of the legal-economic nexus in the foregoing manner, especially through the silent accumulation of common law court cases. That capitalism reigned because capitalists had been successful in achieving legal status for their vision of society, their customs, their conceptions of public purpose, and their interests, over against those of the ancient landlord class. The modern system of rent, price and wages is what it is because of the foregoing legal developments. Lastly, *inter alia*, that change through law of the relative rights of the various parties to transactions was still going on, such that one could expect changes in the legal foundations of capitalism to accommodate the vision of society, the customs, the conceptions of public purpose and the interests of the working class, and to do so in the same manner that the institutionalization of the ideas and interests of the capitalist had taken place.

By 1924 Commons had had several careers. He had been a leading figure in the Social Gospel movement. He had become the leading historian of labor. He had become the advocate of commission regulation and other Progressive institutional innovations, including the strengthening, professionalization and advancement of government at all levels. He had also written several articles and books on topics on the social, political and economic foundations of his more worldly interests. Through these publications he was trying to develop, among other things, the legal and even the psychological foundations of his version of political economy/economics, eventually to culminate in his *Institutional Economics* of 1934.

One of those endeavors was the series of articles, published in 1899–1900 in the *American Journal of Sociology* and later in a book, entitled "A Sociological View of Sovereignty," which this collection celebrates as Commons's contribution to the founding of institutional economics, alongside Thorstein Veblen's *Theory of the Leisure Class*, also of 1899. The arbitrary nature of any such dating is suggested by the fact that in 1895 Commons published a one-page article which was clearly the precursor of his *Legal Foundations of Capitalism* three decades later and, in its own way, of *A Sociological View of Sovereignty* itself.

"Political Economy and Law" was published by Commons in *The Kingdom*, a religiously oriented weekly published in Minneapolis, in the issue of January 24, 1896.[1] The paper attracted a variety of writers, many of whom were associated with the Social Gospel movement. Included were articles with titles such as "The Laboring Classes and the Church," "The Social Evil," "Politics and Religion," "Wants and Wages," "That Word 'Competition,'" and "Natural Laws"; editorials on "Classes and Social Harmony," "Language and Truth," "The Social Failure of Political Economy," and "Individualism"; and reports such as "The Chicago Summer School of Social Economics." John Bascom and Carroll D. Wright were among the contributors.

Commons's article is reprinted below. The capital letters in brackets point to interpretive annotations by the present author following the article.

POLITICAL ECONOMY AND LAW

By John R. Commons

The political economists have been charged by Professor Herron, in a recent number of The Kingdom[,][2] with overlooking ethics. The charge is just and important.[A] But more important is the fact that they have overlooked positive law. In seeking to trace out the workings of self-interest they have taken for granted certain laws as natural and inherent in the constitution of society, such as laws sustaining private property, while other laws have been considered as an artificial and unnatural interference with beneficent self-interest. Protective tariffs, prohibitory statutes, legal protection of women and children, are considered violations of natural law. No economic problem is more important than the just estimate of the part played by customary and statutory law in social evolution.[B]

Law, in the first place, is a part of the environment of every individual. It operates upon him as does the physical environment, by pressure. Law is coercive. It is regulated force.[C] The direction in which it shall work is determined by compromise between the antagonistic interests of society.[D] In primitive times there was no compromise. The strongest ruled by mere might. Pure unmixed arbitrary force reduced the masses of the people to slavery, and compelled them to cultivate the fields for warlike rulers. There was no question of law or human rights. Law first appears when certain interests antagonistic to despotism gained sufficient power to lay down rules which should check the arbitrary coercion by the monarch.[E] These interests were the nobility and the subordinate chiefs. Coercion still kept the masses in slavery and made the land the private property of nobles and monarch.[F]

Later in time the capitalist class, through the representative system, gained a share in making laws. They compelled the ruling classes to lift the pressure which handicapped capitalists, and today they have even shaped the laws to their own preference.[G] Such are the laws enforcing contracts, where the coercive power of the state is enlisted on behalf of the money lender – a thing inconceivable to a medieval duke.[H] Such also are the laws creating and sustaining corporations – "artificial persons" which never die, which always accumulate, and whose contracts with the public and with employes [sic] the power of the state enforces even with the police and the army, if necessary. Such also are laws abolishing entail and primogeniture, making real estate transferable by sale and survey and public record, and thus converting land from an aristocratic inheritance to a plutocratic speculation.

By means of these and other regulations which we call laws, the coercive power of society is lifted from the capitalistic class, a marked advantage in the struggle for life is afforded them, and they are stimulated to exert themselves and accumulate property under the protection of government.

At the same time law has both helped and depressed the masses of the people. It has helped them by abolishing slavery – an institution based solely on force. It has depressed them by maintaining land and capital – by means of which alone they can live – as private property, another institution based on force as truly as slavery.[I] It is only coercion of some kind, however subtle and gloved or justified, which can crowd thousands of people into the tenements of the slums and permit hundreds to spread over roomy homes and palaces and seaside villas.

Ethics effects its telling results by modifying the coercive pressure of society on behalf of those who are weak. Women were the first slaves. Today law protects them from the brutality of men, opens up new trades for them, increases their wages, and gives them shorter hours of work (unless declared unconstitutional by the courts).[J][K]

Ethics also through law, modifies the unchecked coercion of private property by requiring employers to submit disputes with labor to arbitration, by requiring safety appliances, sanitary factories and tenements, and in many other ways which might be mentioned or suggested. Law determines the legal tender, and in its enforcement of contracts can select an expanding or a contracting medium for payment, and so can either take the pressure of competitive society from, or else force it upon, the debtor classes.[L]

Ethics cannot work without coercion. Force is necessary to do good as well as to work oppression.[M] Ethics and religion can justify and stimulate society and social classes to get hold of the law making and law-enforcing power in order to frame new laws and thus give new direction to social coercion. A new environment is then created for individuals, into which they are born, and where they find their motives, ideals and education. It may be an environment where accumulation of private property with accompanying power over others enforced by law is the highest motive and the criterion of success; or it may be an environment where law aided by the state gives no man any coercive control over his fellows, and where, therefore, the highest motives are to gain honor and power through service to others. In the one case the law has shaped an environment where success comes to the shrewd, the brutal, the self-seeking; in the other the law shuts the field against those qualities, and the meek inherit the earth.[N]

ANNOTATIONS

[A] It may be argued that mainstream political economy/economics either omits consideration of ethics, in its quest for ostensible "positive," non-normative scientific status *or* that it has its own ethical/normative preconceptions.

[B] This pair of arguments constitutes two of Commons's central themes, here and throughout his work. One theme is the importance of positive law, for example, in differentially enhancing and restraining the self-interests of different persons. Such law as a thinker or writer or economic agent likes is taken as constitutive of the natural order of things, whereas the rights constituted by the positive law have been artifacts that have evolved through a process of social construction. Thus the second theme is the selective perception of certain actions of government, and of certain rights predicated upon those actions, as "natural" and others as "artificial." By "customary" law Commons means court law (common law in contrast to statute law).

[C] For Commons, economy and society are arenas of both liberty and coercion. It is liberty in so far as individuals or groups of individuals can exercise and effectuate their choice. It is coercion in so far as individuals or groups of individuals are constrained in the domain of their opportunity sets and in the exercise and effectuation thereof. Law, as part of the process and structure, both enhances liberty and imposes coercion, typically differently for different persons or differently for different aspects of a person's situation. That law is coercive is not pejorative for Commons. It is a statement of fact. Law in some form – monarchical edicts, court decisions, statutes by representative assemblies – is a necessity and it is both coercive in and of itself and part of the coercive system of society; as such it is part of the structure and process of both liberty and coercion in economy and society.

[D] Commons eventually developed the concept of the "collective bargaining state," in which processes of adjudication/selection operate to resolve conflicts of interests through what amounts to a civilized – and civilizing – process of compromise. His approach to problem solving was to bring the conflicting parties together, have them mutually inform each other of their interests, and, hopefully, work out solutions acceptable to each, as the parties make mutual concessions. This may be deemed the working out of Pareto optimal solutions in practice, though such was not Commons's language.

[E] Commons's point, in addition to the ubiquity of coercion in society, is the "arbitrary" nature of choice leading to the coercion of those for whom the choices are made. For Commons, democracy, parliamentary government, the inclusion of the customs and interests of hitherto excluded groups or classes, and so on, meant the elimination *pro tanto* of unilateral and therefore arbitrary choice and its consequent coercion. Commons emphasizes not the removal of coercion, for coercion is both inevitable and ubiquitous, but the increasing pluralization of economy, polity and society.

[F] Here Commons points to the evolution of the social and property structures of Western societies, with England the paradigmatic case. In the *Legal Foundations of Capitalism* the details of the evolution – especially in so far as they involve the changing interests to which government/law gives (or is used to give) its support – are presented *en masse*.

[G] Here are two interrelated themes. First, both law and change of law by law are products of a coercive system and process, as well as having coercive impacts. This is particularly evident during the centuries, lasting down to the early years of the twentieth century, in which the landholding class and the rising business class worked out a series of accommodations, in which the former (broadly speaking) were able to retain their land, the system of nobility, and their dominance in the House of Lords; and the latter were to have their interests accepted by the courts and in statutes and to come to dominate the House of Commons. From about the second quarter of the nineteenth century,

119

the conflict between landholding and capitalist interests was transcended by that between both sets of property owners and controllers, and the working class (including individuals as consumers and passive investors). Second, law and interest-protection is a function of who controls the law-making body, either directly or through sharing world views, and who thereby legislates to enhance their own opportunity set. There is a contest for the control of government, and a further and correlative contest over the details of its use; the critical present point being that those in control of government, as Commons here puts it, shape "the laws to their own preference" and advantage. Of course, that is obfuscated by the selective perception which distinguishes between "natural" and "artificial" actions of government, the former eventually (through adoption of the worldview of those who control government) not being perceived as governmentally generated. Commons is also alert to the role of selective perception in sensing the presence and exercise of "power" (typically as a pejorative category) as between instances which are taken to be "natural" and power as such is not sensed, and instances taken to be "artificial," in which power is very much readily identified. He no doubt was also aware of efforts by the self-acknowledged powerful to obfuscate the fact or perception of their power in the minds of others.

[H] This is a solid example of how a government function, the innocuous "enforcement of contracts," is selectively perceived to be systemically, even naturally, given and unobjectionable. A more contentious example would be environmental protection legislation. Such legislation/court decision amounts to the modification of property rights, which rights themselves have evolved through past legislation and court decisions. But at the moment any new legislation is proposed/adopted, the evolved set of property rights is reified or hypostatized and treated as "natural" and the proposed change as "artificial." Another example, historically both important and contentious, concerns the differential status given corporations and unions, each a form of "private" collection action operating under color of law.

[I] Shock at Commons's contemplation of private property – particularly the particular rights which comprise the institution – as the analytical equivalent with regard to force as slavery is another example of selective perception. Commons is not opposed to private property. He is attempting to identify its nature and genesis and, furthermore and very important to him, to establish an intellectual case for further reforms promotive of the interests of the masses as workers and consumers. It is largely these reforms which became designated the "Welfare State." His point is that such law involves government no more and no less than government which supports interests designated as land and capital interests.

[J] This discussion is not only consistent with but arguably an example of the operation of what Adam Smith, in his *Theory of Moral Sentiments*, called the principles of approbation and disapprobation. The working out of these principles, as people critique their own behavior and that of others, is the formation and change of the moral rules – and of the legal rules, as is evident in his *Lectures on Jurisprudence*. From the perspective of the mid-1990s, after several decades of feminist reform of custom and law, the claims made here by Commons seem weak. But they represent steps in the reformation of custom and law.

[K] It is Commons's point, here and elsewhere, that the rights that count are those ultimately upheld by the Supreme Court, "the final faculty of political economy."

[L] The discussion of the supply of money related to the great issue of the period in which this article was written, the coinage of silver as a possible supplement to gold.

[M] Commons's point is, of course, the necessity and inevitability of social control. He is also alert to both the difference between soft and harsh social control and the role of selective perception in seeing coercion (especially in the pejorative sense) in arrangements deemed "artificial" rather than "natural." In the *Legal Foundations* he presents a generalized model, in part following W. W. Hohfeld, of legal-economic relations which is more highly nuanced than simple "coercion."

[N] This paragraph commences with a comprehensive idea of ubiquitous and inevitable coercion and concludes with a somewhat narrower conception in order to portray in a few words the distinction between two types of social order and ethos. That distinction reflects his idealist Social Gospel predilections.

CONCLUSION

It seems clear from the foregoing that the broad themes of what later became the central arguments and detailed analyses of *A Sociological View of Sovereignty* and *Legal Foundations of Capitalism* – and, to a lesser degree, *Institutional Economics* – had been worked out by the time he wrote "Political Economy and Law." If the article by Herron was not merely an opportunity to present his ideas, it may be that in writing his response to Herron – the piece is of course less a response than an extension – Commons was either enabled or compelled to crystallize his ideas, perhaps for the first time.

NOTES

1 The bibliography in Commons's *Economics of Collective Action* (1950, p. 379) incorrectly lists the article as appearing in 1895. The author is indebted to Richard Gonce for locating and providing a copy of the article.
2 See Herron (1895), p. 587. The piece was a signed editorial. Commons's was a signed article.

REFERENCES

Commons, John R. 1896. "Political Economy and Law," *The Kingdom* (January 24), p. 225.
—— 1924. *Legal Foundations of Capitalism*. New York: Macmillan.
—— 1934. *Institutional Economics: Its Place in Political Economy*. New York: Macmillan.
—— 1950. *The Economics of Collective Action*. New York: Macmillan.
Herron, George D. 1895. "The Social Failure of Political Economy," *The Kingdom* (December 27), p. 587.
Veblen, Thorstein B. 1899. *The Theory of the Leisure Class*. New York: Macmillan.

Part III

VEBLEN, *THE THEORY OF THE LEISURE CLASS*

8

VEBLEN AND THE VANISHING OF THE "LEISURE CLASS"

Philippe Broda

INTRODUCTION

The Theory of the Leisure Class (1899) offered Veblen a fame that none of his other writings let him attain. Yet, this first book does not really represent the definitive form of his theory. On the contrary, it is its imperfections that will allow its author to develop a much sounder reflection. The intention here is not to detail the evolution of his supposed evolutionary model but to focus on the quasi-disappearance from his later works of one of the most essential expressions of that book. It is to show that this omission is not primarily a product of chance, a fashion or a personal strategy, but comes from an analytical requirement.

Thus, nobody can contest that the "leisure class" – since it is this that is in question – embodied a central element in Veblen's first book. As announced in the title, he even proposed to build up its theory. Nevertheless, its absence, for example in *The Instinct of Workmanship* (1914),[1] actually goes beyond a simple vocabulary effect; on the one hand, Veblen never thought that the leisure class and its typical behaviour had suddenly ceased to exist, whereas, on the other hand, he deliberately withdrew it from his field of investigation. So, the position adopted in this article is that new theoretical orientations generated his change of attitude towards the leisure class. In addition, it is claimed that they were not the result of a split, a discontinuity. They stemmed from improvements that he made to clear up issues he was conscious about, and within a framework where certain points remained firmly established.

Therefore, the permanent elements of the Veblenian configuration will initially be described. Then, the problems raised by *The Theory of the Leisure Class* will be examined. Finally, we shall look at how Veblen used them as a springboard to give a real consistency to his theory.

VEBLEN'S REGISTERED TRADEMARK

Veblen's theory is founded on the role he assigns to institutions.[2] In *The Theory of the Leisure Class*, they are defined as "prevalent habits of thought with respect to particular relations and particular functions of the individual and of the community" (Veblen 1899: 118). He has not yet put forward the existence of a "cultural scheme". However, he talks about the "aggregate of institutions in force at a given time or at a given point in the development of any society" (Veblen 1899: 118) as a "scheme of life" which reflects the "prevalent spiritual attitude".[3]

The institutions are supposed to evolve according to a process of adaptative selection. But, Veblen underlines that problems of institutional adjustment are inescapable, for men change habits of thought "only tardily and reluctantly, and only under the coercion exercised by a situation which has made the accredited views untenable" (Veblen 1899: 119). Thus, some views which seem to be well suited to an institutional context – even eternal – can be proved completely anachronistic in different circumstances. This consequence of his institutional approach is particularly important because it permits him to oppose preconceived ideas like the irksomeness of labour and the immemorial nature of private ownership.[4] In other words, economic requirements are often faced with a kind of inertia inherent to habits of thought adapted to a different environment. If we remember that, in Veblen's model, the economic interest is widened to all that puts men in relation, either directly or otherwise, with the material means of life and allows them to earn their livelihood, the seeds of his future developments are already present in *The Theory of the Leisure Class*.

Accordingly, when afterwards Veblen comes to reason in terms of a "cultural scheme" emanating from the "complex of the habits of life and of thought prevalent among the members of the community" (Veblen 1919b: 39),[5] he again puts the stress on the lag between the economic institutions and the others. Besides, he insists more strongly on the central place of the former. He asserts that the "economic interest has counted for much in shaping the cultural growth of all communities" (Veblen 1919b: 76). According to him, the ways and means of man during his economic activities sway his behaviour in a wide range of fields, such as scientific knowledge and aesthetics for example. This is why he wonders whether the mental conditioning of the "machine process", which has been the main feature of industry since the beginning of the modern era, could not bring about a collapse of the capitalist system.[6] Now, he does not answer the interrogation: he postulates that the institutional process is "blind", coercive and unforeseeable, like Darwin's natural selection.

This dimension that he ascribes to economic considerations explains his sophisticated analysis concerning the state of the industrial arts and technological borrowings.[7] Notwithstanding, faithful to his first book, Veblen never neglects the power of inertia proper to certain institutions. Furthermore, it is these problems of contradictions, of institutional adjustments, that confirm his early interest in the diverse categories of institutions.

In fact, Veblen discerns two types of outstanding spiritual attitude. The former is guided by the struggle against nature. It supposes a close solidarity among the members of the community. The technological progress is connected with it in the long run, at least implicitly, since the instinct of workmanship is then developed. In the second case, it is the idea of competition between individuals which is underlying to human behaviour. This atmosphere of conflict pushes the necessity of becoming emancipated from the miserliness of nature through industry into the background: the instinct of sportsmanship replaces the instinct of workmanship. Private property represents one of the most essential elements in this kind of cultural logic.

From this division,[8] Veblen undertakes an analysis of the history of mankind. It begins with an era called "savagery", which corresponds to a culture where the first spiritual attitude prevails. This means that, in his opinion, the primitive societies are rather pacific, that they live in a form of harmony. But, technological improvements finally do take place. They supply both the means – more efficient tools and weapons – and the aims – the appropriation of an economic surplus – of an institutional transformation. A second historical phase, which Veblen names "barbarism", then marks a rupture in the solidarity within the community and a development of predatory conducts, which are proper to the second spiritual attitude. Accordingly, the barbarian days symbolize the spirit of competition between men perfectly.

It is obvious that Veblen, with the passage of time, gave importance to varied points. In *The Theory of the Leisure Class*, he argues that the fall of solidarity within the community during the barbarian epoch, the appearance of social groups with relationships of domination between themselves, are related to the emergence of a leisure class. Its existence, indeed, supposes its differentiation from the industrial class. And, in it, he finds the forces of institutional inhibition. The leisure class is "an exponent and vehicle of conservatism or reversion in social structure" (Veblen 1899: 127). Veblen clearly thinks that the technological progress is hampered:

> the strain of self-assertion against odds takes up the whole energy of the individual; he bends his efforts to compass his own invidious ends alone, and becomes continually more narrowly self-seeking. The industrial traits in this way tend to obsolescence through disuse.
>
> (Veblen 1899: 149)

In *The Theory of Business Enterprise* (1904), it is no longer a question of leisure class. Henceforth, his target is businessmen. His analysis endeavours to show how they succeed in ensuring situations of conquest in the modern economy. Actually, they take advantage of a trait specific to the machine era: the interdependence of the industrial processes. It is enough for them to be positioned in the "interstitial adjustments" of this vast apparatus to benefit from guaranteed incomes. So, their selfish interests are satisfied by virtue of a behaviour of obstruction, of parasite.[9] From this point, the Veblenian argument develops around the antagonism between both institutional logics. In "On the Nature of Capital" (1908, in 1919b), he underlines the cultural taking root and the collective dimension of technology (Veblen 1919b: 324–330) whereas, in *The Instinct of Workmanship* (1914), he thoroughly describes the particularities and implications of the conducts motivated by self-help considerations.[10]

Yet, despite these new directions, he never departed from the general framework depicted in *The Theory of the Leisure Class*. In every case, he reached the same conclusion: capitalist civilization is based on the survival of barbarian institutions. This means that it works by drawing on predatory attitudes, on rapacious behaviours stemming from the competition between men. But, and this constitutes another recurrent characteristic of the Veblenian model, such organization of industry induces tremendous waste at a social level. And it is more for this phenomenon of waste than that of exploitation that Veblen reproaches capitalism.[11]

Thus, *The Theory of the Leisure Class* represents an excellent starting point in understanding Veblen's system. None the less, its contents raise a number of questions, which must not be passed over since it is their resolution that provides his theory with its definitive form.

PROBLEMS WITH *THE LEISURE CLASS*

The thesis of *The Theory of the Leisure Class* probably embodies the most radical formulation of the opposition between industrial and non-industrial employments. The superiority of rank of the leisure class is settled on the almost absolute exemption from industrial tasks. Its field of activity mainly includes government, warfare, religious observances and sports (Veblen 1899: 1). This does not signify that non-industrial activities cannot be useful to the community from the productive point of view. But what counts here is that they are not perceived as such by the people. In this regard, the most striking example is indisputably that of hunting:[12] although it contributes to the subsistence of the population it is supposed to be relevant to the category of exploit, not of industry (Veblen 1899: 3).

According to Veblen, this social division between the working and leisure classes corresponds, during the early barbarism, to the sexual differentiation between women and men. Women carry out the industrial works associated with the idea of irksomeness and drudgery, while men are specialized in exploit and prowess. Through this split, we can observe that it is difficult to imagine any intermediate status. The competition between the individuals, the "invidious distinctions" they are seeking, are altogether conflicting with industrial progress.

In this theory, ownership plays a crucial role: everything begins with the appropriation of captive women. By means of the institution of "ownership-marriage", they are then discerned as trophies. Later, this spirit of property is extended both to other persons and to the product of their industry (Veblen 1899: 16). It is this way that the inclination to rivalry between men finds matter to be exercised. Since social position is appraised by the ownership of objects, the "self-esteem" of the individuals stimulates them to display their possessions. Put another way, the aim of the members of the leisure class is to indicate that their economic situation allows them to abstain from working, to show that they are not in need. The mechanisms of "conspicuous leisure" and "conspicuous consumption", that Veblen meticulously breaks down and which are well known, take place here.

Finally, the relationship between consumption and acquisition is inverted. Now, consumption is no longer an end in itself: it is a means of demonstrating his own belonging to the leisure class (Veblen 1899: 17). In this state of mind, far from representing fortuitous accidents or unavoidable results, the phenomenon of waste materializes the best way to show that one stands aside with respectability from industry and economic necessities. Waste affects the sphere of consumption, and it is even possible to say that the barbarian culture directly derives from it.

It is not possible here to present a detailed historical analysis. But it is easy to notice that the Veblenian model of the barbarian universe targets, as a matter of priority, cases like ancient Greece, the Roman Empire, and the feudal societies in the Middle Ages in Europe. In those civilizations, work is dishonourable and it is other activities which are considered as meritorious, whether philosophy, politics or war, for instance. Let us repeat the Veblenian idea that the modern Western world retains the major features of this type of structure. He interprets it according to the tradition of *otium cum dignitate*.[13] And here we find again the sharpness of the contrast between both institutional logics. The model of *otium cum dignitate* is opposed to that of *negotium*, which must be understood in the sense of ordinary economic activity, not of business.

Veblen is aware that the barbarian culture passed through different phases. After a predatory stage, it became "quasi-peaceable" and, later, "peaceful industrial". Meanwhile, this does not prevent him from referring indiscriminately to these historical periods to such a point that he uses the locution "pecuniary emulation" about each of them.[14] He considers that the changes concerning them "are not so much in substance as in form" (Veblen 1899: 59). This permits him to deal rather often with the case of contemporary aristocratic families with a lineage so noble that it forbids them to work and compels them to a life-style worthy of their social status, despite an uncomfortable economic situation.[15] Their situation is supposed to be similar to that of Polynesian chiefs "who, under the stress of good form, preferred to starve rather than carry their food to their mouths with their own hands" (Veblen 1899: 27).

But, as has been already said, in the modern industrial framework, the central personage is the businessman. However, in *The Theory of the Leisure Class*, his conduct is not taken as a model to illustrate the thesis that is defended. Unlike the Polynesian chiefs, the French kings or the impecunious nobility, he is strangely missing. This is because the approach so specific to this work is no longer enough. In order to account for the logic and the behaviour of the businessman – his next book is devoted to this task – Veblen has to alter his analysis. For, with his original book, some issues have to be tackled.

A first observation sheds light on that point. Everybody knows that Veblen was a fervent opponent to capitalism throughout his career. Yet, if one only investigated *The Theory of the Leisure Class*, one would not necessarily draw this conclusion. This assertion may seem provocative, but it is not devoid of arguments. Many upholders of the market system vindicate its existence by stating that it is efficient. Accordingly, the individualism that is expressed in economic competition is perceived as a necessary evil. Now, Veblen guesses that futility and disserviceability are elevated to the rank of institutional principles. But, to generate such values, society has to find itself in a relative state of abundance. Does the surplus wasted in the field of consumption not testify that the capitalist model is, in a way, efficient since it entails this surplus?

This is why some could see in the Veblen of *The Theory of the Leisure Class*, not a radical critic of the functioning of the capitalist economy, but rather a satirist or a moralist.[16] Thus, his conceptions might deserve to be classified as belonging to debates like the *"querelle du luxe"*. The interest of these views is that they can be understood as hinting that the Veblenian theory is then uncompleted. His rejection of capitalism requires a serious examination of the production plan.

More essentially, we remember that Veblen distinguishes several phases in the evolution of the barbarian civilization. He even explains perfectly how the predatory stage, strictly speaking, ended. In fact, as soon as the possessions "come to be valued not so much as evidence of successful foray, but rather as evidence of the prepotence of the possessor of these goods over other individuals within the community" (Veblen 1899: 18), the economic life is organized on the basis of slavery, which is qualified by Veblen as "quasi-peaceful". He also highlights the transition to the "peaceful industrial" society that is characterized by wage-labour. Here, what is determining is not so much the sense given to the appropriation but the nature of the items that one strives to accumulate: it is no longer persons but things

(Veblen 1899: 18–19). Despite this, one problem remains unsolved. How could barbarian civilization, where work and industry are despised and discouraged, foster such a development in the state of the industrial arts? How could the machine technology come out of it?

We must not forget that, even if coercion is a possible answer to the question in a slave society, it is not in a capitalist environment, in which people are presumed to be free. Through his reference to the "instinct of workmanship", Veblen seems to suggest real elements of solution. However, in 1899, he just opens a door, because what he writes on the matter reflects the difficulties he encounters.

A book review by L. F. Ward warmly greeted *The Theory of the Leisure Class* (Ward 1900: 829–837). This was not the case generally. Nevertheless, this favourable opinion did not stop Ward from asking Veblen to enrich his theory through a deeper investigation into the instinct of workmanship. What he had written then on the question was, indeed, manifestly insufficient. He had talked of a "sense of the merit of the serviceability or efficiency and of the demerit of futility, waste or incapacity" (Veblen 1899: 9). This was not convincing, because it was impossible to see how it could find its place in an institutional structure so adverse to the values of industry. The impression given by the instinct of workmanship was that it was acting mainly as a resistance in regard to some rules and canons of reputability of the leisure class (59) and that it was even "the court of final appeal of economic truth or adequacy" (61), knowing that the institutions impose changing standards.

We can also observe that, in this context which lends itself to futile behaviour, the instinct of workmanship was not absent. It was only denatured, diverted from the utility to the ends of the community taken as a whole; that is, industry. It was expressed through competition between men in occupations like sports because they are

> of the same general character . . . even where the element of destructive physical efficiency is not an obtrusive feature. Sports shade off from the basis of hostile combat, through skill, to cunning and chicanery, without its being possible to draw a line at any point.
> (Veblen 1899: 156)

In other words, there are efficient ways to practise sports and even to waste. If this kind of argument can be perceived as a forerunner to his forthcoming theory of the "contamination" of the instincts, it still does not account for the industrial progress that occurred during the different phases of the barbarian times. The explanation for this inability lies in the fact that the instinct of workmanship was then integrated into the radicality of the split between leisure and industry. This appears more clearly, perhaps,

131

in one of the three articles to which Veblen recognized he was indebted for his first book (Veblen 1899: V). He defined the instinct of workmanship as a "quasi-aesthetic sense of economic or industrial merit" (Veblen 1934: 81) whereas, on the other side, the "instinct of sportsmanship" epitomized both the aversion to work and the quest for futilities. Consequently, in terms of instincts, the question becomes: how in a culture where the instinct of sportsmanship is prevalent did the industrial expansion happen?

It is not enough to say that Veblen overcame these multiple challenges, which have a common origin: he did so only at the price of secondary modifications, while still keeping the gist of his primitive ideas. It remains to examine how.

A REAL THEORETICAL CONSISTENCY

The opposition between both classes of spiritual attitudes constitutes the frame of the Veblenian thought. The idea that, in a culture, either the struggle against nature is privileged and there is then a solidarity within the community, or the infightings take precedence in an individualistic and selfish viewpoint, always remained basic. Yet, the continuity it ensures is the source of theoretical changes.

The Theory of the Leisure Class describes societies possessing barbarian traits so that the tendencies to emulate, which are dominant there, are discernible in the eyes of the other men. This makes Veblen concerned with conspicuous phenomena and he frequently uses expressions like "invidious distinctions". This is why his investigation deals especially with the field of consumption. But, in his later works, his analysis of selfishness is partly renewed. The "invidious distinctions" do not occupy the same central place, though they do not stop. It is a question of "self-regard" without specific emphasis on the fact that it depends on the opinion of the community members: egoism is perceived as such. The interest in this approach is that it focuses on the effect of this type of institution with respect to the sphere of production and to its cultural dimension. Thus, if the idea of waste is still present, it takes on a new meaning. It applies primarily to the functioning of the industrial process. In this regard, Veblen even talks of "sabotage".[17]

In the hope of explaining the reality of the economic progress, Veblen comes to mitigate the gap between, on the one hand, industry and solidarity and, on the other hand, waste and individualism. According to him, in very definite circumstances, industrial development and selfishness could cohabit together. Therefore, he refines his analysis of the period that he had previously named "peaceful industrial". He is not content, as he was in his most celebrated book, with timidly noticing that it had reached an "advanced" stage. He sharply dissociates between a "handicraft era" and a "machine era". All this pertains to the idea of theorizing industrial capitalism from its own characteristics, not only from the archaic features that one can find in it.

It is primarily through his description of the modern epoch and its gigantic mechanization that Veblen highlights the existence of the handicraft period that introduces a true innovation in his reflection. Almost every chapter of *The Theory of Business Enterprise* is constructed around this outlook.[18] This grants an intermediate status to this historical phase between the barbarism strictly speaking and the machine era. Accordingly, at an institutional level, it is no longer the purely barbarian customs that account for the mores of the current economy. Another way to expound the point consists in saying that Veblen replaces the predatory stage by the handicraft era as the genuine antecedent of the economic reality.

Veblen's approach to the handicraft era reveals numerous interesting elements. It stretches over a period beginning in about the thirteenth century and lasting until about 1760 for Great Britain, and a little later for elsewhere in the Western world. Its institutional structure only retains the principle of individuation of the barbarian era, not its incitement to laziness. It is no more fully contradictory with the practice of drudgery, of industrial tasks. Indeed,

> so long as work is of a visibly pecuniary kind and is sagaciously and visibly directed to the acquisition of wealth, the disrepute intrinsically attaching to it is greatly offset by its meritorious purpose.
>
> (Veblen 1914: 183–184)

However, it should be pointed out that, in such a context, the combination of self-seeking inclinations and sense of workmanship is built on a hierarchy between both tendencies:

> it is only secondarily, as a means to the emulative end of acquisition, that productive work, and therefore workmanship in its naïve sense, come into the case at all.
>
> (Veblen 1914: 173)

The transformation is meaningful.

Moreover, the leading figure during the handicraft era is not the same person as previously. In social terms, the period saw the emergence of a "class of ungraded free men among whom self-help and individual workmanlike efficiency were the accepted grounds of repute and of livelihood" (Veblen 1914: 276). Besides, Veblen is insistent on the extent of the conflicts between their principles and the values of the aristocratic classes, the conventions of the nobility.[19] It is these individuals whose logic and behaviour explain the activities of the modern "captains of industry", not the aristocrats, and still less, of course, the savage people. Whether it is with the craftsman or the businessman, we can note some appreciable modifications in the state of the industrial arts and in the production without intention of "service-ability". This means that these improvements do not come from a spiritual attitude disclosing solidarity but from egotistic motivations exclusively. Thus, the mentalities are the same in both the handicraft system and the machine era. The difference lies in the nature of their respective techno-logical process.

The Veblenian argument continues in this direction. During the handi-craft epoch, the place of man and his skill in the production line was decisive because the tools were relatively simple. In contrast, since the begin-ning of the machine era, the situation is reversed. The roundabout way of production caused by technology becomes longer and longer. Its improve-ments are such that, now, the individual is overwhelmed and submitted to the discipline of the machine. His role and his talent are lessening. The differences between the habits of thought of the two periods mirror this evolution.[20] During the earlier period, in which the worker stands out, minds are shaped so that the idea of workmanship is present in the inter-pretation of the phenomena. The metaphor of a God clockmaker is quite a good example of the spirit of small-scale production, as well as all the tradition of "natural laws". During the later period, where the machine is essential, theories and generalizations of any kind take on a much more mechanical form. It is the concept of process which is put forward. But the development of the machines involves consequences that spread beyond intellectual constructions.

We know indeed that, for Veblen, the handicraft epoch corresponds to the combination of the self-regarding inclinations, the pecuniary logic, with a sense of workmanship. Then, for as long the machine industry was not highly developed, he considers that the tasks that were relevant to both ways of thinking could be mastered by the same person. The salesman knew and was able to supervise the industrial process (Veblen 1914: 206). But, afterwards, this is no more the case. As a result of economic transformations, especially technological progress, specialization of the occupations becomes advised. Veblen thinks that, since the modern businessmen are "out of effec-tual touch with the affairs of technology as such and incompetent to exercise an effectual surveillance of the processes of industry" (Veblen 1914: 222), a new professional class, the "efficiency engineers", takes care of this field while they themselves focus on salesmanship and the pecuniary traffic.

This division of labour is supposed to endorse the gulf coming after the fragile balance of the handicraft organization between two fundamentally incompatible occupations. Veblen tries to show that, during the machine era, their keeping together within the institutional scheme is responsible for harmful social effects. We again find his primitive thesis of waste, but this time in a framework that really takes the apparent industrial evolution into consideration. His perception of the concept has changed. It is not primarily connected to the idea of idleness and indolence but to the expectation of pecuniary gains.

In order to mention the waste that springs from the obedience of the industrial point of view to the dictates of the business, Veblen emphasizes the cultural dimension, that is collective, of the technology:

> the state of the industrial art is a joint stock of knowledge derived from past experience, and is held and passed on as an indivisible possession of the community at large.
>
> (Veblen 1921: 28)

The materialization of that knowledge also belongs to the group. Hence, the appropriation of any kind of means of production goes against this characterization. The problem, as Veblen understands it, is that the consequences of the self-regarding motivations and of the existence of the institution of ownership are not similar in the different periods.

> So long, or rather in so far, as the "capital goods" required to meet the technological demands of the time were slight enough to be encompassed by the common man with reasonable diligence and proficiency, so the draft upon the common stock of immaterial assets by any one would be no hindrance to any other, and no differential advantage or disadvantage would emerge.
>
> (Veblen 1919b: 339–340)

Presented another way, before the revolution of the machines, the act of making a withdrawal on the inheritance of the community did not prevent other individuals from using their talents. The professional success of the craftsman was founded on his personal ability, not on his obstructive power.[21] Moreover, the productive capacity of the industry "was visibly overtaking the capacity of the market" (Veblen 1921: 36). Later, the situation becomes different. The pecuniary gains are no longer linked to a form of efficiency associated to economic competition. They stem from the control of strategic points in the productive system, from the restriction of output, so that production can be sold at prices satisfying an objective of profitability. These activities of check, of "sabotage", correspond, in the Veblenian theory, to nurturing "vested interests". Of course, the improvements in technology remain a possibility. However, if Veblen talks about waste, it is because he considers production with respect to its potential, to the level that it could reach in the present state of the knowledge, not with respect to a former level.

Thus, the handicraft era appears to be a turning point in Veblen's approach. It restores the instinct of workmanship in comparison with barbarism and it allows him better to construe the modern epoch since, even if it is at odds with it on the idea of waste, both periods share common institutional foundations. This evolution goes necessarily with another evolution, that in the analysis of the instinct of workmanship.

Previously, the instinct of workmanship was mainly attached to the objective of industrial efficiency. In *The Instinct of Workmanship*, which constitutes his most elaborate work on the instincts, Veblen cuts off the inevitability of this link. The instinct of workmanship is no longer connected to a specific end. This makes less confusing the possibility of its "contamination". If every instinct is indeed usually characterized by the end it aims at, the instinct of workmanship is defined from then on by its function to serve "the ends of life, whatever these ends may be" (Veblen 1914: 31). Namely, it is an instinct "auxiliary" to the others.

It is only a question of efficiency, not of industry. There are equally efficient ways to display wasteful behaviour. Now, of course, Veblen assesses it as "chief among those instinctive dispositions that conduce directly to the material well-being of the race" (Veblen 1914: 25). Its grouping with another instinct, the "parental bent", is immediate and benefits the society. But it is not necessary. Instead of serving altruistic dispositions, the instinct of workmanship is also likely to assist the self-regarding inclinations. Actually, it oscillates between the two poles, which are more often than not incompatible and irreconcilable.[22] The advantage of this new exposition is that it increases the number of feasible combinations.

Thus, with the development of the idea of the existence of a historical period, the handicraft era, where the pursuit of individual interests is not catastrophic for the community, Veblen can refer explicitly to the instinct of workmanship and, moreover, in an industrial plan, something he could not afford to do in his over rigid approach from *The Theory of the Leisure Class*. Besides, this allows him to map out the limits of this "invisible hand" through his investigation of the state of the industrial arts.

CONCLUSION

It is well known that, among the criticisms that he formulated against the economic orthodoxy, Veblen set upon John Bates Clark, Laughlin and Davenport with a particular severity, even though these people had helped him during hard moments in his life (Homan 1933: 90). This kind of ingratitude can be also found in the way he deals with an entire part of the population, the leisure class. Its most idle members were, indeed, sometimes zealous supporters of *The Theory of the Leisure Class*.[23] Yet, this did not dissuade him from disregarding it in his later writings, as if it did not exist any more.

It is true that *The Theory of the Leisure Class* laid the foundations of his completed theory, especially through the opposition between two types of spiritual attitudes and the dependence of the contemporary institutions on their predecessors. But the problems that this first book involved also urged him to partially adopt a new line of conduct. Rather than begin from the barbarism to analyse the current world, Veblen started from the particularities of modern civilization and then inquired into their antecedents. In this way, the aristocrat left the centre stage to the businessman, and the idea of irksomeness of labour became less related to that of "conspicuous waste" than to its not very gainful nature during the machine era.

The emergence of the handicraft stage and the new developments on the instinct of workmanship form part of this project. Thus, in Veblen's theory, there is a period in which the individual and collective interests are not wholly contradictory, namely industrial progress is connected to the quest for personal enrichment. This view may seem original in the Veblenian model. But the investigation of the state of the industrial arts by comparing the handicraft technology and the machine process marks the limits of this interlude, and thereby strengthens the consistency of Veblen's construction. For, it is the individualistic spirit of the handicraft era which contains the seeds of the general waste of contemporary capitalism: this state of mind has been connected, in a different technological context, to awful results.

NOTES

1 In fact, this absence is not absolute. Veblen still uses, albeit very scarcely, the expression. But then, it is negatively. For instance, "within the business community there is properly speaking no leisure class, or at least no idle class" (Veblen 1914: 226). Moreover, even when he deals with the "conspicuous consumption", practice specific to the "leisure class", he does not quote it. See, for illustration, Veblen (1904: 325–326).

2 This evidently bears out his ranking within the institutionalist tradition.

3 Worthy of note is the frequent use that Veblen makes of the word "prevalent".

4 On these points, see Veblen (1934: 78–96 and 32–49).

5 About the connection between action and thought in Veblen's theory, see Murphey (1990).

6 Read Veblen (1904), chapters IX and X.

7 On these points, see merely the titles of the chapters II, III, IV, VI and VII in Veblen (1914) as well as Veblen (1915: 17–41).

8 Besides, even if it is only anecdotal, the original dividing line that Veblen states does not run between industrial and non industrial activities. It is concerned with the mastery of "animate" and "inert" forces (Veblen 1899: 6–8).

9 See, for illustration, Veblen (1904: 25–29).

10 *The Instinct of Workmanship* (Veblen 1914), chapter V is enlightening on that point.

11 This is also Adorno's opinion (Adorno 1941: 401).

12 This illustration is not innocent. Veblen attacks the myth of the lonely hunter, symbol of the primitive industry, for Smith and his followers.

13 He himself notes the expression (Veblen 1899: 59).

14 Already from an etymological perspective, it is clear that the idea of "pecuniary" activities applies more to the modern civilization than to the old.

15 See Veblen (1899: 48, 69, 110).
16 The examples are not hard to find: for example, Diggins (1978: 20), Dorfman (1932: 363–409), Mayberry (1969: 319–323).
17 Actually, he identifies four categories of sabotage: the non-using of, at least, part of the productive capacities, the efforts devoted to the marketing of the products, the production of futilities and the lack of co-ordination between the economic agents (Veblen 1921: chapter V). This sabotage is reckoned by him as representing more than 50% of the productive capacities (Veblen 1919a: 79).
18 On the specific point that advertisement is, see Veblen (1904: 50–60).
19 The word "contempt" is even used by Veblen to express the feeling of the aristocracy towards the tradesmen (Veblen 1914: 184).
20 On that point, see, for example Veblen (1919b: 49–55).
21 In Veblen's mind, the economic liberalism through the mechanics of free competition can be justified at that epoch (Veblen 1919b: 340).
22 According to Dobriansky, the instinct of workmanship should be called more accurately "power of creativity directed toward bad or good ends". What confirms this impression of neutrality (Dobriansky 1957: 259).
23 For a cinematographic reference, see James Ivory's *Mr and Mrs Bridge*.

BIBLIOGRAPHY

Adorno, T. W. (1941), "Veblen's Attack on Culture", *Studies in Philosophy and Social Science* 9: 389–413.
Diggins, J. P. (1978), *The Bard of Savagery, Thorstein Veblen and Modern Social Theory*, New York: The Seabury Press.
Dobriansky, L. E. (1957), *Veblenism, A New Critique*, Washington, DC: Public Affairs Press.
Dorfman, J. (1932), "The 'Satire' of Thorstein Veblen's Theory of the Leisure Class", *Political Science Quarterly* 47: 363–409.
Homan, P. T. (1933), *Essai sur la pensée économique contemporaine des anglo-américains {Contemporary Economic Thought}*, Paris: Sirey.
Mayberry, T. C. (1969), "Thorstein Veblen on Human Nature", *American Journal of Economics and Sociology* 28 (July): 315–323.
Murphey, M. G. (1990), "Introduction" in T. Veblen, *The Instinct of Workmanship and the State of the Industrial Arts*, New Brunswick and London: Transaction: VII–LXV.
Veblen, T. (1899), *The Theory of the Leisure Class*, reprint, Mineola, NY: Dover Thrift Editions, 1994.
—— (1904), *The Theory of Business Enterprise*, reprint, New Brunswick: Transaction, 1988.
—— (1914), *The Instinct of Workmanship and the State of the Industrial Arts*, reprint, New Brunswick and London: Transaction, 1990.
—— (1915), *Imperial Germany and the Industrial Revolution*, New York: Huebsch.
—— (1919a), *The Vested Interests and the Common Man*, reprint, New York: Viking Press, 1946.
—— (1919b), *The Place of Science in Modern Civilization and Other Essays*, reprint, New Brunswick and London: Transaction, 1990.
—— (1921), *The Engineers and the Price System*, reprint, New York: Kelley, 1965.
—— (1934), *Essays in Our Changing Order*, in L. Ardzrooni (ed.), New York: Viking Press.
Ward, L. F. (1900), "Book Review: The Theory of the Leisure Class", *American Journal of Economics and Sociology* 5: 829–837.

9

THE THEORY OF THE LEISURE CLASS AND THE THEORY OF DEMAND

E. Ray Canterbery

INTRODUCTION

Mainstream economists are of several minds regarding Veblen's *The Theory of the Leisure Class*. Few, however, would hesitate in mentioning Veblen's contribution of such evocative terms as "conspicuous consumption," "conspicuous emulation," "pecuniary culture," "vicarious consumption," and "the leisure class" to the language of economics. Though little noted, and not yet celebrated, important improvements in demand theory have emanated from *The Theory of the Leisure Class* (hereafter *TLC*). Since the enduring Veblenian contributions to our language are related to consumption, it is hardly surprising that even the mainstream has ratified Veblen with "Veblen effects."

Several of the author's phrases have resurfaced in *Bartlett's Familiar Quotations*, greatly elevating their stature. Three lengthy Veblen quotations made the 1980 edition, all from *TLC*. Notable for the task at hand, all the quotations are relevant to demand theory at both the micro and macro levels. Their worthiness bears reprinting: the first, "Conspicuous consumption of valuable goods is a means of reputability to the gentleman of leisure." The second, slightly longer, is "With the exception of the instinct of self-preservation, the propensity for emulation is probably the strongest and most alert and persistent of the economic motives proper." *Bartlett's* devotes even greater space to the third citation.

> The requirement of conspicuous wastefulness is not commonly present, consciously, in our canons of taste, but it is none the less present as a constraining norm selectively shaping and sustaining our sense of what is beautiful, and guiding our discrimination with respect to what may legitimately be approved as beautiful and what may not.[1]

139

In turn, I will quote much more from Veblen, phrases and ideas equally worthy of *Bartlett's*. In addition to the exquisite styling, these quotations are remarkable, too, for the phrases Veblen bequeathed to the English language. Hereafter, I will show how they have instructed mainstream economics and economics against the stream, to use Myrdal's facile expression. Now is a propitious time to restore Veblen's rightful place in the pantheon of economics. Many have forgotten his place, in his own time, at the top of his profession. In great part, Veblen endured because he illuminated modern society, a society still very much intact, with evolutionary electricity. "What is, is wrong." By applying the law of natural selection to human institutions, broadly defined to include ideas and habits of thought, he found human institutions lagging behind material change, always somehow being out of date. Habits of thought are always conservative, including those habits of thought, as Veblen often claimed, in the institutions of higher learning. Still, if we look closely, we can find Veblenian remnants in today's mainstream. We first will walk through the mainstream and, then, seek alternative vistas.

VEBLENIAN DEMAND THEORY ENTERS THE MAINSTREAM

Veblen entered the mainstream in a classic article by Harvey Leibenstein on "bandwagon, snob, and Veblen effects."[2] Leibenstein distinguishes between *functional demand* or demand for a commodity due to the qualities inherent in the commodity and *nonfunctional demand* or the portion of demand due to qualities external to it. In nonfunctional demand the utility derived from the commodity is enhanced or decreased because others are purchasing and consuming the same commodity or because the commodity bears a higher rather than a lower price tag.

The bandwagon, snob, and Veblen effects are due to *external* effects on utility. The *bandwagon effect* derives from the demand for a commodity increasing because others, too, are consuming the same commodity. *Social taboos* that effect consumption are bandwagon effects in reverse. When the wagon leaves the station, those practicing a social tabu forbidding that particular good will refuse to get on the wagon. The *snob effect* derives from the demand for a commodity decreasing because others are also consuming or increasing their consumption of the same commodity. The snob effect has an opposite but otherwise symmetrical relationship to the bandwagon effect. The snob jumps off the wagon because they do not want to associate with those jumping on. The "Veblen effect" refers to conspicuous consumption in which the demand for a consumer's good is increased because it bears a higher rather than a lower price. Since Leibenstein's operative term *is* price, he is never far from mainstream neoclassical demand theory.

Leibenstein advances the principle of diminishing marginal external consumption effect. The principle suggests that beyond a point, incremental increases in the demand for a commodity by others will have a decreasing influence on a consumer's own demand and, eventually, a zero influence. Not only do incremental increases in total demand become smaller and smaller shares of a larger and larger market demand but there are no cases in which an individual's demand for a good is infinite. Moreover, the income constraint guarantees that a consumer's demand increases eventually will cease. Taking all these influences into proper account, the most plausible demand curve is shaped like a backward S in which the schedule is upward sloping against price in some range, a range exhibiting the "Veblen effect." At some higher price for the good, the budget constraint would preclude further amounts being demanded; at some low price, the good's reason for conspicuousness disappears. From these behaviors emanate the backward S. The backward S, of course, would not apply to all commodities.

Leibenstein gives Veblen too little credit. Veblenian demand clearly includes the bandwagon and snob effects. Besides, Leibenstein defines what he identifies as *the* "Veblen effect" too narrowly. Veblen considered pecuniary emulation to be an individual's strongest motive; in this, Veblen gave everyone sufficient reason to jump on whatever bandwagon passed their doors. To Veblen the *standard of living* shared by a particular class determined the "accepted standard of expenditure." That is, contrary to Leibenstein, price is not necessarily a yardstick in demand. As Veblen put it,

> It does this directly by commending itself to his common sense as right and good, through his habitually contemplating it and assimilating the scheme of life in which it belongs; but it does so also indirectly through popular insistence on conformity to the accepted scale of expenditure as a matter of propriety, under pain of disesteem and ostracism. To accept and practise the standard of living which is in vogue is both agreeable and expedient, commonly to the point of being indispensable to personal comfort and to success in life. The standard of living of any class, so far as concerns the element of conspicuous waste, is commonly as high as the earning capacity of the class will permit – with a constant tendency to go higher.
>
> (pp. 111–112)

Not only are bandwagon effects Veblenian, the person's status within a social class commands them to consume whatever other referential persons in the class are consuming.

Moreover, Veblen rides the bandwagon much farther. Emulation dominates Veblen's Chapter VII on "Dress as an Expression of the Pecuniary Culture," where he writes that "admitted expenditure for display is more universally practised in the matter of dress than in any other line of consumption"

(p. 167). We can imagine hundreds of thousands of women jumping on the shoe-store wagon, as Veblen writes, "the woman's shoe adds the so-called French heel to the evidence of enforced leisure afforded by its polish; because this high heel obviously makes any, even the simplest and most necessary manual work extremely difficult" (p. 171). Of course, much more complex and subtle sociology is at work in *TLC*, including the woman's service as a "chief ornament" around the house and an adequately-adorned "trophy" for her husband. Women comprise an abused class in *TLC*.

Emulation, too, can explain why persons buy high-priced goods that otherwise might fail to be identified as those preferred by a higher social class. What Leibenstein calls the "Veblen effect" is only one element in the complex matrix of emulation. For a large set of reasons, persons buy more of some goods *despite, not because* their prices are higher. In Veblen, the excessive expense of such goods comes from the cost of production side. As he writes, "there are to-day no goods supplied in any trade which do not contain the honorific element in greater or less degree" (p. 157). "Honorific" refers to the amount of cost in excess of what goes to give goods service-ability for their ostensible mechanical purpose. The "proper honorific finish" is more important than price.

When it comes to emulation, the rich are more likely to take note of the higher prices of luxury goods than the middle-class emulator seeking status at any cost. In Veblen's perspective, too, "function" is in the eye of the beholder; a good that confers status serves a higher social purpose. Still, in Leibenstein's and his followers' interpretation, persons increase their demands for status goods *only* because they have higher prices. In this way Leibenstein set the standard for most of the recent mainstream contributions on prestige or status goods. It remains characteristically neoclassical to value goods solely in money prices.

The Leibenstein perspective is unduly limited in other respects. The preference for higher-priced "luxuries" rules out bargain hunters who desire to consume conspicuously as well as the upper middle class or even middle middle class who want to emulate the rich leisure class but must do so by buying cheap imitations or by borrowing, even at the risk of bankruptcy or worse, which might be called the "Gatsby effect." The Gatsby effect, of course, intimates disasters beyond bankruptcy from which recovery *is* possible.

A Gatsby effect barely pushes the Veblenian envelope. Fitzgerald's *The Great Gatsby* is the supreme Veblenian parable of conspicuous consumption, of conspicuous emulation, of pecuniary culture, and of vicarious consumption – even of waste and the leisure class itself. Jay Gatsby wanted to live with Daisy because she was a member of the *established* American aristocracy of wealth. Gatsby lacks the maturity to realize that Daisy cannot be obtained by money alone. Therefore, Gatsby flaunts, in a vulgar version of conspicuous consumption, his nouveau wealth. Despite Daisy's infinite price, Gatsby is most attracted to Daisy's voice (not the supra-price), which he describes as "full of money," because that is the most unrealistic thing about her. Then, too, Daisy is attracted to Gatsby because he reminds her of "an advertisement," the superficial illusion he represents. In the end, of course, Daisy cannot leave the trappings of the old aristocracy and Gatsby cannot escape the greatest Gatsby effect of all – paying the final price, with his life. As in Veblen's *TLC*, the cultural illusions are more important than wealth or money for Fitzgerald's central characters.

Leibenstein also apparently missed Veblen's extensive discussions of the roles of tabus in consumption. Veblen's discussions not only add cultural richness to the subject but make Leibenstein's use of a negative price range problematical. Ceremonial consumption such as "choice articles of food, and frequently also of rare articles of adornment, becomes tabu to the women and children; and if there is a base (servile) class of men, the tabu holds also for them" (p. 69). Under the tabu certain intoxicating beverages and narcotics are reserved for the use of men. Only since the 1960s has the consumption of liquor, cigarettes, cigars, and narcotics become acceptable for women in the United States, all of which remains tabu in the Arab world except for royalty.

Such tabus separate one class from another, members of the "superior class" identifying themselves not only by what they consume but by their power to prevent the consumption of the same items by others. The tabu is the fail-safe way of preventing emulation of the upper classes by the lower classes. As long as the tabu remains culturally intact, even a negative price thought to be the price necessary to pay individuals to induce them to disregard their aversion, contrary to Leibenstein's analysis, will fail to generate consumption by the "lower class." Besides, who or what institution would pay others to consume forbidden goods?

As to snobbery, Fitzgerald's Gatsby again provides instruction. Tom and Daisy Buchanan live in a Georgian Colonial mansion representing established wealth. Gatsby, not unlike the early Robber Barons, owns a pretentious, vulgar imitation of a European mansion, adorned even in brand-new ivy. Even Gatsby's ivy is not in the same league as the Buchanans'. It is clear to the establishment that Gatsby, having no sense of tradition, simply copies the style of others, much as an American university erects a library based upon a medieval Gothic chapel. Worse, Gatsby's sartorial choice is as vulgar and nouveau as his car, his mansion, and his lavish parties. Daisy could never leave Tom for Gatsby because she and Tom are partners in a "secret society" of wealth, one that Gatsby cannot enter because he does not know it. Neither this cultural richness nor the culture of the rich can be entirely captured with Leibenstein's downward shifting demand curves of individual "snobs," reducing their demands for a good because too many others are buying it.

Fitzgerald and tabus, oddly enough, bring us full circle from the *Quarterly Journal of Economics* to the *American Economic Review*. For decades, or so it seems, the *AER* has engaged in reverse emulation, even perhaps snobbery. By their rarity, references to Veblen's work appear to have long been held tabu even to the *AER*, no doubt elevating its presumed professional status. In at least one recent instance, however, the tabu has been lifted, the snobbery surrendered.

VEBLEN REENTERS THE MAINSTREAM

The mainstream has recognized some of the deficiencies in Leibenstein's theory. In particular, Bagwell and Bernheim have attempted to deal with the Veblenian cases that Leibenstein excludes. "In a theory of conspicuous consumption that is faithful to Veblen's analysis," they write, "utility should be defined over consumption and status, rather than over consumption and prices." This does not make high price irrelevant, however, "the prices that one pays for goods may affect status *in equilibrium*."[3] Since individuals like Jay Gatsby consume conspicuously to advertise their wealth, any relation between price and status should signal wealth. Otherwise, "invidious comparison" and "pecuniary emulation" cannot happen, terms insinuating a rank-order in the distribution of wealth. The upper class invites invidious comparison with the lower class whereas the lower class "emulates" the upper class. The upper class, of course, hopes that its costs are sufficiently prohibitive to the lower class that emulation is discouraged, especially by the nouveau riche class. Bagwell and Bernheim use game theory to explain the consequences of these upper-class and lower-class interdependences.

Three findings from Bagwell and Bernheim are persuasive. First, they show that some individuals might prefer to purchase a larger *quantity* of conspicuous goods at a lower price, or a higher *quality* of conspicuous goods at a higher price. For instance, social climbers do not have to be rich to buy Ralph Lauren's Polo brand clothes; yet, the label signals exclusivity. Moreover, if luxury brand "knock-offs" such as fake Rolex watches, Polo shirts, and King Cobra golf clubs cannot be distinguished from the "real things," the thrifty rich can have it both ways by buying the cheaper fakes. Veblen, who often strolled golf courses looking for golf balls, none the less would expect the King Cobra "knock-offs" to have the proper workmanship and polish.

Second, Bagwell and Bernheim rebut the "single-crossing property" of models with asymmetric information.[4] If we define the benefit ratio as the ratio of the utility gains from another unit of a conspicuous good, to the utility losses from another dollar of conspicuous expenditure, the benefit ratio is always higher for the upper-class households under the single-crossing property. (The indifference curves depicting substitutability between inconspicuous and conspicuous goods are, contrary to neoclassical theory, concave rather than convex to the origin. The "single crossing" occurs where the higher-income individual's indifference curve crosses the lower-income individual's indifference curve from below, reflecting the possibilities for cheap emulation.) Contrary to the single-crossing property, Bagwell and Bernheim show that the upper-class households can increase their utilities, without causing imitation, by purchasing more of the conspicuous good at a lower price.

Third, they show that households' conspicuous consumption need not be affected by bankruptcy if the conspicuous good cannot be repossessed (normally, such is the case for a house, even if it is ostentatious). There is a catch, a kind of "Catch 11": If the lower class imitates the upper-class households by matching their every luxury goods purchase, they would default on their loans, foreclosing imitation and foregoing the property protected under Chapter 11. Such an ultimate, even irrational, economic loss – the failure to retain what was pursued as well as the means of pursuit – none the less does not exclude what I have called the Gatsby effect, wherein bankruptcy is its mildest manifestation. As it turned out, Gatsby could not preserve the Daisy he pursued nor the means of pursuit, himself.

Bagwell and Bernheim are faithful to Veblen in still another way. The successful application of game theory to Veblen effects can be done only in a social setting. Neoclassical demand theory always has dismissed interdependent utility functions as either nonexistent or an unnecessary distraction.[5] Game theory cannot: in the case at hand, the upper and lower classes at the least must be aware of each other. People, not commodities, play games, games often involving subtle social nuances signaling superiority. In this sense, the Bagwell-Bernheim approach is truly Veblenian. Whereas houses, automobiles, jewelry, and clothing are often seen by many other individuals through social interaction, and are signets of resource dissipation, the Bagwell-Bernheim model is indeterminant regarding *which* durable, conspicuous goods households will choose. Veblen would have seen indeterminancy as a strength of their results.

Again, the still, cultural waters of Veblen run much deeper. Bagwell and Bernheim's use of game theory becomes an apt metaphor when we reconsider Fitzgerald's parable. Daisy's insincerity betrays her desire to play games with her husband, Gatsby, and others, rather than participate in life where she would be responsible for her actions. Empty gestures signal more to her than genuine emotions. At the center of the American dream as well as Gatsby's own is the belief that sufficient wealth can recapture and fix everything, even the ephemeral, illusory qualities of youth and beauty. Veblen, too, was writing about the great American chimeras.

In any case, though Bagwell and Bernheim do not explore price elasticities, Leibenstein suggests important implications for the price elasticity of demand as well as the nonadditivity of individual into collective demand curves. For the moment, we set aside the issue of how many of these things he describes are truly Veblen effects. If the bandwagon effect dominates, the demand curve is more elastic since reactions to price changes are followed by other reactions, in the same direction. If the snob effect dominates, the demand curve is less elastic since increases in total amounts consumed because of price reductions are countered by some snobs leaving the market. If Leibenstein's "Veblen effect" dominates, the demand curve is less elastic than otherwise, and in part may be positively sloping, making stable equilibrium improbable.

The more important implication – one that pervades Veblen, but eludes Leibenstein – is the critical role of household incomes or the ability to sustain a particular standard of living. If snob effects and conspicuous consumption are truly important, income elasticity overwhelms price effects and price becomes unimportant except as it effects relative real incomes. Moreover, the only constraints keeping persons off the wagon are income and social tabus. If price becomes sufficiently unimportant, the need for price theory (and neoclassical markets) evaporates. This conclusion was not lost on the neoclassicals during the early twentieth century in their pursuit of hegemony or, later, in their snubbing of Leibenstein, though he was closer to the mainstream than was Veblen.

AN ECONOMETRIC ESTIMATE OF "VEBLEN EFFECTS"

Going mainstream these days usually implies econometrics. Econometric tests claiming to estimate "Veblen effects," however, are sufficiently rare to be an endangered species. A small but substantial effort was made by Basmann, Molina, and Slottje.[6] They employ Veblen's distinction between primary consumption and secondary consumption. Rather than functional and nonfunctional qualities of commodities, however, Basmann *et al.* define consumption effects in utility language. *Primary utility* comes from the direct enhancement of life and well-being on the whole through consumption. *Secondary utility* comes from consumption that displays consumers' relative ability to pay, a form of consumption they ascribe to "Veblen effects."

Primary utility is measured from own-use price elasticities. Secondary utility is related to total expenditures, a proxy for real income. Since ability to pay, they say, and I concur, drives Veblen effects, such effects prevail over all social classes from the richest to the poorest. Otherwise, Veblenian emulation is not possible. Capturing both effects, according to Basmann *et al.*, requires the use of a Fechner-Thurstone direct utility function. Using this function, the authors can estimate both kinds of elasticities. A relatively large and statistically significant elasticity for durables with respect to total expenditures is found. The lowest elasticity with respect to total expenditures is for medical services. The results, they say, are consistent with Veblen effects since durables are the most visible items consumed and medical services the least visible.

Inherent in such tests is the problem with the estimated price elasticities of necessities that are necessarily low. The greatest medical expenditures usually happen during the final three to six months of life. Since the rich cannot escape mortality, no matter how much they spend on medical services, even *their* expenditures are price inelastic. As categories, we would expect, even without the benefit of econometric tests, that food and medical services would have lower price elasticities than durables (whose expected lives greatly exceed six months).

Moreover, the high level of aggregation (food, clothing, housing, durables, and medical care) makes these findings less than definitive. For the rich, surely the ownership of estate homes out of the broader category of "housing" is a form of ostentatious consumption. For the middle class, clothing with displayed brand-name labels, not "clothing" per se, is a frequently observed form of visible emulation. Many rich persons advertise their passage to grand, expensive resorts that monitor their health and try to improve it. Moreover, the middle class can advertise their ability to pay by dining, however infrequently, in fine restaurants. Still, the econometric effort was made and the results were published in another leading mainstream journal.

Veblen does write, "goods are produced and consumed as a means to the fuller unfolding of human life; and their utility consists, in the first instance, in their efficiency as means to this end." He adds, "the end is, in the first instance, the fulness of life of the individual, taken in absolute terms." What Veblen calls "secondary utility" is based on emulation which "seized upon the consumption of goods as a means to an invidious comparison, and has thereby invested consumable goods with a secondary utility as evidence of relative ability to pay." The "evidence" of ability to pay, however, is not the same as the *actual* ability to pay. Moreover, he uses the Basmann *et al.* phrase, for "this indirect or secondary use of consumable goods lends an honorific character to consumption, and presently also to the goods which best serve this emulative end of consumption" (p. 154). In what immediately follows, Veblen goes on to discuss the attendant waste or "superfluous expensiveness" in great Veblenian style.

Since so few efforts of this genre have been made, it is judged gallant. The same Bureau of Labor Statistics, however, has tapes with much more detailed consumption data. For instance, the complete data separates meals outside the home from those consumed at home. The consumption data, too, can be separated by income strata so that estimates of price elasticities may differ by income class.

JOHN KENNETH GALBRAITH: VEBLEN AGAINST THE STREAM

Most economists would agree that Veblen's logical successor is John Kenneth Galbraith. Though Galbraith is a best-selling author, he is not mainstream among professional economists. Veblen's influence on Galbraith's demand perspective is most visible in *The Affluent Society*.[7] Galbraith's "conventional wisdom," an established set of ideas used to explain the world and how it operates, providing stability, cohesion, meaning, and predictability in a highly complex environment, parallels Veblen's "vested interests." Since, by its nature, the conventional wisdom denies a change in the environment, it always and everywhere lags behind the times. This "inertia and resistance" comprise Veblen's institutional lag.

In a sense, too, the wealthy had, in Galbraith's view, and despite institutional lag, eventually learned from Veblen. The power to redistribute wealth had shifted toward unions and government. This shift made it downright dangerous for the wealthy to flaunt their wealth by consuming conspicuously, since such display increased the agitation by liberals to redistribute the wealth. Besides, the middle class now could emulate the rich in dress and even in automobiles, especially as the rich downsized to Volvos. At the time, later to be recanted, Galbraith believed economic insecurity among the masses had greatly diminished.

Galbraith concealed behind the "much reduced urgency" of consumption the idea of economic surplus, the means whereby the remaining economic insecurity could be banished. Production had now become the "solvent of the tensions once associated with inequality, and it has become the indispensable remedy for the discomforts, anxieties, and privations associated with economic insecurity." Enhanced production comes at the cost of a paradox, or, in Galbraith's words, "as production has increased in modern times concern for production seems also to have increased."[8]

Galbraith invokes the image of a hierarchy of goods whereby those required for daily living were more important to the average consumer than luxuries. Such a view, long ago advanced by the Austrian Carl Menger, is a contradiction in neoclassical economics in which no rank ordering of goods according to biological need or psychological satisfaction is possible (because cardinal utility is implied). As production surpluses mount (from rising productivity), consumers increasingly must be persuaded regarding adequate consumption. The producer must take on an ancillary role of synthesizing wants "by advertising, catalyzed by salesmanship." That wants are "shaped by the discreet manipulations of the persuaders show that they are not very urgent. A man who is hungry need never be told of his need for food."[9] Ostentatious display is impossible and advertising unnecessary without surpluses; during the Gilded Age, the rich engaged in self-advertisment.

Though it may have escaped the attention of mainstream economics, the existence of economic surplus permeates Veblen's *TLC* from beginning to end. "It has been customary in economic theory," writes Veblen, "to construe this struggle for wealth as being substantially a struggle for subsistence" (p. 24). However, he concludes, "industrial efficiency is presently carried to such a pitch as to afford something appreciably more than a bare livelihood to those engaged in the industrial process" (p. 25). Without surpluses, of course, excesses – of which Veblen finds in themselves, a surfeit – cannot exist. The motive for wealth accumulation cannot be only the satisfaction of physical comfort but must evolve from pecuniary emulation. Put differently, a Jay Gatsby in pursuit of a Daisy must distinguish himself in money terms, even if it is money disreputable for its newness, if not for its source.

In the end even "higher learning" is an expression by, of and for the pecuniary culture. Scholastic discipline conserves the habits of thought believed suitable by the leisure class. Only a leisure class can develop and pursue "esoteric" as well as "exoteric knowledge." The former comprises, as Veblen puts it, "such knowledge as is primarily of no economic or industrial effect, and the latter comprising chiefly knowledge of industrial processes and of natural phenomena which were habitually turned to account for the material purposes of life." Esoteric knowledge becomes part of the surplus, in a sense being surplus knowledge. It serves the agenda of the leisure class by demarcation "between higher learning and the lower" (p. 367). Galbraith, of course, has followed Veblen's lead in his critiques of "higher learning" in economics; Veblen and Galbraith alike have viewed the economics orthodoxy as a system of pecuniary belief suffering serious institutional lag.[10]

Veblen and Galbraith's animus is not so much for the classicals, but for the neoclassicals. After all, the classicals had workers being paid subsistence wages with subsistence often defined culturally. Wage goods provided subsistence. For those political economists, necessity was the mother of convention. The neoclassical economists, to the contrary, presume all income to be discretionary. Relieved of the burden of purchasing necessities, the imaginary consumers are "free to choose" any set of goods and services. Most important for the mathematics (and the theory), the assumption that necessities are unnecessary and luxuries are a special case, guarantees the convexity of indifference curves on which adequate budgets always yield matching marginal utility ratios.

Still, the idea that discretion is the better part of value is an incomplete account of capitalism. In a theoretical system of perpetual scarcity the capitalist can barely be a prime mover. Any self-respecting capitalist is rightly embarrassed when they fail to produce a net surplus. Since the upper 1 percent of households and individuals, *today's* leisure class, now control nearly 40 percent of the USA's total household wealth, a surplus must exist on the income side either in a reflection of production surplus or as rentier income.[11] Though many American households exist at the biological subsistence level, American capitalism is indisputably an economy of surpluses. In what I have called a "supra-surplus economy," a hierarchy of absolute physical necessities and "wants" coexist. "Higher standards of living" usually are associated with the satisfaction of a greater number of wants, not the satisfaction at the margin from one more unit of the same good.[12] The wants of least urgency can be met only by those with incomes or credit sufficient to buy more than basic necessities, a hierarchy of needs and wants implying a lexicographical utility function in which budget constraints for lower-income persons eliminate lower-order goods.[13]

Neoclassical economics has difficulty assimilating Veblen and Galbraith not only because utilities are interdependent or social, but also because surplus production pitted against the income and wealth distributions drives their economics. To the extent that prices are important to Veblen, their role is likely to be perverse; the amounts demanded of a luxury often rises with its price and the incomes of those who purchase it, though the causality need not run from higher price to greater consumption. Since emulation and display need not require a high income, the purchase of "fakes" or labels implies inexplicable waste amid a neoclassical sea of undeniable efficiency. Still, the prices of authentic luxury goods are beyond the means of the middle class. For the neoclassicals, poverty, like richness, cannot be explained except by marginal revenue products, which is not an explanation applicable to either extreme since the importance of the absolutes overwhelms that of the increments. Surpluses, of course, cannot exist in a system in which the quantities that producers are willing to supply exactly match those that consumers are willing to buy. For that matter, surpluses cannot exist where scarcity is the operative assumption defining economic theory. Neoclassical theory is about scarcity and the necessity of parsimony; Veblen and Galbraith's economics is about surpluses and the necessary implications of dreadful waste.

A PARADOX UNMASKED IN MACROECONOMIC DEMAND THEORY

Status goods and interdependent utility functions created an apparently insurmountable problem for neoclassical economics in Alfred Marshall's day. Social interdependence displacing utilitarianism foreclosed the additivity of individual demand curves into an aggregate demand curve. Keynes, like Veblen, placed greater emphasis on habits and instincts as key subjective elements in the propensity to consume[14] and even recognized the desire for ostentation and extravagance as a part of any theory of demand.[15] Keynes's remarks went largely unnoticed until an apparent macroeconomic consumption paradox related to the General Theory was discovered during the 1940s.

Keynes's "fundamental psychological law" emphasizes that as a rule and on the average, as income increases, consumption will increase, but not by as much as the increase in incomes. Thus, the average propensity to consume declines at higher incomes. He never said, however, that all historical movements in income and consumption must conform to this rule. The apparent paradox was found in the data: the average propensity to consume falls with income in cross-section data, confirming Keynes's "law," but is constant in time-series data.

The apparent paradox was seemingly resolved in the late 1940s by James Duesenberry's relative income hypothesis. His hypothesis is based on two assumptions: (1) the household's consumption depends in part upon the consumption patterns of other households (i.e., utility functions *are* interdependent); (2) consumption is in great part dependent upon habitual patterns of behavior and therefore depends in part upon past consumption behavior. These assumptions are purely Veblenian, the first being based on pecuniary emulation and the second on inertia or the unwillingness or reluctance to break with former behavioral patterns.

Duesenberry suggests that the demonstration effect has consumption expenditures by one household inducing expenditures by other households. The level of expenditures by each household is constrained by their absolute levels of income, but the ratio of consumption to income for all families is interdependent. In his second assumption, Duesenberry argues that a household's consumption pattern is irreversible. In a year when income is low relative to past income, households are inclined to sacrifice savings to protect their old standards of living. Evidently, the satisfaction from the higher standard of living influences current consumption behavior. As income rises, households consume more, but not as much more as one might expect from long-run historical data. The households are held back by their habitual patterns of lower consumption and respond only slowly to their new affluence. Therefore, Duesenberry's fundamental psychological postulate is that it is harder for a family to reduce its expenditures than for a family to refrain from making high expenditures in the first place. Such behavior seems plausible, if only because each of us has had the common experience. Moreover, spending to the point of bankruptcy and the Gatsby effect become possible.

Econometrically, Duesenberry estimates a series of short-run consumption functions that exhibit a ratchet effect. The nonlinear short-run function ratchets upward in response to a new peak level of real disposable income, but consumption backslides reluctantly along the new (nonlinear) short-run curve in response to income declines. Duesenberry's relative income hypothesis is consistent with the cross-section data results. A low-income family experiences more pressure from the demonstration effect to attempt to match the consumption patterns of a high-income household. Thus the average propensity to consume for the low-income family is higher as the family sacrifices savings for consumption. Though higher-income households spend more on goods and services, they observe fewer families exhibiting consumption expenditures in excess of their own. Therefore, the average propensity to consume falls as one moves up and through higher-income households.

Duesenberry's hypothesis *was* a mainstream view until Milton Friedman published his permanent income hypothesis in 1957. About the same time

Franco Modigliani and his collaborators (1955) were developing a slightly different explanation for the smoothing-out of consumption over the long run. In a theoretical sense, Modigliani "out-permanents" Friedman's permanent income hypothesis in his suggestion that households attempt to even out their consumption over their entire lifetimes. Friedman and Modigliani went on to win Nobel Prizes, while Duesenberry was relegated to the economics underworld. Today, no macroeconomics text with sufficient sales to remain in print even mentions the relative income hypothesis. That is a pity.

Both Friedman and Modigliani rejected Duesenberry's consumption function. The permanent income and life-cycle theories say that if the influence of the life-cycle differences and transitory earnings could be eliminated, high-income households would save the same shares of their incomes as low-income households. Study after study has failed to support Friedman and Modigliani. In his review of the evidence, Thomas Mayer concluded, "of all the many tests which have been undertaken by friends of the [equal savings shares] hypothesis, *not a single one supports it. . . .*"[16] More recently, Diamond and Hausman produced perhaps the most damaging evidence, concluding that "not only does the level of savings (wealth) rise with permanent income, but it does so in a sharply nonlinear fashion". . . .[17] For permanent incomes below $4770 per year, they found that the savings–permanent income ratio rises by 3.3 percent for each extra $1000 of permanent income; beyond $4700 it rises 5.7 percent for each extra $1000 and beyond $12,076, by 14.2 percent.

If Bill Gates' savings as a share of his permanent income is *lower* than that of another 40-year-old white male different from Gates only because he earns $18,000 per year with little hope for a significant raise, *that* would be quite surprising. Still, if the eighteen-thousand-dollar man were to become unemployed, he would likely borrow funds in an effort to maintain his family's old standard of living, possibly risking the Gatsby effect. Moreover, if Bill Gates' income were to drop a few hundred thousand dollars next year, he probably would not alter his consumption significantly. In short, habit persistence better meets the test of common sense than the permanent income hypothesis. Veblen and Galbraith no doubt would say something amusing about the habitual modes of thinking regarding permanent income in the institutions of higher learning.

VEBLEN AND AN ALTERNATIVE VISION FOR ECONOMICS

Unlike the neoclassicals, Veblen and especially Galbraith have explained why the American economy relies so heavily on advertising and salesmanship. If needs and production are exactly matched, there is no need to spread the word regarding the virtues of any particular product. The market sets the price and consumers pay it without the need for any additional information. Lonely price signals rule the neoclassical world. However, the large gap between the lowest and highest incomes inspires the corporate structure to transcend the role of a simple producer of goods. As Galbraith notes, "mass communication was not necessary when the wants of the masses were anchored primarily in physical need. The masses could not then be persuaded as to their spending – this went for basic foods and shelter."[18]

An excess of income above physiological subsistence leaves a demand wedge for producers. Imperfect competition abhors wedges. Not only does the demand gap (relative to production) lead to advertising, promotion, and salesmanship, it sets into motion forces such as the price markup on unit costs (mostly wages) to fill the space. The money wage – the wage actually negotiated – separates itself from the real wage or labor productivity. The markup depends very much on the firm's ability to further differentiate its product or service. Since products are differentiated with a particular segment of the income distribution in mind, the only relevant "price" elasticities are those prevailing within that part of the income distribution. In this vision non-price competition displaces price competition. It is difficult to imagine the existence of imperfect competition in the absence of excess production capacity.[19]

Since – to a considerable degree – we are what we consume, not surprisingly consumer tastes shape the market for labor. Thus, parallel non-wage-competing forces are found in the modern labor market, forces mirroring those prevailing in goods markets. Our ultimate sociological achievement today is not our work, much less our workmanship, but is whatever standard of living we attain (defined as what we can afford to consume). Once defined by our work and its quality, now we define ourselves by our standard of living. In a Veblenian sense we are "middle class" when we perceive ourselves as very much like everyone else. We believe that everyone is or can be on the same bandwagon. However, producers and marketing experts have much finer classifications for what we can afford and how we can be influenced in accordance with our demographic and economic characteristics. Prices and wages merely comprise background noise in this great social drama.

Duesenberry's aggregate consumption function is consistent with Veblen, Galbraith, and Keynes's visions. It signifies the importance of the income distribution in determining the level of aggregate demand. In neoclassical theory aggregate demand can only be generated by adding individual demand functions that are non-additive. Just as Veblenian demand suppresses the influence of prices at the microeconomic level, Keynes's theory of demand suppresses prices in macroeconomics. Income and output, including capitalism's natural tendency to create overcapacity, drive the system to or away from full employment equilibrium. Relative real incomes are more important than individual prices.

CONCLUSIONS

Often it is said that Veblen's ideas, and Galbraith's, for that matter, cannot be useful for economic theory because they are nebulous, diffused, and irrelevant. As we have seen, however, recent mainstream contributions to demand theory would disabuse anyone of insurmountable difficulties in the use of interdependent or lexicographical utility functions, reflecting Veblenian behaviors. Moreover, direct utility functions and extended linear expenditure systems empirically confirm the importance of standards of living in consumption behavior. Though presently inconspicuous, game theory and econometrics applied to Veblenian demand are persuasive.

That is not all: the Veblenian vision may be broad without being infinite and thereby irrelevant. To theorize about prices in competitive markets is the easy way. Thinking small, however, we are in danger of missing something big. We economists have failed to evolve with the economic system we claim to describe. Not only have technology and education greatly changed, capitalism has evolved through many stages so that it no longer bears even a family resemblance to the nascent industrialization of Alfred Marshall's time much less the merchant capitalism prevailing during the age of Adam Smith. In particular, an economy, even a global economy, with surplus industrial capacity, is not well described by a theory grounded in scarcity. As capitalism has become increasingly complex, too many economists have been content to keep everything except the mathematics simple. Our esoteric self-indulgence places us in danger of becoming the sole consumers of our own production. If that happens, economists will become part of the surplus.

NOTES

1 The three quotations are from John Bartlett, edited by Emily Morison Beck, *Bartlett's Familiar Quotations, Fifteenth Edition* (Boston: Little, Brown and Company, 1980) [1855], p. 685.
2 Harvey Leibenstein, "Bandwagon, Snob and Veblen Effects in the Theory of Consumer's Demand," *Quarterly Journal of Economics*, May 1950. The article was widely reprinted, including its appearance in Edwin Mansfield (ed.), *Microeconomics: Selected Readings*, 3rd edn (New York and London: W. W. Norton, 1971), pp. 12–30.
3 Laurie Simon Bagwell and B. Douglas Bernheim, "Veblen Effects in a Theory of Conspicuous Consumption," *The American Economic Review* 86, No. 3 (June 1996): 350.
4 See, for instance, David M. Kreps, *A Course in Microeconomic Theory* (Princeton: Princeton University Press, 1990). The single-crossing (a.k.a. the Spence-Mirrlees sorting) condition is indigenous to models using asymmetric information.
5 For a model using interdependent utility functions with implications for income redistribution, see E. Ray Canterbery, "Income Redistribution and Rawlsian Justice," *Journal of Economics and Business* 33, No. 3 (Spring/Summer 1981): 188–201. Contrary to the neoclassical conventional wisdom regarding Rawls'

principles of justice, I argue that in the real world such principles can be evaluated and implemented only if interpersonal comparisons are allowed.

6 R. L. Basmann, D. J. Molina, and D. J. Slottje, "A Note on Measuring Veblen's Theory of Conspicuous Consumption," *Review of Economics and Statistics* 70, No. 3 (August 1988): 532–535.

7 John Kenneth Galbraith, *The Affluent Society* (Boston: Houghton Mifflin, 1958).

8 *Ibid.* pp. 119–120.

9 *Ibid.* p. 158.

10 A complete survey and analysis of Galbraith's position is provided in Warren J. Samuels, "Galbraith on Economics as a System of Professional Belief," *Journal of Post Keynesian Economics* 7, No. 1 (Fall 1984): 61–76.

11 These data are from Edward N. Wolff, *Top Heavy: A Study of the Increasing Inequality of Wealth in America* (New York: The Twentieth Century Fund Press, 1995), p. 7. Wolff traces increasing wealth and income inequality to the high returns from increasingly concentrated holdings of financial wealth.

12 See E. Ray Canterbery, "A Theory of Supra-Surplus Capitalism," Presidential Address, EEA, March 6, 1987, printed in *Eastern Economic Journal* 13, No. 4 (October–December 1987): 315–332 and E. Ray Canterbery, *The Making of Economics*, 3rd edn (Belmont, CA: Wadsworth, 1987).

13 The lexicographical utility function is defined and fully explicated in E. Ray Canterbery, "Inflation, Necessities and Distributive Efficiency," in J. H. Gapinski and C. E. Rockwood (eds), *Essays in Post Keynesian Inflation* (Cambridge, MA: Ballinger, 1979), pp. 70–103. This function generates kinked Engel curves because the threshold level of income for a lower-ranked good equals the satiation level of income for the prior higher-ranked good. The value of subsistence expenditures in such a framework can be estimated through the extended linear expenditure system (also discussed).

14 As Keynes put it, the subjective factors "include those psychological characteristics of human nature and those social practices and institutions which, though not unalterable, are unlikely to undergo a material change over a short period of time except in abnormal or revolutionary circumstances" (John Maynard Keynes, *The General Theory of Employment, Interest, and Money* (New York: Harcourt, Brace & World, Inc., 1965) [1936], p. 91).

15 Keynes, *op. cit.*, p. 108.

16 Thomas Mayer, *Permanent Income, Wealth and Consumption* (Berkeley, CA: University of California Press, 1972), p. 348.

17 Peter Diamond and J. A. Hausman, "Individual Retirement and Savings Behavior," Paper presented at SSRC-NBER Conference on Public Economics, Oxford, June 1982, pp. 35–37.

18 John Kenneth Galbraith, *The New Industrial State* (Boston: Houghton Mifflin, 1967), p. 207.

19 For a more detailed discussion of the connections among a theory of demand that relates production to a hierarchy of wants and a theory of the income distribution that relates incomes to job markets as well as to other elements, see E. Ray Canterbery, "Galbraith, Sraffa, Kalecki and Supra-Surplus Capitalism," *Journal of Post Keynesian Economics* 7, No. 1 (Fall 1984): 77–90.

REFERENCES

Akerlof, George A. "A Theory of Social Custom, of Which Unemployment May Be One Consequence." *Quarterly Journal of Economics* 94, No. 4 (June 1980): 749–751.

Bagwell, Laurie Simon and B. Douglas Bernheim. "Veblen Effects in a Theory of Conspicuous Consumption." *American Economic Review*, 86, No. 3 (June 1996): 349–73.

Bartlett, John. *Bartlett's Familiar Quotations*, Fifteenth edition. Edited by Emily Morison Beck. Boston: Little, Brown and Company, 1980 [1855].

Basmann, R. L., D. J. Molina, and D. J. Slottje. "A Note on Measuring Veblen's Theory of Conspicuous Consumption." *Review of Economics and Statistics* 70, No. 3 (August 1988): 532–35.

Canterbery, E. Ray. "Income Redistribution and Rawlsian Justice." *Journal of Economics and Business* 33 (Spring/Summer 1981): 188–201.

—— *The Making of Economics*. Third edition. Belmont, CA: Wadsworth, 1987.

—— "A Theory of Supra-Surplus Capitalism." Presidential Address, EEA, March 6, 1987, printed in *Eastern Economic Journal* 13, No. 4 (October–December 1987): 315–332.

—— "Inflation, Necessities and Distributive Efficiency." In *Essays in Post Keynesian Inflation*. Edited by J. H. Gapinski and C. E. Rockwood. Cambridge, MA: Ballinger, 1979, pp. 79–103.

Diamond, Peter and J. A. Hausman. "Individual Retirement and Savings Behavior." Paper presented at SSRC-NBER Conference on Public Economics. Oxford, June 1982.

Duesenberry, James. *Income, Saving, and the Theory of Consumer Behavior*. Cambridge, MA: Harvard University Press, 1949.

Frank, Robert H. "The Demand for Unobservable and Other Nonpositional Goods." *American Economic Review* 75, No. 1 (March 1985): 101–16.

Galbraith, John Kenneth. *The Affluent Society*. Boston: Houghton Mifflin, 1958.

—— *The New Industrial State*. Boston: Houghton Mifflin, 1967.

Keynes, John Maynard. *The General Theory of Employment, Interest, and Money*. New York: Harcourt, Brace & World, Inc., 1965 [1936].

Kreps, David M. *A Course in Microeconomic Theory*. Princeton, NJ: Princeton University Press, 1990.

Leibenstein, Harvey. "Bandwagon, Snob and Veblen Effects in the Theory of Consumer's Demand." Reprinted in *Microeconomics: Selected Readings*, Third edition. Edited by Edwin Mansfield. New York, London: W. W. Norton, 1971, pp. 12–30.

Mayer, Thomas. *Permanent Income, Wealth and Consumption*. Berkeley, CA: University of California Press, 1972.

Samuels, Warren J. "Galbraith on Economics as a System of Professional Belief." *Journal of Post Keynesian Economics* 7, No. 1 (Fall 1984): 61–76.

Veblen, Thorstein. *The Theory of the Leisure Class*. New York, London: Penguin Books, 1994 [1899].

Wolff, Edward N. *Top Heavy: A Study of the Increasing Inequality of Wealth in America*. New York: The Twentieth Century Fund Press, 1995.

10

VEBLEN'S CONTRIBUTION TO THE INSTRUMENTAL THEORY OF NORMATIVE VALUE

Lewis E. Hill

INTRODUCTION

The purpose of this essay is to specify, to explicate, and to evaluate the contribution of Thorstein Bunde Veblen to the instrumental theory of normative value as it has been developed in the philosophical tradition of pragmatism and in the socioeconomic tradition of institutionalism. The thesis of the paper holds that John Dewey's version of the instrumental theory of normative value was entirely and exclusively procedural and that it was completely devoid of substantive implications. The substance of normative value was contributed to the theory by Veblen in the form of his dichotomy between the benevolent propensities of the human personality that motivate creative behavior and the malevolent propensities of the human personality that motivate destructive behavior. Clarence Ayres achieved a synthesis between the respective value theories of Dewey and Veblen by integrating the Veblenian dichotomy into Dewey's instrumental theory of value. It was in this manner that Ayres transformed Dewey's value theory, which had been exclusively procedural, into the contemporary instrumental theory of normative value, which is both procedural and substantive.

The essay is divided into five parts, the first of which is this introduction. Part Two traces the development of the pragmatic philosophy from Charles Sanders Peirce's logical pragmatism, through the transitional philosophy of William James, to Dewey's instrumental pragmatism and his instrumental theory of normative value. The third part explicates the emergence of Veblen's normative dichotomy of human behavior between the benevolent propensities which motivate creative behavior and the malevolent propensities which motivate destructive behavior. Part Four deals with the development of Ayres' instrumental institutionalism which became the grand synthesis of Dewey's instrumental theory of value and Veblen's dichotomy. The fifth part draws the conclusions from the study.

INSTRUMENTAL PRAGMATISM AND THE THEORY OF NORMATIVE VALUE

Pragmatism is the philosophy which is based upon the presumption that all reality has practical consequences and that, therefore, certainly the best method and perhaps the only method accurately to know and correctly understand reality is through the consideration of practical consequences. In the beginning, pragmatism was an informal folk philosophy that originated on the western geographic frontier during the long history of the American colonies and the United States. Survival on the frontier required an ability to improvise and to innovate in the anticipation of and the adaptation to the unexpected consequences of primitive conditions. This informal folk philosophy provided a set of intellectual tools that could be used to facilitate survival in the harsh and dangerous conditions that prevailed on the frontier (Kallen, 1933).

Charles Sanders Peirce was the first scholar to transform this folk philosophy into a systematic pattern of thought. He stated its basic principle as his pragmatic imperative:

> consider what effects, which might conceivably have practical bearings, we conceive the object of our conception to have. Then, our conception of these effects is the whole of our conception of the object.
>
> (Peirce, 1966: 124)

Peirce proclaimed that the purpose of the pragmatic epistemology is to integrate thought with action in order to solve practical problems.

According to Peirce, the pragmatic process of solving problems proceeds in the following manner: whenever a person encounters a problematical situation, he experiences doubt, his doubt stimulates thought, and his thought creates ideas. Then, the person should use the pragmatic imperative to clarify his ideas to the highest possible degree (1966: 118–124). Scientific inquiry should be used to transform ideas into beliefs through a process known as "fixation." Beliefs become rules of action that are intended to eliminate doubt by solving the problem. If the rule of action effectively solves the problem, then the belief becomes a habit that is repeated every time the same problematical situation occurs (91–112).

Peirce's pragmatic epistemology implies a procedural theory of normative value because it specifies a procedure and a technique that can be utilized to evaluate doubts, thoughts, ideas, beliefs, and actions in order to determine

158

their effectiveness in solving practical problems. Peirce also formulated a substantive theory of normative value, but it was perhaps more metaphysical than scientific because it was derived from his philosophy of religion. Peirce conceived religion to be a sentiment or perception that recognizes First Cause and Final Cause as absolutes and that relates the individual self as a relative being to these absolutes (Peirce, 1966: 350–351). He believed that the distinguishing characteristic of Christianity is the Doctrine of the Two Ways: the Way of Life, which symbolizes all of the affirmative thought and creative behavior that is associated with the Christ; and the Way of Death, which symbolizes all of the negative thought and destructive behavior that is associated with the Antichrist. The Way of Life is the substance of value; the Way of Death is the substance of disvalue (354–355).

Peirce asserted not only that truth always corresponds to reality, but also that truth emerges from agreement among authorities. According to him, a true proposition or idea is the conclusion that all competent scholars would reach if they investigated the question or problem long enough and intensively enough (1966: 130–136). He expressed his concept of truth and reality as follows:

> This great law is embodied in the conception of truth and reality. The opinion which is fated to be ultimately agreed to by all who investigate is what we mean by the truth, and the object represented by this opinion is the real.
>
> (Peirce, 1966: 133)

William James, the second among the originators of the pragmatic philosophy, had a different concept of truth which was more functional and instrumental than factual and logical. James contended that an idea should be evaluated as true or false dynamically, according to what it does, rather than statically, according to what it is. The truth of an idea requires not only that the idea corresponds to some external reality, but also that it proves to be useful in assisting us to adapt to that reality. True ideas help us to distinguish the useful aspects from the harmful aspects of reality and to achieve a harmonious relationship with reality. Moreover, true ideas fulfill our expectations and facilitate the achievement of our objectives, but false ideas deceive and mislead us into wrong courses of action and cause failure in our efforts to achieve our objectives. All true ideas are useful, and, conversely, all useful ideas are true. The truth of an idea is a prediction of its usefulness; the usefulness of an idea is the verification of its truth (James, 1908: 97–238). According to James, "'The true,' to put it briefly, is only the expedient in the way of our thinking, just as 'the right' is only the expedient in the way of our behaving" (222).

James' functional concept of truth presupposes a procedural theory of normative value because it requires the valuation not only of the usefulness of ideas, but also of the desirability or undesirability of the practical consequences of ideas. Clearly, James believed that ordinary people can learn both to predict the consequences of an idea and to judge whether these consequences are desirable or undesirable. This ability to predict and to evaluate consequences is the essence of the instrumental theory of value.

John Dewey, the last of the originators of pragmatism, continued to develop the instrumental theory of normative value. The fundamental principle of his version of the theory held that ideas are intellectual instruments or tools to be used for the purpose of solving practical problems through the process of logical or scientific inquiry (Dewey, 1938: 101–280). Dewey defined inquiry as follows:

> Inquiry is the controlled or directed transformation of an indeterminate situation into one that is so determinate in its constituent distinctions and relations as to convert the elements of the original situation into a unified whole.
>
> (Dewey, 1938: 104–105)

Inquiry is the process which specifies and explicates precisely how ideas are to be utilized in order to solve problems.

The process of inquiry always begins in an indeterminate situation that produces unpredictable and random consequences, rather than predictable and controlled consequences, and causes doubt and uncertainty. The first phase of inquiry is the institution of the problem, which specifies the aspects of the indeterminate situation that threaten to prevent us from achieving our ends in view. In this manner, the indeterminate situation is transformed into a problematical situation and the problem is defined. The second phase of inquiry is the determination of a problem solution. A possible solution to the problem is suggested by the observation and analysis of the factual conditions that are relevant to the cause-and-effect relationships that are involved in the problem. The suggested solution will become an idea when its functional fitness to resolve the problematical situation has been established. Finally, the idea must be symbolized as a set of expected consequences which would result from its implementation. The third phase of inquiry is the use of reasoning to develop the idea into a hypothesis and the hypothesis into a plan of action that becomes the proposed solution to the problem. The fourth phase of inquiry is the implementation of the proposed solution to the problem which is intended to transform the indeterminate situation that constituted the problem into a determinate situation that will constitute the solution (Dewey, 1938: 105–114).

In order to utilize the process of logical and scientific inquiry to solve practical problems, a person must make two kinds of judgments: first, judgments of positive fact concerning cause-and-effect relationships; second, judgments of normative value concerning the goodness or badness of practical consequences. The conventional wisdom among the positivists, who have dominated philosophical thought for the last 150 years, is that only judgments of positive fact are subject to empirical verification or falsification, whereas judgments of normative value can never be either verified or falsified by reference to subsequently observed empirical reality. Therefore, they conclude that only factual judgments possess scientific validity and reliability, and that value judgments should be excluded from the empirical sciences. But Dewey vigorously and profoundly disagreed with this conventional wisdom and with these conclusions. He always insisted that there is no significant difference between judgments of positive fact and judgments of normative value; both are induced empirically by the application of inductive logic to previous experience and both are verified or falsified empirically by the application of inductive logic to subsequent experience (Dewey, 1929: 254–286).

Dewey always contended that judgments of normative value are at least as essential in the process of logical or scientific inquiry as judgments of positive fact. Moreover, he firmly believed that normative value judgments could be empirically verified or falsified with great precision and that a verified judgment of normative value should be accepted as completely valid and thoroughly reliable. Finally, Dewey always held firmly to his conviction that ordinary people are completely competent to induce valid judgments of normative value from their prior experience and to verify these judgments by reference to their subsequent experience. Our lives are controlled by ideas; therefore, we are continuously involved in evaluating the goodness or badness of ideas and the desirability or undesirability of their consequences. These evaluations are normative value judgments. The ideas that we evaluate to be desirable become normative values; the ideas that we evaluate to be undesirable become normative disvalues (Dewey, 1939). Dewey draws the following conclusion from his analysis of the theory of normative value:

> Thus we are led to our main proposition: *Judgments about values are judgments about the conditions and the results of experienced objects; judgments about that which should regulate the formation of our desires, affections and enjoyments.* For whatever decides their formation will determine the main course of our conduct, personal and social.
>
> (Dewey, 1929: 265)

Dewey's theory of normative value is entirely and exclusively procedural; it is completely devoid of substantive implications. He has provided instructions in the procedures and techniques for inducing normative values and value judgments from our past experience, but he never presumed to specify the substance of the normative values that we should induce from our experience or the judgments that we should derive from the application of

161

these values to present conditions in order to control the future course of events. Dewey appears to have had great confidence in the intellectual power of ordinary people to induce sound normative values from their previous experience and to induce logically correct value judgments from these values (Dewey, 1939; Hill and Owens, 1984).

THE VEBLENIAN DICHOTOMY

Thorstein Veblen's major contribution to the instrumental theory of normative value was his dichotomy, which he used to distinguish between the benevolent and malevolent propensities of the human personality and between the creative and destructive patterns of behavior that are motivated by these propensities. This dichotomy transformed Dewey's instrumental theory, which had been exclusively procedural, into a substantive theory of normative value. The dichotomy originated very early in the Judeo-Christian tradition. According to the Old Testament, man was created in the image of God, which symbolizes the benevolent propensities and the creative behavior, but he is guilty of original sin, which symbolizes the malevolent propensities and the destructive behavior (Genesis 1: 2–27 and 3: 1–24). In the New Testament, Jesus of Nazareth is the symbolic embodiment of all affirmative or creative forces; his crucifixion represents a temporary triumph of the negative forces of death and destruction; and his resurrection from the dead represents the final and ultimate victory of life over death and of creativity over destructivity (John 20: 1–18).

Sigmund Freud, the father of contemporary psychoanalysis and psychiatry, expressed the dichotomy scientifically. He imputed the benevolent propensities and the creative behavior to the life instinct; he imputed the malevolent propensities and the destructive behavior to the death instinct (Brown, 1959). Robert Louis Stevenson created a literary analysis of the dichotomy in his greatest novel, *The Strange Case of Dr Jekyll and Mr Hyde* (1886). This novel is the story of the honorable and distinguished Dr Jekyll who discovered a drug which would transform him into the disreputable and uninhibited Mr Hyde. Dr Jekyll personifies good, and Mr Hyde personifies evil. *The Strange Case of Dr Jekyll and Mr Hyde* became the prototypical psychological novel that explicates the conflict between good and evil.

Veblen developed the negative aspects of his dichotomy in his first book *The Theory of the Leisure Class* (1899). This book deals with the exploitative and wasteful behavior of the leisure class, which originated in primitive barbarian cultures when strong men exploited and enslaved the women and the weak men (1–21). The leisure class and ownership developed together because the leisure class owned not only the women and the slaves, but also the things that they produced. The role of the leisure class was exploit; the role of the working class was labor. The warriors and the priests emerged as the leaders of the leisure class (22–34). Since the leisure class is characterized by their abstention from work, they developed patterns of behavior to demonstrate wasteful conspicuous leisure in order to identify themselves with their class (35–67). They demonstrated their prowess through pecuniary emulation by accumulating great wealth and by squandering some of it in wasteful conspicuous consumption (22–34 and 67–101). Exploitation and conspicuous waste became the predominant patterns of behavior that characterized the leisure class.

The affirmative aspects of the Veblenian dichotomy are based on the three benevolent and creative instincts: the instinct of workmanship, the parental bent, and idle curiosity. The instinct of workmanship is the proclivity which motivates humankind to achieve excellence in mastery of technological skills. It is "concerned with the ways and means whereby instinctively given purposes are to be accomplished" (Veblen, 1937: 33–34). The parental bent is the unconditional love which parents feel for their children.

> In the simplest and unsophisticated terms, its functional content appears to be an unselfish solicitude for the well-being of the incoming generation – a bias for the highest efficiency and the fullest volume of life in the group, with a particular drift to the future; so that, under its rule, contrary to the dictum of the economic theorists, future goods are preferred to present good and the filial generation is given the preference over the parental generation in all that touches their material welfare.
>
> (Veblen, 1937: 46–47)

Idle curiosity is an instinctive proclivity for humankind to seek to acquire knowledge for its inherent value rather than any ulterior motive that may be associated with the practical use of the knowledge.

> The fact of this proclivity is well summed up in saying that men are by native gift actuated with an idle curiosity – 'idle' in the sense that a knowledge of things is sought apart from any ulterior use of the knowledge so gained.
>
> (Veblen, 1965b: 5)

These three creative instincts motivate the benevolent propensities in the human personality and the creative aspects of human behavior. Unfortunately these benevolent and creative instincts can become contaminated by negative instincts.

> But where the self-regarding sentiments, self-complacency and self-abasement, come largely into play, as they are bound to do in any culture that partakes appreciably of a predatory or coercive character,

the prerogatives of the ruling class and the principles of authentic usage become canons of truth and right living and presently take precedence of workmanlike efficiency and the fullness of life of the group. It results that conventional tests of validity presently accumulate and increasingly deflect and obstruct the naïve pursuit of workmanlike efficiency, in large part by obscuring those matters of fact that lend themselves to technological insight.

(Veblen, 1937: 47–48)

In *The Theory of Business Enterprise* (1904), Veblen completed his dichotomy by bringing its affirmative and negative aspects together in a single book. He applied the dichotomy to an analysis of the capitalistic economic system, which consists of two contradictory sets of economic forces. The affirmative aspect of this dichotomy is industry, which consists of the application of the technological machine process to the production of an abundance of material goods. The negative aspect of this dichotomy is business enterprise, which involves controlling the machine process in order to limit the output of material goods, to maintain high prices, and to make profits. The problem results from the manner in which the capitalistic economic system subordinates industry and the machine process to business enterprise, which has been granted the overriding power to control the entire system (Veblen, 1904: 1–91). The captains of industry and the entrepreneurs use capitalistic sabotage to limit the inherent productivity of the technological machine process in order to cause scarcity, to maintain high prices, and to maximize profits (Veblen, 1965a: 1–5).

In the higher stages of capitalism the captains of industry are superseded by the captains of finance, who usurp control of the capitalistic system and manipulate it for their own pecuniary gain (Veblen, 1965a: 52–82). These captains of finance promote and finance industrial mergers and consolidations, which increase the monopoly power of big business. During this process of consolidation, the anticipated monopoly profits are capitalized into the asset valuations of the consolidated enterprise in such a manner and to such an extent that the consolidated corporation becomes over-capitalized. This corporate expansion and over-capitalization causes a period of inflationary prosperity, but as soon as it becomes evident that corporate profits cannot support the inflated capital values, a crisis will occur and the boom will collapse into a depression (Veblen, 1904: 92–267). Ironically, Veblen died in 1929, a few months before the stock market crash and the ensuing Great Depression verified the predictions that he had made in 1904.

It was in this manner that Thorstein Veblen formulated his dichotomy between the benevolent and malevolent propensities of the human personality and between the creative and destructive patterns of human behavior. This Veblenian dichotomy became the substantive basis of the instrumental theory of normative value.

164

THE AYRESIAN SYNTHESIS

The late, great Clarence Edwin Ayres synthesized John Dewey's instrumentalism with Thorstein Veblen's institutionalism. In the process, he incorporated Veblen's dichotomy into the instrumental theory of value, and Dewey's instrumental theory of value into institutionalism. Ayres endorsed and emphasized the dichotomy that Veblen had used to distinguish between the benevolent and malevolent propensities of the human personality and between the creative and destructive patterns of human behavior. Ayres included technology, technological behavior, the instinct of workmanship, and industry among the affirmative aspects of the dichotomy; he included institutions, ceremonial behavior, conspicuous waste, and business enterprise among the negative aspects of the dichotomy (Ayres, 1944: 89–202; Ayres, 1951).

Ayres defined technology as organized skill and technological behavior as the use of tools, but he defined both skill and tools very broadly. Skill was defined inclusively enough to include all useful knowledge, which ranges from the skill of laborers, through the industrial know-how of technicians and engineers, to the expertise and ingenuity of pure and applied scientists and the creative talents of artists. Tools were defined to include all useful artifacts from the simplest of hand tools, through all machines and equipment, to intricate and complex scientific instruments. Ayres contended that technology is inherently dynamic and progressive and that all progressive change is caused by technological innovation (1944: 105–124). Veblen had accounted for this dynamism and progressivity by reference to three benevolent instincts: the instinct of workmanship, the parental bent, and idle curiosity (Veblen, 1937: 33–34 and 46–47; 1965b: 5). Ayres, who was writing after the theory of instincts had been discredited by psychological research, explained this phenomenon by reference to the cumulative nature of technology. Each generation inherits the best technology from the previous generation; therefore, any innovation that may be achieved by the current generation will constitute a net increase in and improvement of the inherited technology. Most technological innovations are combinations of previously existing tools; therefore, technological progress accelerates exponentially because each new invention increases the number of tools that are available to be combined with other tools in future innovations (1944: 105–154).

Ayres defined institutions to be customary or traditional socioeconomic and politicoeconomic organizations that rank people in a hierarchical structure and confer authority to the people of higher rank over the people of lower rank. Prototypical examples of institutions are the family, the church, and the state. He insisted that institutions are inherently static and that, therefore, they always resist and oppose progressive change for at least two reasons. First, the predominant class has a vested interest in preserving and maintaining the currently existing institutional structure. Second, most people are motivated by a social inertia to prefer the certainty and security of a known present, rather than uncertainty and insecurity of an unknown future (Ayres, 1944: 177–202). Ayres defined ceremonial behavior to be unproductive and wasteful activities that are associated with institutions and that are authorized and authenticated by institutions. Ceremonial behavior is the opposite of technological behavior. Ayres believed that ceremonial behavior is always wasteful (155–176).

Ayres found normative value in technology, technological behavior, and the other affirmative aspects of the dichotomy; he found normative disvalue in inhibitory institutions, wasteful ceremonial behavior, and the other negative aspects of the dichotomy. Ayres conceived and elaborated the concept of the technological life process to summarize and to symbolize the normative value that inheres in the affirmative aspects of the dichotomy. He always insisted that life is the fundamental basis of all normative value and that the essence of the life process is technological or instrumental. This technological life process is the cause of all progressive change and the substance of all normative value (Ayres, 1944: 205–230). Ayres has written:

> It is in this, the life process of mankind, that values arise. . . . The value judgments which emerge from this process have a basis in fact. When we judge a thing to be good or bad, or an action to be right or wrong, what we mean is that, in our opinion, the thing or act in question will, or will not, serve to advance the life process insofar as we can envision it. . . . In all cases value judgments are judgments with regard to the causal relations between present choices and the future activities of the chooser and of other people.
> (Ayres, 1961: 113–114)

Ayres used this synthesized and integrated theory of normative value as the basis of his theory of economic progress, which proved to be the major component of his own unique instrumental institutionalism. Any theory of economic progress consists of three parts. A theory of normative value must be used to identify progress and to distinguish it from regress. A theory of economic causation must be used to specify the causes of economic progress, which should be sought, and the causes of economic regress, which should be avoided. A theory of economic policy must be used to facilitate the achievement of progress and the avoidance of regress.

According to Ayres, the substance of normative value and the essence of economic progress consists of the benevolent propensities of the human personality and the creative aspects of human behavior which facilitate, strengthen, promote, and enhance the technological life process. Conversely, the substance of normative disvalue and the essence of regress consist of the malevolent propensities of the human personality and the destructive aspects of human behavior which inhibit, weaken, demote, and diminish the technological life process. It is in this manner that the instrumental theory of normative value can be used to identify progress and to distinguish it from regress (Ayres, 1944: 105–124 and 205–230).

Ayres' instrumental theory of normative value implies a technological theory of economic causation which holds that technology and technological behavior are inherently dynamic and that technological innovation is the exclusive cause of all progressive economic change. Institutions and ceremonial behavior are inherently static; therefore, they resist and inhibit progressive economic change. Ayres interpreted economic history as a continuous conflict between the inherently dynamic technology and the inherently static institutions. Fortunately, technology and technological innovation are extremely powerful forces for progress which have ultimately prevailed over the institutional and ceremonial forces of stagnation and regress (Ayres, 1944: 105–204).

Ayres' theory of economic policy recognizes that technology is the source of all progress and that institutions always resist and inhibit progress. Affirmatively, the most important purpose of governmental economic policy should be to ensure the most complete and the least inhibited utilization of the best available technology and to maximize the quantity and quality of technological innovations. Negatively, the most important purpose of governmental economic policy should be to prevent inhibitory institutions and wasteful ceremonial behavior from interfering with the full utilization of technology or with the process of technological innovation (Ayres, 1944: 231–282). It was in this manner that Ayres' theory of economic progress, which became the major thesis of his instrumental institutionalism, began in his instrumental theory of normative value and ended in his theory of economic policy.

During the years since Ayres' retirement in 1968 and his death in 1972, a new generation of institutionalists revised and reinterpreted his dichotomy and his theories of normative value and economic causation. In one of his more insightful essays, William M. Dugger (1995) described and explained this revisionist movement.

> Significant changes have been made in the concepts of inquiry as a consequence of the questions asked by those influenced by the work of Karl Polanyi, J. Fagg Foster, and by a radical group of Veblenian institutionalists. (The groups are not mutually exclusive.) Rising environmental concerns also have had an impact.
>
> (Dugger, 1995: 1014)

These and other institutional economists from this new generation began to question Ayres' sweeping generalizations that held that technology is always progressive and, therefore, good and that institutions are always regressive and, therefore, bad. They learned that perversions of technology

167

can sometimes cause undesirable consequences and that institutions can sometimes cause desirable consequences. This reevaluation of Ayres' dichotomy has led to revisions in his theories of normative value and economic causation.

The locus of Ayres' theory of normative value has changed from technology and technological behavior to the social process and participatory democracy. The logic is clear: if technology cannot be depended upon always to produce reliable normative values and value judgments, then the best alternative is an enlightened electorate participating in a social process that is governed democratically. The locus of Ayres' theory of economic causation has shifted away from an impersonal technology and a mechanistic tool-combination principle and toward intelligent and objective people using ideas as intellectual tools or instruments to solve problems through the process of logical or scientific inquiry. Moreover, the contemporary generation of institutional economists is no longer inclined to condemn institutions as a force that always resists and inhibits progress. Many of them believe that institutions can facilitate and encourage progress. They are much more selective in their condemnation by blaming powerful elites who are defending their vested interests by resisting and inhibiting progress. The old simplistic generalizations of the past have been replaced by a new analytical approach that is more complex, more critical, more discriminating, and more realistic than the original Ayresian synthesis of instrumental institutionalism (Dugger, 1995).

CONCLUSION

The research which has been presented in this essay leads to three conclusions. First, John Dewey developed an instrumental theory of normative value that is entirely and exclusively procedural and which is completely devoid of substantive content. Second, Thorstein Veblen's dichotomy, which he used to distinguish between the affirmative and negative aspects of the human personality and human behavior, constitutes a substantive theory of normative value. Third, Clarence Ayres synthesized Dewey's procedural theory and Veblen's substantive theory in order to create a new instrumental theory of normative value which is both procedural and substantive.

REFERENCES

Ayres, Clarence E. (1951) "The Co-ordinates of Institutionalism," *American Economic Review* 41(2): 47–55.
—— (1944) *The Theory of Economic Progress*, Chapel Hill: The University of North Carolina Press.
—— (1961) *Toward a Reasonable Society*, Austin: University of Texas Press.

Brown, Norman O. (1959) *Life Against Death*, New York: Random House.

Dewey, John (1929) *The Quest for Certainty*, New York: G.P. Putnam's Sons.

—— (1938) *Logic: The Theory of Inquiry*, New York: Henry Holt and Company.

—— (1939) *Theory of Valuation*, Chicago: University of Chicago Press.

Dugger, William M. (1995) "Veblenian Institutionalism: The Changing Concepts of Inquiry," *Journal of Economic Issues* 29(4): 1013–1027.

Hill, Lewis E. and Owens, Donald W. (1984) "The Instrumental Philosophy of Economic History and the Institutionalist Theory of Normative Value," *Journal of Economic Issues,* 18(2): 581–587.

James, William (1908) *Pragmatism: A New Name for Some Old Ways of Thinking*, New York: Longmans, Green and Company.

Kallen, Horace M. (1933) "Pragmatism," *Encyclopedia of the Social Sciences*, New York: The Macmillan Company, 12: 307–311.

Peirce, Charles Sanders (1966) *Selected Writings: Value in a Universe of Change*, Philip Wiener (ed.), New York: Dover Publications, Inc.

Stevenson, Robert Louis (1886) *The Strange Case of Dr. Jekyll and Mr. Hyde*, reprint, Lincoln: University of Nebraska Press, 1990.

Veblen, Thorstein B. (1965a) *The Engineers and the Price System*, New York: Augustus M. Kelley.

—— (1937) *The Instinct of Workmanship*, New York: The Viking Press.

—— (1965b) *Higher Learning in America*, New York: Augustus M. Kelley.

—— (1904) *The Theory of Business Enterprise*, New York: Charles Scribner's Sons.

—— (1899) *The Theory of the Leisure Class*, New York: The Macmillan Company.

169

11

VEBLEN'S *THEORY OF THE LEISURE CLASS* AND THE GENESIS OF EVOLUTIONARY ECONOMICS

Geoffrey M. Hodgson[1]

In Western social science from the First World War to the 1970s, biological metaphors were rarely highlighted and the links between the socio-economic and the biotic worlds were denied (Degler, 1991; Hodgson, forthcoming). In contrast, in the late 1880s and early 1900s there was a widespread opinion that social and biological phenomena were closely related in some manner. The view was often voiced that socio-economic phenomena were explicable in purely biological terms. However, even within this orbit, contrasting views prevailed, as they did for example on the issue of whether cooperation or competition were found in nature, or were "natural" to human society.[2]

Notably, one hundred years ago, biology had a much more limited understanding of the detailed processes of evolution. For instance, there was a prolonged and unresolved controversy on the mechanisms of selection. On the one hand the Lamarckians – of whom Herbert Spencer was a prominent example – believed that the inheritance of acquired characters was a general phenomenon. Ranged against them were the Darwinians, whose position at that time was weakened for lack of a clear understanding of the nature of the "germ plasm" (or gene), and of its mechanisms of replication and transmission.

It was in this context that Thorstein Veblen made a series of contributions that established the possibility of an economics that would break from the static, teleological and individualistic limitations of preceding doctrine in that science. It is surprising, therefore, that Veblen today is often ignored as a founder of modern evolutionary economics. For example, a substantial discussion of precedents to evolutionary thinking in economics by Richard Nelson and Sidney Winter (1982, pp. 33–45) failed to mention Veblen.[3] Potted "histories" of "evolutionary economics" have praised Adam Smith,

Joseph Schumpeter, Friedrich Hayek and several others but ignored this self-proclaimed pioneer of post-Darwinian economics (Langlois and Everett, 1994).

In this essay we focus on Veblen's *Theory of the Leisure Class* (1899) and a number of key articles published during the time of writing of that work.[4] Veblen had a sophisticated understanding of biological theory and he applied its metaphor to socio-economic evolution. Despite the popularity of the *Leisure Class,* its theory of socio-economic evolution has hardly been explored by subsequent commentators. Hitherto, attention has been focused primarily on its discussion of conspicuous waste and consumption, and other related issues. Here a major theme is the theory of socio-economic evolution that Veblen developed in the 1890s. It shall be argued that in these years Veblen's thought underwent a theoretical revolution, stimulated by a number of debates in biology and social theory.

Part I of this essay discusses the genesis of Veblen's evolutionary economics and argues that it resulted from his combined interest both in Marxism and in the principles of evolutionary biology. Part II examines the theory of institutional or socio-economic evolution in Veblen's first and most famous book. It is argued that it was infused with a Darwinian understanding of the evolutionary process. Part III concludes the essay.

THE GENESIS OF VEBLEN'S EVOLUTIONARY ECONOMICS

Several authors have explored the socio-economic context of Veblen's time, including the detailed biography by Joseph Dorfman (1934). Veblen grew up in a new and rapidly changing nation. Especially after the end of the Civil War, America was rapidly becoming industrial rather than agrarian, and more urban and less rural (Mayhew, 1987). It was a time of dramatic institutional growth and change. Further, with a rapidly expanding university system, America was fertile soil for intellectual innovation and diversity.

Veblen's intellectual revolution is dated below to the years 1896–1898. Before we address the nature of that revolution it is necessary to outline in brief some of the debates and issues that impinged on Veblen's thinking up to 1896.[5] Darwin's *Origin of Species* was published in 1859 and his *Descent of Man* in 1871. This led to a widespread discussion in America and Europe concerning human origins and destiny. Although there was no consensus over the precise mechanisms involved, evolutionary biology was the science of the era. In the 1870–1914 period, biological determinism and reductionism were commonplace: it was widely believed that social progress ultimately depended on the human genetic legacy. Such ideas were common amongst both liberals and reactionaries, and led to varied political conclusions.

As Marvin Harris (1968, p. 129) and others have noted, the widespread use of the phrase 'social Darwinism" is highly misleading. In particular, in the 1870–1900 period, in both America and Europe, Charles Darwin was rivalled in standing by Herbert Spencer. To some extent, as Peter Bowler (1983, 1988) explains, Darwinism was itself in eclipse in the scientific community and in precise terms its principles had little influence, even on "evolutionist" social science (Sanderson, 1990, pp. 28–30). Trained in physics and mathematics, and being a brilliant polymath and synthesiser, Spencer made a significant contribution to nineteenth-century biology. He also extended evolutionary ideas to ethics and social science. Spencer's development of a "synthetic philosophy" led to a prolific series of volumes consisting of an ambitious and highly influential synthesis of philosophy, psychology, sociology and other disciplines.[6]

Along with many other nineteenth-century theorists, Spencer's notion of natural causation meant that explanations of social phenomena were reduced to individual and then to biological terms. His Lamarckian conception of evolution operated ultimately in terms of biological characteristics. Consequently, the speed of the underlying evolution of the human organism constrained the pace of socio-economic development. Above all, social evolution depended on "the rate of organic modification in human beings" (Spencer, 1880, p. 366). Explanations of socio-economic evolution had to be reduced ultimately to changes in the human organisms that composed the population.

Hence, in modern parlance, Spencer was a biological reductionist. Even if culture and institutions changed, according to Spencer social evolution occurred only insofar as the biological characteristics of human beings were altered. However, Spencer's acceptance of the Lamarckian principle of acquired characteristics, meant to some degree that acquired habits could be passed on *biologically* through genetic inheritance to the next generation. In the Lamarckian scheme a more rapid evolution of the human organism was thus presumed to be possible.

Veblen first read Spencer in the 1870s when he was a student at Carleton College (Dorfman, 1934, p. 30). During the 1880s, and especially during his years at Yale University, Veblen came under the influence of William Graham Sumner, a prominent advocate of Spencerian evolutionary principles in the social sciences (Dorfman, 1934, pp. 43–6; Riesman, 1963, p. 19). Like many others, Veblen was absorbed by Spencer's and Sumner's ideas of socio-economic evolution (Edgell, 1975; Edgell and Tilman, 1989; Eff, 1989; Murphree, 1959). Spencer visited Yale University in 1882, when Veblen was a postgraduate student there under Sumner's tutelage (Dorfman, 1934, p. 43).

To some degree, Veblen stood aloof from the technical controversies in biology over the possibilities or otherwise of Lamarckian-type inheritance. Initially, it was Spencer's politics that drew critical ink from his pen. Both

Spencer and Sumner were opposed to socialism. In contrast, Veblen was much more sympathetic to socialism and he rejected their laissez-faire dispositions. Significantly, an early article published by Veblen in 1892 addressed Spencer, and was "offered in the spirit of the disciple" (Veblen, 1919, p. 387). However, in this work Veblen began to reject many of Spencer's arguments, including on the question of the feasibility of socialism.[7]

Veblen took up a post at the newly-formed University of Chicago in 1892 and remained there for fourteen years. "It was in Chicago that Veblen had the most sympathetic and stimulating colleagues and where most of his best work was done" (Riesman, 1963, p. 18). There he was influenced by many thinkers, including the friend and leading biologist Jacques Loeb, from whom Veblen was informed of many up-to-date developments in biology. Loeb advocated a particularly mechanistic and reductionist version of Darwinian theory, arguing that all living phenomena could and should be ultimately explained in terms of their physical and chemical constituents. Crucially, Loeb "appears to have helped give Veblen his life-long credo that only a social science shaped in the image of post-Darwinian biology could lay claim to being 'scientific' " (ibid., p. 19). At the same time the influential biologist George Romanes insisted that Darwinism above all meant causal analysis. Instead of taxonomy and the accumulation of facts, "causes or principles are the ultimate objects of scientific quest" (Romanes, 1893, vol. 1, p. 5).[8]

Veblen had earlier been introduced to the writings of William James. The *Principles of Psychology* (1890) proved to be a permanent influence on Veblen and on a great number of thinkers at that time. Like Veblen's former teacher Charles Sanders Peirce, James was critical of Spencer, rejecting his perceived hedonistic utilitarianism in favour of an activist and reconstructive conception of human agency, founded on habits and instincts. Overall, Peirce and James sided with Darwin rather than Spencer, in part because of the deterministic and mechanistic aspects of Spencer's thought (Peirce, 1923, pp. 162–3; 1935, pp. 15–16; James, 1880). Although Peirce expressed reservations about some aspects of Darwinism, he looked favourably upon its central principles of variation and natural selection. For him, these were matters of ontology and logic. By contrast, Peirce rejected Spencer's mechanical philosophy for its failure to accommodate novelty and chance. Similarly, James saw the Darwinian principle of variation as support for a belief in the indeterminacy of the universe and the reality of human initiative. Both James and Peirce "made use of Darwin to uncover spontaneity in nature" (Russett, 1976, p. 77). Although Veblen did not embrace all the radical consequences of these philosophical arguments, there is no doubt that the ideas of James and Peirce had a formative and fundamental influence upon him, establishing Darwinism not merely as a biological but also as a philosophical and methodological creed.[9]

Several related ideas coalesced together in Veblen's examination of Marxism. While editing the Chicago-based *Journal of Political Economy*,

Veblen frequently reviewed works on socialism or Marxism.[10] He was fluent in French and German and thus open to major Continental European influences and developments. In a review of Max Lorenz's *Die Marxistische Socialdemokratie*, Veblen noted that its author (Lorenz, 1896, p. 50) had found a crucial defect in Marxian theory. Veblen wrote:

> While the materialistic interpretation of history points out how social development goes on – by a class struggle that proceeds from maladjustment between economic structure and economic function – it is nowhere pointed out what is the operative force at work in the process. It denies that human discretion and effort seeking a better adjustment can furnish such a force, since it makes man the creature of circumstances. This defect reduces itself . . . to a misconception of human nature and of man's place in the social development. The materialistic theory conceives of man as exclusively a social being, who counts in the process solely as a medium for the transmission and expression of social laws and changes; whereas he is, in fact, also an individual, acting out his own life as such. Hereby is indicated not only the weakness of the materialistic theory, but also the means of remedying the defect pointed out. With the amendment so indicated, it becomes not only a theory of the method of social and economic change, but a theory of social process considered as a substantial unfolding of life as well.
>
> (Veblen, 1897b, p. 137)

Similar criticisms of Marxism recur forcefully in later works (Veblen [1901a], 1919, pp. 313–14; [1906b], 1919, p. 416; [1907], 1919, pp. 441–2). Veblen rightly argued that the mere class position of an individual as a wage labourer or a capitalist tells us very little about the specific conceptions or habits of thought, and the likely actions, of the individuals involved. Individual interests, whatever they are, do not necessarily lead to accordant individual actions. As Veblen (1919, p. 442) pointed out, the members of the working class could perceive their own salvation just as much in terms of patriotism or nationalism as in socialist revolution. The class position of an agent – exploiter or exploited – does not imply that that person will be impelled towards any particular view of reality or any particular pattern of action. Abram Harris (1932, p. 743) later suggested that what had been identified in Marx's writings was "the weakest link in his chain of reasoning".[11]

Veblen's aforementioned "amendment" of 1897 had a number of remarkable features. In this short passage, some crucial and innovative elements of his reasoning can be detected. First, Veblen rejected the proposition that the individual is *"exclusively* a social being, who counts in the process *solely* as a medium for the transmission and expression of social laws and changes" (emphasis added). In other words, Veblen dismissed the idea that the individual's actions are explicable entirely in terms of socio-economic circumstances. Note, however, that Veblen did not replace holistic reductionism with methodological individualism, and thereby attempt to explain socio-economic phenomena exclusively in terms of individuals. In his review, Veblen did not deny that a human is "a social being" or "a medium for the transmission of social laws and changes." He simply rejected an exclusive stress on social determination, and asserted that the human agent is *"also an individual, acting out his own life as such"* (emphasis added). This suggests that humans mould their circumstances just as they are moulded by them. Accordingly, Darwinism was interpreted not narrowly in terms of individuals being selected in a fixed environment, but in an environment that is changed in its interaction with those creative individuals. As Veblen was to write a year later: "The economic life history of the individual is a cumulative process of adaptation of means to ends that cumulatively change as the process goes on, both the agent and his environment being at any point the outcome of the last process" ([1898b], 1919, pp. 74–5).

Second, in Veblen's short review there was an emphasis on the "causes and principles" which Romanes and others had earlier seen as central to Darwinism. The "materialistic" interpretation of history lacked an explanation of "the operative force at work in the process". It did not explain how social forces impel individual actors to think and act. Addressing this hiatus in his subsequent work, and in line with his criticisms of both neoclassical economics and Marxism, Veblen followed James and saw Darwinism as implying that "habit and native propensity", rather than rational calculation of material interest, motivated human beings.

Third, for Veblen in 1897, such explanations of socio-economic evolution must involve individual agents as well as institutions and structures. However, the evolution of individuality must itself be explained: "a theory of social process considered as a substantial unfolding of life as well". In subsequent articles, Veblen thus argued that utilitarian and hedonistic explanations of human behaviour had to be rejected, in part because they did not contain an evolutionary explanation of the origin of the assumed behavioural characteristics. For example, the neoclassical assumption of given preference functions side-steps an explanation of the origin and initial acquisition of those preferences. The assumption that individuals are selfish requires an explanation of the evolution of selfishness. In general, postulates about human behaviour at the socio-economic level themselves require explanation in evolutionary terms (Argyrous and Sethi, 1996). As Veblen ([1898c], 1934, p. 79) wrote with characteristic irony in a critical passage on rational "economic man":

> But if this economic man is to serve as a lay figure upon which to
> fit the garment of economic doctrines, it is incumbent upon the

science to explain what are his limitations and how he has achieved his emancipation from the law of natural selection.[12]

In place of "a passive and substantially inert and immutably given human nature", Veblen ([1898b], 1919, p. 73) saw instincts and habits as the dynamic bases of human nature. Following James and others, they were seen as the prime movers of human cognition and action, explicable in terms of both biological and socio-economic processes of evolution.

Fourth, the methodological injunction that a processual explanation of origin is required, led Veblen to conceive the individual in *both* biological and socio-economic terms. Humans are biotic as well as social beings, so their biology cannot be ignored. In contrast to both Marxism and some versions of neoclassical economics, a viable social science must be linked with biology. This is another implication of Veblen's imperative that socio-economic evolution must be regarded "as a substantial unfolding of life as well." However, in contrast to Spencer's grand synthesis, socio-economic phenomena were not seen as reducible to the biotic substratum. The "theory of the social process" had to be compatible with, but *more* than, the theory of the evolution of human life.

This leads us to another – probably decisive – influence on Veblen in the crucial years of 1896–1898. According to Dorfman (1934, p. 139), in 1896 the zoologist and philosopher C. Lloyd Morgan delivered a lecture at the University of Chicago, key points of which were later published in his book *Habit and Instinct* (1896).[13] Morgan was Professor of Geology and Zoology at the University College, Bristol, in England.[14] Dorfman does not tell us if Veblen attended this lecture or was even availed of its content, but the mention of Morgan in this context must be for no other reason than to suggest a significant direct or indirect influence. Arguably, Morgan's presence in Chicago provided a keystone in the architecture of Veblen's theory of socio-economic evolution. Although it was some years later that Veblen first referred to Morgan, it was with definite approval, showing that Veblen was familiar with Morgan's 1896 book (Veblen, 1914, p. 30 n.).[15]

Lloyd Morgan was a vigorous Darwinian. In opposition to Spencer and other Lamarckians, he contended that acquired habits are not passed on by genetic inheritance. Previously, because of gaps in the theory of natural selection, Darwin himself had flirted with Lamarckian ideas. As Bowler (1988, p. 98) put it: "Darwin himself did not deny a limited role for the inheritance of acquired characters, and he was thus able to admit that the learning of new habits by the animals themselves can play a role." However, Morgan and many other Darwinians had become more resolute in denying the possibility of such inheritance, especially after the publication of August Weismann's (1893) influential work.

This Darwinian stance created an apparent paradox: despite tremendous advances in civilisation in technology in the last few millennia, in *biotic and genetic terms* humankind had evolved only to a very slight degree. Genetically, humans had changed very little in the centuries that had witnessed enormous advances in science, technology and civilisation. To nineteenth-century intellectuals infused with ideas of biological determination, how could such a mismatch be explained?

In contrast, Lamarckian thinking denied this genetic conservatism and thus escaped the problem, by insisting on the possibility that newly acquired habits and other characteristics could readily be passed on genetically from generation to generation. Lamarckians thus saw the development of civilisation as paralleled by the rapid development of the human genotype or organism. As we have seen, Lamarckism permitted a reductionist explanation of socio-economic development in biological terms, as exemplified in Spencer's work.[16]

Rejecting Lamarckism, Morgan then asked: if human beings had evolved only slightly in genetic terms, then *what* had evolved in the last millennium or so of human society? In this period, human achievements have been transformed beyond measure. His answer to the puzzle was as follows:

> This is that evolution *has been transferred from the organism to the environment*. There must be increment somewhere, otherwise evolution is impossible. In social evolution on this view, the increment is by storage in the social environment to which each new generation adapts itself, with no increased native power of adaptation. In the written record, in social traditions, in the manifold inventions which make scientific and industrial progress possible, in the products of art, and the recorded examples of noble lives, we have an environment which is at the same time the product of mental evolution, and affords the condition of the development of each individual mind to-day. No one is likely to question the fact that this environment is undergoing steady and progressive evolution. It is not perhaps so obvious that this transference of evolution from the individual to the environment may leave the *faculty* of the race at a standstill, while the *achievements* of the race are progressing by leaps and bounds.
>
> (Morgan, 1896, p. 340)

In the Lamarckian view, socio-economic evolution proceeded by the acquisition of new habits which could then be passed on by human genetic inheritance, as well as by imitation or learning. Morgan denied that the human genetic endowment was evolving so rapidly. In opposition to Lamarckism, Morgan's Darwinian understanding of evolution led him to promote the idea of an *emergent level* of socio-economic evolution that was not explicable exclusively in terms of the biological characteristics of the individuals involved. Evolution occurred at this emergent level as well, and without any necessary change in human biotic characteristics. Accordingly, the crucial concepts of emergence and emergent properties were liberated by the Darwinian insistence of a barrier between acquired habit and biotic inheritance. The biological and the social spheres became partially autonomous, but linked, levels of analysis. In later works the philosophical concept of emergence was developed by Morgan and others influenced by him.

In Morgan's view of human evolution, the emergent level was the social environment. As this environment itself evolved, the Darwinian process of natural selection brought about slight changes in the human organism. Slow, phylogenetic evolution (that is, involving changes in the genetic material) was thus possible. However, these phylogenetic changes were too gradual to play any significant influence on social evolution itself. Nevertheless, the rapid changes in the social environment were a moving target for the *ontogenetic* development of each human individual. (In biology, ontogeny refers to the growth and development of single organisms, where the genetic material is given.) Significantly, the actual ("phenotyopic") development of any particular organism depends, additionally, on the stimulation and nutrition it receives from its environment.

For example, if a society condemned a segment of the population to strenuous labour then their physique would alter accordingly. If a society provided higher standards of education, nutrition or health care then the development or lifespan of individuals could be improved. However, none of these acquired characteristics would be transmitted to human progeny by genetic inheritance. Primarily, the reproduction and survival of the relevant "environmental" features of the socio-economic system would ensure their replication in the next generation. It is primarily the social system that would change, not significantly the human genotype. As Veblen himself later wrote, in terms redolent of Morgan:

> The typical human endowment of instincts, as well as the typical make-up of the race in the physical respect, has according to this current view been transmitted intact from the beginning of humanity. . . . On the other hand the habitual elements of human life change unremittingly and cumulatively, resulting in a continued proliferous growth of institutions. Changes in the institutional structure are continually taking place in response to the altered discipline of life under changing cultural conditions, but human nature remains specifically the same.
>
> (1914, p. 18)

However, Morgan did not make the objects and mechanisms of socio-economic evolution clear. He did not specify what the social "environment" consisted of. He did not identify the units of selection, the sources of variation and the nature of the selective process. He simply indicated the possibility of "storage in the social environment" through the written record, in social traditions, technology and art. This was, nevertheless, a highly significant point. Morgan's conception of "environmental" evolution implied that, despite change, some degree of inertia and continuity in environmental conditions was necessary, so that appropriate ontogenetic development could occur. In short, the means of preservation of information were necessary for learning. It was left to Veblen to make the crucial next step: institutions rather than individuals became the objects of selection in socio-economic evolution.[17]

Not being himself a biologist, and despite his extensive knowledge of biology, Veblen was too careful to commit himself in the ongoing debate over Lamarckism. Whether acquired characteristics could be inherited or not was in part an empirical question, to be answered by the biologists. These issues were far from resolution in the biology of the 1890s; too little was understood of the mechanisms of genetic inheritance. Veblen did not wish to build his theory on what might be shifting scientific sands, and he took from Darwin what he regarded to be most decisive and enduring: above all his methodological approach.

Morgan's argument directed attention to the phenomenon of socio-economic evolution, and gave it a degree of autonomy from the question of biological inheritance. With Morgan's intervention, the scene was set for Veblen's intellectual revolution: the concept of the evolution and selection of institutions, as emergent entities in the socio-economic sphere. The history of institutional economics is full of strange twists and turns. Its unintended and unacknowledged intellectual paternity, resulting from the ejaculations of a relatively obscure philosopher of biology of Welsh descent while on a foreign tour, is indeed one of the most curious.

It is thus perhaps no accident that shortly after Morgan's visit to Chicago the idea of an evolutionary process of selection of institutions began to appear in Veblen's work. Seemingly, its first appearance in his writings was in yet another book review. Veblen saw in Antonio Labriola's evolutionist Marxism the doctrine that the "economic exigencies" of the industrial process "afford the definitive test of fitness in the adaptation of all human institutions by a process of selective elimination of the economically unfit" (1897a, p. 390).

For Veblen, the institutional structure of society was not merely "the environment", as Morgan had put it. In this quotation Veblen indicated that it consisted of institutional elements that were themselves, like organisms, subject to evolutionary processes of selection. It is also at this time that Veblen began to produce and publish a remarkable series of articles – lasting until 1909 – mostly in the *Quarterly Journal of Economics*, the *American Journal of Sociology* and the *Journal of Political Economy*.[18]

One of the earliest and most important in this series was the 1898 essay "Why is economics not an evolutionary science?" Therein Veblen assembled his critique of neoclassical economics, recognising its central defect of an "immutably given human nature" (Veblen ([1898b], 1919, p. 73). The requirement of an evolutionary explanation of origin obliges us to abandon the assumption of the given individual: "The economic life history of the individual is a cumulative process of adaptation of means to ends that cumulatively change as the process goes on, both the agent and his environment being at any point the outcome of the last process." (Veblen [1898b], 1919, pp. 74–5).

Veblen then nailed his own theses to the church door: "an evolutionary economics must be a theory of a process of cultural growth as determined by the economic interest, a theory of a cumulative sequence of economic institutions stated in terms of the process itself" ([1898b], 1919, p. 77). This was not all that is contained in *The Theory of the Leisure Class,* but it was essentially its core theoretical project. What was also significant was that Veblen did not accept that culture could be or had to be explained in biological terms. As he was to write a few years later:

> If . . . men universally acted not on the conventional grounds and values afforded by the fabric of institutions, but solely and directly on the grounds and values afforded by the unconventionalised propensities and aptitudes of hereditary human nature, then there would be no institutions and no culture.
>
> (Veblen, 1909, p. 300)

Veblen thus suggested that if socio-economic phenomena were determined exclusively by biological factors then the concepts of institution and culture would be redundant. Culture and institutions are irreducible to biological factors alone. Consistent with this interpretation, the concepts of cultural and institutional evolution were developed in *The Theory of the Leisure Class*.[19]

THE THEORY OF THE LEISURE CLASS

Throughout the *Leisure Class*, Veblen grappled with the problem of the relationship between actor and structure. This is indeed the central problem of all social science. As we have seen, Veblen's critique of Marxism was prompted by its apparent overemphasis on the structural determination of individual agency. Veblen's attempted solution to this problem was to conceive of both agency and structure as a result of an evolutionary process. Thus he wrote: "As a matter of selective necessity, man is an agent. He is, in his own apprehension, a centre of unfolding impulsive activity – 'teleological' activity. He is an agent seeking in every act the accomplishment of some concrete, objective, impersonal end" (Veblen, 1899, p. 15). Human purposeful behaviour was a result of evolution itself.

We have noted that Veblen did not commit himself to one side or the other in the debates in biology concerning the possibility or otherwise of the Lamarckian inheritance of acquired characteristics. He did not regard the theses in the *Leisure Class* to be seriously affected by the outcome of the controversy. Thus he wrote:

> Under the guidance of the later biological and psychological science, human nature will have to be restated in terms of habit. . . . The point is not seriously affected by any question as to whether it was a process of habituation in the old-fashioned sense of the word or a process of selective adaptation of the race.
>
> (Veblen, 1899, p. 221)

His openness to possibilities on this question of theoretical biology is evident in another passage in the same work: "class difference in temperament may be due in part to a difference in the inheritance of acquired traits" (Veblen, 1899, p. 248).

It was not until 1901 that the Dutch biologist Hugo De Vries began to publish works explaining the significance of the genetics of Gregor Mendel and proposing a "mutation theory" based upon it. His work caused a stir, and was welcomed with enthusiasm by Veblen's Chicago colleague, Loeb. The rediscovery of Mendelian genetics was eventually to lead to the modern neo-Darwinian synthesis in biology and the victory of the Darwinians over the Lamarckians. But this did not occur until the 1940s, long after Veblen's death. And it was not until 1910 – after his departure from Chicago – that Veblen started work on a paper which incorporated some of De Vries's ideas.[20] Accordingly, the work of neither Mendel nor De Vries played a significant part in the Veblenian revolution of 1896–8.

However, at least from the late 1890s, Veblen was not indifferent between Darwin and Lamarck. Following Romanes, Veblen inclined to Darwinism on methodological grounds. Because Darwin "set to work to explain species in terms of the process out of which they have arisen, rather than out of the prime cause to which the distinction between them may be due", Veblen (1904, p. 369) judged Darwin to be superior to Lamarck. What Darwin had tried to do, albeit without complete success, was to provide a processual explanation of the origin of species where the causal mechanisms involved were fully specified. Although Darwin's "results, as well as his specific determination of the factors at work in this process of cumulative change, have been questioned . . . the scope and method given to scientific enquiry by Darwin . . . has substantially not been questioned" (Veblen, 1904, p. 370).

Darwin rejected religious and teleological explanations of origin or destiny. Veblen rejected them too, while attempting to leave an obscure place for "teleology" in human purposeful behaviour.[21] He interpreted Darwinism as essentially a causal analysis of process, referring in 1906 to "an interpretation in terms of opaque cause and effect" which "might have led to a concept of evolution similar to the unteleological Darwinian concept of natural selection" (Veblen, 1919, p. 416). As he wrote in the subsequent year: "in the Darwinian scheme of thought, the continuity sought in and imputed to the facts is a continuity of cause and effect" (Veblen, 1919, p. 436). While Lamarckian theory lacked an explanation of why organisms produce varied responses to environmental stimuli, Veblen insisted that such purposeful behaviour had itself emerged through evolutionary selection. As he wrote in 1898:

> Like other animals, man is an agent that acts in response to stimuli afforded by the environment in which he lives. Like other species, he is a creature of habit and propensity. But in a higher degree than other species, man mentally digests the content of habits under whose guidance he acts, and appreciates the trend of these habits and propensities. . . . By selective necessity he is endowed with a proclivity for purposeful action. . . . He acts under the guidance of propensities which have been imposed upon him by the process of selection to which he owes his differentiation from other species.
>
> (Veblen [1898c], 1934, pp. 80–5)

Although an advance on both holistic determinism and on conventional Marxism, Veblen's solution was incomplete. As discussed elsewhere (J. Campbell, 1985; Hodgson, 1993, ch. 14) the question of agency remains problematic within a conventional evolutionary framework. Nevertheless, a more complete answer must be able to address the question of the evolution of agency, as Veblen had suggested. Veblen's own attempt to resolve the problem was to see agency and purpose as real, and somehow the result of the causal processes of evolution itself. Having established this point, in the *Leisure Class* Veblen went on immediately to reveal the celebrated "instinct of workmanship":

> By force of his being such an agent he is possessed of a taste for effective work, and a distaste for futile effort. He has a sense of the merit of serviceability or efficiency and of the demerit of futility, waste, or incapacity. This aptitude or propensity may be called the instinct of workmanship.
>
> (Veblen, 1899, p. 15)

Veblen asserted that if normative judgements have to be made, it is upon here that they must be grounded. For Veblen: "Institutions are judged on the basis of their compatibility with the instincts" (Rutherford, 1984, p. 333). The instinct of workmanship "is the court of final appeal in any question of economic truth or adequacy" (Veblen, 1899, p. 99).

Despite their internal limitations and problems, and as argued elsewhere (Hodgson, 1992; 1993, ch. 9), Veblen's writings constitute the first case of an evolutionary economics along Darwinian lines.[22] In the present essay this contention shall be evaluated by use of quotations from the *Leisure Class*. In writings appearing within a year or two of that work, Veblen clarified what he meant by an "evolutionary" or "post-Darwinian" approach. "The prime postulate of evolutionary science . . . is the notion of a cumulative causal sequence," he wrote. In addition, such a science must address "the conditions of variational growth" (Veblen [1900], 1919, pp. 176–7). He saw a "Darwinistic account" in economics as addressing "the origin, growth, persistence, and variation of institutions" (Veblen [1901b], 1919, p. 265).

The Darwinian character of the *Leisure Class* can be addressed in part by considering what are widely accepted today as the three main Darwinian evolutionary principles. First, there must be sustained variation among the members of a species or population. Variations may be blind, random, or purposive in character, but without them, as Darwin insisted, natural selection cannot operate. This is the principle of variation. Second, there must be some principle of heredity or continuity, through which offspring have to resemble their parents more than they resemble other members of their species. In other words, there has to be some mechanism through which individual characteristics are passed on through the generations. Third, natural selection itself operates either because better-adapted organisms leave increased numbers of offspring, or because the variations or gene combinations that are preserved are those bestowing advantage in struggling to survive. This is the principle of the struggle for existence. Consider these three features in turn.

First, there is no clear theory of the source of socio-economic variations in the *Leisure Class*, but it is clear that for Veblen the explanation of their origin was important. Thus Veblen wrote:

> Conspicuous wastefulness does not directly afford ground for variation and growth. . . . The law of conspicuous waste does not account for the origin of variations, but only for the persistence of such forms as are fit to survive under its dominance.
>
> (1899, p. 166)

Veblen (1899, p. 217) also referred to "a selection between the predatory and the peaceable variants". This indicated that for Veblen, and in conformity with Darwin, variation exists *prior* to evolutionary selection. Hence in the *Leisure Class* Veblen recognised the importance of the key Darwinian principle of variation but did not explore it fully. It was later, principally in the *Instinct of Workmanship*, that the principle of "idle curiosity" became a major ongoing source of variety or mutation in Veblen's conception of the evolutionary process.[23]

Second, it is clear from the *Leisure Class* that the institution was regarded as the unit of relative stability and continuity through time, ensuring that much of the pattern and variety is passed on from one period to the next. Veblen wrote that:

> The institutions – that is to say the habits of thought – under the guidance of which men live are in this way received from an earlier time; more or less remotely earlier, but in any event they have been elaborated in and received from the past. Institutions are products of the past process, are adapted to past circumstances, and are therefore never in full accord with the requirements of the present. . . . At the same time, men's present habits of thought tend to persist indefinitely, except as circumstances enforce a change. These institutions which have so been handed down, these habits of thought, points of view, mental attitudes and aptitudes, or what not, are therefore themselves a conservative factor. This is the factor of social inertia, psychological inertia, conservatism.
>
> (1899, p. 191)

In addition:

> Any change in men's views as to what is good and right in human life makes its way but tardily at the best. Especially is this true of any change in the direction of what is called progress; that is to say, in the direction of divergence from the archaic position – from the position which may be accounted the point of departure at any step in the social evolution of the community. Retrogression, reapproach to a standpoint to which the race has been long habituated in the past, is easier.
>
> (1899, p. 196)

The relative stability and durability of institutions made them, for Veblen, key objects of evolutionary selection in the socio-economic sphere.

Third, now turning to the principle of selection, it must first be noted that the phrase "natural selection" made a sparse appearance in the *Leisure Class* and in subsequent works by Veblen. However, its appearance in the *Leisure Class* was extremely significant and played a crucial role in Veblen's argument. In a key passage, Veblen wrote:

> The life of man in society, just like the life of other species, is a struggle for existence, and therefore it is a process of selective adaptation. The evolution of social structure has been a process of natural selection of institutions. The progress which has been and is being made in human institutions and in human character

may be set down, broadly, to a natural selection of the fittest habits of thought and to a process of enforced adaptation of individuals to an environment which has progressively changed with the growth of community and with the changing institutions under which men have lived. Institutions are not only themselves the result of a selective and adaptive process which shapes the prevailing or dominant types of spiritual attitude and aptitudes; they are at the same time special methods of life and human relations, and are therefore in their turn efficient factors of selection. So that the changing institutions in their turn make for a further selection of individuals endowed with the fittest temperament, and a further adaptation of individual temperament and habits to the changing environment through the formation of new institutions.

(1899, p. 188)

It was no accident that Darwin's phrases "natural selection" and "struggle for existence" appeared here. Veblen (1899, p. 207) wrote also of "the law of natural selection, as applied to human institutions". Clearly, for Veblen, the objects of socio-economic, evolutionary selection were habits and institutions. There is thus transparent evidence in the *Leisure Class* that he embraced the three Darwinian principles outlined above.

However, can the relatively infrequent appearance of the words "natural selection" undermine the claim that Veblen was principally an evolutionary economist in a Darwinian genre? The answer must be no, for several reasons. In the first place, irrespective of the frequency of this phrase, Veblen's adoption of the three Darwinian principles in the context of socio-economic evolution was a key event in the history of economic thought. It has been argued at length elsewhere (Hodgson, 1993) that there is no precedent in economic science. In addition – discounting mere repetition of Veblen's own ideas by his followers – it should be noted that it is not until well after the Second World War that Darwinian ideas independently make a sporadic and often imperfectly formulated reappearance in that discipline (Alchian, 1950; Boulding, 1981; Hayek, 1967; Nelson and Winter, 1982). More than half a century passed before Veblen's adoption of Darwinian principles in economics was rivalled.

Furthermore, although the phrase "natural selection" is infrequent, references to an evolutionary concept of selection or selective processes, consistent with Darwinian principles, are abundant in Veblen's writings, including the *Leisure Class*. Confining ourselves to that work alone, here are some additional, confirmatory examples:

A cumulative process of selective adaptation . . . will set in

(p. 13)

As the population increases in density, and as human relations grow more complex and numerous, all the details of life undergo a process of elaboration and selection

(p. 44)

The utility of consumption . . . is an adaptation to a new end, by a selective process

(p. 69)

The situation of today shapes the institutions of tomorrow through a selective, coercive process, by acting upon men's habitual view of things

(p. 190)

In the nature of the case this process of selective adaptation can never catch up with the progressively changing situation in which the community finds itself at any given time; for the environment, the situation, the exigencies of life which enforce the adaptation and exercise the selection, change from day to day; and each successive situation of the community in its turn tends to obsolescence as soon as it has been established.

(p. 191)

There is a cumulative growth of customs and habits of thought; a selective adaptation of conventions and methods of life.

(p. 208)

selective surveillance over the development of men's aptitudes and inclinations. The effect is wrought partly by a coercive, educational adaptation of the habits of all individuals, partly by a selective elimination of the unfit individuals and lines of descent.

(p. 212)

selectively conserving certain traits. . . . Social evolution is a process of selective adaptation of temperament and habits of thought under the stress of the circumstances of associated life. The adaptation of habits of thought is the growth of institutions. . . . a process of selection . . . a selective process . . .

(pp. 213–14)

a selection between stable ethnic types . . . a selection between the predatory and the peaceable variants . . . these concepts of selective adaptation

(p. 217)

probably a result of selection

(p. 225)

by selectively repressing and eliminating those individuals and lines of descent that are unfit

(p. 229)

the educative and selective action of the industrial process

(p. 233)

kept up by a continual selective process. .... This process of selective admission. ... But the precise ground of selection has not always been the same, and the selective process has therefore not always given the same results. .... The ground for selection has changed. ... The training and the selection. ... Life in a modern industrial community ... acts by a process of selection to develop and conserve a certain range of aptitudes and propensities. ... the objective point of the selective process. ... So far as regards the selective conservation of capacities or aptitudes in individuals, these two lines may be called the pecuniary and the industrial.

(pp. 235–9)

Wherever the pecuniary culture prevails, the selective process by which men's habits of thought are shaped, and by which the survival of rival lines of descent is decided, proceeds proximately on the basis of fitness for acquisition. Consequently, if it were not for the fact that pecuniary efficiency is on the whole incompatible with industrial efficiency, the selective action of all occupations would tend to the unmitigated dominance of the pecuniary temperament.

(p. 241)

There is, therefore, a continued selective sifting of the human material that makes up the leisure class, and this selection proceeds on the grounds of fitness for pecuniary pursuits. ... the scheme of life, of conventions, acts selectively and by education to shape the human material

(p. 246)

the trend of the selective process

(p. 319)

This evidence – along with the many other uses of the Darwinian principle of selection in Veblen's other writings – must be considered as decisive. It favours a predominantly Darwinian interpretation of Veblen's work, and in accord with the earlier analyses of Joseph Dorfman (1934), Abram Harris (1934), Forest Hill (1958), Richard Hofstadter (1959), Cynthia Russett (1976), Idus Murphree (1959), Stephen Edgell and Rick Tilman (1989) and many others. It must be emphasised, however, that Veblen's Darwinian economics did not involve the assertion that economic evolution can or must be reduced substantially to biological terms.

It remains merely to be considered why Veblen did not frequently choose to attach the adjective "natural" to the abundant instances of "selection" or "selection process" in his work. He gives no reason but it is not difficult to surmise several. First, and most obviously, Veblen was concerned with the evolution of society, and not of the non-human, natural world. As his attention was directed at society rather than nature, the term "natural" was dropped. Second, the "natural selection" of institutions could be misinterpreted by the reader in terms of "nature" doing the selecting, or that the selection was taking place according to "natural" rather than economic or other social criteria. Dropping the word "natural" would avoid such a misconception. Third, Veblen followed C. Lloyd Morgan and – without using the philosophical term – saw the socio-economic realm as an emergent sphere, irreducible to biological factors alone. Veblen may have avoided using the phrase "natural selection" because it would have linked his theory of socio-economic evolution to those of Spencer and Sumner who had reduced social evolution to natural and biological factors alone. Fourth, economists and others who advocated a "natural" order, or "natural rights", were the persistent objects of Veblen's devastating criticism (e.g. 1914, pp. 258–60, 289–98, 340–3; 1919, pp. 37, 154, 186–202, 280–3, 444; 1934, pp. 33–4). Resistance to the likely interpretations of the word "natural" as "normal" or "predestined" could have led to the rejection of the term, especially when the word "selection" on its own would do. There are thus abundant reasons to explain Veblen's more frequent use of the word "selection" rather than "natural selection" in a Darwinian context. Hence the marginalisation of the word "natural" in his writing should not be taken to imply that Veblen lost any of his Darwinian inspiration.

One of the striking features of the *Theory of the Leisure Class* was its articulation of a relationship between the biological nature of human beings and socio-economic evolution. On the basis of Darwinian imperatives, human beings were attributed with particular traits, the most "ancient and ingrained" of which are "those habits that touch on his existence as an organism" (p. 107). In addition: "With the exception of the instinct of self-preservation, the propensity for emulation is probably the strongest and most alert and persistent of the economic motives proper" (p. 110). On such assumptions concerning human nature, Veblen built his inspirational account of the runaway process of status emulation in modern society.[24] Even Veblen's notion of "conspicuous waste" has strong parallels throughout the natural world, in the evolution of many examples of "costly" signalling between animals, including elaborate mating behaviours, conspicuous plumage, and the celebrated case of the peacock's tail.[25]

Emphatically, and to repeat, this did not mean that everything was reduced to biology. For Veblen, evolution also took place at the socio-economic level, involving important mechanisms and processes that could not be reduced to, nor explained in, biological terms. Nevertheless, Veblen recognised that the account of socio-economic evolution had to be consistent with that pertaining to biological evolution. For him it also involved a liberal transfer of Darwinian metaphors.[26]

However, while Veblen generally saw institutions as units of selection in a process of economic evolution, he did not make the context or criteria of selection entirely clear. Some of the most pregnant passages in this general theoretical regard are on pages 188–98 of the *Leisure Class*. Prompted by the notion that the social "environment"[27] itself evolves, Veblen moved towards, but did not complete, a causal analysis of that evolutionary process. Insofar as an analysis exists, we have to impute it from passages such as the following:

> Institutions are products of the past process, are adapted to past circumstances, and are therefore never in full accord with the requirements of the present. In the nature of the case this process of selective adaptation can never catch up with the progressively changing situation in which the community finds itself at any given time; for the environment, the situation, the exigencies of life which enforce the adaptation and exercise the selection, change from day to day; and each successive situation of the community in its turn tends to obsolescence as soon as it has been established. When a step in the development has been taken, this step itself constitutes a change of situation which requires a new adaptation; it becomes the point of departure for a new step in the adjustment, and so on interminably.
>
> (Veblen, 1899, p. 191)

This clearly suggests a process of imperfect institutional adjustment and cultural lag, in which institutions forever adjust towards "the progressively changing situation". The meaning of the latter is not made entirely clear, however. Did Veblen have a hierarchical conception, in which lower-level institutions are selected and adjusted in the context of a changing social structure? If so, the driving changes in that structure would themselves have to be explained. Alternatively, Veblen could have had in mind a process in which each individual institution was selected or adjusted in the context of the ensemble of all other institutions: a cumulative, bootstrapping process of each institution against the others, in which as a result all of them progressively evolve. The following passage could seemingly be interpreted in either terms:

Social advance, especially as seen from the point of view of economic theory, consists in a continued progressive approach to an approximately exact "adjustment of inner relations to outer relations"; but this adjustment is never definitely established since the "outer relations" are subject to constant change as a consequence of the progressive change going on in the "inner relations."

(Veblen, 1899, p. 192)

Despite a lack of analysis of the precise mechanisms, Veblen was clearly attempting to move towards a general theory of institutional evolution. Although he made remarkable progress in this direction after establishing the notion of "the natural selection of institutions", he did not complete the task. Russett's perceptive verdict was thus apposite:

If Veblen failed to develop an evolutionary methodology, he also failed to develop a comprehensive evolutionary theory to explain in detail how institutions evolve in the cultural environment and what sorts of interaction occur between economic activity and institutional structures. Veblen was something of an intellectual butterfly, and he often lacked the patience to elaborate his ideas into a coherent system. But he teemed with fragmentary insights, and these can be pieced together to suggest the outlines of a Veblenian scheme of cultural evolution – what might be called a "pre-theory" of cultural change.

(1976, p. 153)

The challenge for institutional and evolutionary economists was to complete this task along the lines suggested by Veblen. One hundred years after the publication of the *Leisure Class* this challenge still remains.

CONCLUSION

Veblen's *Theory of the Leisure Class* achieved fame and popularity shortly after its publication. This was, as John Hobson (1939, p. 16) noted, "chiefly due to its satirical commentary upon the upper classes" rather than to its scientific content. Yet Veblen always meant the work to be appreciated as a contribution to social and economic theory, as its original subtitle *An Economic Study in the Evolution of Institutions* suggests.[28] This aspect of the work has received insufficient attention, in part because of a failure of many commentators to appreciate the intellectual environment of the 1890s and thereby the substance and stature of Veblen's intellectual achievement.

It is argued here that Veblen's book was the consummation of a revolution that took place in Veblen's thinking in the years 1896–8. It is possible to trace several key influences. Despite the pre-eminent influence of Spencer at the time, Veblen gravitated towards Darwin. During the 1890s, Veblen became increasingly disenchanted with Spencerian and other forms of biological determinism and reductionism. But, for Veblen, biological determinism and reductionism were not the only issues. For Veblen, the Darwinian rejection of teleology became the basis of a scientific and "post-Darwinian" approach to economics and social science. Like the later German historical school of Gustav Schmoller and others, ideas of historical laws of development and progress were rejected. The exclusion of teleology meant not only the rejection of Spencerian and other notions of mechanical progress towards perfection, but also the displacement of both neoclassical equilibrium theorising and Marxian historicism.

In addition, although sympathetic to socialism, Veblen became increasingly disenchanted with the Marxian treatment of the problem of human agency, especially after reading a critical work on Marxism published by Max Lorenz in 1896. Veblen's 1897 review of the book by Lorenz indicates a novel line of thinking. First, Veblen rejected the idea that the actions of an individual can be explained entirely in terms of social, economic, cultural or other related circumstances. Second, he emphasised the need to have a detailed explanation of the causal processes behind human action. Third, he held that such explanations of socio-economic evolution must involve individual agents as well as institutions and structures. However, the evolution of individuality had itself to be explained. Accordingly, utilitarian and hedonistic models of human behaviour were rejected in part because they lacked an evolutionary explanation of the origin of such behaviours.

In rejecting both the individual and society as the ultimate unit of explanation, Veblen thus distanced himself from both the extremes of methodological individualism and methodological holism, instead embracing an evolutionary framework of explanation along Darwinian lines. What Veblen needed at that stage was a framework of concepts that would support his attempt to build a social theory that did not fall into the traps of biological, individualistic, or holistic reductionism.

There is strong circumstantial evidence that the crucial – but hitherto largely unacknowledged – influence came during or immediately after the visit to Chicago by the British biologist and philosopher C. Lloyd Morgan. (Rick Tilman, 1996, provides a notable exception.) A Darwinian opponent of the Lamarckian theory of biological inheritance, Morgan argued that it was not human individuals that had "evolved" significantly in the last few centuries, but their social environment: "the increment is by storage in the social environment to which each new generation adapts itself . . . this transference of evolution from the individual to the environment may leave the *faculty* of the race at a standstill, while the *achievements* of the race are progressing by leaps and bounds" (Morgan, 1896, p. 340).

Significantly, one year after Morgan's visit to Chicago, the idea of an evolutionary process of selection of institutions first appeared in Veblen's (1897a, p. 390) work. It is also at this time that Veblen switched his primary inclination from reading and reviewing books, to the writing and publication of a remarkable series of creative academic articles. He became much less a commentator and more an innovator. His *Theory of the Leisure Class* was the most substantial product of this period. Institutional economics was thus born.

NOTES

1 The author wishes to thank Hella Hoppe for valuable assistance in drafting this paper and Malcolm Rutherford for discussions. Early sections make use of material from Hodgson (1998).

2 For example, Kropotkin (1902) and Reinheimer (1913) both argued that cooperation rather than competition was prevalent in nature.

3 Note that Nelson and Winter have since recognised that Veblen was a founder of "evolutionary economics" (Nelson, 1995, p. 85; Winter, 1990, p. 271).

4 According to Dorfman (1934, p. 132) the writing of the *Leisure Class* was under way by late 1895.

5 For an overview of several of Veblen's intellectual ancedents, including Kant, Darwin, Spencer, Sumner, Peirce, James, Bellamy, Marx, Schmoller, Tylor, Lewis Morgan and others, see Edgell and Tilman (1989).

6 Another leading economist who came under Spencer's spell was Alfred Marshall (1975, vol. 1, p. 109) who recollected how 'a saying of Spencer sent the blood rushing through the veins of those who a generation ago looked eagerly for each volume of his as it issued from the press.'

7 In later writings Veblen went further in his critique of Spencer. For instance he noted the incompatibility between Spencer's atomistic individualism and a genuinely evolutionary and 'post-Darwinian' conception of socio-economic change (Veblen [1908], 1919, p. 192n). See Hodgson (1993, pp. 127–8).

8 A severe problem of inadequate causal explanation in Lamarckian theory has been highlighted by D. Campbell (1965, 1975). Lamarckian evolution presumes that organisms produce varied responses to environmental stimuli. However, where do the rules that guide the variation in behaviour come from? What inclines the organism to do one thing rather than another? Darwinism attempts an answer to the causal question in terms of genetic mutation or recombination producing new behaviours. Lamarckism lacks such an answer. Campbell contends that the improving rule that promotes new variety in response to the environment has to come from somewhere. Accordingly, Lamarckism may at bottom require a Darwinian explanation. Lamarckism is thus subsumed by Darwinism.

9 Note that the significant influence on Veblen of the psychologist and philosopher William McDougall came later, after the publication of his classic work (McDougall, 1908). Despite later and imputed associations – by Clarence Ayres and others – there is no clear evidence of the influence of John Dewey's psychology or philosophy on Veblen, at least in these early years (Tilman, 1996).

10 The nature and subject matter of Veblen's publications in the period betray his preoccupation with socialist literature. According to the bibliographical list

in Dorfman (1934, pp. 519ff), Veblen published a total of 21 items in the years 1893–1897 inclusive. No less than 17 of these were book reviews. In turn, 11 of these 17 were reviews of books concerned primarily with socialism or Marxism. For details see the appendix below. Incidentally, it is very doubtful if an output of this nature, preoccupation and orientation would be sufficient for Veblen to gain tenure in any department of any research-oriented university in the late twentieth century, despite the fact that Veblen's work in those five years led directly to a tremendous intellectual revolution in economics and social science.

11 Although Lorenz's remarks and Veblen's critique apply most of all to the less sophisticated Marxism found around the end of the nineteenth century, Marx himself lacked an adequate theory of human agency. For a more extensive discussion of Veblen's identification of this "weakest link" in Marx's reasoning, see Hodgson (1996, pp. 406–11).

12 Strikingly, modern evolutionary psychology confirms and elaborates this argument. The literature in this area (Cosmides and Tooby, 1994a, 1993b; Plotkin, 1994; Reber, 1993) gives strong support to the ideas of James, Veblen and others concerning the primacy of habits. The key argument in this modern literature is that postulates concerning the rational capacities of the human brain must give an explanation of their evolution according to established Darwinian principles of evolutionary biology.

13 Lloyd Morgan should not be confused with Lewis Henry Morgan, the famous nineteenth-century anthropologist who greatly influenced both Veblen and Frederick Engels.

14 University College, Bristol became the University of Bristol in 1909, and Morgan remained a fixture of that institution for his entire life. In his later career, Morgan turned increasingly to philosophical issues and was a pioneer of the modern philosophical concept of emergence (Morgan, 1927, 1933). In fact it was he that coined the term. For this reason he is remembered by modern philosophers of biology such as Mayr (1985). His work also influenced Whitehead (1926, p. xxiii) and McDougall (1929, pp. 240-8) among others.

15 The likely influence of Morgan on Veblen in the late 1890s may be detected in the following quotation from the *Leisure Class,* which refers to: 'a process of enforced adaptation of individuals to an environment which has progressively changed ... with the changing institutions under which men have lived. Institutions are not only themselves the result of a selective and adaptive process which shapes the prevailing or dominant types of spiritual attitude and aptitudes; they are ... in their turn efficient factors of selection' (Veblen, 1899, p. 188). Other relevant passages include Veblen (1899, pp. 190–2, 220; 1914, p. 18). These should be compared with Morgan (1896, p. 340) quoted on p. 177 above. However, without any explicit mention of Morgan by Veblen in the 1890s, this evidence is not decisive. What is clear is that from 1897 – in his review of Labriola's book quoted on p. 179 above – and in subsequent writings, Veblen made institutions the objects of selection in socio-economic evolution. This dating is consistent with the presumed effect of Morgan's pronouncements in Chicago in 1896.

16 Later evolutionary social scientists, such as Nelson and Winter (1982) and Hayek (1988), have noted that acquired habits, rules and routines can be passed on and replicated by imitation. Accordingly, something like the Lamarckian inheritance of acquired characters has been seen as possible in the socio-economic domain. However, such an analogy with Lamarckian biology does not necessarily imply the adoption of Lamarckian principles in the biological sphere. Modern biology itself admits the possibility of processes that resemble

Lamarckian transmission at higher levels of abstraction, but do not involve the inheritance of acquired characters at the genetic level (for example, Mayr, 1960; Waddington, 1976). Incidentally, some of these biological ideas were foreshadowed by Morgan (1896, ch. 14) himself.

17 Note the similarity here with modern "dual inheritance" theories of evolution, involving transmission at both the genetic and cultural levels (Boyd and Richerson, 1985; Durham, 1991). Durham gives some interesting special examples of relatively rapid evolution of some limited human traits – such as the development of lactose tolerance since the beginnings of agriculture 6,000 years ago.

18 These essays are collected together in two volumes (Veblen, 1919, 1934).

19 The writing of the *Leisure Class* was well under way when Veblen (1898a) critically reviewed William Mallock's *Aristocracy and Evolution*. While there is much discussion by Mallock of "the pecuniary incentive", Veblen was more optimistic than Mallock concerning the possibility of societies in which forms of non-pecuniary emulation would be pre-eminent. Veblen also uses the opportunity of this review to explore some of the ideas that were to be published in his book in the following year (Dorfman, 1934, pp. 148–9).

20 Dorfman (1934, p. 295). This paper was published three years later (Veblen, 1913). Veblen also refers to Mendelian genetics in subsequent works (1914, pp. 21–5, 69; 1915, pp. 277–8).

21 While Veblen consistently regarded the human agent as purposeful, he never reconciled the notion of purposeful behaviour with mechanical causality: of the Aristotelian "final" and "efficient" types of cause. While "vitalists" such as McDougall (1908) pulled in one direction and resisted the reduction of all causality to mechanism alone, the close and persistent influence of the materialistic scientist Loeb pulled on Veblen in the other direction, towards mechanistic reductionism. It is thus with some justice that Seckler (1975, p. 56) argued that Veblen "teeters between free will and determinism". However, it would be a mistake to suggest that Veblen denied the reality of purposeful behaviour. On the contrary, he emphasised it repeatedly.

22 Several possible prior claimants are considered and rejected in Hodgson (1993). For instance, Carl Menger's work is seen as lacking a full, phylogenetic conception of evolutionary selection. Alfred Marshall's inspiration is seen as coming largely from Spencer rather than Darwin.

23 One of the earliest references to "idle curiosity" is in Veblen ([1906a], 1919, p. 7). See also Veblen (1914, pp. 85–9). Dyer (1986) argued convincingly that Veblen's crucial inspiration for the concept was Peirce's concept of "musement".

24 Note the striking and independent rediscovery of this idea by Boyd and Richerson (1985, pp. 213–40, 286). Without any apparent knowledge of the Veblenian precedent, Boyd and Richerson stressed the adaptive advantages of conformism and described a similarly cumulative process of conformism.

25 Modern biology elaborates mechanisms, by which "costly" signalling between animals may evolve through natural selection, that are strikingly redolent of Veblen's theory of "conspicuous waste". It has been long observed that many species make use of "signalling" to indicate, for example, fitness and an availability to mate. However, the question was raised as to what would prevent low-fitness individuals "cheating" and reproducing, by replicating such signals. Zahavi (1987) and others showed that a signal could provide reliable information about the "quality" of signallers, even in the face of a conflict of interest between signaller and receiver, provided that it was costly to produce. This idea, referred to as the "handicap principle", is that a low-fitness individual would not make use of the signal because the costs involved would exceed the benefits gained.

In these circumstances, those able to produce "conspicuous waste" would thus have an advantage.

26 For recent discussions of the role of biological and other metaphors in economics and other sciences see Hodgson (1993), Maasen *et al.* (1995) and Mirowski (1994).

27 The word is used frequently by Veblen, as if he were echoing C. Lloyd Morgan.

28 In later reprints the subtitle was shortened to *An Economic Study of Institutions*. Contrary to Dorfman (1934, p. 323) this change was made earlier than 1912. A 1908 edition in the possession of the present author has the shorter subtitle. Dorfman suggests, somewhat unconvincingly, that the change was to remove the confusion that the *Leisure Class* was "concerned with the genealogical pedigree of institutions rather than with the present-day functioning of business enterprise, of modern capital". Another possible reason for the alteration was the growing public and academic opinion that social science should be distanced from all biological and evolutionary notions (Degler, 1991; Sanderson, 1990). It is also not clear whether Veblen or his publisher originally suggested the change.

APPENDIX: PUBLICATIONS BY VEBLEN UP TO 1899

1882 "J. S. Mill's Theory of the Taxation of Land", Johns Hopkins University, *University Circulars*, February, p. 176.

1884 "Kant's Critique of Judgment", *Journal of Speculative Philosophy*, July, pp. 260–74. Reprinted in Veblen (1934).

1892 "Böhm-Bawerk's Definition of Capital and the Source of Wages", *Quarterly Journal of Economics,* January, pp. 247–52. Reprinted in Veblen (1934).
" 'The Overproduction Fallacy' ", *Quarterly Journal of Economics*, July, pp. 484–92. Reprinted in Veblen (1934).
"Some Neglected Points in the Theory of Socialism", *Annals of the American Academy of Political and Social Science*, November, pp. 345–62. Reprinted in Veblen (1919).
"The Price of Wheat Since 1867", *Journal of Political Economy*, December, pp. 68–103 and appendix, pp. 156–61.

1893 Review of Thomas Kirkup, *A History of Socialism*, in *Journal of Political Economy*, March, pp. 300–2.
Review of Otto Warschauer, *Geschichte des Socialismus und Communismus im 19 Jahrhundert*, in *Journal of Political Economy,* March, p. 302.
"The Food Supply and the Price of Wheat", *Journal of Political Economy*, June, pp. 365–79.
Review of B. H. Baden-Powell, *The Land-Systems of British India*, in *Journal of Political Economy,* December, pp. 365–79.

1894 Review of Karl Kautsky, *Der Parlamentarismus und die Volkgesetzgebung und die Socialdemokratie*, in *Journal of Political Economy*, March, pp. 312–14.
Review of William H. Bear, *A Study of Small Holdings*, in *Journal of Political Economy*, March, pp. 325–6.
"The Army of the Commonweal", *Journal of Political Economy,* June, pp. 456–61. Reprinted in Veblen (1934).
Review of Joseph Stammhammer, *Bibliographie des Socialismus und Communismus,* in *Journal of Political Economy*, June, pp. 474–5.

Review of Russell M. Garnier, *History of the English Landed Interest (Modern Period)*, in *Journal of Political Economy*, June, pp. 475–7.

Review of Émile Levasseur, *L'Agriculture aux États-Unis*, in *Journal of Political Economy*, August, pp. 592–6.

"The Economic Theory of Woman's Dress," *Popular Science Monthly*, December, pp. 198–205. Reprinted in Veblen (1934).

1895 Review of Robert Flint, *Socialism*, in *Journal of Political Economy*, March, pp. 247–52.

The Science of Finance, translation of Gustav Cohn, *System der Finanzwissenschaft*.

1896 Review of Karl Marx, *Misère de la Philosophie*, in *Journal of Political Economy*, December, pp. 97–8.

Review of Enrico Ferri, *Socialisme et Science Positive*, in *Journal of Political Economy*, December, pp. 98–103.

1897 Review of Richard Calwer, *Einführung in den Socialismus*, in *Journal of Political Economy*, March, pp. 270–2.

Review of G. de Molinari, *La Viriculture – Ralentissement de la Population – Dégénérescence – Causes et Remèdes*, in *Journal of Political Economy*, March, pp. 273–5.

Review of Antonio Labriola, *Essais sur la conception matérialiste de l'histoire*, in *Journal of Political Economy*, June, pp. 390–1.

Review of Werner Sombart, *Sozialismus und soziale Bewegung im 19 Jahrhundert*, in *Journal of Political Economy*, June, pp. 391–2.

Review of N. Ch. Bunge, *Esquisses de littérature politico-économique*, in *Journal of Political Economy*, December, pp. 126–8.

Review of Max Lorenz, *Die Marxistische Socialdemokratie*, in *Journal of Political Economy*, December 1897, pp. 136–7.

1898 Review of Gustav Schmoller, *Über einige Grundfragen der Socialpolitik und der Volkswirtschaftslehre*, in *Journal of Political Economy*, June, pp. 416–9.

Review of William H. Mallock, *Aristocracy and Evolution: A Study of the Rights, the Origins and the Social Functions of the Wealthier Classes*, in *Journal of Political Economy*, June, pp. 430–5.

"Why Is Economics Not an Evolutionary Science?", *Quarterly Journal of Economics*, July, pp. 373–97. Reprinted in Veblen (1919).

"The Instinct of Workmanship and the Irksomeness of Labor", *American Journal of Sociology*, September 1898, pp. 187–201. Reprinted in Veblen (1934).

Review of Robert Turgot, *Reflections on the Formation and the Distribution of Riches*, in *Journal of Political Economy*, September, pp. 575–6.

"The Beginnings of Ownership", *American Journal of Sociology*, November, pp. 352–65. Reprinted in Veblen (1934).

1899 "The Barbarian Status of Women", *American Journal of Sociology*, January, pp. 503–14.

"The Preconceptions of Economic Science, I", *Quarterly Journal of Economics*, January, pp. 121–50. Reprinted in Veblen (1919).

The Theory of the Leisure Class: An Economic Study in the Evolution of Institutions (New York: Macmillan). Subtitle changed in later editions to *An Economic Study of Institutions*.

"The Preconceptions of Economic Science, II", *Quarterly Journal of Economics*, July, pp. 396–426. Reprinted in Veblen (1919).

Review of Simon Patten, *Development of English Thought,* in *Annals of the American Academy of Political and Social Science,* July, pp. 125–31.
"Mr. Cummings's Strictures on 'The Theory of the Leisure Class' ", *Journal of Political Economy,* December, pp. 106–17. Reprinted in Veblen (1934).

REFERENCES

Alchian, Armen A. (1950) "Uncertainty, Evolution and Economic Theory", *Journal of Political Economy,* 58(2), June, pp. 211–22. Reprinted in Witt (1993).

Argyrous, George and Sethi, Rajiv (1996) "The Theory of Evolution and the Evolution of Theory: Veblen's Methodology in Contemporary Perspective", *Cambridge Journal of Economics,* 20(4), July, pp. 475–95.

Boulding, Kenneth E. (1981) *Evolutionary Economics* (Beverly Hills, CA: Sage Publications).

Bowler, Peter J. (1983) *The Eclipse of Darwinism: Anti-Darwinian Evolution Theories in the Decades around 1900* (Baltimore: Johns Hopkins University Press).

—— (1988) *The Non-Darwinian Revolution: Reinterpreting a Historical Myth* (Baltimore: Johns Hopkins University Press).

Boyd, Robert and Richerson, Peter J. (1985) *Culture and the Evolutionary Process* (Chicago: University of Chicago Press).

Campbell, Donald T. (1965) "Variation, Selection and Retention in Sociocultural Evolution", in Barringer *et al.* (1965, pp. 19–49). Reprinted in *General Systems,* 14, 1969, pp. 69–85.

—— (1975) "On the Conflicts Between Biological and Social Evolution and Between Psychology and Moral Tradition", *American Psychologist,* 30, December, pp. 1103–26.

Campbell, John H. (1985) "An Organizational Interpretation of Evolution", in Depew, David J. and Weber, Bruce H. (eds) (1985) *Evolution at a Crossroads: The New Biology and the New Philosophy of Science* (Cambridge, MA: MIT Press), pp. 133–67.

Cosmides, Leda and Tooby, John (1994a) "Beyond Intuition and Instinct Blindness: Towards an Evolutionary Rigorous Cognitive Science", *Cognition,* 50(1–3), April–June, pp. 41–77.

—— (1994b) "Better than Rational: Evolutionary Psychology and the Invisible Hand", *American Economic Review (Papers and Proceedings),* 84(2), May, pp. 377–32.

Degler, Carl N. (1991) *In Search of Human Nature: The Decline and Revival of Darwinism in American Social Thought* (Oxford and New York: Oxford University Press).

Dorfman, Joseph (1934) *Thorstein Veblen and His America* (New York: Viking Press). Reprinted 1961 (New York: Augustus Kelley).

Durham, William H. (1991) *Coevolution: Genes, Culture, and Human Diversity* (Stanford: Stanford University Press).

Dyer, Alan W. (1986) "Veblen on Scientific Creativity", *Journal of Economic Issues,* 20(1), March, pp. 21–41. Reprinted in M. Blaug (ed.) (1992) *Thorstein Veblen (1857–1929)* (Aldershot: Edward Elgar).

Edgell, Stephen (1975) "Thorstein Veblen's Theory of Evolutionary Change", *American Journal of Economics and Sociology,* 34, July, pp. 267–80.

Edgell, Stephen and Tilman, Rick (1989) "The Intellectual Ancedents of Thorstein Veblen: A Reappraisal", *Journal of Economic Issues,* 23(4), December, pp. 1003–26.

Eff, E. Anton (1989) "History of Thought as Ceremonial Genealogy: The Neglected Influence of Herbert Spencer on Thorstein Veblen", *Journal of Economic Issues,* 23(3), September, pp. 689–716.

Harris, Abram L. (1932) "Types of Institutionalism", *Journal of Political Economy*, 40(4), December, pp. 721–49.

—— (1934) "Economic Evolution: Dialectical and Darwinian", *Journal of Political Economy*, 42(1), February, pp. 34–79.

Harris, Marvin (1968) *The Rise of Anthropological Theory: A History of Theories of Culture* (New York: Crowell).

Hayek, Friedrich A. (1967) "Notes on the Evolution of Systems of Rules of Conduct", from Hayek, Friedrich A. (1967) *Studies in Philosophy, Politics and Economics* (London: Routledge and Kegan Paul), pp. 66–81. Reprinted in Witt (1993).

—— (1988) *The Fatal Conceit: The Errors of Socialism, the Collected Works of Friedrich August Hayek*, Vol. I, ed. W. W. Bartley III (London: Routledge).

Hill, Forest G. (1958) "Veblen and Marx", in Dowd, Douglas F. (ed.) (1958) *Thorstein Veblen: A Critical Appraisal* (Ithaca, NY: Cornell University Press), pp. 129–49.

Hobson, John A. (1936) *Veblen* (London: Chapman and Hall). Reprinted 1991 by Augustus Kelley.

Hodgson, Geoffrey M. (1992) "Thorstein Veblen and Post-Darwinian Economics", *Cambridge Journal of Economics*, 16(3), September, pp. 285–301.

—— (1993) *Economics and Evolution: Bringing Life Back Into Economics* (Cambridge, UK and Ann Arbor, MI: Polity Press and University of Michigan Press).

—— (1996) "Varieties of Capitalism and Varieties of Economic Theory", *Review of Political Economy*, 3(3), Autumn, pp. 381–434.

—— (1998) "On the Evolution of Thornstein Veblen's Evolutionary Economics", *Cambridge Journal of Economics*, 22(3), July.

—— (forthcoming) "Decomposition and Growth: Biological Metaphors in Economics from the 1880s to the 1980s", in Dopfer, Kurt (ed.) (forthcoming) *Evolutionary Principles of Economics* (Boston: Kluwer).

Hofstadter, Richard (1959) *Social Darwinism in American Thought*, revised edn (New York: Braziller).

James, William (1880) "Great Men, Great Thoughts, and the Environment", *Atlantic Monthly*, 46, pp. 441–59. Reprinted in James, William (1897) *The Will to Believe* (New York: Harcourt, Brace).

—— (1890) *The Principles of Psychology*, 1st edn (New York: Holt).

Kropotkin, Petr A. (1902) *Mutual Aid: A Factor of Evolution* (London). Republished 1972 (London: Allen Lane).

Langlois, Richard N. and Everett, Michael J. (1994) "What is Evolutionary Economics?" in Magnusson, Lars (ed.) (1994) *Evolutionary and Neo-Schumpeterian Approaches to Economics* (Boston: Kluwer), pp. 11–47.

Lorenz, Max (1896) *Die Marxistische Socialdemokratie* (Leipzig: George M. Wigand).

Maasen, Sabine, Mendelsohn, Everett and Weingart, Peter (eds) (1995) *Biology as Society, Society as Biology: Metaphors*, Sociology of the Sciences Yearbook, 18, 1994 (Boston: Kluwer).

Marshall, Alfred (1975) *The Early Economic Writings of Alfred Marshall, 1867–1890*, edited by J. K. Whitaker (London: Macmillan).

Mayhew, Anne (1987) "The Beginnings of Institutionalism", *Journal of Economic Issues*, 21(3), September, pp. 971–98.

Mayr, Ernst (1960) "The Emergence of Evolutionary Novelties", in Tax, Sol (ed.) (1960) *Evolution After Darwin (I): The Evolution of Life* (Chicago: University of Chicago Press).

—— (1985) "How Biology Differs from the Physical Sciences", in Depew, David J. and Weber, Bruce H. (eds) (1985) *Evolution at a Crossroads: The New Biology and the New Philosophy of Science* (Cambridge, MA: MIT Press), pp. 43–63.

McDougall, William (1908) *An Introduction to Social Psychology*, 1st edn (London: Methuen).

—— (1929) *Modern Materialism and Emergent Evolution* (London: Methuen).

Mirowski, Philip (ed.) (1994) *Natural Images in Economic Thought: Markets Read in Tooth and Claw* (Cambridge and New York: Cambridge University Press).

Morgan, C. Lloyd (1896) *Habit and Instinct* (London and New York: Edward Arnold).

—— (1927) *Emergent Evolution*, 2nd edn. (1st edn. 1923) (London: Williams and Norgate).

—— (1933) *The Emergence of Novelty* (London: Williams and Norgate).

Murphree, Idus L. (1959) "Darwinism in Thorstein Veblen's Economics", *Social Research*, 26(2), June, pp. 311–24.

Nelson, Richard R. (1995) "Recent Evolutionary Theorizing About Economic Change", *Journal of Economic Literature*, 33(1), March, pp. 48–90.

Nelson, Richard R. and Winter, Sidney G. (1982) *An Evolutionary Theory of Economic Change* (Cambridge, MA: Harvard University Press).

Peirce, Charles Sanders (1923) *Chance, Love, and Logic*, ed. M. R. Cohen (New York: Harcourt, Brace).

—— (1935) *Collected Papers of Charles Sanders Peirce, Volume VI, Scientific Metaphysics*, edited by C. Hartshorne and P. Weiss (Cambridge, MA: Harvard University Press).

Plotkin, Henry C. (1994) *Darwin Machines and the Nature of Knowledge: Concerning Adaptations, Instinct and the Evolution of Intelligence* (Harmondsworth: Penguin).

Reber, Arthur S. (1993) *Implicit Learning and Tacit Knowledge: An Essay on the Cognitive Unconscious* (Oxford: Oxford University Press).

Reinheimer, Herman (1913) *Evolution by Co-operation: A Study in Bioeconomics* (London: Kegan, Paul, Trench, Trubner).

Riesman, David (1963) *Thorstein Veblen: A Critical Interpretation* (New York: Charles Scribner's).

Romanes, George (1893) *Darwin and After Darwin*, 2 vols, 2nd edn (London).

Russett, Cynthia Eagle (1976) *Darwin in America: The Intellectual Response 1865–1912* (San Francisco: W. H. Freeman).

Rutherford, Malcolm C. (1984) "Thorstein Veblen and the Processes of Institutional Change", *History of Political Economy*, 16(3), Fall, pp. 331–48. Reprinted in M. Blaug (ed.) (1992) *Thorstein Veblen (1857–1929)* (Aldershot: Edward Elgar).

Samuels, Warren J. (1977) "The Knight-Ayres Correspondence: The Grounds of Knowledge and Social Action", 11(3), September, pp. 485–525. Reprinted in Blaug, Mark (ed.) (1992) *Frank Knight (1885–1972), Henry Simons (1899–1946), Joseph Schumpeter (1883–1950)* (Aldershot: Edward Elgar).

Sanderson, Stephen K. (1990) *Social Evolutionism: A Critical History* (Oxford: Blackwell).

Spencer, Herbert (1880) *The Study of Sociology* (London: Williams and Norgate).

Tilman, Rick (1996) *The Intellectual Legacy of Thorstein Veblen: Unresolved Issues* (Westport, CT: Greenwood Press).

Veblen, Thorstein B. (1892) "Some Neglected Points in the Theory of Socialism", *Annals of the American Academy of Political and Social Science*, 2, November, pp. 345–62. Reprinted in Veblen (1919).

—— (1897a) Review of Antonio Labriola, *Essais sur la conception matérialiste de l'histoire*, in *Journal of Political Economy*, 5(3), June, pp. 390–1.

—— (1897b) Review of Max Lorenz, *Die Marxistische Socialdemokratie*, in *Journal of Political Economy*, 6(1), December, pp. 136–7.

—— (1898a) Review of William H. Mallock, *Aristocracy and Evolution: A Study of the Rights, the Origins and the Social Functions of the Wealthier Classes*, in *Journal of Political Economy*, 6, June, pp. 430–5.

—— (1898b) "Why Is Economics Not an Evolutionary Science?", *Quarterly Journal of Economics*, 12(3), July, pp. 373–97. Reprinted in Veblen (1919).

—— (1898c) "The Instinct of Workmanship and the Irksomeness of Labor", *American Journal of Sociology*, 4, September, pp. 187–201. Reprinted in Veblen (1934).

—— (1899) *The Theory of the Leisure Class: An Economic Study in the Evolution of Institutions* (New York: Macmillan).

—— (1900) "The Preconceptions of Economic Science: III", *Quarterly Journal of Economics*, 14(1), February, pp. 240–69. Reprinted in Veblen (1919).

—— (1901a) "Industrial and Pecuniary Employments", *Publications of the American Economic Association*, Series 3, pp. 190–235. Reprinted in Veblen (1919).

—— (1901b) "Gustav Schmoller's Economics", *Quarterly Journal of Economics*, 16, November, pp. 69–93. Reprinted in Veblen (1919).

—— (1906a) "The Place of Science in Modern Civilisation", *American Journal of Sociology*, 11(1), March, pp. 585–609. Reprinted in Veblen (1919).

—— (1906b) "The Socialist Economics of Karl Marx and His Followers I: The Theories of Karl Marx", *Quarterly Journal of Economics*, 20(3), August, pp. 578–95. Reprinted in Veblen (1919).

—— (1907) "The Socialist Economics of Karl Marx and His Followers II: The Later Marxism", *Quarterly Journal of Economics*, 21(1), February, pp. 299–322. Reprinted in Veblen (1919).

—— (1908) "Professor Clark's Economics", *Quarterly Journal of Economics*, 22(1), February, pp. 147–95. Reprinted in Veblen (1919).

—— (1909) "Fisher's Rate of Interest", *Political Science Quarterly*, 24, June, pp. 296–303. Reprinted in Veblen (1934).

—— (1913) "The Mutation Theory and the Blond Race", *Journal of Race Development*, April, pp. 491–507. Reprinted in Veblen (1919).

—— (1914) *The Instinct of Workmanship, and the State of the Industrial Arts* (New York: Augustus Kelley). Reprinted 1990 with a new introduction by Murray G. Murphey and a 1964 introductory note by J. Dorfman (New Brunswick, NJ: Transaction Books).

—— (1915) *Imperial Germany and the Industrial Revolution* (New York: Macmillan). Reprinted 1964 by Augustus Kelley.

—— (1919) *The Place of Science in Modern Civilisation and Other Essays* (New York: Huebsch). Reprinted 1990 with a new introduction by W. J. Samuels (New Brunswick, NJ: Transaction).

—— (1934) *Essays on Our Changing Order*, ed. Leon Ardzrooni (New York: The Viking Press).

Waddington, Conrad H. (1976) "Evolution in the Sub-Human World", in Jantsch, Erich and Waddington, Conrad H. (eds) (1976) *Evolution and Consciousness: Human Systems in Transition* (Reading, MA: Addison-Wesley), pp. 11–15.

Weismann, August (1893) *The Germ-Plasm: A Theory of Heredity*, translated by W. N. Parker and H. R. Ronnfeldt (London: Walter Scott).

Whitehead, Alfred N. (1926) *Science and the Modern World* (Cambridge: Cambridge University Press).

Winter, Sidney G., Jr (1990) "Survival, Selection, and Inheritance in Evolutionary Theories of Organization", in Singh, Jitendra V. (ed.) (1990) *Organizational Evolution: New Directions* (London: Sage), pp. 269–97.

Witt, Ulrich (ed.) (1993) *Evolutionary Economics* (Aldershot: Edward Elgar).

Zahavi, A. (1987) "The Theory of Signal Selection and Some of its Implications", in V. P. Delfino (ed.) (1987) *International Symposium on Biological Evolution* (Bari: Adriatica Editrice), pp. 305–27.

12

VEBLEN'S FEMINISM IN HISTORICAL PERSPECTIVE

Ann Jennings

Feminist arguments by leading economists have been rare in the history of economics. The best-known exception is Harriet Taylor and John Stuart Mill's *The Subjection of Women* (Mill 1869) though Friedrich Engels's *Origin of the Family* (1884) is also notable and there were assorted, lesser known arguments favoring advances for women among the writings of, especially, the English historical school and the so-called utopian socialists (Folbre 1993). Women's own economic writings on the subject are generally even less visible, except for Charlotte Perkins Gilman's *Women and Economics* (1898), but she lacked training or professional stature as an economist. It is therefore remarkable that relatively little attention has been paid to Thorstein Veblen's feminism. He was probably the most famous American economist of his day and his analyses of the role of invidious social distinctions within economic relationships, rooted in critiques of conventional gender distinctions in society, were central to *The Theory of the Leisure Class* (1899b) and several of his essays.

Previous efforts to increase the visibility of Veblen's feminism do exist; Diggins's (1978) work is especially notable and other useful accounts include Miller 1972; Ryan 1982; Greenwood 1984; Jennings 1992, 1993; Waddoups and Tilman 1992. The purposes of this essay are more comprehensive than any of these. I will explore not only the specific content of Veblen's feminism but also its origins, its relationship to other views in the period (focussing both on evolutionary anthropology as it related to women and on more explicitly feminist arguments and social movements), and conclude with brief remarks on the continuing significance of Veblen's arguments for today's feminism and the now rapidly expanding literature of feminist economics.

I will argue, first of all, that Veblen's feminism was uniquely central to his economic theories. Second, the origins of his feminism were mainly in anthropology rather than in feminist doctrines of the period.[1] Third, his relationship to contemporary feminist thought was not especially close. Finally, in some (though not all) respects his cultural understanding of the oppression of women remains unusually up-to-date with many feminist arguments today. He thus provides an interesting and insightful, though also problematic, model for those currently pursuing the expansion of feminist economics.

VEBLEN ON THE ORIGINS OF THE STATUS OF WOMEN

Veblen's writings on women appeared mainly in the 1890s, beginning with "The Economic Theory of Woman's Dress" (1894), followed by a cycle of essays in the *American Journal of Sociology* ("The Instinct of Workmanship and the Irksomeness of Labor" [1898a]; "The Beginnings of Ownership" [1898b]; "The Barbarian Status of Women" [1899a]), and culminating in his first book, *The Theory of the Leisure Class* (1899b). Though there were occasional references to women in subsequent writings and some discussions in courses he taught over the remainder of his career, there is little evidence of any substantial modification to his early views.[2] Both the primary sources and the content of his discussions of women were anthropological, except for some discussions of contemporary women in *The Theory of the Leisure Class*. He viewed many of the patterns of life in modern society as reflections of much earlier social tendencies and habituated behaviors, despite modifications caused by the growth of human knowledge and the evolutionary adaptation of early tendencies to more modern social circumstances. He also saw anthropological and evolutionary methods as the most appropriate means for discovering the significance of modern social practices and beliefs, including those within the realm of economics. Dorfman (1934, 165) said of the *AJS* essays that they "developed his ideas on the nature of the animistic and hedonistic preconceptions of modern business enterprise in terms of primitive culture." Likewise for the views of gender relations expressed in them; a summary of his early feminist views follows.

"The Economic Theory of Woman's Dress" (1894)

In "The Economic Theory of Woman's Dress," Veblen distinguished between the functions of "dress" as "adornment" and of "clothing" as "affording comfort," noting that adornment predated comfort and protective functions and that "to a great extent [comfort] continues to be in some sort an afterthought" (1894, 66). The economic significance of women's dress "is its function as an index of the wealth of its wearer – or . . . of its owner, for the wearer and owner are not necessarily the same person" (68). In patriarchal society (in which Veblen included his own time) "woman is a chattel"; "it has (ideally) become the great, peculiar, and almost sole function of woman . . . to put in evidence her economic unit's ability to pay" (68) through conspicuously wasteful expenditures. Conspicuous waste was further enhanced by "novelty" ("wearing nothing that is out of date" [72]) and by evidence of "physical incapacity" (73) due to cumbrous and even disabling garb. Though the "ideals" were those of the elite and women's "uselessness" was often a fiction, status emulation nevertheless enforced the standard more widely, recommended concealment of its transgression, and extended it even to men (though to a lesser degree).

The sources for Veblen's arguments about dress and status were clearly anthropological; Frederick Starr, who was Veblen's colleague and friend at the University of Chicago, published a two-part account of "Dress and Adornment" in "primitive" societies in *Popular Science Monthly* (where "The Economic Theory of Woman's Dress" also appeared) in 1891. In it, Starr dismissed the importance of comfort and protection to "dress" in three sentences (Starr 1891, 788). Though Starr focussed more on the aesthetic elements of dress rather than on Veblen's status motives, he did link adornment to marks of distinction, imitation, and fashion and noted the many survivals of "uselessness" in modern dress. Lengthier discussions of imitation and emulation in "primitive" social relations – such as Tarde's accounts, beginning in 1882 and restated in 1890 – were also widely known at the time (Lowie 1937). Veblen's main advance was to develop the continuing significance of imitation and emulation as organizing principles in modern, industrial society and to emphasize their gender dimensions. His anthropological explanation for the gender relationships expressed in dress actually appeared four years later, however, and were couched within his larger attacks on the predatory animus of modern business practices in the *AJS* essay series.

"The Instinct of Workmanship and the Irksomeness of Labor" (1898a)

"The Instinct of Workmanship and the Irksomeness of Labor" was the first article in Veblen's *AJS* cycle and it was also the broadest argument of the three. It appeared in September, 1898 and generally focussed on how human beings could have survived as a species if, as was commonly held in economics, they were naturally averse to the useful effort (work) that produced their own sustenance. This, Veblen remarked, would make them "an anomaly in the animal world. . . . it is incumbent upon [economics] to explain . . . how [they have] achieved [this] emancipation from the law of natural selection" (79). Yet, since expressions of the irksomeness of labor were common enough, Veblen thought they must have some factual basis. Human beings had somehow achieved a unique position from which they were "now able, without jeopardy to the life of the species, to play fast and loose with the spiritual basis of [their] survival" (80). Veblen's answer, in brief, was that human beings were "endowed with a proclivity for purposeful action," an agency that had propelled them beyond the constraints confronting other species. They had "turn[ed] the forces of the environment to account" (80), and had thereby created room for an "aversion to labor that [was] in great part a conventional aversion only" (81).

Several ideas that were central to Veblen's subsequent writing were announced in these positions. First was his use of "instinct psychology," the more progressive of the two main tendencies in psychological theory at the time.[3] Veblen held that human beings (and other species) had innate "spiritual" (read: psychological) tendencies including (for human beings) first and foremost "the instinct of workmanship," the "ubiquitous human impulse to do the next thing" (1898a, 81). Second was the role of culture, by which the tendency to purposeful activity was molded into specific forms, habits, and beliefs and bent to specific, conventional objectives. Third was the Darwinian evolutionary principle of change in relationship to an environment – though human achievements and change had made the cultural and conventional constraints of the social environment more compelling, if somewhat looser, than those of brute nature. Culture amended the natural environment of the human species as it molded human nature itself.

Veblen's main target in "The Instinct of Workmanship" was almost certainly Spencer's view that human evolution recorded a progression from relatively violent, militaristically organized struggles for life and subsistence to more peaceable, contractual economic relationships. Veblen deemed Spencer's sequence implausible. Though Veblen accepted the then standard anthropological stages of "savagery," "barbarism," and "civilization," he thought savagery must have been largely peaceable and only in the subsequent stage of barbarism could decidedly predatory behaviors reign. The fighting disposition was too destructive for survival under the earliest human conditions when the means of life were scarce. Predatory habits and relationships among human beings were incompatible with the diligent efforts needed to obtain sustenance and to develop the useful techniques that would eventually improve the margins for survival. They also presumed "something to prey upon" (87) and must have developed later, within expanded possibilities due to earlier, more peaceable and workmanlike accomplishments. Nevertheless, Veblen did include predatory inclinations among the original array of human spiritual elements. He held only that they must have been less prominent than workmanship under early cultural conditions.

The vital importance of cultural conditions was indicated, to Veblen, by the basic sociality of human beings. "[H]is muscular form is [not] specialized for fighting. . . . [a]nd he did not become a formidable animal until he had made some considerable advance in the contrivance of implements for combat" (85–6). "[A]rchaic man was necessarily a member of a group, and . . . could [not] have survived except on the basis of a sense of solidarity strong enough to throw self-interest into the background." Under earlier conditions of savagery, "[n]otions of economic rank and discrimination between persons [that Veblen later called invidious distinctions] . . . [were] almost, if not altogether, in abeyance." Self-interest emerged as an accepted human motive only in tandem with later, more predatory modes of life that Veblen identified with "the beginnings of barbarism" (92).

With barbarism, self-interest subordinated solidarity, men's workmanlike efficiency was redirected to the purposes of fighting capacity, and much greater scope for status and emulation appeared. In this stage,

> the able-bodied barbarian of the predatory culture, who is at all mindful of his good name, severely leaves all uneventful drudgery to the women and minors of the group. He puts in his time in the manly arts of war and devotes his talents to devising ways and means of disturbing the peace. That way lies honor.
>
> (94)

Social divisions, initially by gender, ensued which, with accumulations of wealth continuing up to the present day, yielded a "shameful" and "indecorous" class association of labor with poverty. Hence its social and conventional "irksomeness."

"The Beginnings of Ownership" (1898b)

"The Beginnings of Ownership" appeared two months later, in November 1898. Both the speculative themes and the critiques of earlier anthropologists continued in it with little break, although discussions of women's social positions were much more evident. The essay began with attacks on two common theories of property: the natural rights theory, according to which property became a natural but earned right; and the "ethnological" view that property originated in personal articles such as the "customary use of weapons and ornaments by individuals" (34). The natural rights view was flawed by its reliance on "conjectural history" (33) and by its assumption of originally isolated individuals. "[I]t overlooks the fact that there is no isolated, self-sufficing individual. . . . men are always guided by the experience of others" (33). Production required both a community and "technical knowledge," without which there was "no accumulation and no wealth to be owned" (34).

By contrast, the ethnological view based on developments out of personal use seemed (at first brush) less problematic. It nevertheless involved relatively large logical leaps as well as an implicit projection of modern views of property onto early social arrangements and beliefs. Veblen said,

> [in] the apprehension of the savage and the barbarian the limits of his person do not coincide with the limits which modern biological science would recognize. His individuality is conceived to cover

... a pretty wide range of facts and objects that pertain to him more or less immediately.

(36)

This "quasi-personal fringe" shaded off gradually, as did individuality itself, but the objects in question were "personal to him in a vital sense. They are not a congeries of things to which he stands in an economic relation and to which he has an equitable, legal claim." They were part of him "in much the same sense as his hands and feet are his" (37). The "penumbra of personality" continued even when the objects were given away or otherwise separated from him though, if they "escaped" their "organic relation" to him (by lapse of time, for example) they would pass to another person's personal sphere or (in some cases) "into the common stock of the community" (39). This was not ownership, nor full legal discretion over the object.

"Ownership" required a new category in thought that was not an outgrowth of notions of personal influence. An object could imaginably belong to one person by "personality" and another by "ownership" as, indeed, do locks of hair (for example) or photographs even today. The concepts could coexist in some objects but remained quite distinct, without displacing one another. Thus ownership required an alternate foundation. Nor could rights by labor fill the gap. There were far too many cases where labor did not confer ownership of what was produced. Veblen turned, instead, to tenure by prowess and seizure, particularly the seizure of other persons who, by virtue of their own personality, could not have been imagined to fall within the personal fringe of their captors.

Veblen argued that the seizure of members of other groups had sufficiently distinct social implications to ground novel ownership concepts without disrupting prior social practices. Property and ownership arose under barbarism, when belligerent predatory impulses could flourish with less threat to productive effort and with greater potential rewards. As outsiders, captives had no claims within the group consumption patterns of their captors, nor were captives traditionally shared by the group, nor were they extensions of a captor's personality. Instead, they became trophies, expressing the predatory excellence of their captor. Women, Veblen speculated, were probably the first objects of property. They were easier to subdue than men and, due to the gender divisions between predatory and productive activities he had noted in his previous essay, women were "worth more to the group than their maintenance" (47). They also served their captor's vanity by permitting him to place his domination in continuing evidence within his original group; they became constant vehicles for self-interested, competitive display among men.

Eventually the capture of women became a customary right of exclusive individual abuse of women: marriage. "This ownership-marriage seems to be the original both of private property and of the patriarchal household.

206

Both of these great institutions are, accordingly, of an emulative origin" (48). Marriage by capture as the origin of modern marriage was a fairly standard belief among late nineteenth-century anthropologists.[4] Veblen took a more controversial position in stating that "[t]he appropriation and accumulation of consumable goods could scarcely have come into vogue as a direct outgrowth of primitive-horde communism, but it comes as an easy and unobtrusive consequence of the ownership of persons" (49). It was controversial for two reasons. The first, already noted, was its rejection of earlier theories of property; the second was its parallel rejection of earlier theories of "communistic marriage," or, less euphemistically, of "primitive promiscuity."[5]

"The Barbarian Status of Women" (1899a)

Veblen's third *AJS* article, "The Barbarian Status of Women," appeared in January 1899 and completed the cycle in which Veblen gave his reformulated anthropology of the origins of contemporary belief and practice. In it he recalled much of his earlier argument and explained how fighting strength and predation hardened into a status system linked to gender and an established "code of proprieties" (54), social repute, and virtue. By habituation and (social) selection under predatory barbarism, males grew "tolerant of any infliction of damage and suffering" (54); since men had also become the "superior class," their views of the matter set the standards to which the whole community became habituated as "common sense." Marriage by capture became the "enlightened," most honorable form of marriage while other, more peaceable forms fell "under polite odium" and any "masterless, unattached woman consequently lost caste" (56). Thus a "remedy" to "save the requirements of decency" and "permit the marriage of women from within the group" (57) emerged. "Ceremonial capture" – " 'protective mimicry,' to borrow a phrase from the naturalists" – arose, so that "a woman of high birth should not be irretrievably outclassed by any chance-comer from outside" and in order to keep men who married within the group "in countenance" (57).

When joined with his arguments in "The Instinct of Workmanship and the Irksomeness of Labor," the further progression leading up to women's enforced idleness, incapacitating dress, and use as objects of vicarious leisure and consumption – as discussed in "The Economic Theory of Women's Dress" – can be inferred. Continuing accumulation led to social divisions and class distinctions among men on the basis of property and wealth which could be amplified by preventing the erstwhile productive efforts of wives and children and by inflating the wasteful, unproductive requirements of full propriety. Veblen provided more explicit discussions of the process in *The Theory of the Leisure Class*, where most of the *AJS* arguments were restated and their implications were extended.

Further implications

In *The Theory of the Leisure Class* (1899b) Veblen suggested more clearly that class distinctions emerged out of early gender distinctions. There he said

> dress has subtler and more far-reaching possibilities than [the] crude, first-hand evidence of wasteful consumption only. If . . . it can also be shown that [the wearer] is not under the necessity of earning a livelihood, the evidence of social worth is enhanced to a very considerable degree.
>
> (1899b, 120)

Later, "obvious physical discomfort . . . or disability" also accrued "in behalf of some one else to whom she stands in a relation of economic dependence . . . [or] servitude. . . . [I]n the modern civilized scheme of life the woman is still . . . perhaps in a highly idealized sense . . . the man's chattel" (127). The ability to maintain large numbers of dependents who performed no labor – or, as in the case of liveried servants and those charged with the punctilious maintenance of extravagant households, no useful labor – was a more advanced method of displaying "the ability to pay." Though productive but uneventful drudgery had once fallen to women, useful drudgery now (ideally) fell to a lower, propertyless class of persons and most useful labor was discredited in some degree within the canons of propriety and status. Ownership based on masculine exploit evolved into a larger, more general and finely wrought system of social distinctions and dependencies that encompassed both gender and class.

Veblen developed his arguments about the relationship between ownership and emulation further, into an attack on orthodox economic doctrines.

> Whenever the institution of private property is found . . . the economic process bears the character of a struggle between men for the possession of goods. It has been customary in economic theory, and especially among those economists who adhere with least faltering to the body of modernized classical doctrines, to construe this struggle for wealth as being substantially a struggle for subsistence. Such is, no doubt, its character . . . during the earlier and less efficient phases of industry. . . . [and] where the "niggardliness of nature" is so strict as to afford but a scanty livelihood. . . . But in all progressing communities an advance is presently made beyond this early stage of technological development. . . .
>
> [I]t is only when taken in a sense far removed from its naive meaning that the consumption of goods can be said to afford the incentive from which accumulation invariably proceeds. The motive

that lies at the root of ownership is emulation. . . . It is of course not to be overlooked that in a community where nearly all goods are private property the necessity of earning a livelihood is a powerful and ever-present incentive for the poorer members of the community. . . . On the other hand, so far as regards those members and classes who are chiefly concerned in the accumulation of wealth, the incentive of subsistence or physical comfort never plays a considerable part. Ownership began and grew into a human institution on grounds unrelated to the subsistence minimum. The dominant incentive was from the outset the invidious distinction attaching to wealth, and . . . no other motive has usurped the primacy at any later stage of development.

(1899b, 34–6)

In these passages, Veblen dismissed the scarcity principles underlying standard economics; "the economic problem" was not scarcity, except in the perverse sense of a treadmill – that is, accumulating more and more only to keep one's place in the pack. The net result was no overall improvement since the benefits of emulation required an advance in *relative* position in the pack. It was a zero-sum game in which scarcity confronted only those whose social position left them struggling for basic subsistence. Even in those cases, however, the scarcity was not due to natural or even technological limits on resources; it was due entirely to the distribution of resources, the use of property as a means of emulative display, and waste. Standard economic scarcity arguments were conventional defenses of (mainly liberal) views of private property that Veblen also found seriously flawed.

Veblen's critique of modern society and standard economics rested on his initial distinction between production and exploit. The distinction first manifested itself in society, however, as a set of gender distinctions. For this reason it can be said that for Veblen, more than for any other economist of his time and perhaps as much as any since, gender was a central, original element of his view of modern economic relationships. This still leaves the problem of assessing the relevance and strengths of Veblen's arguments for today's readers. Before turning to that question, however, his views should be placed in historical context, alongside other arguments from Veblen's own day. I begin with contemporary accounts in anthropology, followed by a description of late nineteenth-century feminism.

NINETEENTH-CENTURY VIEWS OF SOCIAL EVOLUTION AND WOMEN

Veblen was by no means the only nineteenth-century scholar to consider women's status and roles (or class distinctions) from the standpoint of evolutionary anthropology. Indeed, although feminist interpretations of anthropological arguments were not as common as interpretations that supported the status quo of gender inequality, even feminist readings were not unique to Veblen. Among those whose use of evolutionism and anthropology favored social advance for women were Antoinette Brown, Charlotte Perkins Gilman, Lester Frank Ward, and Henry Louis Morgan (see Rosenberg 1975). Veblen's evolutionism, however, was less biologically-based and much more focussed on the evolution of social conventions than most renderings of evolutionary arguments, feminist or otherwise, at the time. His subversion of Spencerian social evolutionism was central to his unusual position.

Spencerian thought – the general beliefs that biology and evolution could explain much in human behavior and social relationships and that evolution took the progressive course of "survival of the fittest" – was widely influential in the late nineteenth century. Even those rejecting some or all of Spencer's particular views were responding, for the most part, to issues that Spencer had moved to center stage. Many of Spencer's basic principles were not entirely new or original to him. His division of human history into the stages of savagery, barbarism, and civilization had been fairly standard in anthropology since about 1800 and his Lamarckism was of similar vintage (Stocking 1987). His associationist psychology can be dated to Hume (though Spencer amended it with Lamarckism; see note 3) and even Spencer's (1876) alternate, militarism-contractualism stage theory of social organization was given earlier by Maine (1860). Though Spencer became the central figure in nineteenth century social evolutionism, the ground had already been prepared for him.

It was probably the advent of Darwin that provided the catalyst, and the "scientific" imprimatur, for Spencer's rise to fame. In any case, evolutionism was the rage in the late nineteenth century and, in that sense, Veblen's use of evolutionary anthropology was entirely in keeping with the times. Nor was the highly speculative style of Veblen's rendering of anthropological origins at all unusual (c.f. Ward's "Our Better Halves" [1888], described below). Methodical ethnographic field studies, such as Boas's studies of the Eskimo (1884–85) and Kwakiutl (1895) and fieldwork organized through the Smithsonian Institution to study the native tribes of the US only began in earnest in the 1880s. Veblen was as familiar with ethnographic results as any of his contemporaries.

Though Veblen represented himself as a "disciple" of Spencer (Veblen 1892)[6] he was by no means an obedient or uncritical disciple. Veblen's critique of Spencer's progression from militaristic to contractual social organization has already been noted; his larger critique of Spencer concerned Spencer's teleology, his biologism, and his psychology: that is, it concerned almost all of Spencer's basic views of human nature and history (see Jennings and Waller 1998). Although Veblen's instinct psychology did maintain a set of biologically innate human dispositions, instincts were given all of their specific content through cultural learning, habituation, social conventions and – not to be overlooked – the creative activities of human beings. Moreover, Veblen held that the basic instinctual endowment of human beings had "been transmitted intact from the beginning of humanity" (Veblen 1914, 18).[7] Thus instinctual endowments did not explain states of social development; they could be deemed "constant" or "exogenous" in human behavior, in sharp contrast to Spencer's Lamarckian biological determinism. Veblen was also convinced that human cultural evolution was not necessarily "progressive" – the social selection of habits according to dominant social conventions and status did not assure that social "fitness" meant social betterment, given the prevalence of destructive predatory norms. In modern business competition, predation involved private property and financial conquest, rather than physical force,[8] but was none the less wasteful and violent for all its "legal" underpinnings – for Veblen, "legal" defined only the "limits of permissible fraud" (1899b, 181). Spencerian teleology was self-congratulatory and animistic, imputing to history a mindfulness and consciousness that Veblen rejected. Veblen's position implied the culturally relative formation and recreation of purposes by actual human beings.

Numerous anthropologists had considered the origins of women's social status and marriage before Veblen. Among them were Bachofen (1861), Maine (1861), McLennan (1865), Lubbock (1870), Morgan (1871; 1877), Spencer (1876), and Westermarck (1891), to name only the most famous.[9] Most of these writings were firmly in the tradition of Spencerian evolutionary meliorism. They tended to see modern patriarchal monogamy, with women sanctifying the home while stalwart and competitive men provided both sustenance and protection, as the crowning achievement of civilization's evolutionary advance. The best known Victorian evolutionists writing on women were supremely confident of the virtues of their own social arrangements and, by comparison, of the cruelty and inferiority of any alternatives (see Fee 1974). Most of them were thus opposed to any "advancement" of rights for women; Morgan and Westermarck were the main exceptions.

Veblen's own positions were most similar to those taken by Westermarck. Obviously projecting modern Western social values and beliefs about women into their speculative versions of earlier social forms, all of the scholars listed above, except for Spencer and Westermarck, regarded women as *unproductive*. Moreover, all except Westermarck (and to a lesser degree Morgan) held that, in the earliest stage of social life, sexual relationships must have included "communal" access to women. Bachofen and Morgan also believed that the existence of matrilineality in some contemporary "primitive" groups implied that matriarchal family forms had preceded patriarchal families (see Fee 1974; Thomas 1909). Veblen rejected all of these positions (and summarily dismissed Engels's "world historic defeat of the female sex," which was based almost exclusively on Morgan's accounts).[10] Only Westermarck accepted each of Veblen's characteristic views of the origins of marriage and the status of women, including: the economic value of women's productive efforts; the absence of any original state of sexual promiscuity; the absence of an earlier stage of matriarchy and the importance of marriage by capture (Thomas 1909).

Veblen was not alone, however, in bending anthropology and evolutionism to feminist perspectives. Ward, for example, argued in "Our Better Halves" (1888) that women embodied the evolutionary principle of "heredity," while men embodied the principle of "variability" (an apparent reference to the three central principles of Darwinian natural selection: heredity, variation, and selection). Though he did not challenge conventional views that women were mentally and physically inferior to men (if also morally superior) he reasoned that it must be women's social and evolutionary advance that would improve the human race (a proposition abetted by his Lamarckian view of heredity). "The attempt to move the whole race forward by elevating only the sex that represents the principle of instability, has long enough been tried. . . . Woman *is* the race and the race can be raised up only as she is raised up" (1888, 275). Gilman said in her autobiography (1935) that Ward's "gynaecocentric theory" was one of only two main scholarly inspirations for her own *Women and Economics* (1898). In her later work (Gilman 1911) she also borrowed the evolutionary concepts of "katabolism" and "anabolism" from Veblen's colleague at Chicago, W.I. Thomas (1897). Anabolism was seen as a feminine metabolic trait, involving "innately passive, nurturant, industrious, and uncreative" characteristics, while katabolism implied "a male personality that was essentially belligerent, passionate, selfish, lazy, and competitive" (Rosenberg 1975, 145).[11]

Veblen's reading of the anthropological record took an alternative, third course. He sharply dismissed both the paeans to patriarchy and the view that women innately possessed different traits than men. Though he did suggest that women might possibly be slightly more (innately) disposed to workmanship and communitarian (or "parental") purposes than men, he argued mainly that those concerns were relegated to women following their subordination to masculine status principles of belligerence and exploit. Workmanship and communitarian inclinations must have been just as common to both men and women in the early stages of peaceable savagery, when survival required the general suppression of any self-interested and bellicose frame of mind. Later, men's social dominance required the conventional and proprietary repression of any such traits in women. Moreover, since women were "protected" from competitive pursuits, they acquired much more scope to exercise their normalized moral traits. Though Veblen, with some notable qualifications (see below, pp. 219–20), applauded women's more useful and socially auspicious inclinations by comparison with the destructive competitive exploits reserved for men, he saw the gender distinctions themselves as only conventionally exclusive. These views also put him at some distance from the main tendencies within nineteenth century feminism.

LATE NINETEENTH-CENTURY FEMINISM

There are a number of ways that feminism can be defined. A loose and relatively inclusive definition is sufficient for purposes here: feminism seeks to explain and correct inequities linked to sex and/or gender differences (where sex is now widely understood as a biological, and gender a social trait). Variations then result from differences in either the visions and foundations of equity or the remedies envisioned for inequities. Feminism has encompassed relatively formally organized programs and groups devoted to specific remediation efforts as well as scholarly writings and more amorphous historical trends that have at least somewhat self-consciously expanded social possibilities for women.

For expositional purposes, nineteenth-century American feminism can be discussed in terms of four general movements and two main ideologies. The four movements considered here are the woman's suffrage movement, the temperance movement, the "new woman" movement, and the settlement movement. The two main ideologies that informed these movements were "liberal feminism," based on principles of natural rights, individualism, and public–private distinctions, and a "woman's nature" argument based on beliefs that women naturally possessed special moral and maternal capacities that were both essential to a good society and too often undervalued or threatened by men's more aggressive behavior.[12]

The abolitionist origins of nineteenth-century American feminism closely connected the liberal and the "woman's nature" positions at the outset. Classical liberal arguments concerning the "rights of man," to a public voice in government for all private adults, were central to the anti-slavery movement. The public–private distinctions grounding liberalism were also being redefined due to industrialization in the period, however, and new forms of gender distinctions emerged with them. As the public domain increasingly encompassed all paid work outside the home, the private domain became centered on women's homemaking and childrearing activities (Matthaei 1982; Nicholson 1986; Jennings 1992, 1993). Men's competitive nature was socially viewed as appropriate to the public arenas of both government and wage labor, while women became identified with the cooperative moral and nurturant functions of the private family.[13] In the context of the anti-slavery movement, however, this gave women some special standing, as the guardians of morality, in light of the evident immorality of denials of natural rights under slavery. Thus, although woman's sphere was deemed to be the home, questions of public morality licensed at least some expansion of the feminine domain under the rubric of "social homemaking" – a metaphorical device that also grounded demands for greater educational access for women (how else could they adequately fulfill their domestic mission of raising up adequate sons and citizens of the republic?), new feminine occupations, and other public opportunities as the century unfolded (Matthaei 1982).

Woman's suffrage

The suffrage movement demanded "a permanent, public role for women" (DuBois 1975, 66) initially linked to similar demands on behalf of black/African slaves. The demand was based on individual merit, the right to achieve full individual potential and the right to self-government. All persons capable of education were deemed equally capable of representing themselves in government and entitled, from birth, to the right to do so. Though few at the time really believed that black slaves, male or female, and white women were fully as capable as white men, achievements by women within the anti-slavery movement gave ample evidence that they were as least as deserving of the vote as male slaves. Further, to deny suffrage to women while granting it to black men – as rightfully feared by early abolitionist women such as Elizabeth Cady Stanton, Susan B. Anthony, and Lucretia Mott – might subordinate white women to white and black men due only to their sex (and not to their abilities or potential). They saw no legitimate grounds for thinking white (or black) women less capable of self-direction than black men (Eisenstein 1987).

Women's demands were eventually subordinated to "the negro's hour," however, despite Stanton's protests that without votes the emancipation of "Southern black women . . . was but another form of slavery" (Eisenstein 1987, 79). The Fourteenth Amendment extended the franchise to black men but left women to continue their own struggle for the vote with far less support than before. Once separated from abolitionism, the conflict between public–private distinctions as the basis, on one hand, for political enfranchisement and self-government and, on the other hand, for gendered understandings of morality and the family became more evident in the woman's suffrage movement. Woman's suffrage positions rooted in the classical liberal arguments advanced by Stanton and Anthony were perceived as a direct threat to the family.[14]

At issue was whether the individual or the family was the basic unit of society. Though usually only implicit, the point was sometimes made explicitly, as by Mary Putnam Jacobi. "The American state, she explained, is based on 'individual cells,' not households" (DuBois 1975, 66). This then raised the concern that pressing women's interests in terms of the former might destroy the latter. "Without directly attacking women's position within the private sphere suffragists touched the nerve of women's subordinate status by contending that women might be something other than wives and mothers" (ibid.). For this reason, and because women's maternal roles and special morality were embraced by most woman's suffrage activists too, women's rights to political self-determination were always (albeit uncomfortably) combined with some acceptance of women's special nature. Leading suffragists also demanded laws to make the exercise of women's special roles freer and less exposed to domestic tyranny and abuses by men – and many supported the temperance movement.

Temperance

Woman's suffrage remained a small, middle-class movement throughout the nineteenth century and did not achieve a large following (even) among women, probably because of its perceived threat to the family, the lack of alternatives to domesticity for most women, and the emulative aspirations of many working-class women to a more complete domesticity.[15] The temperance movement, by contrast, grew to much larger proportions and crossed class lines to a much greater degree. Up to 30 percent of its local leaders were from the working class (Degler 1980, 316). Its leading figure, Frances Willard, consciously expanded the goals of the Woman's Christian Temperance Union to include a broad range of improvements in women's well-being. Like opposition to alcohol consumption itself, however, most of the WCTU's activities focussed on the condition and security of women in the family or on social homemaking extensions of maternal roles.[16] The WCTU was centered on the principle of women's special nature, not liberal arguments concerning natural rights beyond the family, though it eventually also embraced woman's suffrage as necessary for legislation in defense of the family. It consciously sought greater influence and equity for women, brought women into the public arena in relatively large numbers, and was relatively successful in large part because of its consistency with the popular consensus about women's special nature.

The "new woman" movement

The "new woman" movements represented another feminist front around the turn of the century though it lacked the formal organizations of suffrage and temperance. Without official spokespersons or doctrines it must be defined in terms of its popular image of a new kind of woman and of the feminist contributions of the women who fit that image in the period. Identified and named in the 1880s, the new woman was popularly typified by the "Gibson Girl," a model of physical health who had discarded her mother's tightly constraining corsets and heavy gowns, rode bicycles, worked for wages (at least before marriage), and possessed an air of cheerful competence and autonomy (Smith-Rosenberg 1985). She was feminine in a new way. In large part she reflected and continued the increasing visibility of women, the expansion of women's higher education, and new professional opportunities that had been opening up to women under the auspices of social homemaking. She was generally understood as a middle-class, educated, single woman seeking morally rewarding work, beyond domesticity, to develop her abilities and contribute to society.

The ideological foundations for the social trend represented by the "new woman" were, of course, amorphous. Associated with the burgeoning women's colleges and new coeducational opportunities for women, however, those fitting the description were also responsible for many challenges to erstwhile "scientific" views of women's intellectual inferiority, their biologically different nature (from men's) and their widely supposed physical infirmity. These women initiated much of the scholarly research that eventually deposed older scientific doctrines while they worked for advanced degrees, especially at the University of Chicago and Columbia University (Rosenberg 1982; Haddock Siegfried 1996).[17]

New women were far more likely to pursue life-long careers and far less likely to marry than women in the general population. Career choice and marital status were connected, of course: it was still not generally believed that women (unlike men) could successfully combine work and marriage – though some did. Many new women remained in academe (teaching mostly at women's colleges), others moved into careers in the new state and federal government protective and regulatory agencies founded during the Progressive Era, while still others spent much of their lives in settlement houses.

The settlement movement

The settlement movement, which first appeared in the US around 1890, was originally modeled on English experiments that combined communal living with efforts to help the poorest members of the working class. The English model was associated with universities and run by male reformers but the American version, though usually also linked to colleges or universities, was organized and operated primarily by women. Jane Addams's Hull House, in Chicago, was founded in 1889 and maintained very close (though informal) ties to the University of Chicago. Ties to trade unionism and other nonacademic groups were also formed, as in the case of Lillian Wald's Henry Street Settlement in New York City (Tax 1980). By 1911 there were at least 400 settlement houses across the US (Hayden 1981).

The settlement movement is perhaps best viewed as the most organized expression of contemporary women's "social homemaking" mission and the emerging women's profession of social work. Hull House was established both to offer middle-class women a safe and satisfying homelife apart from marriage and to assist poor working-class and immigrant women and children in improving their domestic and educational standards, escaping intolerable circumstances, and assimilating to American social norms. It was not merely a charitable enterprise, however; it sought to imbue the most advanced approaches to childrearing and education, nutrition, domestic finance, and the new "domestic science" of the day.[18] Thus its ties to the University of Chicago were important as a source for new "best practices" while it in turn provided a laboratory for the new ideas being developed by researchers in the period (Hayden 1981; Haddock Siegfried 1996). John Dewey served on its board of directors and was one of many frequent

216

academic visitors and speakers at Hull House. Veblen also reportedly spoke at Hull House but had far less presence there,[19] for reasons that may become apparent.

VEBLEN AND FEMINIST MOVEMENTS

Late nineteenth-century feminism was primarily a middle-class movement. Despite the enlistment of some working-class women to the cause of temperance and the contributions of settlement workers to unionism, the leadership of woman's suffrage, temperance, the settlements, and the most visible images and representatives of the new woman were all middle-class. Though Veblen was a critic of the narrow, subservient prescriptions for women's lives they also opposed, he applied his cultural interpretations and criticisms to them, too.

Veblen said little about the ideological foundations of women's movements themselves but his views can be readily inferred from his other arguments. The liberal feminism of Anthony and Stanton (as well as Harriet Taylor and John Stuart Mill) rested on a claim of natural rights that Veblen rejected along with the whole of natural law philosophy (see Diggins 1978).[20] Universal, individualistic "rights of man" arguments were fundamentally antithetical to Veblen's cultural relativism and his anti-teleological attacks on "animism" in social philosophy. Nor did Veblen admire the individualism that such feminism claimed for women and, unlike most others in the period, he never implied that women were *any* less innately capable than men. In fact, he largely credited women with responsibility for the technological advances that allowed the transition from savagery to barbarism to take place (1898a; 1899b; 1908, 185; 1914).

The "woman's nature" feminism of Ward, Gilman, Willard, and, in some degree, most other feminists of the period can also be seen, ultimately, as based in nature, albeit biological rather than metaphysical nature. Though Veblen shared the preference for communitarianism and conscientious workmanship that woman's nature arguments advanced, he largely rejected foundations in any biological exclusiveness of feminine and masculine dispositions. Once again, the gender division of roles and dispositions was largely conventional; biologically, both men and women were (at least almost) equally possessed of nurturant, workmanlike and competitive instinctual capacities. While most feminists wanted to reweight the social importance of what they deemed naturally or biologically masculine and feminine traits, Veblen wanted to reweight the social importance of *culturally* masculine and feminine traits and hoped for a lesser role for culturally masculine predation and exploit. In this regard, Veblen's feminism was unusually prescient and well-ahead of its time.

Veblen's only explicit discussions of the objectives of contemporary feminism appeared in *The Theory of the Leisure Class*. His most favorable comments concerned the new woman movement; his remarks on the settlement movement were more ambivalent, while temperance and woman's suffrage were mentioned only in passing. In all cases, however, the context for the discussions was the larger social regime of status that reflected and ordered, according to exigent social conditions, the original human impulses of community and workmanship versus self-seeking exploit. Though Veblen favored the expansion of economic opportunities for women, in the main he questioned whether feminist reforms would have the dramatic social consequences that either their advocates hoped or their detractors feared.

His brief references to temperance and suffrage illustrate his basic orientation. He described the consumption of alcohol as an aspect of invidious distinctions: "Drunkenness and other pathological consequences of the free use of stimulants . . . tend . . . to become honorific. . . . as manly attributes. . . . The same invidious distinction adds force to the current disapproval of any indulgence of this kind on the part of women, minors, and inferiors" (1899b, 62). What was deemed proper (or even required) for men of high standing was immoral for all others. But when discussing the conservative and self-protective function of the leisure class and its "prescriptive example" (138) in society he also said that

> it is not unusual to hear those persons who dispense salutary advice and admonition to the community express themselves forcibly upon the far-reaching pernicious effects which the community would suffer from such relatively slight changes as the disestablishment of the Anglican church, an increased facility of divorce, adoption of female suffrage, prohibition of the manufacture and sale of intoxicating beverages, abolition or restriction of inheritances, etc. Any one of these innovations would, we are told, "shake the social structure to its base," "reduce society to chaos," "subvert the foundations of morality," "make life intolerable," "confound the order of nature," etc.
>
> (139–40)

Veblen explained these apocalyptic attitudes as simply an "aversion to change" and

> to the bother of making the readjustments which any given change will necessitate; and this solidarity of the system of institutions of any given culture or of any given people strengthens the instinctive resistance offered to any change in men's habits of thought, even in matters which, taken by themselves, are of minor importance.
>
> (140)

The conservatism of the leisure class also resulted in conservative lower classes, however, because of the need to devote energy and resources to readjustments:

The accumulation of wealth at the upper end of the pecuniary scale implies privation at the lower end of the scale. It is commonplace that, wherever it occurs, a considerable degree of privation among the body of the people is a serious obstacle to any innovation.

(141)

Veblen explained both the apparent radicalism of suffrage and temperance and the excessive resistance to changes of such "minor importance" in terms of the entrenchment of mental habits and social inequality. We can infer that he favored the changes he listed but doubted any dramatic consequences.[21]

At least some feminist leaders of the period partially shared his assessment. Gilman (1935, 186–7), for example, said she had "worked for equal suffrage when opportunity offered, believing it to be reasonable and necessary, though by no means as important as some of its protagonists held." Gilman's (1898) alternative emphasis was much closer to the logic of the new woman movement. She focussed on the need for women to achieve economic independence. But she also saw a division of labor between men and women as efficient and compatible with basic differences in their natures. She advocated the professionalization of housework and childrearing; these responsibilities should not isolate women or make them dependents but should, instead, become public pursuits.

By contrast with Gilman, Veblen would not have favored professionalizing housework; he saw most of it as devoted to a decorous wastefulness and to tastes that reflected invidious distinctions:

> [T]he greater part of the customary round of domestic cares to which the middle-class housewife gives her time and effort is of ... a decorative and mundificatory character. ... [T]he taste to which these effects of household adornment and tidiness appeal is a taste which has been formed under the selective guidance of a canon of propriety that demands just these evidences of wasted effort.
>
> (68–9)

Such invidious wastefulness was present in the settlement movement too:

> The solicitude of the "settlements," for example, is in part directed to enhance the industrial efficiency of the poor and to teach them the more adequate utilization of the means at hand; but it is also no less consistently directed to the inculcation, by precept and example, of certain punctilios of upper-class propriety in manners and customs. ... Those good people who go out to humanize the poor are commonly, and advisedly, extremely scrupulous and silently insistent in matters of decorum and the decencies of life.

219

They are commonly persons of an exemplary life and gifted with
a tenacious insistence on ceremonial cleanness in the various items
of their daily consumption. . . . The economic reform wrought is
largely of a nature of a permutation in the methods of conspicuous
waste.

(224–5)

Veblen explained that these pursuits had originated in a reversion, among
women of leisure protected from pecuniary struggle by their husbands' or
fathers' means, to more workmanlike impulses:

The exception from pecuniary stress has been carried further in the
case of the leisure-class woman of the advanced industrial communities than in any other considerable group of persons. The women
may therefore be expected to show a more pronounced reversion to
a noninvidious temperament than the men. . . . The tendency
to some other than invidious purpose in life has worked out in a
multitude of organizations, the purpose of which is some work of
charity or social amelioration. . . . [including] the agitation for
temperance and similar reforms, for prison reform, for the spread
of education, for the suppression of vice, and for the avoidance of
war by arbitration, disarmament, or other means; such are, in some
measure, university settlements, neighborhood guilds, [etc.]

(220–1)

Though social reform reflected "an effective skepticism with respect to the
full legitimacy of an emulative scheme of life" (221) and there were "some
motives of a non-emulative kind" (222), nevertheless "many of the efforts
now in reputable vogue for the amelioration of the indigent population of
large cities are of the nature, in great part, of a mission of culture" (223).
That is, they largely upheld existing cultural standards and proprieties.

Such criticisms of social reforms expressed Veblen's belief in the conservative drag of cultural habits rather than any wholesale condemnation of
reform efforts. Like other social pursuits, both the goals of reform and the
available means were cultural products that could not be expected to exhibit
radical or revolutionary breaks with existing conditions. But, in some sense
at least, this also made more genuine radicalism appear utopian. Veblen's
own social vision was probably much more radical than that of most
reformers but his lack of active commitment to radical change (or even
explicit public support for less radical reformism) can be partly explained
by his aversion to impractical and futile (utopian) schemes.[22]

Other than anthropology, the roots of Veblen's feminism are murky. He
made only a single reference to any feminist writer (but see note 21) though
we know he was impressed by the descriptions of a noninvidious society in

Edward Bellamy's *Looking Backward* (1889) and that he read Ibsen. At least as important, however, was his constant exposure to feminist ferment at the University of Chicago. It was probably the leading center of the new woman movement at the time. By 1900 women made up half the undergraduates and received 20 percent of the doctoral degrees. They flocked to the classrooms of sympathetic scholars such as Veblen, Thomas, and Dewey (Rosenberg 1982). This may explain why Veblen gave his most unqualified approval to the new woman movement rather than to more formal projects like suffrage, temperance, and the settlements.

Veblen saw great significance in the new woman movement; it "marks a reversion to a more generic type of human character, or to a less differentiated [read: less invidious] expression of human nature" (233–4). Invidiousness, subservience, and wasted effort were mutual conditions for one another and more useful social inclinations would thus require a diminished emphasis on social status.

> [T]hat less manageable body of modern women who, by force of youth, education, or temperament, are in some degree out of touch with the [received] traditions of status . . . and in whom there is, perhaps, an undue reversion to the impulse of self-expression and workmanship – these are touched with a sense of grievance too vivid to leave them at rest.
>
> In this "New-Woman" movement – as these blind and incoherent efforts to rehabilitate the woman's pre-glacial standing have been named – there are at least two elements discernible, both of which are of an economic character. [They] . . . are expressed by the double watchword, "Emancipation" and "Work." Each of these words is recognized to stand for something in the way of a widespread sense of grievance. . . . [T]here is a demand, more or less serious, for emancipation from all relation [*sic*] of status, tutelage, or vicarious life. . . . The demand comes from that portion of womankind which is excluded by the canons of good repute from all effectual work.
>
> (231–2)

These were the same women who heavily populated Veblen's courses and among whom he established some close and long-lasting friendships. In them he saw evidence to confirm what his reading of the anthropological record already showed, namely that

> the woman is endowed with her share – which there is reason to believe is more than an even share – of the instinct of workmanship,[23] to which futility of life or of expenditure is obnoxious. She must unfold her life activity in response to the direct, unmediated

221

[nonvicarious] stimuli of the economic environment with which she is in contact. The impulse is perhaps stronger upon the woman than upon the man to live her own life in her own way and to enter the industrial process of the community at something nearer than the second remove.

(232)

SOME ASSESSMENTS

The amorphous links between Veblen's writing and the feminism of his day does not make him less of a feminist. He clearly favored both work and emancipation for women and his doubts about far-reaching effects from reforms flowed easily from his larger evolutionary views of social change. Moreover, his use of evolutionary anthropology to support his positions was entirely understandable in that context; he repeatedly said that explanations of social change required a "genetic" (cause-and-effect) account of unfolding sequence, which no explicitly feminist writings of the period could offer. Nor should his differences from the bulk of contemporary feminism be exaggerated. In many ways they were no greater than his differences from the best-known arguments from nineteenth-century anthropology, which he used but also freely criticized.

From today's vantage point, the intimate association between Veblen and anthropology raises a number of important questions and may, in turn, make him vulnerable to the same sorts of criticisms he lodged against his contemporaries. For example, his speculative style of reasoning probably exceeds the tolerance of today's readers in at least the same degree as that of his contemporaries exceeded his. And we can readily find his own work as contaminated by the racialism of hundred-year-old anthropology as he found that the settlement movement was by social proprieties of the day (but see Jennings and Waller 1998). These are not minor issues in any assessment of Veblen's contributions or usefulness. But they are concerns that Veblen would also have acknowledged.

In the preface to *The Theory of the Leisure Class* Veblen issued the following caveat:

A more explicit statement of the theoretical position involved is made in a series of papers published in Volume IV of the *American Journal of Sociology*. . . . But the argument does not rest on these — *in part novel* — generalizations in such a way that it would altogether lose its possible value as a detail of economic theory in case these novel generalizations should, in the reader's apprehension, fall away through being insufficiently backed by authority or data.

(1899b, xx, emphasis added)

He knew that his *AJS* speculations might not hold up and, in fact, they were largely missing from the accounts of social evolution he gave in *The Instinct of Workmanship* (1914), which he regarded as his only important book. What survived there was, first, that women had been largely responsible for the technological advances that subsequently permitted the free play of predation and exploit by men and, second, that the genetic endowment of instinctual proclivities did not vary much across social groups or by sex but was variably expressed and molded by social conditions. A strong case can be made that these positions were the central elements of his feminism in the 1890s too, but readers should form their own judgments of the matter.

Nor did Veblen expect to transcend the constraints imposed on him by his intellectual milieu. All thought, he argued, was socially "contaminated" in this way (Veblen 1914, 54; see also Samuels 1990 and Jennings and Waller 1998), since the specific purposes that motivated human activities were always conditioned by specific social circumstances (see Jennings and Waller 1994). Samuels (1990) contends that by recognizing that his own positions necessarily fell within the circle of cultural understandings, however, he was aligning himself with the post-modern currents that would come to dominate Western philosophy in the twentieth century. Certainly his view that masculine and feminine personalities were culturally, not biologically, determined is also more consistent with current feminist distinctions between sex and gender than were most feminist arguments from 1900 (though active feminist debates about sex–gender distinctions continue productively today; see Butler 1990).

Veblen's feminism can also be faulted for its apparent tendency to singular explanations of the origins and evolution of women's unenviable social position. There are two useful responses to this problem. First, it remains a problem for current feminism, too. The resurgence of American feminism in the 1960s and 1970s brought with it a renewed interest in just such universalized origin stories, whether based on anthropology, Freudian psychology, or Marxian materialism (see Firestone 1970; Sacks 1975; Rubin 1975; Rosaldo 1980). These have subsequently (and probably deservedly) lost ground, to the point where "totalizing" theories themselves have been implicated by both anthropologists and feminists in maintaining invidious distinctions in societies around the world (see Stocking 1991; Said 1979; Mohanty *et al.* 1991; Spelman 1988; Riley 1988; Hill Collins 1990). The debates continue but the recognition, shared by Veblen, that there is never a full "escape" from cultural bias has increased, not decreased, the importance of (hopefully more self-critical) historical and anthropological explanations of social inequalities.

The second response relates to the relative absence of references to women in Veblen's writings after 1900. We can speculate that he simply chose not to recover the same ground again but one other possibility exists, namely that he also came to doubt the adequacy of singular explanations of social inequalities. He never repeated his initial account of the origins of private property in the seizure of women; student notes from his lectures (Thompson 1904; Lubin 1917–18; Yoder n.d.) suggest a growing awareness of the ethnological variability of social relationships and gender. He increasingly associated the patriarchal family with pastoral societies (e.g., those of Biblical peoples) and John G. Thompson (1904, 13) recorded the following: "Only by normalizing the data to the point of sterility can you connect, definitely, a certain organization of the family with a certain industrial [technological] organization or condition. – Veblen."[24]

The fact that Veblen wrote so little about women after 1900 also raises one final question. Though feminism was clearly central to Veblen's economic analysis in *The Theory of the Leisure Class*, was it also implicit in his later works in economic theory, the most notable of which are *The Theory of Business Enterprise* (1904) and *Absentee Ownership* (1923)? The matter cannot be resolved here but the answer may hinge on how "feminist economics" is defined; Veblen offers an interesting case to explore in this regard.

There seem to be two main approaches to what constitutes feminist economics. One, perhaps more common, is to see feminist economics as "the economics of women." The other is to use the insights of feminist philosophy, history, and anthropology to challenge the gendered cultural foundations and biases of economic theories themselves, whether received orthodoxy or such heterodoxies as Marxism and neo-Marxism, post-Keynesianism, and Institutionalism ("old" and "new"). One goal of the latter view of feminist economics is to make gender issues fundamental at the outset of analysis. It raises doubts that gender concerns can be adequately or consistently addressed as an afterthought in theory. Just as Harding (1986) found that "the science question in feminism" was more radical than "the feminist question in science," however, "the economics question in feminism" raises a larger set of critical questions for economics than does the approach labeled "the economics of women."

The economics question in feminism includes, but raises further challenges to economic analyses of women whenever the latter are undertaken with theories containing inherent gender biases in their philosophical and methodological foundations, their conceptual categories, their theoretical premises, or the boundaries of analysis. And, in societies with unequal power and status relationships, social theories will typically contain such biases in some degree. A very promising line of critical feminist research has resulted from these insights (e.g., Ferber and Nelson 1993). Another aspect of the issue, however, is whether feminist economics is properly a field of study within economics (as in the economics of women) or, instead, should flow from methodological or metatheoretical dispositions and extend the implications of feminist principles even to fields where women and gender issues do not (presently) seem important (e.g., Jennings 1994). Of course, by stating the question in these terms I have already hinted at my personal response.

It would be terribly parochial to suggest that feminist economics was not feminist whenever it was not discussing women in particular – and no better than saying that economics would be feminist if discussions of gender (or other social) inequities could be deferred indefinitely (as they can be in much of current economic theory). Feminist economics is not limited to questions specifically about women. Thus it is not clear what Veblen's silence on women's issues in his later work implies about whether that work was as informed by feminism as his earlier work. Much more effort is needed to explore that question. The matter is far from trivial; it goes to the heart of what the aspirations of feminist economics can or should be. Accommodation to feminist principles (of whatever form, and there are now many) may be at least as important to judging the strengths of economic theories as the presence or merits of particular explanations of inequality. And, given the dearth of feminist arguments in the history of economics, there may be much more to learn from Veblen's example than simply whether his specific explanations have withstood the test of time.

NOTES

1 The major influences on Thorstein Veblen's economic thought are fairly clear and well-known. He was first taught economics by John Bates Clark when Clark was still under the influence of his German education and the German Historical School of economic thought. He encountered Herbert Spencer's social evolutionism early on (probably while still an undergraduate), was taught by Spencer's disciple, William Graham Sumner, at Yale and wrote his now missing dissertation on Spencer and Kant. He sat in briefly on C.S. Peirce's lectures at Johns Hopkins and his exposure to Kantian philosophy encouraged his interest in instinct psychology and the work of William James. His Norwegian background fed his concern with both anthropology and the hereditary bases of human behavior. His early lectures on socialism at the University of Chicago revealed and extended his engagement with Marxism, its allies, and its critics. He was also intrigued by Edward Bellamy's utopian novels. Finally, perhaps the greatest influence of all was Charles Darwin. Though all these influences are reasonably well known, the particular role of most remains somewhat unclear (Tilman 1996). Veblen read very widely but seldom cited his sources; he was also a highly original thinker, borrowing selectively and reinterpreting much of what he borrowed. Moreover, to my knowledge, no careful analysis of the origins of Veblen's feminist views has previously been undertaken.
2 See Veblen (1901, 272–3; 1907, 435; 1908, 186; 1914, 69, 94, 144). Veblen taught at the University of Chicago (1892–1906), Stanford University (1906–1909), the University of Missouri (1910–1918) and at the New School for Social Research (1919–1923). His course, "Economic Factors in Civilization," which was taught at Chicago, Stanford, and Missouri, regularly contained remarks on the status of women, their economic contributions, and the patriarchal family. Numerous sets of student course notes have survived (see

225

Thompson 1904; Lubin 1917–18; Yoder n.d.; among others; all are in the Dorfman papers at Columbia University).

3 The other main psychological theory of the day was associationism. It rested on Humean empiricism and held that our only knowledge of the world came through our senses, that repeated sequences of events produced associations among experiences, and that such experiential associations yielded the sole supportable meaning of reality. Moreover, regularities in experience were the only possible meaning of "causation," while sense-based hedonism became the only basis for human values (Robinson 1982). The best-known nineteenth century advocates of associationism were Mill and Spencer; the former added utilitarian arguments, while the latter appended the Lamarckian inheritance of originally naive human associations (and Benthamite preferences) to produce evolutionary advances in human knowledge and tastes. Mill accepted Spencer's version of associationism as definitive (Stocking 1987). Veblen, in turn, found such representations of knowledge and causation completely incoherent. He dismissed associationism's naive empiricism, its positivism, its pre-Darwinian teleology, its hedonism, and its passive view of human nature in favor of Kantian apperception, Jamesian instinctual purposefulness, and causal concepts linked to Peircean abduction (see Jennings and Waller 1998). Without the latter, the event irregularities involved in evolutionary change would be inexplicable.

4 Most of the leading evolutionary anthropologists of the period held such a belief; Morgan was the main exception. They usually did not regard it as "customary right of exclusive individual abuse," however, or else held that it had evolved into a loving relationship in which patriarchy became a means of elevating women to their proper, adored place.

5 Diggins (1977) argues that Veblen's attempted reformulation of theories of private property also targeted Marxian accounts of the conjuncture of original forms of private property with original forms of alienation. According to Diggins, Veblen found that Marxian private property required that alienation must have preceded it, *and vice versa*. This is certainly a plausible interpretation of some of Veblen's concerns. The *AJS* articles were written at a time when he was deeply engaged with socialist writings; he wrote and published numerous reviews of socialist works in *The Journal of Political Economy* (which he edited) in the period and was also teaching a thorough course on the "Varieties of Socialism" at the University of Chicago. But Veblen was almost certainly also attacking existing theories of the evolution of marriage in human society, most of which posited an early period in which women were the "common possession" (Thomas 1909, 530) of the men in the group. Veblen denied that such a period had occurred, probably following the arguments of Westermarck (1891).

6 Perhaps because Spencer had led the way in studying social evolution and because Veblen did borrow several important ideas from him (Jennings and Waller 1998; Eff 1989; Edgell and Tilman 1989).

7 Though this quote is somewhat later (1914), and reflects Veblen's eventual grounding of "the stability of racial types" in the the work of Hugo de Vries (after the rediscovery of Mendel – see Jennings and Waller 1998), Veblen had reached nearly the same conclusion by 1899, arguing that biology was the "remoter cause" of differences in human behavior, while culture was the "proximate cause" (Veblen 1899c, 99).

8 As Boas had found that competition by property and goods (Potlatch) was a latter-day substitute for physical demonstrations of prowess among the Kwakiutl (Boas 1895, 343). Veblen was certainly aware of the account, citing it in both Veblen 1914 and in his lectures.

9 Veblen was familiar with most of these writings. Student notes from Veblen's classes, though from a somewhat later period (Thompson 1904; Lubin 1917–18; Yoder n.d.) also cite Maxime Kovalevsky (1890) and O.T. Mason (1894). Both of these sources were likely known to Veblen in the 1890s and Mason was almost certainly one of Veblen's main sources on the technological contributions of women to social development. See Fee (1974) for a good discussion of Veblen's main predecessors on the anthropology of women and the family; W.I. Thomas (1909), Veblen's colleague at the University of Chicago, also published an interesting contemporary reader, digest, and bibliography of these and other topics in anthropology; and see Lowie (1937).

10 Patriarchal, ownership-marriage with male heads of household, Veblen argued, was not necessarily antithetical to matrilineal systems of descent. Matrilineality indicated, at most, a longer period before the predatory stage of culture had been reached. There was no implication of "the prior existence of a maternal household of the kind in which the woman is the head and master of a household group. . . . Still less does it imply a prior state of promiscuity." Coercive marriage was most probably preceded by noncoerced unions, "terminable at will by either party" (1899a, 63), under more peaceable social conditions. These remarks are probably directed at Morgan; of Engels (and Bebel) he said: "The efforts of Engels (*Ursprung der Familie*) and Bebel (*Die Frau*) would scarcely be taken seriously as scientific monographs even by hot-headed socialists if it were not for the lack of anything better" (Veblen 1907, 435).

11 Thomas himself later rejected his own argument, however, in light of research by women graduate students at Chicago, most notably Helen Thompson (Woolley)'s *The Mental Traits of Sex* (1903), which refuted biological causation arguments. See Rosenberg (1975). Gilman knew Veblen but apparently met him after 1900. She reported to Dorfman that "I have met Thorstein more than once. A dry quizical [*sic*] man, as I remember. . . . The Theory of the Leisure Class was recommended to me by my old friend Dr. E.A. Ross, who wrote me that he had enjoyed it more than any book since my Women and Economics. To me it seemed clear and impressive; and, though rather stiff and labored in parts, illuminated by the most brilliant and penetrating satire I ever saw" (Gilman 30 August 1933). Becky Meyers, Veblen's stepdaughter, also said that "T[horstein] must have known Charlotte P. Gilman. I recall Anne V[eblen, his second wife and Becky's mother] telling us stories in 1909 of Gilman, of whom she was very fond. How G[ilman] tryed [*sic*] to saw lumber like a man while swearing under her breath" (Meyers 26 February 1982). Veblen's address book (1929). also included Gilman's name.

12 For the classic review of positions and difficulties in liberal feminism (as well as other feminist stances) see Jaggar (1983). Current woman's nature arguments include Gilligan (1982). Degler (1980) argues convincingly that suffrage did not become a successful mass movement until it abandoned its liberal stance in favor of arguments linked to social homemaking and maternal morality.

13 Folbre (1991) has shown how official government statistics were modified over the nineteenth century to reclassify women's domestic activities from work to "leisure"; even women's paid labor was often excluded from official labor statistics unless women were the household's primary source of income (Peterson 1990). Thus, although "labor" was primarily associated with distinctions among men by the end of the nineteenth century, it still retained important gender dimensions. Women were not regarded as proper wage-earners and "a woman's wage" was virtually an oxymoron (Kessler-Harris 1990).

14 Stanton's and Anthony's views are analyzed in Eisenstein (1987), DuBois (1975), and Degler (1980). The classic account of suffrage arguments is Kraditor (1965).

15 Women's domesticity was a middle-class norm that was only gradually achieved among the urban working class over the nineteenth century. Even then, it was primarily skilled, native-born white men who achieved the "family wages" necessary to separate spheres. That it inspired emulation was reflected in both family wage struggles by men and the concealment of remunerative labor by women, even in official statistics (Folbre 1991; Peterson 1990). The norm only intensified wage disadvantages for working-class women who needed to earn but lacked the skills or refinements for feminine occupations such as clerical work and sales, however, and maintained their dependence on men's wages – as was intended, given that women's independence implied immorality (Kessler-Harris 1990).

16 Degler (1980, 318), for example, notes that "by 1889 [Willard] had [established] 39 departments in the WCTU, organized under headings like labor, women, health, social purity, peace and arbitration, as well as temperance."

17 Thompson (Woolley) (1903), for example, found no support for innate differences in talents or mental abilities between men and women in controlled experimental studies, though she argued that cultural factors, such as differences in class, educational opportunities, and social norms and encouragements, probably did cause differences among the general population.

18 On developments in domestic science see Strasser (1982) and Hayden (1981); on the variety of programs at Hull House see Hayden (1981).

19 Addams wrote two letters, both very brief, to Dorfman about her contacts with Veblen. In the first she said, "I knew Mr. Veblen when he was in Chicago and the Arts and Crafts Society to which you refer used to meet at Hull House. However, I seem unable to recall anything of special interest connected with him" (Addams 3 June, 1930). In the second letter she reported that "he spoke once or twice at Hull House but I never felt that I knew him intimately nor do I have much more impression of him than I have gained from reading him" (Addams 17 [September?] 1932).

20 But also see Eisenstein's (1987) view of the "radical feminist" aspects of Stanton's thought, and Jaggar (1983) for a classic survey of radical feminism. Briefly, radical feminists tend to hold that sex and sexuality are the basic root of women's oppression and/or that gender is a more basic form of oppression than class. A "woman's nature" argument concerning the special virtues of women is also important in some radical feminist accounts (e.g., Gilligan 1982).

21 Veblen's reiteration of his scorn for those who opposed women's demands contained the only reference to any feminist anywhere in his work:

> The good and beautiful scheme of life, then – that is to say the scheme to which we are habituated – assigns to the woman a "sphere" ancillary to the activity of the man. . . . It is unfeminine in her to aspire to a self-directing, self-centered life . . . [and] is a menace to that social order which expresses . . . the traditions of pecuniary culture. "All this fume and froth of 'emancipating woman from the slavery of man' and so on is, to use the chaste and expressive language of Elizabeth Cady Stanton inversely, 'utter rot.' The social relation of the sexes are fixed by nature. Our entire civilization . . . is based on the home." . . . [T]he existing moral order, of necessity and by the divine right of prescription, places the woman in a position ancillary to the man.
>
> (1899b, 230)

But it is Veblen's unnamed source who quotes Stanton, not Veblen himself. Much later, in student notes from his course on "Economic Factors in

Civilization," Veblen again affirmed the limited probable consequences of woman's suffrage:

> At present the patriarchal family does not seem to be in as good shape as formerly. This has come about with the extending of suffrage to women and the fact that the father no longer has exclusive control of children. . . . The patriarchal family . . . is still right and is still fundamentally and eternally good but it is not as fundamentally and eternally good as it used to be. . . . In modern times there is no exigency that falls much upon the patriarchal family so that there is no particular decay of the patriarchal family. It does not greatly matter. . . . In time of exigency decay may go on. A campaign or crusade against this particular institution may have some bearing. The resulting process of change is rather slight and slow because on the whole it does not greatly matter. There is no strong selective force engaged in the crusade.
>
> (Lubin 1917–18, 28)

NB: the "extending of suffrage to women" most likely refers to passage by the US House of Representatives, which occurred January 10, 1918 but was followed by a defeat in the US Senate (Catt 1923). Final ratification did not occur until August 1920.

22 Nevertheless, there were utopian elements in some of his economic thought, especially on the subject of "the engineers," on whom Veblen eventually pinned his hopes for a more efficient, less acquisitive and predatory set of economic arrangements. These hopes reflected some scientistic elements in his thought; see Rutherford (1992); Mirowski (1987).

23 A phrase he attributed to Sarah McLean Hardy (Gregory), one of his students and a long-time friend; see Dorfman (1934, 197).

24 The remark appeared in a discussion of social forms among native American groups and clearly reflected Veblen's extensive familiarity with ethnographic materials. Stocking (1987) credits Boas with considerable responsibility for the growing importance of ethnography and the eventual displacement of earlier (generally unilinear) accounts of cultural evolution by much more relativist and diffusionist ethnologies in anthropology. Boas was also the first to use the plural term, "cultures," rather than the singular; Veblen may well have taken note.

REFERENCES

Addams, Jane (1930) Letter to Joseph Dorfman, 3 June, Dorfman Archive, Box 61, Columbia Rare Book Room, Columbia University.

—— (1932) Letter to Joseph Dorfman, 17 [September?], Dorfman Archive, Box 61, Columbia Rare Book Room, Columbia University.

Bachofen, J.J. (1861) *Myth, Religion, and Mother Right*, trans. R. Manheim (1967), Princeton: Princeton University Press.

Bellamy, Edward (1889) *Looking Backward*, Boston: Houghton Mifflin.

Boas, Franz (1884–85) "The Central Eskimo," *Bureau of American Ethnology*, Washington: Smithsonian Institution: 399–659.

—— (1895) "Social Organization of the Kwakiutl," *National Museum Report*, Washington: Smithsonian Institution: 311–738.

Butler, Judith (1990) *Gender Trouble*, London: Routledge.

Catt, Carrie Chapman (1923) *Woman Suffrage and Politics*, New York: Charles Scribner's Sons.

Degler, Carl (1980) *At Odds*, New York: Oxford University Press.

Diggins, John (1977) "Animism and the Origins of Alienation," *History and Theory* 16 (May): 113–36.

—— (1978) *The Bard of Savagery*, New York: The Seabury Press.

Dorfman, Joseph (1934) *Thorstein Veblen and His America*, New York: Viking Press.

DuBois, Ellen (1975) "The Radicalism of the Woman Suffrage Movement," *Feminist Studies* 3 (Fall): 63–71.

Edgell, Stephen and Tilman, Rick (1989) "The Intellectual Antecedents of Thorstein Veblen," *Journal of Economic Issues* 23: 1003–26.

Eff, Anton (1989) "History of Thought as Ceremonial Genealogy," *Journal of Economic Issues* 23: 689–716.

Eisenstein, Zillah (1987) "Elizabeth Cady Stanton: Radical Feminist Analysis and Liberal Feminist Strategy," in Anne Phillips (ed.) *Feminism and Equality*, New York: New York University Press: 77–102.

Engels, Friedrich (1884) *The Origin of the Family*, as reprinted 1972, New York: International Publishers.

Fee, Elizabeth (1974) "The Sexual Politics of Victorian Social Anthropology," in M. Hartman and L. Banner (eds) *Clio's Consciousness Raised*, New York: Harper and Row: 23–39.

Ferber, Marianne and Nelson, Julie (eds) (1993) *Beyond Economic Man*, Chicago: University of Chicago Press.

Firestone, Shulamith (1970) *The Dialectic of Sex*, New York: William Morrow.

Folbre, Nancy (1991) "The Unproductive Housewife," *Signs* 16 (3): 463–84.

—— (1993) "Socialism, Feminist and Scientific," in M. Ferber and J. Nelson (eds) *Beyond Economic Man*, Chicago: University of Chicago Press: 94–110.

Gilligan, Carol (1982) *In a Different Voice*, Cambridge, MA: Harvard University Press.

Gilman, Charlotte P. (1898) *Women and Economics*, as reprinted 1990, New York: Harper and Row.

—— (1911) *The Man-Made World*, New York: Charlton Co.

—— (1933) Letter to Joseph Dorfman, 30 August, Dorfman Archive, Box 61, Columbia Rare Book Room, Columbia University.

—— (1935) *The Living of Charlotte Perkins Gilman*, as reprinted 1990, Madison: University of Wisconsin Press.

Greenwood, Daphne (1984) "The Economic Significance of 'Woman's Place' in Society," *Journal of Economic Issues* 18 (September): 663–80.

Haddock Siegfried, Charlene (1996) *Pragmatism and Feminism*, Chicago: University of Chicago Press.

Harding, Sandra (1986) *The Science Question in Feminism*, Ithaca: Cornell University Press.

Hayden, Delores (1981) *The Grand Domestic Revolution*, Cambridge, MA: MIT Press.

Hill Collins, Patricia (1990) *Black Feminist Thought*, Boston: Unwin Hyman.

Jaggar, Alison (1983) *Feminist Politics and Human Nature*, Totowa, NJ: Rowman and Allanheld.

Jennings, Ann (1992) "Not the Economy," in W. Dugger and W. Waller (eds) *The Stratified State*, Armonk, NY: M.E. Sharpe: 117–49.

—— (1993) "Public or Private?" in M. Ferber and J. Nelson (eds) *Beyond Economic Man*, Chicago: University of Chicago Press: 111–29.

—— (1994) "Towards an Expansion of Feminist Macroeconomics," *Journal of Economic Issues* 28 (June): 555–65.

Jennings, Ann and Waller, William (1994) "Evolutionary Economics and Cultural Hermeneutics," *Journal of Economic Issues* 28 (December): 997–1030.

—— (1998) "The Place of Biological Science in Veblen's Economics," *History of Political Economy* (forthcoming).

Kessler-Harris, Alice (1990) *A Woman's Wage*, Lexington: University Press of Kentucky.

Kovalevsky, Maxime (1890) *Tableau des Origines at de l'Evolution de la Famille et de la Propriété*, Stockholm.

Kraditor, Aileen (1965) *The Ideas of the Woman Suffrage Movement, 1890–1920*, as reprinted 1971, Garden City, NY: Doubleday-Anchor.

Lowie, Robert (1937) *The History of Ethnological Theory*, New York: Holt, Rinehart and Winston.

Lubbock, John (1870) *The Origin of Civilization and the Primitive Condition of Man*, London: Longmans Green.

Lubin, Isador (1917–18) Course notes for Veblen's Economic Factors in Civilization, Dorfman Archive, Box 67, no. 8, Columbia Rare Book Room, Columbia University.

Maine, Henry Sumner (1860) *Ancient Law*, 4th edn. 1870, London: J. Murray.

Mason, O.T. (1894) *The Share of Woman in Primitive Society*, New York: D. Appleton.

Matthaei, Julie (1982) *An Economic History of Women in America*, New York: Schocken.

McLennan, John (1865) *Primitive Marriage*, Edinburgh: A & C Black.

Meyers, Becky (1982) Letter to Jack Diggins, 26 February, Dorfman Archive, Box 62, Columbia Rare Book Room, Columbia University.

Mill, John Stuart (1869) "The Subjection of Women," as reprinted in Alice Rossi (ed.) (1970) *John Stuart Mill and Harriet Taylor Mill: Essays on Sex Equality*, Chicago: University of Chicago Press.

Miller, Edythe (1972) "Veblen and Women's Lib," *Journal of Economic Issues* 6 (September): 75–86.

Mirowski, Philip (1987) "The Philosophical Basis of Institutional Economics," *Journal of Economic Issues* 21: 1001–38.

Mohanty, Chandra, Russo, Ann and Torres, Lourdes (eds) (1991) *Third World Women and the Politics of Feminism*, Bloomington: Indiana University Press.

Morgan, Lewis Henry (1871) *Systems of Consanguinity and Affinity of the Human Family*, Smithsonian Contributions to Knowledge, Vol. 17. Washington: Smithsonian Institution.

—— (1877) *Ancient Society*, as reprinted 1964, Cambridge, MA: Harvard University Press.

Nicholson, Linda (1986) *Gender and History*, New York: Columbia University Press.

Peterson, Janice (1990) "What's in a Number?" unpublished paper, State University of New York at Fredonia.

Riley, Denise (1988) *Am I that Name?*, Minneapolis: University of Minnesota Press.

Robinson, Daniel (1982) *Towards a Science of Human Nature*, New York: Columbia University Press.

Rosaldo, Michelle (1980) "The Use and Abuse of Anthropology," *Signs* 5 (3): 389–417.

Rosenberg, Rosalind (1975) "In Search of Woman's Nature, 1850–1920," *Feminist Studies* 3 (Fall): 141–54.

—— (1982) *Beyond Separate Spheres*, New Haven: Yale University Press.

Rubin, Gayle (1975) "The Traffic in Women," in R. Reiter (ed.) *Toward an Anthropology of Women*, New York: Monthly Review Press: 157–210.

Rutherford, M. (1992) "Thorstein Veblen and the Problem of the Engineers," *International Review of Sociology* 3: 125–50.

Ryan, Barbara (1982) "Thorstein Veblen: A New Perspective," *Mid-American Review of Sociology* 7 (2): 29–47.

Sacks, Karen (1975) "Engels Revisited," in M. Rosaldo and L. Lamphere (eds) *Woman, Culture and Society*, Stanford: Stanford University Press: 207–22.

Said, Edward (1979) *Orientalism*, New York: Vintage Press.

Samuels, Warren (1990) "The Self-Referentiability of Thorstein Veblen's Theory of Preconceptions of Economic Science," *Journal of Economic Issues* 24: 695–718.

Smith-Rosenberg, Carroll (1985) *Disorderly Conduct*, New York: Oxford University Press.

Spelman, Elizabeth (1988) *Inessential Woman*, Boston: Beacon Press.

Spencer, Herbert (1876) *Principles of Sociology*, New York: D. Appleton.

Starr, Frederick (1891) "Dress and Adornment, I and II," *Popular Science Monthly* 39: 488–502; 787–801.

Stocking, George W. Jr (1987) *Victorian Anthropology*, New York: Free Press.

—— (1991) *Colonial Situations*, Madison: University of Wisconsin Press.

Strasser, Susan (1982) *Never Done*, New York: Pantheon Books.

Tarde, Gabriel (1890) *Les Lois de l'imitation*, Paris.

Tax, Meredith (1980) *The Rising of the Women*, New York: Monthly Review Press.

Thomas, W.I. (1897) "On a Difference in the Metabolism of the Sexes," *American Journal of Sociology* 3 (July): 31–63.

—— (1909) *Source Book for Social Origins*, Chicago: University of Chicago Press.

Thompson, John G. (1904) Course notes for Veblen's Economic Factors in Civilization, Dorfman Archive, Box 69, no. 36, Columbia Rare Book Room, Columbia University.

Thompson (Woolley), Helen (1903) *The Mental Traits of Sex*, Chicago: University of Chicago Press.

Tilman, Rick (1996) *The Intellectual Legacy of Thorstein Veblen*, Westport, CT: Greenwood Press.

Veblen, T. (1884) "Kant's Critique of Judgment," as reprinted in L. Ardzrooni (ed.) (1934) *Essays in our Changing Order*, New York: Viking: 175–93.

—— (1892) "Some Neglected Points in the Theory of Socialism," as reprinted in T. Veblen, 1919, *The Place of Science in Modern Civilization*, New York: B.W. Huebsch: 387–408.

—— (1894) "The Economic Theory of Woman's Dress," as reprinted in L. Ardzrooni (ed.) (1934) *Essays in our Changing Order*, New York: Viking: 65–77.

—— (1898a) "The Instinct of Workmanship and the Irksomeness of Labor," as reprinted in L. Ardzrooni (ed.) (1934) *Essays in our Changing Order*, New York: Viking: 78–96.

—— (1898b) "The Beginnings of Ownership," as reprinted in L. Ardzrooni (ed.) (1934) *Essays in our Changing Order*, New York: Viking: 32–49.

—— (1899a) "The Barbarian Status of Women," as reprinted in L. Ardzrooni (ed.) (1934) *Essays in our Changing Order*, New York: Viking: 50–64.

—— (1899b) *The Theory of the Leisure Class*, as reprinted 1953, New York: Mentor Books.

—— (1899c) "The Preconceptions of Economic Science I," as reprinted in T. Veblen, 1919, *The Place of Science in Modern Civilization*, New York: B.W. Huebsch: 82–113.

—— (1901) "Gustav Schmoller's Economics," as reprinted in T. Veblen, 1919, *The Place of Science in Modern Civilization*, New York: B.W. Huebsch: 252–78.

—— (1904) *The Theory of Business Enterprise*, as reprinted 1978, New Brunswick, NJ: Transaction.

—— (1907) "The Socialist Economics of Karl Marx and his Followers – II," as reprinted in T. Veblen, 1919, *The Place of Science in Modern Civilization*, New York: B.W. Huebsch: 431–56.

—— (1908) "Professor Clark's Economics," as reprinted in T. Veblen, 1919, *The Place of Science in Modern Civilization*, New York: B.W. Huebsch: 180–230.

—— (1914) *The Instinct of Workmanship and the State of The Industrial Arts*, as reprinted 1990, New Brunswick, NJ: Transaction.

—— (1923) *Absentee Ownership*, as reprinted 1967, Boston: Beacon Press.

—— (1929) Address Book of Thorstein Veblen, Carleton College Archives.

Waddoups, Jeffrey and Tilman, Rick (1992) "Thorstein Veblen and the Feminism of Institutionalism," *International Review of Sociology* 3: 182–204.

Ward, Lester Frank (1888) "Our Better Halves," *Forum* 6 (November): 266–75.

Westermarck, E. (1891) *The History of Human Marriage*, London: Macmillan.

Yoder, Fred (no date) Course notes for Veblen's Economic Factors in Civilization, Dorfman Archive, Box 67, no. 11, Columbia Rare Book Room, Columbia University.

13

VEBLEN AND THE
ANTHROPOLOGICAL
PERSPECTIVE

Anne Mayhew

It is widely known that, in *The Theory of the Leisure Class*, and indeed in
all of his work, Thorstein Veblen employed an "anthropological approach"
to his descriptions of modern economies. In this paper I will explore the
meaning and consequences of these anthropological roots. Changes that were
occurring in anthropology itself, even as Veblen was writing *The Theory of
the Leisure Class,* have tended to obscure the multiple meanings that anthropology had for Veblen. The divergent paths of economic anthropology and
of institutional economics in this century will also be explained.

VEBLEN'S ANTHROPOLOGICAL ROOTS

During the 1870s and 1880s, while Veblen was a student at Carleton, Johns
Hopkins, and Yale, and during the interlude of unemployment while he
read on the family farm, the body of thought that was becoming the modern
discipline of anthropology was profoundly affected by "Darwinism." Old
ideas and evidence about the progression of human society from savagery
to civilization were reformulated as Darwinian or, much more accurately,
as Spencerian evolution (Lowie, 1937, p. 19; Eggan, 1968, p. 122; Stocking,
1968, pp. 110–38).

Several things about the work of the major creators of this new anthropological conception of the human record (E. B. Tylor, Sir Henry Maine,
Lewis Henry Morgan) are important in understanding how Veblen fitted
into the anthropological mold.[1] The first is that the work of the "historical
evolutionary school" did not derive directly from Darwin. Robert Lowie
(1937, p. 19), George W. Stocking Jr (1968, pp. 110–132), and most
recently Ann Jennings and William Waller (HOPE, forthcoming) have all
emphasized that, as Lowie put it,

the idea of progressive development from savagery to civilization was much older than Darwin or even Lamarck. However, when evolution became not merely an approved biological principle but a magical catchword for the solution of all problems, it naturally assimilated the earlier speculations about cultural change as obviously congruous with its own philosophy.

(Lowie 1937, p. 19)[2]

When Veblen described his own approach "as Darwinian," he was putting himself in the camp of the anthropologists. A number of Veblen's ideas, and particularly those in *The Theory of the Leisure Class*, were in many ways identical to the mainstream view of anthropologists and other social theorists who, in the 1880s and 1890s, had taken "evolution" as the organizing principle for their comparative work.

In *The Theory of the Leisure Class*, Veblen adopted the stages theory of human society that was a central feature of the historical/evolutionary school in anthropology. Veblen is notoriously difficult to read with confidence because his sharp wit makes it hard to know when analysis shades to satire. Further, Veblen sometimes "made up" prehistory in order to poke fun at the modern world (as in "An Early Experiment in Trusts"). There is, therefore, the danger that Chapter 1 ("Introductory") of *The Theory of the Leisure Class* may strike the modern reader as an example of using prehistory solely for satire. It would be easy to think that the initial words of the book – The institution of a leisure class is found in its best development at the higher stages of the barbarian culture (Veblen, 1899 [1967], p. 1) – were written only in order to set the stage for the sardonic treatment of the modern leisure class that follows.

Veblen's description of the stage of human history at which a leisure class appeared, and his description of the evolution of that class in subsequent stages, was quite straightforward anthropology as well as a satirical social commentary. For example, Lewis Henry Morgan, in presenting his version of evolutionary history (originally published in 1877) had described the same stages that Veblen uses in *The Theory of the Leisure Class*. According to Morgan, there were three periods of savagery, three of barbarism, and the current "status of civilization." Each of these "Ethnical Periods" had a particular "mode of life" – a particular technological base – and there were cultural patterns characteristic of that mode (Morgan, 1877 [1964], p. 15). These "ethnical periods" were part of a sequence that was universal and "a natural as well as necessary sequence of progress" (p. 11).

Veblen's own arguments about what drives social change bear great similarity to Morgan's materialistic conception of history and discussion of the "ratio of human progress" associated with the various stages. Morgan says that it is "probable that the great epochs of human progress have been identified, more or less directly, with the enlargement of the sources of subsistence" (p. 24). Further, it is possible to read Morgan as saying that it was change in the "arts of subsistence" that drove all other change. This is the interpretation that Leslie A. White offers in his "Introduction" to the 1964 edition of *Ancient Society*, and it is this interpretation that, as White says, endeared the work to Marx and Engels (p. xxxiii).[3]

The racial analysis that is part of *The Theory of the Leisure Class* was also part of the anthropology of the 1890s. Passages such as the following were quite within the mainstream of that discipline at the time that it was written:

> The man of our industrial communities tends to breed true to one or the other of three main ethnic types: the dolichocephalic-blond, the bracycephalic-brunette, and the Mediterranean – disregarding minor and outlying elements of our culture. But within each of these main ethnic types the reversion tends to one or the other of at least two main directions of variation; the peaceable or ante-predatory variant and the predatory variant. The former of these two character-istic variants is nearer to the generic type in each case, being the reversional representative of its type as it stood at the earliest stage of associated life of which there is available evidence, either archae-ological or psychological.
>
> (Veblen 1899 [1964], p. 215)

This and similar passages appear to the modern reader to be nonsense at best or, at worst, racially bigoted and offensive. For Veblen and his contemporaries however, ethnicity and race were assumed to be essentially the same. Discussions of racial variation were in fact discussions of what we would today call ethnic or cultural differences. In the passage just cited, Veblen is mixing what we would think of as quite separate biological and cultural characteris-tics, and doing so in a way that makes no sense in modern social science.

It is difficult for those of us who live in the late twentieth century to appreciate the way in which scholars of the late nineteenth thought of race, and therefore easy to think that they were "racists" as we have come to use that term. Stocking's discussion of the role given race in the widespread Lamarckianism of the social sciences at the end of the nineteenth and the beginning of the twentieth century is a good source for understanding the complexity of this issue. Stocking provides convincing evidence that, in the social science community in the US at the time,

> [t]he assumption that the processes of race formation were in large part social, and operated in the present through the biological mech-anism of the inheritance of acquired characteristics, provided a theoretical rationale for the widespread casual misapplication of the term "race" to various national and cultural groups.
>
> (Stocking 1968, p. 245)

It is in this anthropological context that Veblen's racial (and to the modern ear, racist) analysis is to be understood.

Viewed as work done within anthropology, rather than within economics, Veblen's efforts (most famously in "Why Is Economics Not an Evolutionary Science?" [1898] (1990)) to find a genetic, causal explanation for evolution takes on rather different meaning. That essay is most often read as criticism of the progress of economics, and it certainly is that. It was also a plea for importation into economics of the anthropological approach.[4]

Veblen was also in process of developing what was still a fairly inchoate theory of how evolutionary change occurred. His own articulation of the anthropological perspective described human activity rather than satisfaction of desires as the essence of humanness and,

> the desires under whose guidance the action takes place are circum-
> stances of temperament which determine the specific direction in
> which the activity will unfold itself in the given case. These circum-
> stances of temperament are ultimate and definitive for the individual
> who acts under them, so far as regards his attitude as agent in the
> particular action in which he is engaged. But, in the view of
> the science, they are elements of the existing frame of mind of the
> agent, and are . . . the products of his hereditary traits and his past
> experience.
>
> (1990, p. 74)

This passage and those that follow show Veblen to have been working out for economics a theory of evolutionary change that not only involved heavy borrowing from anthropology but also a new direction of theorizing about change as well. However, Veblen's evolutionary theories did not arouse much interest among anthropologists. By the time Veblen published *The Theory of the Leisure Class,* the nature and focus of anthropological research and theory was already changing substantially, and much of what Veblen borrowed and used in *Leisure Class* was left behind in the anthropological attic.

Fred Eggan describes two "great syntheses" of thought in the anthropology of the last half of the nineteenth century. The first synthesis was that of the historical evolutionists; the second "centered around the regional formulation of ethnographic data – their ordering in space" (1968, p. 122). In the second synthesis, the natural environment, diffusion, and migration were the important causes of cultural variation, not progress through a rela-tively invariant set of historical stages. The problem was that these two syntheses produced drastically different "histories."[5] Eggan observes that this could be ignored for quite some time as "the evolutionists were largely concerned with social and religious institutions and the anthropogeographers dealt mainly with material culture" (p. 123).

Eventually, however, a reconciliation of sorts was forged, primarily by Franz Boas (Eggan, 1968, pp. 127–129). It was a lopsided reconciliation. The ideas of a universal history of mankind and of comparing the social patterns of diverse peoples were not explicitly abandoned. Nevertheless, the focus of research was that of the ethnogeographers: it was the culture of particular peoples – and the contacts that they had had with others, and the resulting cultural diffusion – that was now of importance to anthropologists.[6]

The pivotal figure in this shift of focus was Franz Boas. To understand what Boas did, and how he did it, it may help to suggest that Boas was to the change in anthropological thought what Keynes was to the rejection of "classical economics" in favor of the "Keynesian economics" of the 1930s, 1940s, 1950s, and 1960s. Or, as easily, one could say that Boas played much the same role in anthropology as Adam Smith played in economics when he defined the "mercantilist" philosophy that was to be rejected in favor of his own program of laissez-faire. What Keynes and Smith each did was to summarize for his generation the growing perception of shortcomings in current thought, and to articulate a new orthodoxy. And this is just what Boas did.

According to George Stocking, Boas's key statement (a much shorter revolutionary statement than either Smith's *The Wealth of Nations* or Keynes' *The General Theory*!) was a paper he read to the American Association for the Advancement of Science in 1896. In that paper, "The Limitations of the Comparative Method of Anthropology," Boas said that "modern anthropology" (meaning evolutionary anthropology) had assumed that the similarities of human culture had common causes, thus allowing evolutionary anthropologists to recreate a general human history through comparative methods and reconstruction (Boas, 1896; Stocking, 1968). But Boas, using his own work among the Kwakiutl, went on to argue that "apparently similar phenomena could be the end results of such varied and complex historical, environmental, and psychological factors that the similarity of their causes could no longer be assumed" (Stocking, 1968, p. 210). Boas's attack on the proposition that like phenomena meant like causes was the equivalent of Keynes's attack on Say's Law. And, in much the same way that rejection of Say's Law cleared the ground for Keynes to build his own analytical apparatus, so too were Boas and his students freed from the need to contribute to a general history or to a theory of social evolution.

Boas reconstructed an anthropology that focussed on the local and the particular. He did assert his commitment to the older goal of producing "general laws of human development" but, as Stocking puts it, "there is no doubt that the extension of his critique of evolutionary anthropology did much to stamp the next half-century of American anthropology with a strong anti-evolutionary bias" (1968, p. 211). As did Smith and Keynes in economics, Boas attacked a fairly stereotypic version of the ruling paradigm – in Boas's case, the evolutionary approach. He was also, as were those great figures in economics, as much the articulator of a major change in approach already underway as he was sole creator of a new paradigm. Even before Boas broke with evolutionary anthropology, the discipline of anthropology was becoming less the territory of "arm-chair scholars" than a province to be entered only by accomplishment of "field work." Under Boas's influence fieldwork became a demanding process. According to Lowie, Boas's unique historical position in anthropology was the consequence of the fact that he was "the first anthropologist who combined ample field experience with an unrivaled opportunity to train investigators" (Lowie, 1937, p. 129). Boas's influence was such that fieldwork among "exotic" peoples became the distinctive feature that set anthropologists apart from other social scientists.

There were other important consequences of the Boasian revolution as well.[7] Although E.B. Tylor is often given credit for creating the modern definition of "culture," the actual history of the idea is more complex.[8] Stocking reports that it is not until 1915 that social scientists begin to speak of "cultures" as opposed to "culture." Intertwined with abandonment of the idea of a unilinear progression from savagery to civilization was ongoing work in experimental psychology that cast doubt on the idea that there were mental differences that were "racial" (in the late-nineteenth-century sense). From these two attacks on the foundations of the evolutionary/historical school there emerged the new concept of "cultural determinism" (Stocking, 1968, Chapter 9). This is the idea – familiar to all institutionalists – that the patterns of behavior and their justifications, the rules and the folkviews that explain those rules, are a cultural whole into which individuals are enculturated.[9]

The Boasian revolution rejected the proposition that all people were part of a universal history, but in doing so it also gave great prominence to the idea that all people shared the universal trait of being products of their cultures. The revolution also gave different meaning to a phrase that had been used in anthropology from at least the time of Adolf Bastian and his work in the 1860s: the "psychic unity of mankind" (Bastian, 1860). In its newer form this unity implied equality among peoples, whereas the older evolutionary thinking implied a ranking. The new view also allowed for a uniformity of human needs and reactions.

It seems likely that Veblen's possible contributions to the discourse of anthropology ceased to be recognized as such for two reasons. First, the anthropology of *The Theory of the Leisure Class* appeared to be part of the now rejected evolutionary/historical anthropology of Tylor and Morgan. In "Christian Morals and the Competitive System" (1910), in "The Mutation Theory and the Blond Race" (1913), in "The Blond Race and the Aryan Culture" (1913), and even in *Imperial Germany and the Industrial Revolution* (1916), Veblen continued to use much of the older vocabulary. Secondly, Veblen's work after the publication of *The Theory of the Leisure Class* seldom dealt with the cultures and economies of exotic peoples (although such works on western economies as *The Theory of Business Enterprise* could certainly be described as the first ethnographic history of western civilization).

However, the substance of all Veblen's work is Boasian. For Veblen, as for Boas, human patterns of behavior and their meaning were culturally defined and created. This was true for Veblen even as early as *The Leisure Class*. Consider, for example, this passage from *The Leisure Class*, in which Veblen is explaining what he means when he uses the term "waste":

> expenditure must be classed under the head of waste in so far as the custom on which it rests is traceable to the habit of making an invidious pecuniary comparison – in so far as it is conceived that it could not have become customary and prescriptive without the backing of this principle of pecuniary reputability or relative economic success.
>
> (1899 [1964], p. 100)

In short, what is waste depends upon the specific cultural history – an eminently Boasian perception. Or consider *Imperial Germany*: there it is specific culture*s* (with an s) that change, and the changes are described in a manner consistent with the then new ideas of culturally-molded psychology and behavior:

> In respect of the stable characteristics of race heredity the German people do not differ in any sensible or consistent manner from the neighboring people; whereas in the character of their past habitu- ation – in their cultural scheme – as well as in respect of the circumstances to which they have latterly been exposed, their case is at least in some degree peculiar. It is in the matter of received habits of thought – use and wont – and in the conditions that have further shaped their scheme of use and wont in the recent past, that the population of the country differs from the population of Europe at large.
>
> (1915, p. 6)

It was not Veblen's approach that set him apart from the emerging anthro- pological paradigm. Though he used a language of race and of stages that was out-of-date, his concepts of culture and cultural change were consistent with the new anthropology. What separated him was subject matter. Veblen and his followers focussed largely on the United States and the US economy. Anthropologists wrote of peoples (and sometimes economies) that were given little or no attention outside of anthropology. This divergence of disciplinary interests made it more and more difficult to see Veblen's legacy as the variant of anthropology that it was.

Veblen also continued to develop his thought about human mental processes along lines that were in many ways parallel to those developing in anthropology and sociology. The separation of the concepts of race and culture that was a critical part of the "Boasian revolution" caused new questions to be raised. As Stocking puts it,

> so long as social theorizing was carried on within the framework of unilinear social evolutionism and the organic analogy, the important questions of the nature of cultural change were begged.
>
> (1968, p. 263)

A shift of focus in sociology, as well as in anthropology, led to "concern with the processes of *social* heredity" (Stocking, 1968, p. 263). What Veblen wrote about instincts and about the importance of emulation as a universal, driving force of human behavior was his effort to deal with this anthropological/sociological concern. (This is, of course, why Veblen was so hard for economists to understand: he was answering questions that derived from other disciplines, not questions that came from the puzzles of economics.) Although Veblen owes his instinct theories more to James and McDougall than to the anthropologists and sociologists (Rutherford, 1994, pp. 56–57), the issues with which he dealt and many of the resolutions that he proposed were consistent with the new ideas in the other social sciences.

VEBLEN'S ANTHROPOLOGICAL ROOTS AND HIS INSTITUTIONALIST LEGACY

To this point I have argued that Veblen's anthropological roots were profound, and by no means limited to the universal evolutionary history that was disowned by anthropologists in this century. This argument leads me to three propositions: about Veblen's legacy to institutional economics, about the relationship between institutionalism and anthropology after Veblen, and about the development of the sub-discipline of economic anthropology over the course of the twentieth century.

My first proposition is that Veblen's profoundly anthropological legacy to institutional economics has helped to differentiate institutionalism from other approaches in economics.[10] The twin concepts – of culture as cultures into which all of us are by place and time of birth enculturated (or into which some are later acculturated) and of the psychic commonality of mankind – come through Veblen's work in the form of his emphasis on institutions as "habits of use and wont," and as the instincts that he attributed to all humankind. These propositions about human culture and the humans that make and are shaped by it remain the differentiating characteristics between the original (sometimes called the old) institutionalism and the new institutionalism, Marxist economics in its many variants, and the varieties of neoclassicism as well.

For Veblen, as for many institutionalists, the process of enculturation explains the tastes and preferences that are exogenous in neoclassical economics and makes them social rather than individual. These social "tastes" change as part of the evolutionary process. What also change as a part of this process are the specific goals – minimization of transfer costs or greater efficiency – that are the exogenous givens in the "new institutionalism." An issue that recurs among those economists who have of late rediscovered institutions will serve to illustrate my point and, at the same time, to illustrate the power of Veblen's legacy. Those who are identified as new institutional economists are distinctive among economists for their explicit recognition that inherited patterns ("routines," "habits," "institutions,") are important features of economic systems. However, they come to this recognition from the decidedly non-anthropological perspective of neoclassical economics. From this perspective all such patterns must be (a) treated as if they were "chosen," and (b) thought of as selected in aid of "efficiency" or some other goal that is exogenous to the processes whereby the "institutions" are chosen.[11] Thus, as Rutherford puts the dilemma in describing the work of Douglass North (a major contributor to the new institutional economics): the chosen task of "endogenizing" institutions must remain incomplete.[12]

No such incompleteness need plague the followers of Veblen and practitioners of the old institutional economics. In keeping with the anthropological roots of the approach, goals and means of achieving them are part of a cultural mix that changes over time. History and the common nature of humans (their "instincts" in Veblen's language) become the sources of explanation.

Adopting this approach means that all legitimate criteria emerge from the systems that produce the results; there are no meta-criteria left with which to judge the results of history and humanness. This lack of meta-criteria has proven unacceptable to most neoclassical economists and to most Marxists, modern and otherwise. Although Veblen did share with Marxists and Fabians a strong dislike for the status quo, his analysis was markedly different, and this has tended to isolate the old institutional economists from the new institutionalist economists, and from most other economists.

Unfortunately, institutional economists have also become increasingly isolated from the group that might have been expected to be intellectually most supportive: anthropologists, particularly those anthropologists interested in economic aspects of society. How and why this happened was described from the anthropological perspective by Melville Herskovits in 1948.

Herskovits notes that "the data on which economic theorists have based their definitions and principles pertain to a single culture, our own" (1952,

p. 45). This means, says Herskovits, that "from the point of view of the comparative study of culture, the 'laws' derived from these data are the equivalent of a statistical average based on a single case" (p. 45). He finds the work of Marshall, Keynes, and Marx (among others) to suffer from the same "cultural particularism."

Herskovits notes, however, that Veblen, "gave more consideration than either the neo-classical group or the Marxians to economic problems susceptible of investigation in non-machine, non-pecuniary societies" (1952, p. 50). But, says Herskovits, those who have followed Veblen have also failed to do work of anthropological interest because "even Veblen's followers . . . have tended to restrict their field of interest to matters that are specifically related to our economic order" (p. 50). Herskovits continues:

> Ayres, the neo-Veblenian who has perhaps most retained the point of view of what may be termed classical institutionalism, in theory, at least continues in the tradition of recognizing the usefulness of cross-cultural terms of reference. But the matter is different in practice; one finds in his work a minimum of ethnographic documentation to supplement the historical, psychological, and philosophical arguments he employs in developing his hypotheses. This is especially true, for instance, in his discussion of the problems of price, of value, and of technology. Here the appeal to the concepts and data of the single historical stream of Euroamerican culture often makes his conclusions highly vulnerable from the point of view of cross-cultural analysis.
>
> (Herskovits, 1952, p. 51)

Of Gambs he wrote:

> A more striking example of how neo-institutionalists fail to take advantage of cross-cultural data is to be found in Gambs's discussion of institutionalist economics. Like Ayres, though in a more critical vein, he takes Veblen as his starting-point. But one misses completely in his work those references to 'the Polynesian islanders,' 'the Andamans,' 'the Todas,' and 'the Pueblo communities' which at the outset of Veblen's book [*The Leisure Class*] establish the pattern and his entire system and concern data that form the background against which his argument concerning certain aspects of our own economy is implicitly projected.
>
> (Herskovits, 1952, p. 51)

When Herskovits wrote in the 1940s, the subdiscipline of economic development that did produce work that was both Veblenianly anthropological and about different cultures had yet to emerge.[13] Even after the emergence of such work, it remained true that most institutionalists focussed on the US (and, more recently, Europe) and so remained effectively apart from anthropology.

Oddly, a major interaction between economics and anthropology – a lively intellectual exchange that involved both economists and anthropologists – erupted a dozen or so years after Herskovits wrote. It focussed on a book that was written in 1944: Karl Polanyi's *The Great Transformation*. Polanyi had not developed his interest in anthropology through Veblen, nor were his questions specifically anthropological. But he did call his work to the attention of anthropologists by his use of the kind of anthropological data that Herskovits found so wanting in the work of Gambs. In *The Great Transformation* Polanyi sought to establish that the self-regulating market system that emerged in the ninteenth century was a system unlike markets in other times and places and very unlike economic systems that had no markets. In order to make his case Polanyi needed to show that there were other ways in which societies could provision themselves, and to do so he made use of the work of Bronislaw Malinowski and Richard Thurnwald. It was this use of ethnographic data about cultures that made Polanyi's work of interest. Even though Polanyi's core argument – that the self-regulating market system that is idealized in neoclassical models was not "natural," and was in fact instituted in the nineteenth century – was not an issue in anthropology, the question of how to interpret much of the ethnographic data was a major issue.

The irony was that the interaction between anthropologists and economists over Polanyi's work – the "formalist–substantivist debate" – was about the wish of economic anthropologists for precisely the kind of acultural or metacultural theory that Boasian anthropology denied them. Those who chafed at this denial and wanted to incorporate cross-culturally invariant economic behavior into their work attacked Polanyi and his economist colleagues for their Boasian particularism (see Mayhew, 1980). The formalists wanted a general theory of the economy and thought they had found it in the neoclassical theory of choice.

The formalist–substantivist debate subsided, but the search among economic anthropologists for a general and usable theory that would allow non-culturally-specific descriptions of economies has continued. A strong motivation for this search has been increased emphasis by anthropologists on intracultural variation and on human agency: aspects of society that are difficult to incorporate into a strict model of cultural determinism (Mayhew, 1987a). To solve this problem the economic anthropologists continued their search. Marxism was popular for a time; more recently, in one of the annual volume of papers emerging from the meetings of the Society for Economic Anthropology, the new institutional economics has been touted as a body of theory that may be applicable to tribal and peasant societies (Acheson, 1994, pp. 4–29).

James Acheson's essay on his hopes for the future of the new institutional economics and anthropology contains sad testament to the loss of understanding of what Veblen was about, and to the failure of institutional economists to find common ground with anthropology in the post-Boasian world of the social sciences. Acheson writes:

> Institutional economics has come to the forefront of economics at two periods. In the interwar years, institutional economics was the dominant theoretical framework when the work of John R. Commons and Thorstein Veblen dominated the field. ... Both Veblen and Commons were essentially concerned with the injustices caused by laissez-faire capitalism in the United States in the late 19th and early 20th centuries. Veblen concentrated on destroying the old economic order; Commons on building a new one.
>
> (Acheson, 1994, p. 5)

According to Acheson the old institutionalism faded as neoclassicism replaced it, but the new institutionalism once again holds hope for anthropologists. Any recognition of the anthropological roots of the old institutional economics has been lost. The new institutional economics is no more likely to prove useful to anthropologists than Marxist and neoclassical thought have been; for the metacriteria of choice and judgment that are involved in all of these economistic approaches are quite simply incompatible with the strong Boasian legacy of the cultural and social determination of patterns of behavior.

CONCLUSION

An important legacy that Thorstein Veblen left to institutional economics was his anthropological perspective. When he wrote *The Theory of the Leisure Class* this perspective consisted of the idea of unlinear evolution, of the identity of what we would call racial and ethnic variation, and of the importance of the cultures produced by this variation in accounting for individual behavior and belief. At roughly the same time that Veblen wrote this classic work, a revolution in anthropology discarded the idea of unlinear evolution.

In the Boasian perspective that came to dominate anthropology, emphasis was placed on the importance of cultures rather than culture, and on ethnic (not racial) variation across time and space. Veblen shared this perspective, and in all of his work he brought the anthropological perspective to the study of capitalism in the US and elsewhere. For Veblen, economic systems of modern industrial nations were as much cultural systems as were those of the non-industrial peoples whom the anthropologists studied. However, the new anthropological commitment to the importance of fieldwork among "exotic" peoples was not part of Veblen's approach. Because such fieldwork or, at the very least, use of the data from such fieldwork became the defining characteristic of the anthropological perspective, institutional economists became more and more isolated from economic anthropologists and from anthropologists in general. The emergence of the sub-discipline of economic anthropology has done little to alter this sad state of affairs. For institutional economics, anthropology has been equally remote, serving in most cases only as a repository of sometimes useful anecdotes about ceremonial behavior.[14]

Recognition of the importance of Veblen's anthropological perspective can help to illuminate the common ground that anthropologists and the old institutional economics ought to occupy. Such recognition is also important in defining what it is that makes "Veblenian" a continuingly appropriate descriptor for the old institutional economics.

NOTES

The author thanks Walter C. Neale for contributing clarity to the argument presented here, and for greatly improving her understanding of Sir Henry Maine.

1 The diversity of this conception, even among the creators of the historical/ evolutionary paradigm, is beyond the scope of this paper. Nevertheless, it is worth noting that the creators "often fought among themselves, and their formulations of stages of development differed in important respects" (Eggan, 1968, p. 124).

   In the case of Sir Henry Maine, however, the stages are of a different sort altogether. He proposes no stages prior to the historical (written) record (the Homeric epics are the "earliest" source for Greek and Roman law). He explicitly limits his argument to the histories of Indo-European cultures. His "stages" – all defined in terms of legal ideas and procedures – are those of divinely-inspired judgments (*themistes*, "dooms"), heroic kingship, oligarchies, and written codes: no savages or barbarians. He does subscribe to "the Patriarchal Theory" on the grounds of a comparative jurisprudence drawn from the "legal testimony" of "the Indo-European stock, the Romans, Hindoos, and Sclavonians" (Maine, 1861 [1977], p.118). But he goes on to remark that "the difficulty, at the present stage of inquiry, is to know ... of what races it is *not allowable* to lay down that the society in which they are united was originally organized on the patriarchal model" (pp. 2–3).

2 Fred Eggan notes that, of the English and continental scholars who made major contributions to "the development of classical evolution" (Bachofen, Maine, McLennan, Spence, and Tylor), none were "directly influenced by Darwin though the development of social and cultural evolution grew out of the same intellectual climate that gave rise to *Origin of Species* (1859) and flourished under the stimulus of biological evolution" (Eggan, 1968, p. 124). Lewis Henry Morgan, according to Eggan, "accepted Darwinian evolution – except for man. His ultimate codification of social and cultural evolution in *Ancient Society* (1877) stands or falls without reference to Darwin's great contributions" (Eggan, 1968, p. 124). For the importance of Spencer as opposed to Darwin see Hodgson (1993, Chapter 6) and on the variety of ideas of evolution that were part of anthropology during the nineteenth century, see Stocking (1968).

3 David Seim (1996) argues that Veblen was seriously remiss in not giving Morgan sufficient credit for having presented the "Veblenian" argument earlier.

4 The first lines of the essay are: "M.G. de LaPouge recently said, 'Anthropology is destined to revolutionise the political and the social sciences as radically as bacteriology has revolutionised the science of medicine' " (Veblen, 1990, p. 56).

5 It might be noted that both of these "histories" were what Maine called "speculative history" (Maine, 1861 [1970]).

6 On this see Hodgson (1993), Jennings and Waller (forthcoming), and my paper, "On the Difficulty of Evolutionary Analysis" (in process).

7 I call it Boas's revolution because he did train so many of the people who followed his prescriptions. However, as Stocking observes, "Boas was not a systematic theoretical thinker. He did not draw together and present to anthropological posterity a 'theory' of culture, which the historian can take in a certain sense as the 'given' content of his work" (1968, p. 196). In constructing my argument in this paper I have relied heavily on Stocking's account of "Boasian" thought and Stocking in turn relied heavily on the work of the "anthropologists who have gone on to treat culture in more systematic ways" and who were trained by Boas and were "bound to him by an ambiguous network of psychological, institutional, and intellectual relationships" (p. 196). These people, Stocking notes, revered Boas as "founder" of their discipline and "[i]t would therefore be very surprising if the culture concept which they elaborated were not strongly influenced by his thought" (Stocking, 1968, p. 196).

8 For more on how the modern definitions of culture emerged, and on how that story has been told by mythmakers and historians alike, see Lowie, 1937, Chapter 7 on "Edward B. Tylor," and Stocking, 1968, Chapter 4 on "Matthew Arnold, E.B. Tylor, and the Uses of Invention," and Chapter 9 on "Franz Boas and the Culture Concept in Historical Perspective."

9 I use here W.C. Neale's definition of an institution (Neale, 1987). Other equally anthropological descriptions of the complex of whole of cultural patterns could be substituted.

10 See Mayhew, 1987a and 1987b.

11 For discussion of this problem and the way it has been approached by various proponents of the new institutional economics, see Malcolm Rutherford (1994), 43–50.

12 This incompleteness manifests itself clearly in the work of those who follow in the Coasian tradition in the study of industrial organization. They are keenly interested in routines and habits and in application of a "Darwinian" approach to transmission and mutation of such routines through time. However, the general commercial goals of the firms in which these routines are followed and changed are assumed to be unchanging. Put differently, when Coase asked his famous question about why firms existed, he assumed (he left exogenous) the goal of cost minimization that could be pursued through the firm or through the market.

13 Examples of this work are Adams (1986), Barber (1961), Neale (1969), Rosen (1975), Van Roy (1971).

14 An exception is David Hamilton's plea for treating modern western economies in the same way that ethnographers have treated the economies of "exotic" peoples. See Hamilton (1991).

REFERENCES

Acheson, James (1994) "Welcome to Nobel Country: A Review of Institutional Economics," in James M. Acheson, *Anthropology and Institutional Economics*, Lanham, MD: University Press of America, pp. 3–42.

Adams, John (1986) "Peasant Rationality: Individuals, Groups, Cultures." *World Development* 14, February, pp. 273–82.

Barber, William J. (1961) *The Economy of British Central Africa*, Stanford, CA: Stanford University Press.

Bastian, Adolphe (1860) *Der Mensche in der Geschichte*, Leipzig: Otto Wigand.

Boas, Franz (1896) "The Limitations of the Comparative Method of Anthropology," *Science* 4: 901–8.

Dorfman, Joseph (1934) *Thorstein Veblen and His America*, reprinted Clifton, N.J.: Augustus M. Kelly, 1972.

Eggan, Fred (1968) "One Hundred Years of Ethnology and Social Anthropology," in J.O. Brew (ed.), *One Hundred Years of Anthropology*, Cambridge, Mass.: Harvard University Press.

Hamilton, David (1991) "The Meaning of Anthropology for Economic Science," *Journal of Economic Issues* 25, December: 937–49.

Herskovits, Melville J. (1952) *Economic Anthropology*, New York: Alfred A. Knopf. [First published in 1948 as *Man and His Works*.]

Hodgson, Geoffrey M. (1993) *Economics and Evolution: Bringing Life Back into Economics*, Ann Arbor, MI: The University of Michigan Press.

Jennings, Ann and William Waller (forthcoming) "The Place of Biological Science in Veblen's Economics," *History of Political Economy*.

Lowie, Robert H. (1937) *The History of Ethnological Theory*, New York: Holt, Rinehart and Winston.

Mayhew, Anne (1980) "Atomistic and Cultural Analyses in Economic Anthropology: An Old Argument Repeated," in John Adams (ed.), *Institutional Economics*, Boston: Martinus Nijhoff Publishing.

—— (1987a) "Culture: Core Concept Under Attack," *Journal of Economic Issues*, 21, June: 587–603.

—— (1987b) "The Beginnings of Institutionalism," *Journal of Economic Issues* 21, September: 971–98.

—— (forthcoming) "On the Difficulty of Evolutionary Analysis," *Cambridge Journal of Economics*.

Maine, Sir Henry (1861) *Ancient Law*, reprinted Gloucester, Mass.: Peter Smith, 1970.

Morgan, Lewis H. (1877) *Ancient Society*, reprinted Cambridge, MA: The Belknap Press of Harvard University Press, 1964.

Neale, Walter C. (1969) "Land Is To Rule," in Robert Eric Frykenberg (ed.), *Land Control and Social Structure in Indian History*, Madison: University of Wisconsin Press.

—— (1987) "Institutions," *Journal of Economic Issues*, 21, September: 3–15.

Polanyi, Karl (1944) *The Great Transformation*, New York: Rinehart & Co.

Rosen, George (1975) *Peasant Society in a Changing Economy*, Urbana: University of Illinois Press.

Rutherford, Malcolm (1994) *Institutions in Economics: The Old and the New Institutionalism*, New York: Cambridge University Press.

Seim, David L. (1996) "The Morganian Revolution," unpublished MA Thesis, Colorado State University, Fort Collins, CO.

Stocking, George W., Jr (1968) *Race, Culture, and Evolution*, New York: The Free Press.

Van Roy, Edward (1971) *Economic Systems of Northern Thailand*, Ithaca, NY: Cornell University Press.

Veblen, Thorstein (1899) *The Theory of the Leisure Class*, reprinted New York: The Viking Press, 1967.

—— (1904) "An Early Experiment in Trusts," *Journal of Political Economy*, 12, March: 270–9.

—— (1904) *The Theory of Business Enterprise,* New York: Charles Scribners Sons.

—— (1910) "Christial Morals and the Competitive System," *International Journal of Ethics* 20, January: 168–85.

—— (1913a) "The Mutation Theory and the Blond Race," *Journal of Race Development* 3, April: 457–75.

—— (1913b) "The Blond Race and the Aryan Culture" *University of Missouri Bulletin, Sciences Series* 2, April: 39–57.

—— (1915) *Imperial Germany and the Industrial Revolution,* New York: The Macmillan Co.

—— (1990) *The Place of Science in Modern Civilization,* Introduction by Warren J. Samuels, Brunswick, NJ: Transaction Publishers. [First published in 1898.]

14

THE RHETORICALITY
OF THORSTEIN VEBLEN'S
ECONOMIC THEORIZING

A critical reading of *The Theory of the Leisure Class*[1]

David Sebberson and Margaret Lewis

INTRODUCTION

We live in a time self-conscious about the way theory is constructed. How we are to even think about issues, let alone address them, is a question that haunts both the academy and the culture at large. As part of this debate, we are led to question and reconsider how we engage in or practice our economic theorizing. As we hope to demonstrate in this paper, we believe that reading Thorstein Veblen's *The Theory of the Leisure Class* from a contemporary perspective will allow us to see not only an alternative economic theory but also a radically alternative *practice* of economic theorizing, the understanding of which is arrived at through understanding Veblen's discursive practices, which are richly rhetorical.

From the beginning, *The Theory of the Leisure Class* has been described by many as social satire, thereby placing the work in the realm of literature. Some readers have asserted that, in fact, *The Theory of the Leisure Class* is nothing more than literature. For example, in 1950, Kenneth Burke, one of the preeminent rhetoricians of the twentieth century, argued that the satirical elements precluded *The Theory of the Leisure Class* from being a serious work of science, calling Veblen's work "satire masked as science" (Burke 1950: 131). Others, particularly institutional economists and social scientists outside of economics, have read Veblen differently, viewing *The Theory of the Leisure Class* as social science (see, e.g., Samuels 1990 and 1992). And still others have argued that *The Theory of the Leisure Class* is, in fact, both literature and science (see, e.g., Dorfman 1972 and Eby 1994). How then are we to read *The Theory of the Leisure Class*? Is it the discourse of science, is it the discourse of literature, is it both, or is it, as we will argue, a different sort of discourse?

Veblen himself seems ambivalent about how to categorize his book. In the preface to *The Theory of the Leisure Class* Veblen writes,

> It is hoped that no one will find his sense of literary or scientific fitness offended by the recourse to homely facts, or by what may at times appear to be a callous freedom in handling vulgar phenomena or phenomena whose intimate place in men's life has sometimes shielded them from the impact of economic discussion.
>
> (Veblen 1931: viii)

How are we to interpret Veblen's prefatory statement? By hoping not to offend the reader's literary or scientific sensibilities, Veblen is creating an aporia – a trope of difficulty, doubt, deliberation, an expression of hesitancy over alternatives – that unsettles the complacent dichotomy between science and literature, suggesting that his theory will not fit easily in either category, and, in the process, is creating an opening for seeing an alternative mode of discourse for economic theory. Thus Veblen's text can be read not as the text of simply a scientist or a litterateur (or even a combination of the two) but as something other. That is, in order to understand Veblen's text, we must move beyond the dichotomous discourse modes of science and literature to a third mode: rhetoric.

Now what, it is perfectly reasonable to ask, is the significance of seeing a text as rhetorical rather than as scientific or literary? In other words, what is the significance of seeing the rhetoricality of Veblen's economic theorizing?

To understand the significance of rhetoricality as a mode of discourse for economic theorizing, we are going to develop a complex argument. In the first part of the paper, "The Rhetorician's Question," we will consider Veblen from a contemporary pragmatic position; more specifically, we will examine how Veblen's work embodies tensions that obtain first between scientific and literary discourse and then between practical reasoning or ethical know-how (*phronesis*) and technological production or technical know-how (*techne*). In the second part of the paper, "The Economist's Response," we will explore how communicative action informs *The Theory of the Leisure Class*, demonstrating Veblen's critique of systematically distorted communication. Then, using a definition of rhetoric that goes beyond the popular definition of a means of persuading a particular audience to adopt a particular belief, we will explore how Veblen's text is essentially rhetorical. We will argue finally that Veblen practiced a way of theorizing that grounded economic theory in neither the literary world of self-expression nor in the scientific world of disinterested description but rather in the rhetorical world of social action. Moreover, only by acknowledging the rhetoricality of Veblen's discourse can we understand fully his economic theory. Section

251

headings followed by brief statements in italics provide an overview of the argument and strategies used to develop it. By going over these italicized parts, the reader can get a sense of the argument without the immediate burden of learning the more technical details of rhetorical philosophy and analysis.

As a preliminary consideration, we must address the significance of social action in economic thinking. Turning to one of the tenets of institutional economics, of which Veblen is a founder, we maintain that the study of economics is undertaken to make the world a better place in which to live; that the goal of studying economics, of coming to an economic under-standing, reflects a goal of progress and thus social action.[2] And, as we will argue, situating economic understanding in the world of social action demands the mode of discourse appropriate for such action. That mode of public discourse is rhetoric. By understanding the rhetoricality of Veblen's theorizing we can see a praxis that, while looking like mere social satire to both literary critics and non-institutional economists, is indeed a form of theory-in-praxis – theory in a pragmatic tradition that enables social action. It is coming to this understanding of an alternative mode of economic theorizing and the rhetorical mode of discourse appropriate for such theo-rizing, while simultaneously coming to an understanding of *The Theory of the Leisure Class*, that is the end of this article.

1 THE RHETORICIAN'S QUESTION – WHAT KIND OF BOOK IS THIS, ANYWAY?

Starting with a question about whether The Theory of the Leisure Class *is science or literature leads us to consider issues in pragmatism, the philosophical tradition in which Veblen writes. To help us in our consideration, we draw on the work of Richard J. Bernstein, a contemporary American philosopher whose work includes careful examinations of neo-pragmatism and hermeneutics, and Jürgen Habermas, a contemporary German social philosopher whose theory of communicative action grows in part out of a critical response to pragmatism on the one hand, and hermeneutics on the other. Our question about science or literature turns out to be an important one for seeing how Veblen's work embraces social action, for* The Theory of the Leisure Class *attempts neither pure science nor pure literature (satire). Instead, it is an exercise in critical social science whose goal is social action in general and emancipation in particular. Moreover, our philosophers help us to see not only Veblen's concern with technical know-how but also with practical reasoning and ethical know-how. This is important because Veblen believes that economy and society are not driven by any transcendent purpose, which can be matched and repli-cated in some abstract theory. Rather, economy and society are matters of social construction, which requires the interest of human actors who draw on their ethical know-how to reason practically.*

The problem with literature

If we follow the neo-pragmatic lead of privileging the literary over the scientific, we lose the impetus for social action because the literary encourages only passive observation.

It is commonplace in Veblenian scholarship to mention that Veblen was working in the pragmatic tradition of the late nineteenth to early twentieth century. Veblen's work is typically associated with that of Peirce, James, and Dewey, for whom, according to contemporary philosopher Richard J. Bernstein, the scientist is the cultural hero (Bernstein 1986: 88), which is certainly the case for the Veblen of causality and matter-of-fact. But establishing the scientist as cultural hero has proven to be problematic for contemporary neo-pragmatists because of the modernist emphasis on detached science, removed as it is from the context of human action, divorced from the ethical and political complexities in which science is actually situated. To compensate for the detachment of the early pragmatist's scientific hero, a contemporary neo-pragmatist like Richard Rorty, for example, instead chooses as his cultural hero the novelist, or litterateur (Bernstein 1986: 88). According to Rorty, the one who tells the most compelling moral story, as epitomized in the literary narrative, wins. Here we see that the same aporia between literature and science expressed by Veblen in his preface to *The Theory of the Leisure Class* persists generally across generations of pragmatists and neo-pragmatists in the identification of different cultural heroes: which alternative are we to choose? But why does the aporia – the hesitancy and doubt – over science and literature matter?

From a contemporary postmodern perspective – a perspective developed after Auschwitz, Hiroshima, and the silent spring – the scientist is not so easily a cultural hero, for the scientist's disinterested gaze has come to look like blindness, and rationality like the mask of irrationality.[3] But is the turn away from the scientist as cultural hero to the novelist less problematic? Not if we are concerned with the discourse necessary for social action. For as Bernstein argues, while Rorty considers

> novelists . . . the most effective moral educators in a liberal society
> . . . Rorty's praise of novelists who educate not by didacticism but
> by imaginative concrete description depends on a dubious pre-
> supposition which he never justifies and for which there seems to be
> little, if any, concrete empirical evidence. Rorty thinks that novels
> do have "force," they do make a difference in how we act in our every-
> day lives. . . . But where is the evidence to support such a claim?
> (Bernstein 1992: 285)

And besides the significant evidentiary problems associated with Rorty's cultural hero, how do we, as readers of a novel, move beyond being passive observers? That is, while novels do serve societal roles, they do not make the same demands on their readers as those of practical discourse necessary for responsible social action. In other words, even if we accept Rorty's position, how do we move from being readers of books – mere spectators – to actors in society?

Both Bernstein and Habermas have recognized this limitation of the novelist as cultural hero in a liberal society, where public deliberation is a necessary element for social action. Bernstein, for example, criticizes Rorty for believing "there can be no rational argument" about the political question of what constitutes serious conflicts within society:

> Rorty never thematizes this question. Rorty's politics seems to be one in which there is *no* public space – the space in which human beings come together to *debate* and *argue* with each other. . . . For public debate presupposes what Rorty seems to want to eliminate – that we can be locked in *argument* with each other.
>
> (Bernstein 1992: 284–5)

German philosopher Jürgen Habermas raises a similar concern about privileging literary discourse over public discourse. Habermas is reluctant to reduce practical discourse, including economic texts, to literary texts, which he characterizes as "the world-disclosing productivity of language" (Habermas 1987: 333). If all discourse is literary text, Habermas argues, "social praxis disappears in the anonymous hurly-burly . . . of ever new worlds from the imaginary dimension" (1987: 330). The reason for this is that

> [i]n everyday communicative practice speech acts retain a force that they lose in literary texts. In the former setting they function in contexts of action in which participants cope with situations and – let's say it – have to solve problems. . . . [But literary texts] remove the burden of acting from the reader. . . . Literature does not invite the reader to take a position of the same kind that everyday communication invites from those who are acting.
>
> (Habermas 1992: 223)

Thus, for Habermas, literary speech acts are "illocutionarily *disempowered*" (1992: 223), a characteristic inappropriate in practical discourse designed for social action. Thus both Bernstein and Habermas draw out the limitations of literary texts for the ethical and political discourse necessary for social action.

What are the implications here for Veblen's work? If we label *The Theory of the Leisure Class* as social satire and categorize it as merely literature, à la Burke, we render Veblen's text nothing more than a story whose efficacy ends when the reader lays down the book. And even if we recognize the rich literary dimensions of *The Theory of the Leisure Class* as a way of understanding Veblen's theory as a part of the cultural practices of his day, described so well by Waller and Robertson (William Waller and Linda R. Robertson 1990), the empowering force of Veblen's text as practical discourse is still obscured, thereby confining the potential for ethical and political action implicit in the text. But in reading Veblen from the common perspective of Bernstein and Habermas outlined above, we see an economic theorist who is committed to constructing economic theory as practical discourse, who moves considerably beyond "imaginative concrete description" (in Bernstein's words) less to disclose the world of the leisure class than to address what Veblen calls "homely facts" and "vulgar phenomena" – the substance of "everyday communicative practice," as Habermas puts it, where "participants cope with situations and . . . have to solve problems." Thus to read Veblen merely as a novelist is to disempower him.

The problem with science

If instead we reduce pragmatism to technological reason, as the first pragmatists are often understood to do, we reduce ethical and political issues of social action to technical problems of production. When this happens, there is no legitimate way to discuss the ethical, political, and social context in which production takes place.

If seeing Veblen in light of Rorty's literary neo-pragmatism is not satisfactory because it closes down the sort of public place and discourse necessary for social action, is it any more satisfactory to invoke in an unqualified way not Veblen-the-litterateur but rather Veblen-the-scientist, especially the scientist of machine processes? This question raises a different sort of problem, one where pragmatism intersects not with literature, but with hermeneutics. The problem can be framed as follows: just as reducing action-oriented discourse to literary discourse erases the possibility of public argument and action – insulates, e.g., economics from ethically and politically responsible action – so too does reducing all practical concerns to terms of technology undermine the possibility for responsibly engaged human action, insulating economic activity again from the ethical and the political.

The conflict between the technological and the practical is a recurrent theme in hermeneutic philosophy, and sometimes that conflict is expressed explicitly in terms of antagonism towards pragmatism. By bringing in hermeneutics' differentiation between technical reason and practical reason, we can recuperate the impulse for social action in Veblen. One way to understand the conflict between the technical and the practical, from a hermeneutic perspective, is through the Aristotelian concept of *phronesis*, a concept appropriated by hermeneutic philosopher Hans-Georg Gadamer and explained by Bernstein. Commenting on Gadamer, Bernstein invokes not only the Aristotelian term *phronesis*, but also *episteme* and *techne* – terms

255

that reflect different intellectual practices. *Episteme* is commonly considered scientific knowledge, knowledge of "what is universal and what exists 'of necessity,' and takes the form of . . . scientific demonstration" (Bernstein 1986: 99). Because *episteme* is concerned with necessity, it is not a practice appropriate for human action, which is characterized not by necessity but by contingency. On the other hand, *phronesis* is to be distinguished not only from *episteme* but also from *techne*. As Bernstein puts it, *techne* is "technical know-how" and *phronesis* is "ethical know-how" (1986: 100). In explaining further the differences between *phronesis* and *techne*, Bernstein summarizes three distinctions that he sees Gadamer making.

1   *Techne* has to do with a skill for producing something; "[b]y contrast, the subject of ethical reason, of *phronesis*, man always finds himself in an 'acting situation'" (1986: 100).
2   In technical reasoning one does not have to consider "that the means which allow it to arrive at an end be weighed anew on each occasion," but in ethical know-how, "there can be no prior knowledge of the right means by which we realize the end. For the end itself is only concretely specified in deliberating about the means appropriate to *this* particular situation" (1986: 100).
3   Of *phronesis* Bernstein quotes Gadamer: This knowledge "is not in any sense technical knowledge or the application of such. . . . The person with understanding does not know and judge as one who stands apart and unaffected; but rather, as one united by a specific bond with the other, he thinks with the other and undergoes the situation within him" (Bernstein 1986: 100).

Hence Bernstein summarizes Gadamer: "We can learn from Aristotle what 'practice' really is and why it is not to be identified with the 'application of science and technical tasks'" (Bernstein 1986: 102–3). One way to view current cultural crises, then, is to see modern Western culture as a culture that has erased *phronesis*, reducing the line of all legitimate problem-solving to a science–technology axis. Philosophical hermeneutics is an attempt to reclaim that deliberative space that scientism shuts down.

We have introduced the difference between *phronesis* and *techne*, hermeneutics and pragmatism, in terms of conflict because that is typically the way it is played out. In coming to terms with Veblen, however, we find it more fruitful to think not in terms of conflict but rather in terms of tension. To anticipate our point here, we believe that while *techne* plays a key role in *The Theory of the Leisure Class*, *techne* does not exist so much at the expense of *phronesis* as in tension with it. Thus to understand Veblen's mode of theorizing we must first see the presence and interplay of *techne* and *phronesis* and the way they are manifest in the text. Some close textual analysis is needed to bear out this point.

Close reading 1: Terms of technology

Veblen's commitment to the technological seems to obliterate the possibility for practical reasoning and ethical know-how.

Sprinkled throughout *The Theory of the Leisure Class* are statements that appear to privilege *techne* at the expense of *phronesis*. For example, early on Veblen defines industry as "effort that goes to create a new thing with a new purpose given it by the fashioning hand of its maker out of passive ('brute') material" (Veblen 1931: 12). Later, Veblen asserts that "[t]he lasting evidence of productive labour is its material product" (1931: 44). Here there seems to be no room at all for ethical know-how. Indeed, there is a radical synecdoche of human agency that represents all of human "purpose" as originating in the "fashioning hand," not, for example, in the critical or practical mind or in the ethical or political will (to use traditional locations of understanding and motivation). Synecdoche, as the trope of representing the part to stand in for the whole, is concerned with scale manipulation (Lanham 1991: 148). Here the scale is tipped entirely towards the technical: purpose is legitimated by makers in the realm of *techne*, not interpreters and actors in the realm of *phronesis*.

Towards the end of *The Theory of the Leisure Class* are two more passages, somewhat more developed, that make such strong statements about *techne* that they seem to place *phronesis* under complete erasure. The first discusses industrial organization and the nature of the worker under such organization:

> The industrial organisation assumes more and more of the character of a *mechanism*, in which it is man's office to discriminate and select what natural forces shall work out their effects in his service. The workman's part in industry changes from that of a prime mover to that of discrimination and valuation of *quantitative sequences* and *mechanical facts*. The faculty of a ready apprehension and unbiased appreciation of causes in his environment grows in relative economic importance and any element in the complex of his habits of thought which intrudes a bias at variance with this ready appreciation of *matter-of-fact sequence* gains proportionately in importance as a disturbing element acting to lower his industrial usefulness. Through its cumulative effect upon the habitual attitude of the population, even a slight or inconspicuous bias towards accounting for everyday facts by recourse to other ground than that of *quantitative causation* may work an appreciable lowering of the collective industrial efficiency of a community.
>
> (Veblen 1931: 284–5, emphasis added)

Consider the concentration of terms here: "mechanism," "quantitative sequences," "mechanical facts," "matter-of-fact sequence," "quantitative causation." All is quantity, facticity, and mechanism. Again there is a sort of radical synecdoche operating here that represents the practical in terms of the technical – "technocracy" is the term Adorno uses to summarize what he sees as Veblen's bleak view of the world where "emancipation from the realm of utility is nothing but the index of . . . purposelessness" (Adorno 1981: 75). Again there is a radical shift in scale as agency is reduced from that of a "prime mover" to a discriminator and valuator of sequence and fact. *Techne* rules as its "cumulative effect upon the habitual attitude" spreads. If habitual attitudes are increasingly shaped by *techne*, what room is there for public space that is not an industrial space? What room is there for deliberation that is not deliberation about technical applications?

Veblen's line of thinking about quantity and mechanical sequence culminates in the following way:

> The habit of mind which best lends itself to the purposes of a peaceable, industrial community, is that matter-of-fact temper which recognises the value of material facts simply as *opaque items in the mechanical sequence*. . . . To meet the requirements of the highest economic efficiency under modern conditions, the world process must habitually be apprehended in terms of quantitative, dispassionate force and sequence.
>
> (Veblen 1931: 304–5, emphasis added)

Once more the scale of *techne* shifts; *techne* has become ubiquitous, dominating now "the world process." While the end here is "a peaceable, industrial community," which is certainly desirable, at the same time, it is founded on a sort of silence and blindness: the *opacity* of material fact. Here the trope of metonymy – reduction – comes into play, articulating the effect, the opaque, that reality is reduced to in a world of facts and sequences. But in an opaque world, what room is there for deliberation? *Phronesis*, ethical know-how, depends on vision, but what vision can there be through the opaque? Opacity not only precludes vision but also engenders silence: what can one *say* about opaque facts and mechanical sequence? What is there to argue about? This rendering of Veblen obliterates the possibility of engaged social action as surely as does rendering Veblen a literary satirist. Sardonic litterateur or mechanistic scientist? The aporia that Veblen expressed in his preface seems unsatisfactorily resolved in terms of the practical and the technical: there is no doubt or hesitancy here about choosing alternatives – the technical is the only route.

Close reading 2: Terms of practical reasoning and ethical know-how

Veblen's choice of words offers evidence of practical reasoning and suggests a commitment to ethical know-how that balances Veblen's commitment to technology.

As we suggested above, *techne* does not erase *phronesis* so much as it exists in tension with it. Throughout Veblen, we see characteristics of *phronesis* outlined by Bernstein (1986: 100): the economic theorist as an ethical agent in an acting situation; the economic theorist "deliberating about the means appropriate" to the particular situation; the economic theorist in the midst of what he is theorizing about – a "person with understanding [who] does not know and judge as one who stands apart and unaffected."

The following passage from the Introduction to *The Theory of the Leisure Class* illustrates this tension and serves as a counterstatement, balancing *phronesis* against the *techne* governing the passages cited earlier:

> The *ground* on which a *discrimination* between facts is habitually made changes as the *interest* from which the facts are habitually viewed changes. Those features of the facts at hand are salient and substantial upon which the dominant *interest* of the time throws its light. Any given *ground* of distinction will seem insubstantial to any one who habitually apprehends the facts in question from a different *point of view* and values them for a different *purpose*. The habit of distinguishing and classifying the various *purposes* and directions of activity prevails of necessity always and everywhere; for it is indispensable in reaching a working theory or scheme of life. The particular *point of view*, or the particular characteristic that is pitched upon as definitive in the classification of the facts of life depends upon the *interest* from which a *discrimination* of the facts is sought. The grounds of *discrimination*, and the norm of procedure in classifying the facts, therefore, progressively change as the growth of culture proceeds; for the end for which the facts of life are apprehended changes, and the *point of view* consequently changes also. So that what are recognised as the salient and decisive features of a class of activities or of a social class at one stage of culture will not retain the same relative importance for the *purposes* of classification at any subsequent stage.
>
> (Veblen 1931: 9, emphasis added)

If terms like "mechanism," "quantitative sequence," and "mechanical facts" govern passages where *techne* comes to the fore, then consider the terms in this passage, which does not involve *techne* at all: "interest," repeated twice; "ground," "point of view," "purpose," and "discrimination" all repeated three times. These terms clearly invoke the ethical know-how of *phronesis* and exemplify "what 'practice' really is and why it is not to be identified with the 'application of science and technical tasks'" (Bernstein 1986: 102–3). For in this passage, Veblen is laying out the practical dimension in which his economic theorizing is to participate. At stake here are not issues of production but issues of action. Nor are means simply a function of undebatable prior knowledge when Veblen discusses how changing cultural grounds affect interest and change points of view and purposes, which in turn alter the understanding of facts. And certainly it is not the blind application of technical knowledge but rather the understanding of "one united by a specific bond with the other" (Bernstein 1986: 100) that is "indispensable in reaching a working theory or scheme of life" as Veblen puts it.

Thus the above passage suggests the presence of *phronesis* in *The Theory of the Leisure Class*. But to see how *phronesis* plays more than an incidental role and is actually constitutive of Veblen's thought – and consequently to comprehend the significance of Veblen's rhetorical mode of economic theorizing – we must now examine the relation between hermeneutics, communicative action, and rhetoric.

2 THE ECONOMIST'S RESPONSE – WHAT DO YOU MEAN, IT'S RHETORICAL?

Now you've done it: you've just argued that phronesis *as well as* techne *is a presence in Veblen, and you've also let the hermeneutics genie out of the bottle. Hermeneutics embraces tradition and prejudice; Veblen has no use for tradition and prejudice – how can you put "Veblen" and "hermeneutics" in the same sentence?*

Not to worry. Here's what we'll do. Using Bernstein and Habermas again, we'll show first how hermeneutics is actually part of pragmatic thought and then how Veblen advances pragmatic thought by engaging its hermeneutic element. After that, we'll move away from hermeneutics towards rhetoric. Habermas remains crucial, providing a critique of hermeneutics that leads to the concept of communicative action. Communicative action is important because it leads to the ideas of systematically distorted communication, emancipatory social science, and an understanding of rhetoric that is critical rather than performative. These ideas are important because they shed light on what Veblen is about: The Theory of the Leisure Class *analyzes systematically distorted communication to recreate economics as an emancipatory social science; to write such an emancipatory economics requires an equally emancipatory mode of discourse, namely critical rhetoric.*

Here's another way of putting it: Existing institutions, including language, contribute to the process of the social construction of social reality. To a large extent – to too large an extent, Veblen believes – those institutions and that language give effect to preconceptions of teleology (often serving to ideologically freeze present arrangements) and to practices of competitive emulation. The creation of noninvidious institutions requires language that neither reifies existing arrangements nor obfuscates their social construction, but that is a mode of discourse calling attention to and emphasizing the facts of choice and of the social valuational process actually at work. At present, this process includes linguistic mediations and symbolic expressions that do quite the opposite. The Theory of the Leisure Class *is thus a critique of systematically distorted communication and calls for a focus on a language that gives social action its due and is emancipatory.*

Pragmatism, hermeneutics and the move to communicative action

Veblen advances pragmatic thought by tapping its hermeneutic potential, moving beyond Peirce's semiotics of representation to a hermeneutics of communicative action – that is, a mode of rationality grounded in dialogue and aimed at the mutual understanding necessary for healthy social action.

That hermeneutics – grounded in human dialogue and aimed at interpretation – constitutes a significant element of Veblen's thought as well as our understanding of it has been demonstrated effectively in different ways, for different reasons, by Mirowski (1988), Samuels (1990), and Jennings and Waller (Jennings and Waller 1994). Thus our intention here is not to rehash or engage their arguments but rather to draw on the basic insight of a hermeneutical dimension in Veblen. But we then wish to move from hermeneutics to communicative action, a discourse theory that grows out of hermeneutics while responding to its limited potential for critique and social transformation. A framework that distinguishes communicative action from hermeneutics allows us to see that Veblen makes a significant advance in pragmatic theorizing in general as well as lays the groundwork for reconstructing economics from what Habermas calls empirical-analytic science into critical, emancipatory social science.

Our first point in creating a framework that brings communicative action to the fore is to see the connection between turn-of-century pragmatism and twentieth-century hermeneutics, a connection that Bernstein makes for us when he notes first that Habermas recognizes the key role of dialogue in human action: "a humane collective life depends on the vulnerable forms of innovation-bearing, reciprocal and unforcedly egalitarian everyday communication" (Bernstein 1992: 55), and second, that Habermas's conviction derives "from the pragmatist inheritance" (Bernstein 1992: 55). Bernstein further argues that both Habermas and the pragmatic tradition "share an understanding of rationality as intrinsically dialogical and communicative. And both pursue the ethical and political consequences of this form of rationality and rationalization" (Bernstein 1992: 48). In locating these traits in specific pragmatists, Bernstein notes that Peirce's idea of "a self-corrective critical community of inquirers without any absolute beginning points or finalities," Dewey's "'task of democracy' ... in the face of all those tendencies in the contemporary world which seek to undermine, crush, and deform communicative rationality," and Mead's "linkage of dialogic communicative rationality and the institutionalization of democratic forms of life requir[ing] a new understanding of the genesis and development of practical sociality" (Bernstein 1992: 48) are echoed in the contemporary work of Habermas. Thus by focusing on the communicative dimension of rationality, Bernstein illuminates the hermeneutic element in the pragmatic tradition.

At this point, it is not difficult to see how Veblen's thought can be characterized in a way that situates him easily along this hermeneutic–pragmatic axis. Like Peirce, Veblen posits a community of inquirers – economists – as, to use Bernstein's words, a "self-corrective critical community . . . without any absolute beginning points or finalities." This is clear in *The Theory of the Leisure Class* when Veblen strikes the major chord of his theory: that economic activity is grounded not in the allocation of scarce resources but rather in the distinction between practices of industry and practices of exploit, a distinction, Veblen points out, that has "received but slight attention at the hands of economic writers" (Veblen 1931: 8). Veblen likewise shares an affinity with Mead's "linkage of dialogic communicative rationality and the institutionalization of democratic forms of life," although Veblen establishes this linkage negatively rather than positively through his critique of the antidemocratic institution of the leisure class and its use of symbols to draw invidious distinctions. We see the strongest affinity, however, between Veblen and the way Bernstein characterizes Dewey, where the "task of democracy" focuses on "all those tendencies . . . to undermine, crush, and deform communicative rationality." Indeed, we see the very *practice* of Veblen's theorizing as an investigation into just how deformed communicative rationality has become through the institution of the leisure class, a point which we will take up again, and in greater detail below, but first we need to discuss how Veblen represents an advance in Peirce's semiotics.

To understand Veblen's advance of Peirce, we must begin by distinguishing hermeneutics from semiotics, a distinction that derives from the hermeneutically-defining trait of dialogue.[4] Habermas points out the importance of this distinction in his critique of Charles Sanders Peirce. In discussing issues of postmetaphysical thinking, Habermas turns to Peirce, noting the importance of his semiotic turn:

> He showed how causal symptoms and spontaneous expressive gestures . . . can be interpreted on the model of linguistic signs. He thereby opened new realms to semiotic analysis: for example, the extraverbal sign world, in the context of which our linguistic communication is embedded.
>
> (Habermas 1992: 107)

But while Habermas appreciates Peirce's groundbreaking work, he sees "the bad legacy of Platonism . . . reproduced even in the work of anti-Platonist Peirce" (109) as a particular limitation. The problem as Habermas sees it generally lies in

> Peirce's semiotic conception of the universal as a sign-mediated representation together with his interpretation of evolution as a

learning process. Both allow communication, in which the tendency to universalization asserts itself, to be seen from only *one* side: communication is not for the sake of reaching mutual understanding between ego and alter about something in the world; rather, interpretation only exists for the sake of the representational and the ever more comprehensive representation of reality. This privileging of the sign's representative relation to the world above the sign's communicative relation to the interpreter causes the full-fledged interpreter to disappear behind the depersonalized interpretant.

(Habermas 1992: 109)

Thus while Peirce has laid a semiotic ground for science as interpretation, a ground upon which Veblen will build his economics, Peirce has not provided the ground for communicative action that would reconstruct the social sciences in general, and economics in particular, as emancipatory sciences. If cast in terms of *phronesis*, Peirce's semiotics tend to turn toward logic rather than ethical know-how.

Habermas ends his discussion of Peirce by invoking George Herbert Mead as the second-generation pragmatist who advances Peirce's insight into the realm of social action (Habermas 1992: 110). We would argue that it is Veblen who makes such a move, taking Peirce's semiotic insight out of the realm of sign-mediated universal and into the realm of ethical and political *praxis*.[5] When Veblen grounds economic activity not in the rational allocation of scarce resources but rather in the symbolic communication of social status and the interpretation of signs, Veblen's integration of economic and social practices of valuation moves beyond a semiotic interpretation of signs into a hermeneutic analysis of a complex dialogical exchange of what society values in the everyday communication that takes place when money talks.

Thus far, in considering the move from hermeneutics to communicative action, we have made two points: (1) that there is a connection between hermeneutics and pragmatism and (2) that Veblen made a specific contribution to the hermeneutic element of pragmatism by making an advance on Peirce's semiotics. Our next point is that Habermas's critique of hermeneutics clears the way for us to see how Veblen's practice of economic theorizing lays the ground for reconstructing economics as critical and emancipatory.

The limits of hermeneutics: The problem of systematically distorted communication

While hermeneutics helps us understand Veblen in terms of pragmatism and ethical know-how, it is not adequate to see the full range of Veblen's theorizing, which moves beyond hermeneutics to analyze systematically distorted communication, residing in the traditions and prejudices of the leisure class's institutions of invidious distinctions.

While communicative action grows out of hermeneutics, it does challenge the hermeneutical concepts of tradition and prejudice with the concepts of critique and systematically distorted communication. Habermas developed these concepts in his extended debate with Gadamer regarding the tension between tradition and critique, focusing his argument in the essay, "On Hermeneutics' Claim to Universality." The line of argument pertinent here can be sketched in the following manner:

1 Hermeneutics invokes a situatedness shaped by prejudices and formed by tradition.

2 "The hermeneutical elucidation of unintelligible or misunderstood expression must always refer back to a prior consensus which has been reliably worked out in the dialogue of a convergent tradition (Habermas 1988a: 313).

3 (a) But "Hermeneutical consciousness is incomplete so long as it has not incorporated into itself reflection on the limit of hermeneutical understanding" (Habermas 1988a: 302),

(b) and " 'the hermeneutical approach can be upheld only if one starts from the recognition that the context of tradition, as the locus of possible truth and real accord, is at the same time the locus of real falsehood and the persistent use of force' " (Habermas 1988a: 314).

4 (a) Thus "hermeneutical consciousness proves inadequate in the case of systematically distorted communication" (Habermas 1988a: 302),

(b) where the inadequacy of hermeneutical consciousness leads to "pseudocommunication, in which a disruption of communication is not recognized by the parties involved. Only a newcomer to the conversation notices that they misunderstand each other. Pseudocommunication produces a system of misunderstandings which remain opaque because they are seen in the light of a false consensus" (Habermas 1988a: 302).

5 To counter pseudocommunication we need to consider what "we know from depth-hermeneutics . . . that the dogmatism of the traditional context is the vehicle . . . for the repressiveness of a power relationship which deforms the intersubjectivity of understanding as such and systematically distorts colloquial communication" (Habermas 1988b: 314).

We can see from this line of argument how central the problem of systematically distorted communication is for Habermas: it is recurrent in his critique of hermeneutics as we have outlined it here, and like the grit that prompts the oyster's pearl, it shapes his theory of communicative action. There is, however, another, albeit related, element to his critique of hermeneutics, mentioned in 3(a) above, which has to do with the limit of hermeneutical understanding.

For Habermas, hermeneutics grounded exclusively in tradition and dialogue is problematic because it "hypostatizes language . . . and . . . tradition [and] binds itself to the idealist presupposition that linguistically articulated consciousness determines the material being of life practice" (Habermas 1988b: 173). But, Habermas counters, while "revolutions in the conditions of the reproduction of material life are in turn linguistically mediated . . . a new practice is not set in motion by a new interpretation. Rather old patterns of interpretation are also attacked and overthrown 'from below' by new practices" (173). Habermas summarizes his position:

> The linguistic infrastructure of society is a moment in a complex that, however symbolically mediated, is also constituted by the constraints of reality: by the constraint of external nature, which enters into the procedures of technological exploitation, and by the constraint of inner nature, which is reflected in the repressions of social relationships of power. These two categories of constraint are not only the object of interpretations; behind the back of language, so to speak, they affect the very grammatical rules in accordance with which we interpret the world. *The objective context in terms of which alone social actions can be understood is constituted conjointly by language, labor, and domination.* The process of tradition is relativized both by systems of labor and by systems of authority; it appears as an absolute power only to an autonomous hermeneutics.
>
> (Habermas 1988b: 174)

Here we see a theoretical position that can account for the complexity of Veblen's practice of theorizing, which examines human economic activity as embedded in such basic cultural practices as working *and* talking, tool making *and* symbol using, *techne* and *phronesis*, and how these cultural practices both shape and are shaped by domination that has been institutionalized.

Now we can see how the different parts of our argument begin to come together. Regarding the tension between *techne* and *phronesis*, we see that Veblen is not reducing issues of ethical know-how to those of technical production but rather is exploring the fact that the machine process defining the technology of Veblen's day becomes a practice "from below" that forms a constraint impinging upon the culture's symbolic practices. As Habermas puts it, "the instrumental sphere of action . . . can . . . subject traditional patterns of interpretation to the constraints of the labor process. A change in the mode of production entails a restructuring of the linguistic world view (1988b: 173). We can now construct Veblen's practice of economic theorizing in the following way, using terms and insights from Habermas. Economic activities are embedded in cultural practices; as such, economic theory must take into account cultural practices of valuation that are mediated linguistically and expressed symbolically. At the same time, economic theorizing is itself a discursive practice engaged in social action, demanding ethical know-how. While both economic activity and theorizing about economic activity can thus be seen as hermeneutical in so far as they are grounded in acts of interpretation and dialogical exchange, for *phronesis* to be an actual presence in the practice of economic theorizing, it must be conceived in more powerful ways than the tradition and prejudices that hermeneutics offers. It must also take into consideration material constraints represented on the one hand by technological exploitation – Veblen's machine process – and on the other by repressions of social relationships of power – Veblen's institutions of the leisure class. By keeping these constraints in mind, Veblen explores the systematically distorted communication underlying economic activity. As such his analysis examines frozen power relations with the aim of transforming economics from an empirical-analytic science into an emancipatory one.

A definition of emancipatory social science

Based on an understanding of systematically distorted communication, emancipatory social science identifies dependence on ideologically frozen relations of power and seeks to transform them; this interest in emancipation characterizes Veblen's economic theory.

Before detailing the transition to emancipatory social science as represented in *The Theory of the Leisure Class*, we must first elaborate on the difference between an empirical-analytic science and an emancipatory science, a distinction made by Habermas, who defines three different types of science: the empirical-analytic sciences, the historical-hermeneutic sciences, and the sciences of social action or emancipatory sciences. In the empirical-analytic sciences,

> [t]heories comprise hypothetico-deductive connections of propositions, which permit the deduction of lawlike hypotheses with empirical content. The latter can be interpreted as statements about the covariance of observable events; given a set of initial conditions, they make predictions possible.
>
> (Habermas 1971: 308)

Habermas contrasts this with the historical-hermeneutical sciences by noting that theories in the latter type of sciences

> are not constructed deductively and experience is not organized with regard to the success of operations. Access to the facts is provided by the understanding of meaning, not observation. The verification of lawlike hypotheses in the empirical-analytic sciences has its counterpart here in the interpretation of texts. Thus the

rules of hermeneutics determine the possible meaning of the validity of statements of the cultural sciences.

(Habermas 1971: 309)

To the extent that Veblen engages in interpreting the signs of invidious distinction, he is practicing a historical-hermeneutic science. But we would argue that his economic theorizing goes beyond to embrace this trait of what Habermas calls the science of social action:

> The systematic sciences of social action, that is economics, sociology, and political science, have the goal, as do the empirical-analytic sciences, of producing nomological knowledge. A critical social science, however, will not remain satisfied with this. It is concerned with going beyond this goal to determine when theoretical statements grasp invariant regularities of social action as such and when they express ideologically frozen relations of dependence that can be in principle transformed. ... The methodological framework that determines the meaning of the validity of critical propositions of this category is established by the concept of *self-reflection*. The latter releases the subject from dependence on hypostatized powers. Self-reflection is determined by an emancipatory cognitive interest. Critically oriented sciences share this interest with philosophy.

(Habermas 1971: 310)

As we will discuss below, we believe that *The Theory of the Leisure Class* goes beyond both the traditional empirical-analytic and historical-hermeneutic sciences and represents economics as an emancipatory science – that it is a critical social science engaged in expressing "ideologically frozen relations of dependence that can . . . be transformed."

We can summarize our consideration of Veblen from a perspective that moves from hermeneutics to communicative action in the following way. A common hermeneutic thread runs through early pragmatist thought, to which Veblen contributes by advancing Peirce's semiotic insight. As we have argued, Veblen moves Peirce's emphasis on the representation of reality to an emphasis on issues of reaching mutual understanding about something in the world; this move towards reaching understanding simultaneously calls forth the dimension of *phronesis* or ethical know-how. But grasping the hermeneutical cast of Veblen's thought is not sufficient for understanding the full complexity of his theorizing. For this we need to turn to Habermas's refinement of hermeneutics, communicative action, which challenges hermeneutic reliance on tradition and prejudice with the concepts of critique and systematically distorted communication. By seeing Veblen from the perspective of communicative action, we can appreciate

267

his radical reconstruction of economics into an emancipatory science. As a final note in understanding how a critique of systematically distorted communication relates to communicative action and the three types of science just identified, we again turn to Habermas, this time to his schematic organization for social actions, represented by the following diagram (Habermas 1984: 333):

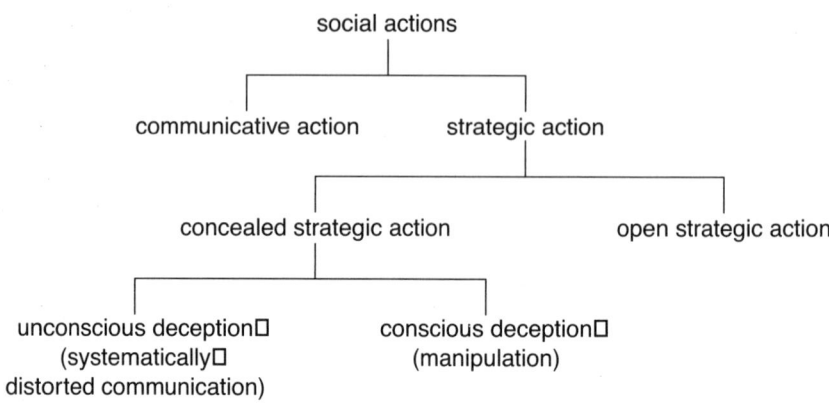

According to Habermas's scheme of social actions, the empirical-analytic sciences would fall under the category of open strategic action in so far as they are concerned with "purposive rationality" (Habermas 1971: 308). Such openly strategic action is perfectly appropriate for those processes of inquiry where technical control and its accompanying purposive rationality are desirable. A problem arises, however, when "action theory . . . remain(s) fixated on purposive rationality as the only aspect under which action can be criticized and improved" (Habermas 1984: 332). Such fixation in the sciences can lead to varieties of concealed strategic action; this occurs when processes of inquiry (the aforementioned different types of sciences) that are practical rather than technical and that are engaged in social action rather than removed from it, are reduced by a radical metonomy to variations of technology and means-end rationality. To recover these practical processes of inquiry, Habermas constructs them as either hermeneutical or critical social sciences, which are governed not by strategic action, oriented toward success, but by communicative action, oriented toward understanding and emancipation. By reading *The Theory of Leisure Class* as a critique of systematically distorted communication that opens up the possibility for economics as a critical social science, we would place Veblen on the side of communicative action, not on the side of strategic action, where he would be placed if seen exclusively in terms of technology and instrumental reason.

Close reading 3: Veblen's critique of systematically distorted communication

Veblen views economic activity as grounded in colloquial discourse distorted by emulation and expressions of exploit, prowess, and status. For Veblen, leisure-class institutions are congealed linguistic constructions that create systems of misunderstanding and prevent people from realizing their potential as active social agents.

To support our claim that Veblen grounds his economic theory in a critique of systematically distorted communication, we turn now to the text of *The Theory of the Leisure Class*. From the beginning, Veblen makes it clear that he does not view economic activity as a "struggle for subsistence" grounded in what he puts in scare quotes as "niggardliness of nature" (Veblen 1931: 24). Instead Veblen views economic activity in terms of emulation, which is grounded not in nature but in communication. Moreover, exploit, the precursory motive for emulation, is also grounded in communication.

First, a few words about exploit: most succinctly, exploit is rhetoric run amok. When Veblen distinguishes "between animate and inert things," he is distinguishing between that with which it is believed you can communicate and that with which you cannot. Prowess is not only an expression of physical exploit but also of rhetorical exploit: it is the rhetorician-priest who has the power to exploit "active objects" by persuading them as they are "assimilated to the human agent" (Veblen 1931: 12). Consider how Veblen describes this sort of exploit: "exploit, so far as it results in an outcome useful to the agent, is the conversion to his own ends of energies previously directed to some other end by another agent" (12–13). This could just as easily describe the power of the classical orator as represented by Gorgias, for example, where the orator's agency lies in his ability to redirect the energies of others through the drug-like power of his speech. Veblen defines prowess as "force or fraud" (14), precisely the sort of criticism Plato leveled at the sophists in *Gorgias*. This is not to say that Veblen is dismissive of rhetoric but to suggest that his critique of exploit can be seen in part as critique of systematically distorted communication. Linguistic power is misused to create a limiting environment that reduces human action either to exploitative activity or irksome labor rather than being used positively as communicative action and a ground for praxis.

The habit of systematically distorted communication begun in exploiting the "animate" evolves into habits of distorted communication that ground emulation. We can see this grounding in the vocabulary of signification that Veblen uses when discussing varieties of emulation. For example, in chapter III, "Conspicuous Leisure," the terms "mark" and "code" appear frequently, complemented by an array of terms of signification: "index," "voucher," "evidence," "badge," "insignia," "expression," and "symbol" and its derivatives "symbolic" and "symbolized." In the following chapter, "Conspicuous

Consumption," the term "mark" is again used frequently, supplemented by "insignia," "badge," "code," "signature," and "advertising" and "advertisement." The term "expression" appears eight times in five pages of the chapter on "The Pecuniary Standard of Living," and the terms "code," "mark," and "expression" return in "Pecuniary Canons of Taste." As much presence as these terms have throughout *The Theory of the Leisure Class*, however, "canon" is ubiquitous. With its various meanings of rule, law, edict, aphorisms, and sacred text, it is a term rich with connotations for discourse and attitudes towards it. Perhaps the meaning of "canon" with the richest potential for understanding Veblen's critique of systematically distorted communication is the following one, as taken from *The Oxford English Dictionary*: "In monastic orders, a book wherein the religious of every convent have a fair transcript of the rules of their order, frequently read among them as their local statutes." Here is a condensed description of the communicative practices that undergird emulation. It is as if every member of society has ever on display a transcript of the rules that are being read and interpreted: marks of status, codes of hierarchies, indices of exploit, and expressions of prowess constitute the basic communication and order of society that govern all economic activity.

Within the lexical texture of marks, codes, and canons, Veblen offers some explicit examples of the basic communicative nature of pecuniary emulation. In discussing manners, for example, Veblen characterizes them as "an *expression* of the relation of status, – a *symbolic* pantomime of mastery on the one hand and of subservience on the other" (Veblen 1931: 47, emphasis added). Of pecuniary strength he remarks that "[i]n order to impress . . . transient observers, and to retain one's self-complacency under their observation, the *signature* of one's pecuniary strength should be *written in characters* which he who runs may *read*" (87, emphasis added). One of the most explicit examples integrating communication and economic activity comes in Veblen's discussion of "Pecuniary Canons of Taste," in which he indicates his "present purpose . . . [as] determining what economic grounds are present in the accepted *canons* of taste and what is their *significance* for the distribution and consumption of goods" (165, emphasis added). A more developed example of grounding economic activity in communication occurs in a discussion of "Dress as an Expression of the Pecuniary Culture." In this discussion, Veblen traces the evolution of communication from unwieldy symbols such as powdered wigs to "subtler contrivances":

> These *indices* and others which resemble them in point of the boldness with which they point out to all observers the habitual uselessness of those persons who employ them, have been replaced by other, more delicate methods of *expressing* the same fact; methods which are no less evident to the trained eyes of that smaller, select circles whose good opinion is chiefly sought. The earlier and cruder method of *advertisement* held its ground so long as the public to

270

which the exhibitor had to appeal comprised large portions of the community who were not trained to detect delicate variations in the evidences of wealth and leisure. The method of *advertisement* undergoes a refinement when a sufficiently large wealthy class has developed, who have the leisure for acquiring skill in *interpreting* the subtler *signs* of expenditure. . . . The result of all this is a refinement of methods, a resort to subtler contrivances, and a spiritualisation of the scheme of *symbolism* in dress.

(Veblen 1931: 186–87, emphasis added)

What is particularly remarkable about this passage is not simply the various terms of communication (marked in italics) but also the transformation from bold indices and crude advertisements to spiritualized symbolism. Here we see instantiated a critique of systematically distorted communication. Keeping in mind Habermas's line of argument regarding the limits of hermeneutics, we see that Veblen is playing the role of "newcomer" who sees the indices, signs, symbols, and advertisements of exploit, prowess, and status as forms of "pseudocommunication" that creates a "system of misunderstandings" about what constitutes truly worthwhile economic activity. Moreover, Veblen's remarking on the transformation from crude methods of advertisements to a spiritualizing scheme of symbolism and the training in education that accompanies it together show a recognition of the repressiveness of power relationships, the deformity of intersubjective understanding, and colloquial communication systematically distorted. From this focal point in Veblen's text, we can interpret the signifying practices of emulation as pseudocommunication establishing systematically distorted communication. Additionally, we can view institutions not only as traditions found by habits of mind but as systematically distorted communication congealed into systems of authority and domination.

By engaging in a critique of systematically distorted communication, Veblen is providing an analysis that would transform economics into an emancipatory science. His viewing of economic activity as grounded in colloquial discourse distorted by emulation and expressions of exploit, prowess, and status results in a critical social science attempting to release the subject from hypostatized powers as it distinguishes invariant regularities of social action from ideological frozen relations of dependence that can be in principle transformed. But this emancipatory impulse to reconstruct economics as a critical social science requires a mode of discourse adequate for its articulation: critical rhetoric.

From critique to critical rhetoric

Veblen moves from a critique of systematically distorted communication that limits both economic practices and economic theory to a use of rhetoric capable of articulating complexity and situating economic theory in the day-to-day business of getting a living. To understand the complexity of Veblen's theory and his theorizing about economics, we need to understand the complexity of his rhetoric, which is critical and action-oriented rather than persuasive and performance-oriented. Critical rhetoric is grounded in reflecting on traditions and prejudices and in judging anew seemingly natural schemes of values, assumptions, and perspectives.

Traditionally, hermeneutics – the art of interpretation – complements rhetoric – the art of persuading and convincing. But as Habermas points out, hermeneutics is transformed from art to critique when it becomes philosophical and reflective. Moreover, this transformation is enabled in part by philosophical hermeneutics's learning from the experiences of rhetoric (Habermas 1988a: 294). By examining these rhetorical experiences, we will sketch out a critical rhetoric complementary to both philosophical hermeneutics and communicative action, arguing that Veblen practices such a critical rhetoric as a mode of discourse for transforming economics into a critical social science.

From Habermas, we can compile for rhetoric the following maxims, which serve as a basis for reconstructing rhetoric as critical praxis rather than as an art of persuasive techniques.[6]

1 Rhetoric is the appropriate mode of discourse for "situations where practical questions are brought to decision" (Habermas 1988a: 294).

2 Reflection on . . . convincing and persuading . . . serves in the interest . . . of a philosophical inquiry into the structures of colloquial communication" (Habermas 1988a: 294).

3 "Classical antiquity . . . reserved to rhetoric the realm of the merely 'plausible,' as opposed to that in which the truth of statements is discussed on theoretical grounds" (Habermas 1988a: 296).

4 Rhetoric is concerned with "practical questions . . . which can be reduced to decisions about the acceptance or rejection of standards, of critique of evaluation and norms of behavior" (Habermas 1988a: 296).

5 "Practical questions . . . remain bound to the context of the colloquial language" (Habermas 1988a: 296).

6 "The element of force . . . remains an ineradicable part of any consensus" (Habermas 1988a: 296).

7 "The rhetorical experience . . . teaches us . . . to respond spontaneously to changing states of affairs . . . to change ingrained schemata of interpretation, to learn (and teach others) to see things understood on the basis of tradition differently and to judge them anew" (Habermas 1988a: 296–7).

8 "The rhetorical experience . . . teaches us to see the connection between language and praxis" (Habermas 1988a: 297).

9 In the process of *self-reflection*, the subject becomes aware of unconscious presuppositions which underlie accomplishments he has taken for granted" (Habermas 1988a: 298).

From these insights by Habermas, we can construct the following statement defining critical rhetoric: critical rhetoric moves beyond the art of persuasion into the realm of *practical discourse*, where humans deliberate about the standards, criteria, norms, and values that come into play in day-to-day living. But issues of force and power also come into play during the course of such deliberations. By drawing out the critical impulse of rhetoric that urges us to judge anew ingrained schemata and traditions and coupling this with the process of self-reflection, the rhetorician engages colloquial language to lay open and articulate elements of force and power that may distort deliberation and judgment necessary for human action. The critical rhetorician must therefore be aware of how force and power are masked in colloquial language and how they impinge upon praxis. To complete this definition, we need to turn momentarily to Aristotle's *Rhetoric*.

While it would not be appropriate here to develop an elaborate reconstruction of Aristotle in terms of critical rhetoric, two points are pertinent. First, Aristotle explicitly states that rhetoric is an offshoot of ethics and politics as well as the counterpart to dialectic (Aristotle 1954: 1356a). This statement clearly ties rhetoric to the ethical know-how of *phronesis* and provides a ground for considering rhetoric as a critical praxis rather than a performance *techne*. Second, Aristotle also states explicitly that there are three modes of persuasion that are manifest in discourse: the character of the speaker, or *ethos*; the putting of the audience into an appropriate frame of mind, or *pathos*; and the words or account of the speech itself, or *logos* (1356a). While these three modes of proof can be seen from a traditional performative perspective of persuasion drawing on non-critical traits of colloquial speech – a personable speaker manipulating the emotions of the audience to accept an account of something – they can be reconstructed to develop the critical dimensions of colloquial speech. That is to say, colloquial speech carries with it the potential of self-reflection and critique, a potential that is actualized in critical rhetoric when *ethos* entails judging and enjoining the ethical dimensions of discourse, when *pathos* entails judging and enjoining the appropriateness or emotional dimensions of discourse, and when *logos* entails judging and enjoining what is included in or excluded from the accounts of discourse. Thus a critical rhetorician must deliberate and judge appropriately, not simply deliver a persuasive performance, in order to engender social action.

Close reading 4: Veblen's use of critical rhetoric

A rhetorical analysis of The Theory of the Leisure Class *demonstrates how critical rhetoric (as opposed to scientific exposition or literary satire) informs Veblen's mode of theorizing. The analysis discusses deliberation and contingency as the realm of rhetoric; the use of rhetorical proofs ethos, pathos, and logos; and the function of irony as a governing trope. Veblen does not offer a theory of critical rhetoric but provides an example of critical rhetoric in the making as he articulates an economic theory aimed not at the revelation of universal truths but rather at an emancipation from social practices that stand in the way of getting a living – practices that need to be deliberated over and transformed.*

Having outlined some basic characteristics of critical rhetoric in such a way that it can be seen as the mode of discourse appropriate for communicative action, we would like to turn one last time to *The Theory of the Leisure Class* to see how critical rhetoric manifests itself as the mode of discourse that shapes Veblen's practice of economic theorizing.

The earliest evidence of the rhetoricality governing *The Theory of the Leisure Class* comes in the prefatory statement quoted above, where Veblen articulates the aporia between science and literature, expressing doubt about the "fitness" of his work in either category. In addition to this aporia, Veblen indicates that the substance of his theory relies on "recourse to homely facts or by what may at times appear to be a callous freedom in handling vulgar phenomena or phenomena whose intimate place in men's life has sometimes shielded them from the impact of economic discussion" (Veblen 1931: viii). "Vulgar phenomena" suggest to us the realm of rhetoric as Aristotle understood it. For Aristotle, the realm of rhetoric was not the realm of necessity nor was it exactly the same as the realm of the poetic, the construction of drama and narrative. Instead, "[t]he duty of rhetoric is to deal with such matters as we deliberate upon" (Aristotle 1954: 1357a). Aristotle goes on to say that

> [t]he subjects of our deliberation are such as seem to present us with alternative possibilities: about things that could not have been, and cannot now or in the future be, other than they are, nobody who takes them to be of this nature wastes his time in deliberation.
> (Aristotle 1954: 1357a)

Moreover it is rhetoric that is the discourse not only for deliberation but also for action. As Aristotle continues, "it is about our actions that we deliberate and inquire, and all our actions have a contingent character; hardly any of them are determined by necessity" (1357a). Now it is this realm of contingency, deliberation, and action, the dispensing with necessity and inevitability, that suggests for us that rhetoric is the mode of discourse operating in *The Theory of the Leisure Class*. In addition, Veblen's invocation of "homely facts" and "vulgar phenomena" resonates richly with the Habermasian maxim for critical rhetoric that pertains to practical questions remaining bound to the context of the colloquial language, for it is precisely about homely facts and vulgar phenomena that colloquial language speaks. The invocation of "intimate phenomena" that had shielded men from economic discussion also signals critical rhetoric, suggesting a critique of norms, a judging anew of traditions and a change of ingrained schemata

274

of interpretation, and even a philosophical inquiry into the structures of colloquial communication. Finally, the "callous freedom" that infuses Veblen's invocations is the freedom of rhetoric's call to act transformatively in its critical mode, engaged in self-reflection and calling into question the unconscious presuppositions that underlie those previously intimate phenomena.

The second indication that Veblen is engaged in critical rhetoric is the manner in which *ethos, pathos*, and *logos* come into play in *The Theory of the Leisure Class*. As we noted above, when these terms are employed in the context of critical rhetoric, they call forth issues of ethics, appropriateness, and inclusiveness of accounts. A brief consideration of material, much of which we have already examined, will be adequate to understand these rhetorical elements in Veblen's work.

Given the way the rhetoric of *The Theory of the Leisure Class* works, we will consider *logos* first. From the standpoint of critical rhetoric, questions of *logos* cannot be reduced to questions of logic. Instead, critical rhetoric draws on another definition of the term – account. In *The Theory of the Leisure Class*, we see called into account human activities and conditions that had been excluded from the accounts of other economists. Thus Veblen will include in his account what has hitherto been excluded: the distinction between worthy and unworthy employments (Veblen 1931: 8). Similarly, Veblen sees a lack on the part of accounts of "the classical tradition . . . [where] man's 'power over nature' . . . [is] the characteristic fact of indus-trial productivity" (10). And again, Veblen criticizes "classical doctrines . . . [which] construe [the] struggle for wealth as being substantially a struggle for subsistence" (24). Consequently, Veblen expands the *logos* of economic theory to include much more than behavior that rationally allocates scarce resources, which brings us to arguments derived from a critical appropriation of *pathos*.

Pathos traditionally has to do with the emotions, and in strategically conceived rhetoric, their manipulation to succeed in winning arguments. In critical rhetoric, however, *pathos* takes on the issue of appropriateness in different ways. One way that *pathos* works is in close relation to *logos*, asking whether the account being given has the appropriate depth and dimensions that emotions add to human life. Is the *pathos* right, the economic theorist employing critical rhetoric may ask, to reduce economic activity to allo-cating scarce resources? What emotional elements need to be considered in developing arguments that acknowledge the complexity for providing material well-being? Thus as Veblen expands the *logos* of economic theory, he does so by drawing arguments from considerations of *pathos* such as prowess, status, and, especially, emulation.

Just as a critical use of *pathos* can enhance understanding, so too can a critical use of *ethos*. A critical appropriation of *ethos* moves beyond the persua-siveness of a speaker's character to an incorporation of ethical arguments.

Veblen makes arguments from *ethos* in three ways. First, Veblen makes particular arguments about women as trophies and property and about their mutilation, all of which derive from *ethos*. Second, at the other extreme from particular arguments about women, is the ubiquitous term "habit." Veblen is always speaking about habits of thought and habits of mind. This construction takes on considerable rhetorical significance when we consider that the original definition of *ethos* is habit. Thus just as the frequent use of lexical references to signifying practices informs a critique of systematically distorted communication, so too does a frequent use of "habit" signal the presence of *ethos*, the ethical domain, which is culturally created and cumulative and which shapes our praxis, bringing forth the dimension of *phronesis* and ethical know-how within which economic activity takes place. This general presence of *ethos* is particularized in the third way that arguments from *ethos* are present. Again we rely on particular terms. As we noted before, Veblen initiates his theory by distinguishing between two types of employment, worthy and unworthy. Far from being simply technical terms, they carry with them an ethical force as do other such key conceptual terms as "exploit," "waste," and "invidious." Even though Veblen claims of the last two that they are simply technical terms (34, 97), they can be seen as drawn from *ethos* when we consider this statement by Veblen: "An invidious comparison is a process of valuation of persons with respect of worth" (34). Any process of valuation, we would argue, derives from *ethos*. But the ethical dimension of Veblen's terms, along with his insistence on their status as technical terms can best be explained by what we see as the third indication of Veblen's employment of critical rhetoric – his use of irony.

Irony, Lanham notes, is one of Kenneth Burke's four master tropes and performs the function of dialectic (Lanham 1991: 102). Lanham also says that "generally speaking, the more sophisticated the irony, the more is implied, the less stated" (92). As a figure of speech, the presence of irony is not a defining characteristic of critical rhetoric. Recognizing irony's *dialectical* function, however, does allow us to see the dialectical dimension of Veblen's critical rhetoric. The significance of irony's dialectical quality lies in its saying one thing while simultaneously making a counterstatement through implication. The meaning of irony thus lies neither in what is stated nor what is implied but in the dialectical tension between the two. This dialectical tension between statement and implication is a tension that simultaneously creates distance and engagement. On the scale of inquiry, it is the principle at work in critical social science, which demands simultaneously the distance necessary for discerning behavioral regularities and the engagement necessary for transformation. On the scale of critique, it demands the ironic tension of being able to analyze what is being expressed explicitly while simultaneously engaging the structures of power that go unstated. On the scale of Veblen's critical rhetoric, it allows for an *ethos* that articulates the distance necessary for economic analysis while simultaneously, from an ethical position, calling into question the mask of objectivity worn by the classical economists. Consider the terms that are specifically called into ironic play: "invidious," "leisure," and "waste," where "invidious" is used in a "technical sense" (Veblen 1931: 34), where "leisure" is simply "non-productive consumption of time" (43), and where "waste" is not to carry its normal "undertone of deprecation" (97). What is the unspoken counterstatement to these terms? For "invidious," it is "rational" – in its technical sense, of course; for "leisure," "subsistence," which must connote nothing more than the productive use of time, and for "waste," "efficiency," which certainly should not carry the normal undertones of appreciation. Veblen has taken three terms that govern classical economic theory and has turned them on their heads. He is using his terms in a technical way, just as classical economists do, but he is also using them from an ethical perspective. Unlike the classical economists, however, Veblen is aware that economic theory is not objective, disengaged, and neutral, but rather is situated in complicated ways as historical and cultural activity. Veblen's irony, then, is an irony of both distance and engagement that embraces the dialectical complexity of human life.

If economic theory is to account accurately for complexity, it must be constructed in a mode of discourse capable of articulating complexity. Critical rhetoric is such a mode of discourse in so far as it criticizes norms, traditions, and schemata of interpretation that all go to shape the way we draw arguments, come to understanding, and act – all of which come into play in *The Theory of the Leisure Class*. Furthermore, the critical reconstruction of *ethos*, *pathos*, and *logos* allows for rich arguments that fully integrate accounts and rationality with considerations of ethics and appropriateness. Again all these elements come into play in *The Theory of the Leisure Class*. Finally, when informed by irony, critical rhetoric functions dialectically, playing what is explicit and overt against what goes unsaid, which, finally, is the trope that organizes the discourse of *The Theory of the Leisure Class*. With all this in mind, we would like to close with why we see the rhetoricality of Veblen's thought as significant.

The significance of Veblen's rhetoricality

Only by understanding the rhetorical dimension of Veblen's thought can we understand his practice of theorizing about economics and understand the full complexity of his economic theory. Without understanding Veblen's rhetoric, his theory can seem one-dimensional and dated, too heavily situated in the technology of the industrial age. Understanding his rhetoric, however, allows us to see an additional dimension of his theory: one grounded in social action and emancipation.

The rhetoricality of *The Theory of the Leisure Class* is significant on two counts. First, critical rhetoric represents a practical mode of discourse for economic theorizing. As such, Veblen advances pragmatic thought in general and economic theory in particular in the direction of critical, emancipatory social science. In effect, we see Veblen inventing in practice a language for the sort of theory that is situated in human praxis and aimed at transformation. Second, we see in the rhetoricality of *The Theory of the Leisure Class* a dimension of Veblen's theory that is not otherwise easily seen: the dimension of *phronesis* – ethical know-how – and social action, which exists not as a separate, abstract *a priori* theory but as embedded in the rhetorical texture of Veblen's theorizing practice. This act of embedding theory, which is within text and which can be recovered only through interpretation, is the very embodiment of pragmatism governed by critical hermeneutics and articulated by critical rhetoric. Only by comprehending the critical rhetoricality of Veblen's thought can we comprehend his theory of social action.

Most easily seen are Veblen's theories of machine processes and institutions; together they constitute a compound theory of production. The first part considers human productivity, while the second part considers constraints to that productivity. In Habermas's terms, these can be construed as technology and domination. As such, Veblen is a theorist of *techne* and production, which is represented in Figure 1:

Theory of production 1: machine processes (technology)	Theory of production 2: institutions (domination)

Limiting Veblen as simply a theorist of *techne*, however, is irksome, for it constrains our instincts that Veblen is articulating theory more complex than *techne* would allow. And merely redefining *techne* – or technology – to include action as well as production is not particularly satisfying from a pragmatic perspective: by maintaining a distinction between action and production, *phronesis* and *techne*, we more readily maintain a way to contextualize problems of production and thus solve them.

Put in slightly different terms, by seeing Veblen as only a theorist of production, we can see his theory in only negative terms. That is, once the constraints of institutions have been removed, what is the context of production? To say that institutions can be enabling as well as constraining is, like the redefinition of technology, not entirely satisfactory, at least in the case of understanding Veblen's theory. For Veblen, institutions are congealed systems of distorted communication. Thus as powerful as Veblen's theory of production is in negative terms, by itself, it lacks the power of positive theory.

We can see the positive element of Veblen's theory – the element that grounds issues of production in the context of social action governed by *phronesis* — when we examine the rhetoricality of *The Theory of the Leisure Class*. This is represented in Figure 2.

Theory of production 1: machine processes (technology)	Rhetoric of action	Theory of production 2: institutions (domination)

By attending to the practice of critical rhetoric that Veblen uses to articulate *The Theory of the Leisure Class*, we see emerge a dialectic between production and social action that operates in the same manner as the dialectic of irony. Explicit and on the surface, Veblen's theory speaks to the production of technological know-how and the constraints imposed by ineffective institutions. But implicit in the rhetoric that goes on behind the back of explicit theory, so to speak, is the discourse of ethical know-how and the rhetoric of social action. To read Veblen's theory as one of machines and institutions is to read only half of Veblen's theory. The other half of Veblen's theory comprises ethical know-how and social action. But this other half of Veblen's theory cannot be easily extracted or summarized as "content"; instead, it can only be grasped as an interpretation of Veblen's rhetoric. It is in grasping, finally, the dialectic of irony that we grasp the dialectic between economic theory and rhetorical practice, the dialectic between production and social action. And it is in grasping the full dialectical meaning of *The Theory of the Leisure Class* that we grasp it not as predictive science or as literary narrative but as critical social science whose goal is emancipation.

EPILOGUE: THE RHETORICIAN AND THE ECONOMIST AGAIN

So what you're saying is that the only way you can fully appreciate the complexity of Veblen's economics is to understand his rhetoric — that his theory and manner of theorizing are embedded in his language, just as he believes economic activity itself is embedded in language and communication.

Yes. By reading Veblen from a contemporary perspective that foregrounds rhetoric, we see his theory becoming revitalized and appropriate again. Let's face it. In the post-industrial age, we don't make steel so much as exchange symbols, images, and information, the exchange of which carries social, political, and ethical implications.

And Veblen's economic theory speaks to this sort of economy in ways that neo-classical economics cannot, hobbled as it is by scarcity and the behavior of rational economic man who behaves rather than acts. With Veblen we see instead the actions of rhetorically oriented, symbol-using people engaged in social action and striving for emancipation from institutional arrangements that limit human potential as they limit our abilities in the day-to-day work of getting a living. That, after all, is the ground of economic exchange as well as economic change.

NOTES

1 We wish to thank Warren Samuels for both his encouragement and his excellent editorial suggestions, which have contributed greatly to whatever strengths this article may have.

2 According to the Association for Evolutionary Economics (AFEE) membership invitation, "AFEE economists develop cogent and relevant theories for formulating sound economic policies. They develop economics as a social science to join causal explanation to social action." Included among "The Tenets of Institutionalism" are the following statements: "Economics is a policy science; economic inquiry is significant only to the extent that it is relevant to problem solving" and "Social value judgments are a part of inquiry and must themselves be objects of analysis" [Association for Evolutionary Economics].

3 This is a commonplace perspective all the way from the critical theory of Max Horkheimer and Theodor W. Adorno [1982] to the revision of that tradition by Jürgen Habermas [1971] to the hermeneutic philosophy of Hans-Georg Gadamer and Paul Ricoeur [1981] to the French poststructuralism of Michel Foucault [1980] and Jean-François Lyotard [1988] to the feminist critiques of science by Sandra Harding [1986] and Helen E. Longino [1990].

4 While interpretation is arguably the most basic trait of hermeneutics, an equally defining trait is dialogue.

5 Thus we would argue that Veblen went farther than Mirowski's claim that in his earlier works, including *The Theory of the Leisure Class*, "Veblen's antinomies resonated with the pragmatist philosophy" of Peirce [Mirowski 1988: 72].

6 In effect, we are moving rhetoric as a social action from the side of strategic action – either open or deceptive – to the side of communicative action. This has the practical effect of fitting the mode of discourse with the process of enquiry.

REFERENCES

Adorno, Theodor W. 1982. *Prisms*. Trans. Samuel and Shierry Weber. Cambridge, Mass.: MIT Press.

Aristotle. 1954. *The Rhetoric and the Poetics of Aristotle*. Trans. W. Rhys Roberts. New York: The Modern Library.

Association for Evolutionary Economics. n.d. "An Invitation to Creative and Relevant Scholarship." Lincoln, Nebr.: Association for Evolutionary Economics.

Bernstein, Richard J. 1986. *Philosophical Profiles*. Philadelphia: University of Pennsylvania Press.

—— 1992. *The New Constellation: The Ethical-Political Horizons of Modernity/Postmodernity*. Cambridge, Mass.: MIT Press.

Burke, Kenneth. 1950 [1969]. *A Rhetoric of Motives*. Berkeley: University of California Press.

The Compact Edition of the Oxford English Dictionary. 1971. Glasgow: Oxford University Press.

Dorfman, Joseph. 1972. *Thorstein Veblen and His America*. Clifton, N.J.: A.M. Kelly.

Eby, Claire Virginia. 1994. "Thorstein Veblen and the Rhetoric of Authority." *American Quarterly* 46 (2): 139–73.

Foucault, Michel. 1980. *Power/Knowledge: Selected Interviews and Other Writings 1972–1977*. New York: Pantheon Books.

Gadamer, Hans-Georg. 1988. "The Rehabilitation of Authority and Tradition." In *The Hermeneutic Reader*: 261–67. Edited by Kurt Mueller-Vollmer. New York: Continuum.

Habermas, Jürgen. 1971. *Knowledge and Human Interests*. Trans. Jeremy J. Shapiro. Boston: Beacon.

—— 1984. *The Theory of Communicative Action: Volume 1: Reason and the Rationalization of Society*. Trans. Thomas McCarthy. Boston: Beacon Press.

—— 1987. *The Philosophical Discourse of Modernity: Twelve Lectures*. Trans. Frederick Lawrence. Cambridge, Mass.: MIT Press.

—— 1988a. "On Hermeneutics' Claim to Universality."

In *The Hermeneutic Reader*: 294–319. Edited by Kurt Mueller-Vollmer. New York: Continuum.

—— 1988b. *On the Logic of the Social Sciences*. Trans. Shierry Weber Nicholsen and Jerry A. Stark. Cambridge, Mass.: MIT Press.

—— 1992. *Postmetaphysical Thinking: Philosophical Essays*. Trans. William Mark Hohengarten. Cambridge, Mass.: MIT Press.

Harding, Sandra. 1986. *The Science Question in Feminism*. Ithaca and London: Cornell University Press.

Horkheimer, Max and Adorno, Theodor W. 1982. *Dialectic of Enlightenment*. Trans. John Cumming. New York: Continuum.

Jennings, Ann and Waller, William. 1994. "Evolutionary Economics and Cultural Hermeneutics: Veblen, Cultural Relativism, and Blind Drift." *Journal of Economic Issues*. 27 (4): 997–1030.

Lanham, Richard A. 1991. *A Handlist of Rhetorical Terms*, 2nd edn, Berkeley: University of California Press.

Longino, Helen E. 1990. *Science as Social Knowledge: Values and Objectivity in Scientific Inquiry*. Princeton: Princeton University Press.

Lyotard, Jean-François. 1988. *The Differend: Phrases in Dispute*. Minneapolis: University of Minnesota Press.

Mirowski, Philip. 1988. "The Philosophical Bases of Institutionalist Economics." In *Evolutionary Economics: Volume I*: 51–88. Edited by Marc R. Tool. Armonk, NY: M.E. Sharpe, Inc.

Plato. 1975 [1925]. *Gorgias*. Trans. W. R. M. Lamb. London: Heinemann. (New York: Putnam's. Loeb Classical Library.)

Ricoeur, Paul. 1981. *Hermeneutics and the Human Sciences: Essays on Language, Action and Interpretation*. Cambridge: Cambridge University Press.

Samuels, Warren J. 1990. "The Self-Referentiability of Thorstein Veblen's Theory of Preconceptions of Economic Science." *Journal of Economic Issues* 24 (3): 695–718.

Tilman, Rick. 1992. *Thorstein Veblen and His Critics, 1891–1963*. Princeton: Princeton University Press.

Veblen, Thorstein. 1931 [1899]. *The Theory of the Leisure Class*. New York: The Viking Press (New York: Macmillan Company).

Waller, William and Robertson, Linda R. 1990. "Why Johnny (Ph.D., Economics) Can't Read: A Rhetorical Analysis of Thorstein Veblen and a Response to Donald McCloskey's *Rhetoric of Economics*." *Journal of Economic Issues* 24 (4): 1027–44.

15

GEORG SIMMEL AND THORSTEIN VEBLEN ON FASHION FIN DE SIÈCLE

Rick Tilman

INTRODUCTION

Although Thorstein Veblen (1857–1929) and Georg Simmel (1858–1918) were important contemporaries in the shaping of modern social theory, scholars have paid little attention to their intellectual relationship. Indeed, with one possible exception, no systematic effort to compare their work exists including their most influential books, Veblen's *The Theory of the Leisure Class* (1899) and Simmel's *The Philosophy of Money* (1900).[1] Although Veblen never cites or mentions Simmel, the two both published in the *American Journal of Sociology*, which was edited by Albion Small from 1895 to 1926 at the University of Chicago where Veblen taught. Most of the material by Simmel was translated from German by Small himself and included a section from *The Philosophy of Money*. Veblen was undoubtedly familiar with some of what Simmel published in the *AJS*: fifteen articles between 1896 and 1910. Simmel may well have read Veblen's contributions to it, amounting to four articles between 1898 and 1906. Even so, there is no indication of direct mutual intellectual influence although the two men probably were in reading contact with each other.[2]

Simmel was a founder of formalism in sociology and its apologist in economics, while Veblen was an antiformalist in both disciplines. To illustrate, Simmel was greatly influenced by the marginalist revolution in neoclassical economics, especially the work of the Austrians and particularly that of Carl Menger (1840–1921); but Veblen's institutionalism was a main source of dissent from the conventional wisdom.[3] Simmel was also more inclined to view economics *per se* as the science of exchange as measured by price, although he believed the economy clearly had an aesthetic dimension to it; for Veblen such a paradigm was too narrow and he, instead, viewed economics as the study of social provisioning. Simmel's taxonomic analysis of forms in sociology diverted his attention from questions of social causation. Veblen, on the other hand, denounced taxonomic endeavors and preferred to examine the forces that move specific groups and classes of human beings to create concrete cultural and social forms. Even in the discipline of history the two seemed to diverge; Simmel considered history to be an inscrutable realm of movement and flux while, at least in principle, Veblen thought no social processes including prehistory and history to be beyond human scrutiny and understanding. In rough fashion, then, Simmel falls into the formalist and antihistoricist camps while Veblen adhered to antiformalism and historicism.

Both Veblen and Simmel believed that Western culture had entered a period of deepening cultural crisis that was connected with far-reaching socioeconomic changes. Where they sometimes disagreed was over the nature and the causes of the turn-of-the-century crisis and the lens through which these might be viewed. My focus will be on fashion as I attempt to show how Simmel and Veblen differ in their views of this crisis, but I shall also consider how the former complements the latter's theoretical perspective. It should be understood at the outset, however, that by "fashion" Simmel means not only clothing and apparel but what is fashionable in morals, aesthetics and other facets of the cultural apparatus; whereas, Veblen more narrowly signifies garb, jewelry and ornamentation as "fashion." To illustrate, Simmel comments on the changing role of fashion in this vein:

> It may almost be considered a sign of the increased power of fashion, that it has overstepped the bounds of its original domain which comprised only personal externals, and has acquired an increasing influence over taste, over theoretical convictions, and even over the moral foundations of life.
>
> (Simmel, 1957, p. 548)

His definition thus exceeds the parameters of "fashion" established by Veblen by a considerable margin since Veblen uses the term "convention" to indicate theoretical, aesthetic and moral consensus rather than "fashion." However, the significance of their different terminology and styles of thinking will become more evident as I examine (1) the impact of money in the objectification and rationalization of culture including fashion in their work; (2) the role of fashion in status emulation; (3) fashion as a class phenomenon; (4) the refinement of Veblenian and Simmelian "microeconomics" with fashion as a focal point; and (5) Simmel's depoliticization versus Veblen's politicization of fashion.

Before I proceed with the analysis, however, "fashion" must be located within the overall approaches of each writer in more detail. In Veblen it is an aspect of the "pecuniary standard of living" and "canons of taste" and, more generally, of the broader social environment (Veblen, 1964). But in

Simmel it is an aspect of "the style of life" and, more generally, of the whole cultural complex set out in the "synthetic part" of *Philosophy of Money*. (1978, chapters 4–6). It is thus possible to contrast the meanings of "pecuniary" and "money" for Veblen with the meanings of "standard of living" and "style of life" in Simmel. If space permitted, it would also be possible to specify the particular understandings of class, status and market they had and, in addition, their contrasting analyses of the cultural and political crisis.

In any case, some of the most penetrating social theorizing and criticism on the subject of fashion was done by Simmel and Veblen. Yet their fundamental outlooks on fashion were different in that Simmel viewed it in a more positive light as a blend of contradictions, while Veblen saw it as mostly wasted labor and materials ostentatiously displayed in anticipation of status enhancement. In short, the former saw its contradictory nature and the ambiguous role it performed in turn-of-the-century Berlin; whereas the latter castigated its role in intensifying emulatory rivalry even while it functioned simultaneously as a social bonding agent in Chicago and other cities with which he was familiar.

OBJECTIFICATION AND RATIONALIZATION OF CULTURE BY MONEY

In his *Philosophy of Money* Simmel considers exchange to be both "paradigmatic and symbolic of society as a whole." (Frisby, 1992, p. 12) In Veblen's *Theory of the Leisure Class* money is largely viewed as symptomatic of particular kinds of power and emulatory status systems that are linked with class. For Simmel a major consequence of the widespread use of money in modern culture is that it serves to "objectify" human relations, that is, it introduces and intensifies the quantification of all material relations including thought processes. Rhythms and patterns of human behavior lose their asymmetries and adopt more predictable parameters; whim and fancy lose their eccentricity, while irrational forms of conduct become less idiosyncratic. The adoption of money and the intensification of its use in everyday life as a means of exchange thus inculcates a rationality which is not confined to the mere pursuit of self-interest but, unfortunately, leads to a social order where means began to absorb or destroy ends. These ends may be moral or aesthetic but Simmel argues that their very existence is threatened by means, that is, the monetization of economy and culture.

For Veblen the "objectification" of society is only in part a monetary phenomenon; it is due to the spread of "matter-of-fact" knowledge that accelerates at the point of convergence of science and technology. What Veblen calls the "machine process," in particular, imposes its own discipline on the human psyche. Along with the industrial culture of which it is a part, it compels psychological conformity in terms of the quantifying impact of weight and tale, process understood as cause and effect, precision of measurement, uniformity and adjustment of response to technological imperatives, adherence to time schedules, accuracy of accounting and inventory, and so forth. For Veblen (1975, chapters 2 and 9) these related processes will continue toward dominance of modern culture and may bring with them not only greater functional rationality but, also, (hopefully) more substantial rationality, that is, greater capacity for choosing humane ends. Simmel seems to fear, however, that the increasing monetization of economy and society is producing means (free exchange) that will destroy ends that are morally, aesthetically and culturally valuable. Nevertheless, the causal variables are so complex, subtle and difficult to diagnose that for both Veblen and Simmel the future remains somewhat unpredictable; social trends can be identified but they do not necessarily point beyond the immediate future. For Veblen emulatory consumption and the resurgence of atavistic continuities such as institutional religion and nationalism may defeat or at least retard the development of substantial rationality. To Simmel it appeared that the community is susceptible to the blandishments of a monetized economy and society for reasons that can only accelerate its cultural and aesthetic decay. At the turn of the century, the cultural crisis of industrial society forced both of these thinkers to face the future with psychic unease born out of the recognition that a transition was underway whose outcome was difficult to predict and whose consequences might well be undesirable. Not surprisingly, this transition often manifested itself in the worlds of fashion, social convention and ornamentation which were increasingly subject to instability and rapid change.

THE ROLE OF FASHION IN STATUS EMULATION

For Simmel, what Veblen negatively portrays as conspicuous consumption, waste, and exemption from useful labor has a different meaning. Simmel tends to accent the positive, or at least, not to dwell on the morbid aspects of emulatory behavior while Veblen's view of it as pathological is well known. However, with regard to the relationship between advertising and consumer demand, Simmel comments to the effect that commodity production itself must be followed by giving things an enticing external appearance over and above their usefulness. That is, one must attempt to excite the interest of the buyer by means of the external attraction of the object. Simmel calls this process "aesthetic productivity." Thus, when it comes to "fashion," some degree of convergence in Simmel and Veblen is, nevertheless, apparent despite their other differences over it. To further illustrate: for Veblen, clothing – women's dress in particular – has three characteristics in a capitalistic economy. It must be novel, wasteful and cumbersome; that is, it must be fashionable, unnecessarily expensive, and inhibit the free movement necessary for useful labor. Nevertheless, for the two men, even in the case of women's dress, emulation serves different functions: what is mostly waste and futility in Veblen's analysis, is to Simmel enticement, sensual and intense, if transient. However, in one of his most "Veblenian" glosses on social emulation, Simmel writes that:

> Every fashion is essentially the fashion of a social class; that is, it always indicates a social stratum which uses similarity of appearance to assert both its own inner unity and its outward differentiation from other social strata. As soon as the lower strata attempt to imitate the upper strata and adopt their fashion the latter create a new one. Wherever fashions have existed they have sought to express social differences. Yet the social changes of the last hundred years have accelerated the pace of changes in fashion, on the one hand through the weakening of class barriers and frequent upward social mobility of individuals and sometimes even of whole groups to a higher stratum, and on the other through the predominance of the third estate.
>
> (Simmel, 1978, p. 461)

Simmel continues:

> The first factor makes very frequent changes of fashion necessary on the part of leading strata because imitation by the lower strata rapidly robs fashions of their meaning and attraction. The second factor comes into operation because the middle class and the urban population are, in contrast to the conservatism of the highest strata and the peasantry, the groups in which there is great variability. Insecure classes and individuals, pressing for change, find in fashion, in the changing and contrasting forms of life, a pace that mirrors their own psychological movements. If contemporary fashions are much less extravagant and expensive and of much shorter duration than those of earlier centuries, then this is due partly to the fact that it must be made much easier for the lower strata to emulate these fashions and partly because fashion now originates in the wealthy middle class.
>
> (Simmel, 1978, p. 461)

Simmel has succinctly summarized several of Veblen's ideas regarding social emulation and, interestingly, anticipated microeconomist Harvey Leibenstein's development of them. Although no direct evidence exists that Simmel had read Veblen at this point in his career, he probably was aware of Veblen's articles in the *American Journal of Sociology*; if so, the similarity in this part of their analysis is easier to explain.

Both Veblen and Simmel were early theorists of what is today regarded as "want creation" which means, of course, the creation of ever-new needs. Simmel writes that:

> The seller must always seek to call forth new and differentiated needs of the enticed customer. In order to find a source of income which is not yet exhausted, and to find a function which cannot readily be displaced, it is necessary to specialize in one's services. This process promotes differentiation, refinement, and the enrichment of the public's needs, which obviously must lead to growing personal differences within this public.
>
> (Simmel, 1964, p. 420)

Of course, to Veblen one result of "enticed" consumption is the creation of jobs, the main function of which is to produce consumer goods for purposes of status enhancement, thus only compounding the existing problem of exemption from useful labor. Also, he did not share Simmel's enthusiasm for the promotion of "differentiation, refinement, and the enrichment of the public's needs" because he did not believe these served what he called "the generic ends of life." This is not to claim, however, that Veblen believed all novel goods and services were waste and futility. It is to suggest that it was their status-enhancing not more utilitarian functions upon which he focused in his indictment of emulatory consumption.

Simmel also held a more positive view of the way individuals used their leisure time than did Veblen, although they were both social theorists for whom leisure is an important subject of investigation. David Frisby (1992) writes with regard to Simmel's discussions of leisure:

> First, leisure can be viewed as an ideological denotation for the emptier "fillings-in of time and consciousness." In other words leisure as a concept requires the same kind of deconstruction as did the nineteenth-century notion of "recreation." Second, Simmel insists that leisure is not an autonomous sphere that can be examined without reference to work, to "the serious things in life." Third, leisure is never associated *a priori* with creativity, with creative subjectivity. "Free" time is not necessarily "creative" time. One reason for this which Simmel draws to our attention is that forms of leisure can be and usually are commodified, and the "activity" of consumption is a passive one.
>
> (Frisby, 1992, p. 134)

In Veblen's analysis the leisure class and others who emulate it use their leisure time in wasteful and pernicious ways that are not fulfilling; these include horse and dog racing, breeding of animals for purposes of display, dram drinking and treating, football, and other sports and games based on force and fraud, and so on (Veblen, 1975, p. 89). Frisby comments that:

> What [this] connotes is *non-productive consumption of time*. Time is consumed non-productively (1) from a sense of the unworthiness of productive work, and (2) as an evidence of pecuniary ability to afford a life of idleness. Such "non-productive consumption of time" indicates both a critical stance *vis-à-vis* classical political economy and, with its emphasis upon "consumption" rather than "use" of time, some accord with the concerns of the economists who had heralded the "marginalist revolution" in their discipline.
>
> (Frisby, 1992, pp. 118–19)

Veblen's sometimes puritanical hatred of waste, that is, nonproductive consumption of time as a form of emulatory display thus set him off from Simmel, who had a more positive attitude toward the prevailing uses of leisure time than his American contemporary.

Although Simmel was not as focused as Veblen on status emulation, that is, ostentatious display, conspicuous waste and conspicuous exemption from useful labor, he was not unaware of these aspects of human behavior. Indeed, on several occasions in *Philosophy of Money* he alludes to emulatory display in ways that parallel Veblen's analysis; also, these examples are linked with manifestations of the ego, or lack thereof, along Veblenian lines in that they have to do with the sense of self-worth. Nevertheless, even when Simmel describes the emulatory behavior of classes, groups or individuals, it is evident that he is pursuing a different line of analysis. It is the individual's psyche that he is bent on understanding: the "inner person," so to speak, not so much the status rivalry of Veblen-satirized humankind. To illustrate the point further, Simmel refers to the status-enhancing value of certain goods, in this case, Indian wampum (1978, p. 155). It is clear, however, that this is not the focus of Simmel's analysis; rather it is the scarcity value, that is, the unmet or satisfied needs of the individual that are at stake. Indeed, what Simmel develops in much of *Philosophy of Money* is not really a theory of status emulation; rather, it is a theory of price formation which is only indirectly linked with the status aspirations of groups or individuals:

> Many commodities are available in such abundance that they cannot all be consumed by the well-to-do members of society and they have to be offered to the poorer strata of society if they are to be sold at all. The prices of such goods cannot be higher than these strata are able to afford. One might refer to this as "the law of consumer's prices limitation," according to which the price of a

commodity can never exceed the amount that the social strata to whom the available supply must be offered is able to pay. This may be interpreted as an application of marginal utility theory to the social scene; instead of the least urgent need that can still be satisfied by a commodity, it is the need of those with the least ability to pay that becomes decisive for price formation.

(Simmel, 1978, p. 219)

The emulatory strain and competitive rivalry so characteristic of human behavior in Veblen's *Theory of the Leisure Class* is often absent in Simmel's *Philosophy of Money* since it is less focused on status phenomena. Worldly prestige obviously matters both to those who possess it and those who do not. Yet, as Simmel points out, money and what it will buy is not to him what it is to Veblen, narrowly interpreted, namely, a social fulcrum for conspicuous consumption, conspicuous waste and exemption from useful labor: that is, status enhancement. Rather, for Simmel's upper class it is psychologically, at least, an easement to material consumption without distraction or discomfort (Simmel, 1978, p. 220). And, for those classes able to emulate it, it performs the same role. In what Veblen might well have regarded as a perverse analysis, Simmel wrote that:

one can observe that, where very low prices for necessary foodstuffs prevail, the culture as a whole progresses only slowly and luxury articles, in which a considerable amount of mental labor is invested, are extremely dear. In contrast, increases in the price of basic food-stuffs usually go hand in hand with a reduction in the price and further increase in luxuries. It is characteristic of lower cultures that indispensable foodstuffs are very cheap whereas higher means of life are very expensive, as is still the case, for example, in Russia in comparison with central Europe. The cheapness of bread, meat and shelter, on the one hand, does not create the pressure that forces the worker to struggle for higher wages, whereas the expen-siveness of luxury goods, on the other hand, pushes these goods completely out of his view and prevents their dissemination. It is primarily making dear what was originally cheap and making cheap what was originally dear ... that implies and brings about an increase in intellectual activities.

(Simmel, 1978, p. 422)

Simmel thus suggests that what Veblen called "idle curiosity," or critical intelligence, can only flourish where emulatory consumption is so intense that it creates insatiable appetites for luxury goods; otherwise, the underly-ing population will merely acquiesce in its traditional stupor. The competi-tive strain and rivalry brought about by striving for uncommon goods, their possession and enjoyment, is what leads to cultural and intellectual growth; whereas in Veblen's scheme of things, emulatory consumption and waste are not only self-defeating, they are likely to inhibit the exercise and growth of altruism, proficiency of workmanship, and most importantly for our purposes, intellectual curiosity (Veblen, 1975, chapters 1–6).

Just as Veblen was aware of the Western cultural crisis at the turn of the century, so was Simmel:

> The rootless, arbitrary character of modern personal life is the expression of this fact: the vast, intricate, sophisticated culture of things, of institutions, of objectified ideas, robs the individual of any consistent inner relationship to culture as a whole, and casts him back again on his own resources. . . . The cultural malaise of modern man is the result of this discrepancy between the objective substance of culture, both concrete and abstract, on the one hand, and, on the other, the subjective culture of individuals who feel this objective culture to be something *alien*: which does violence to them and with which they cannot keep pace.
>
> (Simmel, 1976, p. 251)

What, then, given the existence of this cultural malaise, keeps society from coming apart at the seams? Veblen's answer was, of course, emulatory consumption. The prime social bonding agent in modern civilization is the shared desire of all classes to engage in conspicuous consumption and ostentatious display. This factor, alone, while it does not completely offset or mitigate the cultural crisis does, none the less, give a common thrust to social change; emulatory strain and competitive rivalry hold sway, but so long as the rules of the status game are widely accepted, society will not self-destruct.

FASHION AS A CLASS PHENOMENON

In the analysis of fashion Veblen and Simmel agree that it is a class phenomenon and, furthermore, it is the upper social strata that are the catalysts in promoting differentiation. As Simmel puts it: "fashions of the upper classes develop their power of exclusion against the lower in proportion as general culture advances, at least until the mingling of the classes and the leveling effect of democracy exert a counter-influence" (Simmel, 1957, p. 546). For both theorists fashion thus was a class phenomenon in the sense that the economically dominant classes are the proactive fulcrum in promoting change while the lower classes are mostly reactive in following the example of those above them. In Simmel's words: "The very character of fashion demands that it should be exercised at one time only by a portion of the given group, the great majority being merely on the road to adopting it" (1957, p. 547).

To Veblen, however, fashion is also a social emulatory process providing individuals with no important distinctive traits; indeed, the feeling fashionable individuals have that their appearance is noteworthy is itself mostly evidence of the massive illusions that exist in a fashion-conscious society. But, to Simmel, fashion induces both individualism and social integration. The individual maintains both his distinctiveness and personal honor and at the same time signifies his social circle and class (Simmel, 1957, p. 544). As he puts it in "Fashion":

> Thus fashion represents nothing more than one of the many forms
> of life by the aid of which we seek to combine in uniform spheres
> of activity the tendency towards social equalization with the desire
> for individual differentiation and change.
>
> (Simmel, 1957)

It is Simmel's view that the study of the history of fashions is always an analysis of the necessity of adjusting the two counter-tendencies of individualism and uniformity to each other; indeed, he claims that the varied psychological elements of fashion must all adhere to this basic principle. In Simmel's analysis, importantly, the two counter-tendencies, "individualism" and "social uniformity" help to produce a realm of "freedom" or "breathing-space" (1957, p. 544). In Veblen's view, individuals engaged in emulatory processes, especially fashion and dress, are trapped by their own vanity, but Simmel suggests the real significance of this "freedom" lies in the fact that:

> fashion is also a social form of marvelous expediency, because, like
> the law, it affects only the externals of life, only those sides of life
> which are turned to society. It provides us with a formula by means
> of which we can unequivocally attest our dependence upon what
> is generally adopted, our obedience to the standards established by
> our time, our class, and our narrower circle, and enables us to with-
> draw the freedom given us in life from externals and concentrate
> it more and more in our innermost natures.
>
> (Simmel, 1957, p. 554)

Thus, what to Veblen is a network of invidious distinctions, an inescapable web of honorific prowess and emulatory waste that permeates and contaminates every vital aspect of human existence unless its pervasive impact is checked, is interpreted quite differently by Simmel. Simmel's Germanic cultural focus manifests itself when he uses Goethe as an historical example of someone who strictly adhered to the dictates of fashion and thus reaped the reward of inner freedom, that is, the enjoyment of an unconstrained social breathing space.

> Speaking broadly, we may say that the most favorable result for the aggregate value of life will be obtained when all unavoidable dependence is transferred more and more to the periphery, to the externals of life. Perhaps Goethe, in his later period, is the most eloquent example of a wholly great life, for by means of his adaptability in all externals, his strict regard for form, his willing obedience to the conventions of society, he attained a maximum of inner freedom, a complete saving of the centers of life from the touch of the unavoidable quality of dependence.
>
> (Simmel, 1957, p. 554)

Simmel also believes, however, that the individual courting of "fashion" can be given an ironic twist so that the uniformity of appearance, which for example, creates a certain equality of condition, nevertheless, provides opportunity for the manifestation of power and ego (Simmel, 1957, pp. 554–5). Yet, despite his recognition that fashion induces both individuality and conformity, he also focuses on the extreme degree to which the emulatory response can be personalized (p. 544). Individual consciousness and personal identity are thus shaped through the intense personalization of social emulatory processes having to do with fashion. The critic, including Veblen, might well ask whether such individuals are really "free" and, if so, what significance does such "freedom" bequeath?

However, Simmel embellishes Veblen's theory of status emulation by pointing to the fact that fashions are absolutely indifferent to the functional needs of the individual; evidence of this is provided by the fact that fashion may recommend something materially appropriate in one case, esoteric in another and aesthetically neutral in a third. Indeed, he argues that "formal social motivations" are the ones with which fashion is mostly concerned. Simmel then focuses on what he perceives as the key variable, a variable largely ignored by his American contemporary:

> The reason why even aesthetically impossible styles seem *distingue*, elegant, and artistically tolerable when affected by persons who carry them to the extreme, is that the persons who do this are generally the most elegant and pay the greatest attention to their personal appearance, so that under any circumstances we would get the impression of something *distingue* and aesthetically cultivated. This impression we credit to the questionable elements of fashion, the latter appealing to our consciousness as the new and consequently most conspicuous feature of the *lout ensemble*.
>
> (Simmel, 1957, p. 544)

At this point, Simmel's analysis is contrastable with Veblen's in that the role of the distinguished and aesthetically cultivated individual in the dissemination of fashion has no significant part in the latter's methodologically holistic analysis because the individual is submerged in the social aggregate. At most, individuals can only exemplify social trends for they cannot exist in isolation from others, and as fashion exemplars, individuals possess no meaningful distinctive traits anyway.

Nevertheless, Veblen and Simmel regarded the fashion of their time from a class perspective. Both are explicit in claiming the dynamism of fashion lay in its being a manifestation of social distance between the upper classes and other classes; a social elite emphasizes its particular social position by continuous changes in outward appearance. The constant shifts are due to the fact that, after a certain lapse of time, those styles of the elite spread to other groups, thus losing their original social anchorage. The cycle of fashion is thus repeated anew, but now with something added to signify and, perhaps, intensify social distance.

Veblen and Simmel were in agreement that by the turn of the century fashion had come to have an increasingly powerful influence on the social consciousness. Their analyses both stressed the class basis of fashion. Simmel wrote "great, permanent, unquestionable convictions are continually losing strength, as a consequence of which the transitory and vacillating elements of life acquire more room for the display of their activity." Thus the "transitory and vacillating elements of life," that include "fashion," acquire a social dominance that significantly encroaches on long-held convictions regarding aesthetics, morals, politics and religion. For this reason alone, changes in fashion cannot be ignored or down-played. However, Veblen was much less concerned than Simmel regarding the loss of traditional views and values because he believed they constituted the backbone of "imbecile institutions" and change-inhibitory lag (Veblen, 1918, chapters 5 and 7; 1904, chapters 9 and 10). However appealing these might seem to the conventionally-minded, they were anachronisms which, in the final analysis, would only prove to be obstacles to scientific and technological progress.

THE REFINEMENT OF VEBLENIAN AND SIMMELIAN "MICROECONOMICS"

Veblen's social theory posits human beings who, presumably because they suffer from ego deficiency and status anxiety (the two having a symbiotic relationship) are continuously striving to enhance their self-esteem or sense of self-worth. This is why they are so given to emulatory behavior since, when it is successful, it binds them ever more tightly to those they seek to emulate by rewarding them with more social deference. Critics argue that Veblen's social psychology tends to ignore the role of emotion in his delineation of social roles because of his focus on emulation; there is, for example, little analysis of love and hate and not much emphasis in his work on the modern phenomenon of the increase in nervousness and the importance of the inner realm as a retreat from too much external stimulation. In short, Veblen's portrait of the "inner" man or woman is a narrow one since it largely ignores traits and processes that do not fit his preconceptions of "homo emulatorus" who, arguably, is merely his substitute for such highly stylized types as the neoclassical economist's "economic man" and the sociologist's "oversocialized man."

Perhaps the most useful of Simmel's ideas regarding emulatory consumption and fashion are those which so closely parallel Veblen they can be used as complementary to expand, elaborate and refine his theory of status emulation. Although not specific enough to codify as in Leibenstein's taxonomy of them, they are heuristically intriguing and lend themselves to further refinement of Veblen's larger theory of consumption within the matrix of his historical anthropology. While Simmel's ideas were based on personal observation of Hohenzollern Berlin rather than Victorian Chicago, and refined by reading many of the sources so familiar to Veblen, Simmel stated them roughly simultaneous with Veblen's articulation of them in 1899. To describe emulatory behavior Veblen coined the phrases "conspicuous consumption," "conspicuous waste" and "conspicuous exemption from useful labor." It was his hypothesis that a powerful competitive strain exists in capitalist society causing individuals to seek more status through these behaviors. An individual's sense of self-worth is based on what they believe others think of them and this is largely a function of ability to consume, waste or be conspicuously exempt from useful work. Thus ostentatiously displayed behavior of these kinds is a means of improving the self-image through status enhancement (Veblen, 1975, chapters 2 and 4).

In *Theory of the Leisure Class*, the primary measure of status, and thus self-worth, is ability to pay. In modern terms this might be called the "Rolex watch effect." Since a Rolex is no more functional than a quartz watch, its most important function is as a status signal. In Harvey Leibenstein's post-Veblenian analysis the original emulatory process is labeled "Veblen effects," that is, the higher the price of a good or service the more status it yields.

Leibenstein (1950) also identifies and labels two related types of emulatory consumption "bandwagon effects" and "snob effects." "Bandwagon effects" are characterized by consumers emulating their peers. These occur in industrial societies with a relatively large middle class where the economies are characterized by mass production and consumption. The object of this type of consumption is not, as in Veblen effects, to get ahead of the Jones family, but rather to keep up by joining them on the bandwagon.

"Snob effects" seem inevitable once mass consumption makes it impossible to gain adequate status by ostentatious display of commodities that many others can obtain. In Leibenstein's analysis, snobbery requires the consumer to possess esoteric knowledge as a consequence of sophisticated cultural indoctrination. Thus, only initiates can take part in an emulatory process of this sort. The secrets of "good taste" and "breeding" are limited to the very few with the cultural expertise to enjoy such unique (and expensive) artifacts as Impressionist paintings or boxes at the opera. The point of snobbery, however, is not to get ahead of the Jones's, as in Veblen effects, or to join the Jones's on the bandwagon, but to be different from them through possession and display of cultural expertise and artifacts beyond their aesthetic grasp.

Robert Steiner and Joseph Weiss (1951), in turn, have added a still further refinement to Veblen's theory of emulatory consumption which they call "counter-snobbery." Because snobbery will no longer satisfy the snob's status needs, they turn against it by reverting to a simpler, more austere life style in which the acquisition of material wealth and its display play an insignificant role. Emulatory consumption can thus be summarized under four categories: Veblen, bandwagon, snob and counter-snob effects. As here shown, these have social consequences and visible manifestations which are similar in one respect in that they aim at status enhancement, but they may differ from one another in other important respects.

As indicated in Leibenstein's refinement of Veblen's theory of status emulation, mass production and mass consumption produce "bandwagon effects." Simmel describes the upper classes' reaction to this democratization of consumption as follows:

> Social forms, apparel, aesthetic judgment, the whole style of human expression, are constantly transformed by fashion, in such a way, however, that fashion – i.e., the latest fashion – in all these things affects only the upper classes. Just as soon as the lower classes begin to copy their style, thereby crossing the line of demarcation the upper classes have drawn and destroying the uniformity of their coherence, the upper classes turn away from this style and adopt a new one, which in its turn differentiates them from the masses; and thus the game goes merrily on. Naturally the lower classes look and strive towards the upper, and they encounter the least resistance in those fields which are subject to the whims of fashion; for it is here that mere external imitation is most readily applied.
> (Simmel, 1957, p. 545)

Status anxiety is produced by competitive consumption patterns and, according to Simmel, status frenzy results among various groups within the upper social strata:

> The same process is at work as between the different sets within the upper classes, although it is not always as visible here as it is, for

example, between mistress and maid. Indeed, we may often observe that the more nearly one set has approached another, the more frantic becomes the desire for imitation from below and the seeking for the new from above. The increase of wealth is bound to hasten the process considerably and render it visible, because the objects of fashion, embracing as they do the externals of life, are most accessible to the mere call of money, and conformity to the higher set is more easily acquired here than in fields which demand an individual test that gold and silver cannot affect.

(Simmel, 1957, p. 545)

In the Leibenstein refinement of Veblen and the Steiner–Weiss corollary, "snobbery" and then "counter-snobbery" result; that is, those fearing democ-ratization of consumption engage in display of exotic artifacts and esoteric knowledge that can only be appreciated by those who are literate in the cultural legacy of Western civilization, i.e., its art, literature, music and sculpture. Then, when democratization of cultural literacy encroaches on the practice of "snobbery," the "snob" turns to "counter-snobbery" to demar-cate and elongate the social distance between themselves and the encroachers. This "counter-snobbery" consists of reversion to a simpler and more austere life style which, of course, is visibly displayed for others to admire and emulate, although the display is no longer ostentatious but pretends to be self-effacing. Simmel's readers will recognize the relationship between "counter-snobbery" and his discussion of "ascetic poverty" (Simmel, 1978, p. 251).

Many status emulators in the Veblenian analysis engage in conspicuous consumption, waste and exemption from useful labor in order to enhance their sense of self-worth by commanding more social honor or deference. At times Simmel's status emulator roughly parallels that of Veblen except that his distinctive traits and individual eccentricities are more likely to be in view. It appears that fashion provides an ideal field for individuals with dependent personalities, whose self-identities, however, demand a certain amount of attention and stroking from peers. Fashion elevates even the insignificant individual by making him the embodiment of a class, the distillate of a common spirit (Simmel, 1957, p. 545). Simmel's humor and his originality as a thinker are exemplified in this portrait of the "dude" who has no real equivalent in Veblen's social landscape:

In the dude the trial demands of fashion appear exaggerated to such a degree that they completely assume an individualistic and peculiar character. It is characteristic of the dude that he carries the elements of a particular fashion to an extreme; when pointed shoes are in style, he wears shoes that resemble the prow of a ship; when high collars are all the rage, he wears collars that come up to his ears; when scientific lectures are fashionable, you cannot find him anywhere else, etc, etc. Thus he represents something distinctly individual, which consists in the quantitative intensification of such elements as are qualitatively common property of the given set of class. He leads the way, but all travel the same road.

(Simmel, 1957, p. 549)

Thus the specific social role of individual fashion leaders, in this case the "dude," a role largely ignored by Veblen, turns out to be social property induced by individual mimesis into a distillate of group trends. There is a sense, however, in which Simmel helps enrich understanding of status emulation and emulatory behavior and thus embellishes the Veblenian tradition. In certain respects, for example, he gives a more detailed and intimate appraisal of the motivation for adorning oneself, say, with jewelry or other trinkets than does Veblen. As Simmel puts it:

One adorns oneself for oneself, but can do so only by adornment for others. It is one of the strangest sociological combinations that an act, which exclusively serves the emphasis and increased significance of the actor, nevertheless attains this goal just as exclusively in the pleasure, in the visual delight it offers to others, and in their gratitude. For even the envy of adornment only indicates the desire of the envious person to win like recognition and admiration for himself; his envy proves how much he believes these values to be connected with the adornment. Adornment is the egoistic element as such: it singles out its wearer, whose self-feeling it embodies and increases at the cost of others (for, the same adornment of all would no longer adorn the individual). But, at the same time, adornment is altruistic: its pleasure is designed for the others, since its owner can enjoy it only insofar as he mirrors himself in them.

(Simmel, 1964, p. 339)

Thus, what for Veblen is merely an egoistic act aimed at status aggrandizement, is portrayed by Simmel as morally more complex since it has both an egoistic and an altruistic impulse. Simmel thus specifies the moral dualism of adornment, but his complex explanations of motivation ultimately lead to depoliticization. Nevertheless, Simmel converges with Veblen, but embellishes his own theory (and potentially Veblen's) with these penetrating comments:

[I]n adornment, the sociological and aesthetic emphasis upon the personality fuses as if in a focus; being-for-oneself and being-for others become reciprocal cause and effect in it. Aesthetic excellence and the right to charm and please, are allowed, in this decree, to go only to a point fixed by the individual's social sphere of significance. It is precisely in this fashion that one adds, to the charm which adornment gives one's whole appearance, the sociological charm of being, by virtue of adornment, a representative of one's group, with whose whole significance one is "adorned." It is as if the significance of his status, symbolized by jewels, returned to the individual on the very beams which originate in him and enlarge his sphere of impact. Adornment, thus, appears as the means by which his social power or dignity is transformed into visible, personal excellence.

(Simmel, 1964, p. 343)

CONCLUSION: SIMMEL'S DEPOLITICIZATION VERSUS VEBLEN'S POLITICIZATION OF FASHION

Simmel's analysis of the private psyche is, of course, more "balanced" than Veblen's but this contributes to the apolitical nature of his analysis of fashion and social convention. Two commentators on Simmel bring out this point. E.V. Walter states: "Simmel internalizes and psychologizes freedom, moving it from the realm of external relations to the inner life" (Walter, 1965, p. 162). R.H. Weingartner adds:

Simmel feels deeply the need to dominate the current of experience and to transcend it. But for him, mastery does not primarily mean manipulation. Unlike John Dewey, whose goal is to use and change the world, to bend it to the will of men, Simmel's hope and need is to grasp it intellectually, to comprehend it, to contemplate it.

(Weingartner, 1962, p. 183)

On this point, Simmel's thinking seems to be dominated by a social stoicism and political quietude which may be part of his Kantian inheritance (Davis, 1973, p. 321). The great subtlety of Simmel's ideas regarding consumption, fashion and adornment, interestingly, depoliticize his larger social theory; that is, his attention to shades and nuances of human behavior downplayed by Veblen give much of his work an apolitical cast upon which it is difficult to base public policy. It should be noted, also, that Simmel's analysis lacks the satirical qualities which give Veblen's analysis of adornment such power. No real effort is made by Simmel to mock or discredit such behavior, or to politicize wasteful consumption in hopes of curbing it or otherwise altering it. Nevertheless, although they may lack direct political import, Simmel's points about greed, avarice and cynicism and his blasé attitudes regarding fashion and consumption are relevant to his argument (Simmel, 1978, pp. 255–59).

Although Simmel was not indifferent to considerations of power, it was social and cultural power in the broader sense that interested him, not political power measured in the narrower sense as ability to use coercion and impose binding sanctions; this is what critics presumably mean when claiming he was "apolitical." This is linked, of course, with his disinterest in using manipulative state power to carry out social engineering schemes. What followed from his seeming neglect of political power was that throughout his academic career he rarely focused on the genesis, process or consequences of public policy. Veblen, on the other hand, paid more attention to policy and to the role of government in bringing it about, although he did not have a particularly strong policy orientation either. But the latter can hardly be accused of being apolitical for he is much more value-expressive regarding specific social institutions and cultural practices than Simmel. His readers, particularly in the case of emulatory consumption, fashion and ornamentation, have little difficulty determining what he thinks about them, although differing policy orientations are derived by interpreters from both his social theory and doctrinal preachments (Tilman, 1992 and 1996). Nevertheless, Veblen is an important figure in American dissenting economics because his satire aimed at discrediting atavistic practices and exploitative processes which he both identified and mocked, a claim which cannot be made for Simmel.

But Simmel, too, had intellectual descendants who were politically involved. Although Simmel had major aesthetic concerns and a tendency towards social stoicism and political quietism, his direct intellectual heirs such as Karl Mannheim and especially George Lukacs, were active critics of public policy and politically involved. More generally, the relationship of Simmel to critical theory and the Frankfurt School is worth considering since their dissenting views had political significance. Both Veblen and Simmel are regarded in some circles as eccentric and marginal and dismissed as politically irrelevant, yet both have adherents who stress the political relevance of their work.

The creation of the Association of Evolutionary Economics and the publication of its organ, the *Journal of Economic Issues*, have since 1966 provided a forum for the study of Veblen and his ideas. More recently the Association for Institutional Thought (1979), the European Association for Evolutionary Political Economy (1988), and the International Thorstein Veblen Association (1993), provide evidence of the continued growth of a dissenting tradition with Veblenian roots. Veblen's theoretical and doctrinal arsenal as a dissenter from the neoclassical paradigm in economics and mainline sociology is thus more widely accessible to a new generation of social scientists. As might be expected, no such organizations with political/doctrinal objectives can be directly traced to Simmel in spite of his influence on the social sciences and the recent renewal of interest in his work.[4] Veblen poses clearer political and moral objectives than Simmel because his cultural perspective is more overtly biased and more ethically delineated. As a consequence, Veblen's disciples, the institutionalists, however diverse and eclectic they may be, have coagulated into an international political movement with ideological objectives. While Simmel has influenced many social scientists and humanists, no Simmelian movement as such exists as an organized political body with explicit or identifiable doctrinal aims. Not surprisingly, this is previsaged in their social theorizing and criticism in *Theory of the Leisure Class* (1899) and *Philosophy of Money* (1900) and other writings fin de siècle which deal with fashion.[5]

NOTES

1 See Smith, 1988, pp. 47–56; he believes that Veblen and Simmel are alike in the following ways; "both are centrally concerned with the inner meaning of market relations within contemporary capitalism and the underlying connections between these relations and other aspects of capitalist urban culture." But, Smith hastens to add, "their two analyses, produced in consecutive years around the turn of the century, are strikingly different," and he stresses the differences in outlook between Veblen and Simmel. Also, cf. Joas, 1993, pp. 27–29; Mestrovic, 1993, pp. 13–14, 74–7, 124–5, 249–50, 276–8; Sellerberg, 1994, pp. 59 ff. For analysis of the emerging culture which Veblen and Simmel emphasized, although his focus is Britain rather than the United States or Germany, see Richards, 1990.

2 The two main depositories with unpublished Veblen materials, the Thorstein Veblen Collection, University Library, Carleton College, Northfield, Minn., and the Joseph Dorfman Papers, Rare Book and Manuscripts Room, Butler Library, Columbia University, New York, have no documents directly relevant to their relationship.

3 See Veblen, 1930, pp. 56–179, 231–51, 324–86. Laidler and Rowe, 1980, argue that close parallels exist between Simmel and the Austrians, especially Carl Menger. On the whole, Simmel's neoclassicism and Veblen's institutionalism are thus far removed from each other.

4 To further illustrate, Lawrence A. Scaff (1988) writes that Simmel's "political traits of the war years must, for example, seem like hopelessly apolitical musings of the aesthetic consciousness" (p. 5); his "cultural prowess was gained at the price of his political innocence. His version of Nietzsche was poorly suited to political combat" (p. 13); "Simmel could not be called a feminist; his interests were, as always, guided by an intriguing cultural-philosophical problem, rather than by a concern for political justice" (p. 21).

5 The author thanks Colin Loader, University of Nevada, Las Vegas; David Frisby, University of Glasgow; Dennis Smith, Aston University, Birmingham; and John Brown, Georgia Southern University for aid when the manuscript was in its formative stages. The usual disclaimers hold.

REFERENCES

Davis, Murray S. 1973. "Georg Simmel and the Aesthetics of Social Reality," *Social Forces* 51 (March): 320–329.

Frisby, David. 1992. *Simmel and Since: Essays on Georg Simmel's Social Theory*. London: Routledge.

Joas, Hans. 1993. *Pragmatism and Social Theory*. Chicago: University of Chicago Press.

Laidler, David and Nicholas Rowe. 1980. "Georg Simmel's *Philosophy of Money*: A Review Article for Economists," *Journal of Economic Literature* 18 (March): 97–105.

Leibenstein, Harvey. 1950. "Bandwagon, Snob and Veblen Effects in the Theory of Consumer's Demand," *Quarterly Journal of Economics* 64 (May): 183–207.

Mestrovic, Stjepan G. 1993. *The Barbarian Temperament Toward a Postmodern Critical Theory*. London and New York: Routledge.

Richards, Thomas. 1990. *The Commodity Culture of Victorian England*. Stanford: Stanford University Press.

Sellerberg, Ann-Mari. 1994. *A Blend of Contradictions: Georg Simmel in Theory and Practice*. New Brunswick: Transaction Publishers.

Simmel, Georg. 1900. *The Philosophy of Money*. Reprinted 1978, London: Routledge & Kegan Paul, 1978. Trans. by Tom Bottomore and David Frisby.

—— 1976. *Georg Simmel: Sociologist and European*. Edited with Introduction by Peter Lawrence. Middlesex: Thomas Nelson and Sons Ltd.

—— 1964. *The Sociology of Georg Simmel*. Edited with Introduction by Kurt Wolff. New York: The Free Press.

—— 1957. "Fashion," *American Journal of Sociology* 62 (May): 541–558; originally published in *International Quarterly* 10 (October, 1904): 130–155.

—— 1900. "A Chapter in the Philosophy of Value," trans. by Albion Small, *American Journal of Sociology* 5 (March): 577–603.

Smith, Dennis. 1988. *The Chicago School: A Liberal Critique of Capitalism*. London: Macmillan Education, Ltd.

Steiner, Robert and Joseph Weiss. 1951. "Veblen Revised in the Light of Counter-Snobbery," *Journal of Aesthetics and Art Criticism* 9 (March): 263–268.

Tilman, Rick. 1996. *The Intellectual Legacy of Thorstein Veblen: Unresolved Issues*. Westport, CT: Greenwood Press, Chap. 5.

—— 1992. *Thorstein Veblen and his Critics, 1891–1963*. Princeton: Princeton University Press.

Veblen, Thorstein. 1904. *The Theory of Business Enterprise*. New York, Charles Scribners Sons.

—— 1918. *The Instinct of Workmanship*. New York: B.W. Huebsch.

—— 1930. *The Place of Science in Modern Civilization and Other Essays*. New York: Viking Press.

—— 1964. "The Economic Theory of Women's Dress" in *Essays in Our Changing Order*. New York: Augustus M. Kelley: 65–77.

—— 1975. *The Theory of the Leisure Class*. New York: Augustus M. Kelley.

Walter, E.V. 1965. "Simmel's Sociology of Power: The Architecture of Politics." In *Essays on Sociology, Philosophy and Aesthetics*, Kurt Wolff, ed. New York: Harper and Row: 139–166.

Weingartner, R.H. 1962. *Experience and Culture: The Philosophy of Georg Simmel*. Middletown, CT: Wesleyan University Press.

16

A NEOINSTITUTIONAL THEORY OF SOCIAL CHANGE IN VEBLEN'S *THE THEORY OF THE LEISURE CLASS*[1]

Marc R. Tool

What pertinence does Thorstein Veblen's widely read but insufficiently understood volume, *The Theory of the Leisure Class* (1899), have for those guiding social and economic change in contemporary economies? What does it offer beyond provocative captions and social satire? It is the purpose of this essay to demonstrate something of the continuing relevance of Veblen's contribution by identifying and exploring various aspects of his theory of social change, first introduced in his *Leisure Class*.

As Veblen's first book, *Leisure Class* contains in embryonic form major constructs and analyses more fully developed in his later works. With the addition of the also early methodological essays of his *Place of Science* (1919), an initial exposure to the theoretical core of much of his subsequent writing is provided. Veblen was the unintended founder of American institutional economics. He "compelled a whole generation of economists to search their hearts lest the truth be not in them" (Homan 1928, 107). His philosophical and theoretical contributions continue to undergird and inform contemporary neoinstitutional analysis and policy (Bush 1994, 291–6).

This essay, characterizing his theory of social change, includes the following five components: Part I presents Veblen's general theory of social change as a process of overcoming institutional rigidities and transforming institutional structure. Part II examines Veblen's broad analytical approach to inquiry. Part III considers sources of social change with special reference to human agency. Part IV explores the character of change with particular attention to the Veblenian dichotomy. Part V identifies impediments to social change generated by invidious distinctions. Illustrative material is introduced as space constraints permit.

I VEBLEN'S GENERAL THEORY OF SOCIAL CHANGE

For Veblen, social change is a process of institutional adjustment and transformation. Any human community may be viewed as an "economic mechanism," the structural fabric of which is institutional. "These institutions are
habitual methods of carrying on the life process of the community in contact
with the material environment in which it lives" (1899, 193). Institutions
are "prevalent habits of thought with respect to particular relations and particular functions of the individual and the community" (190). Communities
are under continuing pressure from changing circumstances to modify their
structural fabric. "The readjustment of institutions and habitual views to an
altered environment is made in response to pressure from without" (193).
The old ways no longer well enough serve contemporary demands. Those who
are sheltered from the "action of the environment in any essential respect"
will be slow to recognize the need for change, and may well resist efforts to
modify structure.

Although Veblen speaks often of incessant habituation of behavior and
mind sets and of cultural rigidities, he recognizes that

> any one who is required to change his habits of life and his habitual
> relations to his fellow-men will feel the discrepancy between the
> method of life required of him by the newly arisen exigencies, and
> the traditional scheme of life to which he is accustomed.
>
> (1899, 195)

Given the general interdependence of exchange relations, the appearance of
"pecuniary exigencies" will sometimes be a stimulus for structural change.

Veblen's general theory of social change then rests on the analytical recognition that economies are comprised of structure, most of which has become
habitual. Social change requires the adjustment of the institutional fabric.
Individuals are confronted with pressures to modify habits of mind and
behavior. The predictable differential impact of change leads some to support
and some to oppose institutional modification.

II APPROACH TO INQUIRY

What is Veblen's approach to social and economic inquiry? Upon what sort
of knowledge base does Veblen's theory of social change rest? The short
answer is scientifically warranted esoteric knowledge–factual knowledge,
continuously generated, publicly available, open to challenge. Veblen distinguishes between knowledge claims that are evidentially grounded and those
that are not:

The habit of mind which best lends itself to the purposes of a peaceable, industrial community, is that matter-of-fact temper which recognizes the value of material facts simply as opaque items in the mechanical sequence. It is that frame of mind which does not instinctively impute an animistic propensity to things, nor resort to preternatural intervention as an explanation of perplexing phenomena, nor depend on an unseen hand to shape the course of events to human use. To meet the requirements of the highest economic efficiency under modern conditions, the world process must habitually be apprehended in terms of quantitative, dispassionate force and sequence.

(1899, 304–5)

That is, inquiry is an empirical, objective and processual quest to explain in causal terms.

Esoteric knowledge – non-factual, authoritative, private, privileged – is pursued by members of the leisure class in part to demonstrate their irrelevancy to the world of industry and productive labor. They are engaged in a quest for honorific status.

The canons of reputable living act to throw . . . intellectual interest as seeks expression among the [leisure] class on the side of classical and formal erudition, rather than on the side of the sciences that bear some relation to the community's industrial life.

(1899, 382)

In contrast the artisan class draws knowledge from its industrial connection that "requires a constant recognition of the undisguised phenomena of impersonal, matter of fact sequence and an unreserved conformity to the law of cause and effect" (322).

More generally, Veblen's approach to social and economic inquiry may be characterized as anthropological, historical, analytical, and scientific.

Anthropological

Veblen advised his better students to read, as did he, in the then newly emerging anthropological literature in order to gain "a view of man in perspective and more in the generic than is ordinarily attained by the classical economists" (quoted in Dorfman 1934, 133). Veblen had a continuing interest in behavioral traits of primitive cultures (1899, 6). He engaged in comparative cultural analysis in pursuit of fundamental characteristics, continuing attributes and regularities, and culturally acquired habits of mind and conduct. He was examining "the sequence of cultural evolution" (8). He argues that the continuity of any community is dependent upon its economic institutions.

Historical

Corollary with the foregoing is Veblen's exploration of the transition of cultures through time. All cultures are processual: generally structures change slowly; sometimes they change rapidly. His whole analysis encompassed the idea of cultural transformations. Veblen draws developmental distinctions between and among (a) early primitive cultures (Eskimos, Aniu: small groups, peaceable, sedentary, poor), (b) lower barbarian cultures (Polynesian, Icelandic: differentiation of function but preclass societies), (c) higher barbarian cultures (feudal Europe and Japan, Brahmin India: employments define classes; leisure and lower classes distinct), and (d) contemporary industrial cultures (US, Germany: leisure class preeminent in status and perhaps dominion) (1899, 1–21). He speaks then not only of cultural differences but of historical transformations of cultures.

Analytical

Veblen developed original analytical constructs – including instinct of workmanship, idle curiosity, parental bent, economic efficiency, leisure class, invidious distinctions, conspicuous consumption – to explain in causal terms motivations and habituations that drive conduct, determine the structural ordering of economies, identify sources of productivity, arrange the distribution of income, and define the loci of power. He sought to understand how the institutional fabric is constituted, how it functions, and what the actual consequences of its operations are. His analyses examine a social order in process; his mode of inquiry is then necessarily processual. It incorporates concepts that have a provisional status, that can be adapted to observable changes in institutional form and substance. Construct creation was one of Veblen's fortes.

Scientific

For Veblen, scientific inquiry is a quest for "an articulate recognition of causal sequence in phenomena, whether physical or social" (1899, 386). "The exigencies of modern industrial life," he insisted, "have enforced the recognition of causal sequence in the practical contact of mankind with their environment" (387). The rudimentary pursuit of such systematized knowledge is impaired by "anthropomorphic sentiment," by "an expression of an archaic, animistic habit of mind," by "professions of devotional zeal" and the like (178).

Science is a pursuit of "knowledge for its own sake, the exercise of the faculty of comprehension without ulterior purpose" (1899, 383). The pursuit of scientific knowledge in universities – the "higher learning" – is retarded, regrettably, by judgments of status (382), by invidious distinctions rooted in gender (376), and by resistance from established scholars. "New views, new departures in scientific theory, especially new departures which touch the theory of human relations at any point, have found a place in the scheme of the university tardily and by a reluctant tolerance, rather than by a cordial welcome" (380).

In sum, Veblen's theory of social change is culturally embedded, processually constituted, analytically cogent, and scientifically warranted as explanatory of causal phenomena.

III HUMAN AGENCY AS SOURCE OF CHANGE

In *Leisure Class* and elsewhere, Veblen views men [in this context, generic for persons] as discretionary actors. "As a matter of selective necessity man is an agent. He is, in his own apprehension, a centre of unfolding impulsive activity. ... He is an agent seeking in every act the accomplishment of some concrete, objective, impersonal end" (1899, 15). People are culturally emergent. In purposive interaction with the culture, they acquire habits of mind and habits of behavior (212–30). People live only in the presence of others. Accordingly, terms and conditions of interrelations are from infancy learned and imbedded in the psyche; they constitute habits. "Human nature will have to be restated in terms of habit" (221). People are cultural products even as they are agents in revising the habitual patterns that have become customary and governing.

Given such continuing cultural interdependence and interaction, an individual's personal quest for identity and recognition, for being well thought of, may, in Veblen's view, take either of two forms: First, the engaged individual may be

> possessed of a taste for effective work and a distaste for futile effort. He has a sense of the merit of serviceability or efficiency and of the demerit of futility, waste, or incapacity. This aptitude or propensity may be called the instinct of workmanship.
>
> (1899, 15)

Second, where a culture, through long habituation, honors the

> predatory habit of life ... it becomes the able-bodied man's [non generic] accredited office in the social economy to kill, to destroy such competitors in the struggle for existence as attempt to resist or elude him, to overcome and reduce to subservience those alien forces that assert themselves refractorily in the environment.
>
> (1899, 14–15)

It is Veblen's view that in "the primitive phase of social development" where the culture is peaceable, sedentary, and without elaborate ownership

306

arrangements, "the efficiency of the individual can be shown chiefly and most consistently in some employment that goes to further the life of the group" (1899, 16). The instinct of workmanship fosters esteem and generates emulation in support of "industrial serviceability." If and when a culture passes into a predatory phase of life, however, the magnitude and character of esteem and consequent emulation dramatically changes. "[M]en who constitute the inchoate leisure class . . . must be habituated to the infliction of injury by force and stratagem" (7–8). Activity becomes more and more exploitative. "Tangible evidences of prowess – trophies – find a place in men's habits of thought. . . . Aggression becomes the accredited form of action . . . the . . . worthy form of self-assertion is contest" (17). Seizure becomes an approved means of acquiring goods. They love to "reap where then have not strewn" (14).

Human agency can therefore be exercised in either of two ways: first by engaging in productive work, of which industrial employment guided by the instinct of workmanship is a general characterization; second by engaging in exploitation and seizure guided by the "habitual bellicose frame of mind" reflected in coercive combat. In a "sequence of cultural evolution" from peaceable to predatory phases, cultural conceptions of human worth shift from the former to the latter. Indeed "labour acquires a character of irksomeness by virtue of the indignity imputed to it" (1899, 17). An invidious distinction emerges: industrial labor is demeaning, and therefore irksome; predatory labor may become the main source of social approval. "Industrial employment" gives way, significantly but not entirely, to "exploit and acquisition by seizure." Coercion and intimidation become mechanisms of agency implementation. Shifts reflect altered conceptions of worthiness.

Discretion exists for human agents. Its exercise may often be culturally supported but it will, over time, reflect changes in habits of mind. Meanings of purposiveness will be revised. The predatory proclivity may at times override the instinct of workmanship.

For Veblen, institutional change then is not deterministic in the sense of conformity to some natural or historical law. Veblen offers no great-man theory, "law of motion" dictum, or preternatural account of social change. He sees all cultures as continuously evolving but not according to any predetermined pattern. Habits govern behavior but habits are themselves subject to discretionary alteration when perceived circumstances suggest or demand revision.

He writes:

> Institutions are products of the past process, are adapted to past circumstances, and are therefore never in full accord with the requirements of the present. . . . This process of selective adaptation can never catch up with the progressively changing situation in which the community finds itself at any given time; for the

environment, the situation, the exigencies of life which enforce the adaptation and exercise the selection, change from day to day; and each successive situation of the community in its turn tends to obsolescence as soon as it has been established.

(1934, 191)

What Veblen offers is a recognition of the incessant need for continuing institutional adjustment. The growth of warranted knowledge permits the identification of structure that has become "obsolescent." For Veblen, the institution of the leisure class is one such.

It is clear that Veblen does not advocate a purposive shift to some recipe-like ismic model – capitalism, socialism, communism. He sees economies as processually evolving, complex structural entities. There is nothing in Veblen's *Leisure Class*, for example, comparable to the normative use, by neoclassicists, of the capitalist competitive model as a definer of direction for economic and social change (Tool 1986, 104–25; Tool 1995, 197–211).

Veblen acknowledges that an habitual inquiry approach will define the way factual material is perceived and that the approach, over time, will be refined and the material changed. "The habit of distinguishing and classifying the various purposes and directions of activity prevails of necessity always and everywhere; for it is indispensable in reaching a working theory or scheme of life" (1899, 9). Social change is discretionary; it can be directed as a matter of fact and judgment.

In sum, Veblen's theory of social change affirms that people are culturally emergent, discretionary agents, whose acquired habits of mind and conduct encompass, for example, the constructive instinct of workmanship and/or the destructive predatory bent.

An illustration: A particularly compelling application of Veblen's conception of agency, reflecting the differing impact of the instinct of workmanship and the predatory bent, can be touched upon here only briefly.

In the years following the breakup of the Soviet Union, the discretion held by the central planning bodies was dissolved. Under pressures from Western advisors to "privatize," "stabilize," and "liberalize" the economy, discretion devolved upon plant managers, union groups, and local bureaucrats, but seemingly without guiding patterns or controls that sufficiently embody or reflect the instinct of workmanship. In the absence of effective constraints, opportunistic and criminal Mafias moved in and exploited an unstable and deeply factious political setting. Through bribery, intimidation, payoffs and other forms of coercion, they evidently took control over much of the economy (Goldman 1995, 21; Vanhecke 1995, 15). This substantial dominion served their own invidious interests, not that of the larger community. Control of supplies, prices, deliveries, and labor generated local monopolies and cartel-like bodies responsible to no public body. Accordingly, there was little, if any, continuing or substantive accountability.

Other agents, observing this concentration of control, were left with very limited options – that of joining with or accommodating to Mafia interests. The Mafias' income levels permitted priority claims on such luxury goods as were available domestically and abroad and generated social status for a newly formed "leisure class."

IV CHARACTER OF CHANGE

The Veblenian dichotomy

As captioned by post-Veblenian institutionalists, the Veblenian dichotomy is a construct that facilitates an appraisal of the character and import of social change. The fundamental Veblenian distinction, a dichotomy connoting mutually exclusive paired constructs, originates with his concept of instincts, two of which – workmanship and predation – were mentioned above. For Veblen, as I elsewhere write, "*instincts* are not the hereditary transmission of choice behavior; they are 'native proclivities' which consciousness and intellect channel into culturally acknowledged modes of behavior" (Tool 1986, 35).

Veblen identifies two sorts of instincts: one set supports the life process generally; the other set provides "contaminants" of that process. The former includes the instincts of workmanship, parental bent, and idle curiosity. Workmanship, "occupies the interest with practical expedients, ways and means, devices and contrivances of efficiency and economy, proficiency, creative work and technological mastery of facts," and a "proclivity for taking pains" (Veblen, 1914, 33–4). The parental bent is a proclivity that exhibits "an unselfish solicitude for the well-being of the incoming generation – a bias for the highest efficiency and fullest volume of life in the group, with particular drift to the future" (46–7). Idle curiosity is a drive to "seek knowledge, and value it. . . . men are by native gift actuated with an idle curiosity – 'idle' in the sense that a knowledge of things is sought apart from any ulterior use of the knowledge so gained" (Veblen 1918, 5). The latter proclivities, the contaminants, encompass impulses to predatory behavior and invidious emulation. Practices of exploit, prowess, pecuniary acquisition, and dominion illustrate predation. Practices of conspicuous display and conspicuous waste illustrate invidious emulation (Veblen 1918, passim). Evident is a distinction between constructive proclivities that generate and sustain the wellbeing of communities and contaminating proclivities that sabotage the community's ability to generate and distribute the material means of life.

The Veblenian dichotomy, per se, extends beyond, but does not abandon, the presumed instinctual proclivities of individual persons identified above. What is evident and operative in virtually *all* of Veblen's writings in political economy is a *general* dichotomous principle of institutional assessment and judgment presented in a large number of different forms and versions (Tool 1986, 36–7). That principle juxtaposes ceremonial versus technological or invidious versus noninvidious structure and conduct. For Veblen, the term *invidious* means a "comparison of persons with a view to rating and grading them in respect of relative worth or value" (1899, 34). In *Leisure Class* Veblen says:

> Institutions – the economic structure – may be roughly distin-
> guished into two classes or categories, according as they serve one
> or the other of two divergent purposes of economic life. . . . [T]hey
> are institutions of acquisition or of production. . . . [T]hey are pecu-
> niary or industrial institutions. . . . [T]hey are institutions serving
> either the invidious or the non-invidious economic interest. The
> former category have to do with "business," the latter with industry.
> (1899, 208)

Thus institutions either do or do not enhance human life as a whole and achieve the largest and most serviceable production of goods and services.

His concern is to minimize the damage generated by a leisure class. That class is committed to pecuniary emulation, invidious display, and the pursuit of a life reflecting a "conspicuous exemption from all useful employment" achieved by primary involvement in occupations relating to "government, war, sports, and devout observances"(1899, 40). "Abstention from labour," he says, "is the conventional evidence of wealth and is therefore the conventional mark of social standing" and of worthiness. "Productive labor . . . becomes intrinsically unworthy" (41).

The normative Veblen

The Veblenian dichotomy is the original and primary source of neoinsti-
tutionalists' normative analysis; it undergirds their social value theory (Tool 1986, 33–84). Veblen, however, disclaims, perhaps mischievously, any such normative intent or responsibility. He contends, for example, that he has "nothing to say in the way of eulogy or depreciation of the office of the leisure class as a vehicle of conservatism or reversion in social structure" and that "right" and "wrong" are "used without conveying any reflection as to what ought or ought not to be" (1899, 206–7). Disclaimers notwithstanding, Veblen's dichotomy constitutes an embryonic normative construct.

Digressing briefly, the logic of the matter cannot be at issue. Any credible theory of social change must be normative as well as positive. If social inquiry is to be addressed to problem solving (its only *raison d'être*), there is no way of identifying a problem for inquiry without applying some conception of a difference between what is and what ought to be. The "ought" is a *integral* part of inquiry (Tool 1993, 127–31). Principles of oughtness can be and have been drawn from Veblen's warranted approach to inquiry alluded to above.

Veblen actually utilizes his basic dichotomy as an encompassing governing normative tenet. His inquiry is everywhere driven by an intellectual *purposiveness* that seeks to explain reality in order to foster identification and revision of the "imbecile" institutions that prevent a community from solving its problems of adequate provisioning and more equitable distribution. He distinguishes, on the one hand, between those activities that actually enhance the community's ability efficiently to generate and sustain the flow of real income, and on the other hand, those activities that invidiously divert resource creation and use to comparatively noncontributive forms reflected in invidious display, conspicuous consumption, and ceremonial waste. In so doing, the latter demeans the artisan and industrial members of the community and sabotages their ability to generate and distribute real income. Veblen is indeed a normative theorist; his analytical approach undercuts his normative disclaimers.

Character of change

If we build on the Veblenian distinction in *Leisure Class* between institutions that promote acquisition, pecuniary, and invidious ends-in-view, on the one hand, and on the other, those that promote production, industry, and noninvidious interests, we can identify which are the progressive forces for social change and which are the regressive forces. (For definitive treatments that extend and refine this initial distinction between progressive and regressive change, see Bush 1988 and Bush 1994).

Progressive change in *Leisure Class,* and in Veblen's subsequent writings (Tool 1986, 34–7), is technological and non-invidious. It is accomplished where energy and activity are institutionally coordinated to support the acquisition of matter-of fact knowledge, its application in the tangible performance of productive skills, and the incorporation of competent workmanship. Progressive change is in pursuit of productive efficiency, of technological advancement, and of industrial development for the community generally. Veblen believes that the economy should be managed so that its institutions produce the "largest and most serviceable output of goods and services," with the "most economical use of the country's material resources and man-power (Veblen 1917, 168–9). The community's interest in serviceability and the common man's interest in productive employment and a decent income are to be enhanced by social change.

Regressive change, in contrast, is ceremonial or invidious. It occurs where energy and activity are institutionally coordinated to support acquisition of ownership, competitive advertising, ceremonial status claims, vested interests (a "prescriptive right to get something for nothing"), invidious emulation, and a "conscientious withdrawal of efficiency" in support of business interests (1899, 36–7). "The interest of the community at large demands industrial efficiency and serviceability of the product, while the business interests of the concern as such demands vendibility of the product" (Veblen 1904, 157–8).

Positively stated, progressive change is the quest to direct all effort "to enhance human life," to "elaborate the material means of life" (Veblen 1899, 10) and to reaffirm the dignity and worth of those engaged in providing these "material means of life." Negatively stated, progressive change is to erode the status, power, and parasitic waste of the leisure class. In the most general sense, *Leisure Class* is addressed to repeated demonstrations of the significance of the Veblenian dichotomy in distinguishing between invidious and noninvidious purposes, between what is and is not in service of public purposes.

In sum, Veblen's theory of social change demonstrates, but does not admit, that social and economic inquiry must be normative as well as positive, and be concerned with "what ought" as well as "what is." He actually derives his normative tenet through an historical and analytical review and assessment of conduct and motive, on the one hand, and an examination and assessment of the *character* of consequences invoked, on the other.

Moreover, the Veblenian dichotomy provides an approach for the *evaluation* of the purposes to be served in and by the provision of the means of life and experience. Whose interests are to be served, and to what ends, and with what consequences? The Veblenian dichotomy suggests what sorts of questions to ask, what kinds of inquiry to pursue; it does not spin out automatic or ritualistic responses.

An illustration: Perhaps the most obvious analytical application of the Veblenian dichotomy is directly to address the character of production. What goods and services ought to be provided? To what productive purposes ought any modern economy direct its human and physical resources? When we ask what activities must be undertaken to enhance the community's ability efficiently and noninvidiously to generate and sustain the flow of real income, the response, reflecting Veblen, comes easily. Create and utilize institutions whose primary functions include, for example, the industrial production of goods, production of food and fiber, production and dissemination of reliable knowledge, transport of goods and persons, communication of word and image, protection of environmental quality and ecological balances, provision of medical care, and education of the young (Tool 1985, 108). What is critical for Veblen is that any such categories of activities be undertaken with as little deference to ceremonial and invidious considerations and constraints as is possible.

The same cannot be said of some aspects of the four activity categories – warfare, sports, devout observances, and government – especially selected by Veblen in *Leisure Class*, that are addressed frequently to predatory conduct and invidious emulation. These are noncontributive labor; they do not help extend the community's ability efficiently and noninvidiously to provide and enhance the flow of goods and services. In each of the following four areas, the normative distinction between instrumental or technological interests and invidious or ceremonial interests and institutions will be suggested; the former precedes the latter.

Concerning warfare: While the procurement of military matériel and personnel for defensive purposes, to ensure the continuity of efficiently warranted production, can be justified by a Veblenian, procurement cannot be defended for aggressive and expansionist purposes. The past funding of "star war" missilery and the massive sale of military weaponry to destabilize Third World countries appear to fall outside rational defense needs.

Concerning sports: Organized sports for the young, professional sports as entertainment, and physical activity generally to maintain good health obviously have some defensible warrant. However, the ritualization of habitual conflict, the diversion of university funding to commercial sports programs, the monopolistic control over funding of professional sports, and the public provision and cultivation of status options for the leisure class (golf courses, polo grounds, yacht harbors) fall outside that threshold.

Concerning devout observances: The exploratory organizational quest for peace-fostering theological insights, provision of emotional support for the disturbed, the generation of communitarian impulses, and the like, can perhaps be agreeably sustained in a Veblenian assessment. But the imposition of doctrinaire and autocratic or cultish "religious" beliefs and behavior that demean, intimidate, generate dependency, or impair reasoned reflection cannot be so defended.

Concerning government: Governments have continuing and essential democratic and noninvidious functions to perform to facilitate the determination and administration of public policy. A Veblenian critique invokes an assessment of how that process, for example, is often diverted to serve especially the interests of the leisure class through subsidies, tax expenditures, vested interest funding of campaigns, lobbyists' influence on legislation, and the like.

V IMPEDIMENTS TO CHANGE

In *Leisure Class*, as noted, Veblen's referential content for "invidious" is "a comparison of persons with a view to rating and grading them in respect of relative worth or value" (1899, 34). Invidious distinctions, then, are "aesthetic or moral" characterizations in which human differences – ancestry, ethnicity, gender, race, wealth, caste, class, age, *et al.* – are used as indices of comparative or relative rank, worth, and status. Who is and is not to be judged as meritorious? "[A] process of valuation of persons in respect of worth" (34) defines who is to be regarded as inferior and who as superior.

Veblen's primary use of this construct in *Leisure Class* is to explain the differential significance attributed to categories of employment, beginning with the earliest cultures. He wrote:

> [T]he distinction between exploit and drudgery is an invidious distinction between employments. Those employments which are to be classed as exploit are worthy, honourable, noble; other employments, which do not contain this element of exploit, and especially those which imply subservience or submission, are unworthy, debasing, ignoble. The concept of dignity, worth, or honour, as applied either to persons or conduct, is of first-rate consequence in the development of classes and of class distinctions.
>
> (1899, 15)

Veblen roots the origins of the leisure class in the emergence of this distinction between exploitative and ordinary productive work and its application to the organization of the economic order. What is construed to be worthy activity, exploit, becomes the primary source of social esteem and invidious acclaim. Invidious display fostering invidious emulation becomes the accepted standard of social and personal appraisal. Ownership of property, acquired initially by exploit, later by purchase or inheritance, becomes a conspicuous indicator of achieved status and entitlement to a deferential share of the community's resources. There are many ways in which the leisure class secures and retains its position of status and influence:

One is *conspicuous leisure* (1899, 35–7): The term "leisure" for Veblen, "does not connote indolence or quiescence"; it connotes "non-productive consumption of time" spawned by "a sense of the unworthiness of productive work" and as an indication of the "pecuniary ability to afford a life of idleness" (43). Conspicuous leisure wastes potential productive talent and generates resistance to economic or social change that might impinge adversely on status and/or pecuniary income.

Another is *conspicuous consumption* (1899, 68–101). "Unproductive consumption of goods is honourable, primarily as a mark of prowess and perquisite of human dignity"; in addition, "it becomes substantially honourable in itself" (69). Conspicuous consumption encourages the skewing of production to meet significant demands for high-cost and unhealthy goods, exotic merchandise and services; and encourages unproductive and unhealthy emulation among more ordinary folk.

A third is *conspicuous waste*. Any purchase that augments the "consumer's good fame must be an expenditure of superfluities. In order to be reputable it must be wasteful" (1899, 96). A wasteful expenditure "does not serve human life or human well-being on the whole" (97). "Nothing should be included under the head of conspicuous waste but such expenditure as is incurred on the ground of an invidious pecuniary comparison" (99). "The

314

test to which all expenditure must be brought . . . is the question whether it serves directly to enhance human life on the whole – whether it furthers the life process taken impersonally" (99). Conspicuous waste drains productive effort and resources that might otherwise be used for non-invidious purposes: "[I]t does not enhance human life on the whole"; it enhances the life of a self-serving and power-conscious elite. It "guides the formation of habits of thought as to what is honest and reputable in life and in commodities" (116). It helps elevate invidiousness into a standard of judgment and social ordering.

What all of these manifestations of leisure-class motive and behavior demonstrate, of course, is their near total irrelevance for the development and growth of an economy that is able to provide the material means of life for all members of the community.

Indeed, a view shared by many neoinstitutionalists is that Veblen's characterizations of invidious distinctions, when generalized well beyond distinctions between invidious and noninvidious *employment*, provide a powerful explanatory construct to undergird a credible theory of social change. Distinguishing between invidious and noninvidious judgments and behaviors permits any community to identify real problems and to fashion institutional adjustments to restore congruity and efficiency to the productive process. Why and how is this so?

When human differences are viewed invidiously, some persons are in consequence defined as inferior and unworthy, while others are construed to be superior and worthy. This motive and behavior of demeaning categorizations precludes, erodes, or destroys a sense of communal interdependence and mutual responsibility by setting invidiously defined group against invidiously defined group. Invidiously identified differences do not constructively or significantly enhance the problem-solving capabilities of any social segment. On the contrary, invidious discrimination in educational access and career options, for example, limits or denies the acquisition of needed knowledge and skills. The ability of the community to develop pertinent warranted knowledge and to apply it to the production and distribution of real income is sabotaged. Technological judgments are prevented from pragmatically generating needed institutional adjustments. Problematic consequences are attributed to invidiously defined groups. Substantive analysis identifying the factual determinants of problems is left undeveloped. The task of rationally reordering the fabric to enhance its productive capabilities is ignored. The achievement of a sense of mutual commitment to public purposes is forestalled. Without this mutuality to invoke inquiry and propose substantive structural change, problems will remain unresolved. Constructive social change will be aborted. Conflicts over invidious claims and counterclaims will comprise the universe of "discourse."

Invidious distinctions, then, profoundly *impair* the collective ability to create a viable and learning community, to generate a sharing and egalitarian

315

community, and to ensure the adequacy and continuity of the provisioning process within the community. When invidious judgments are endemic, social dialogue is reduced to placing blame and conduct is directed to getting even. Those made to feel unworthy or inferior live blighted, undeveloped, and hence unfulfilled lives. Their quest for self-esteem and recognition for workmanship are ignored. The emulation by the underclass of predatory conduct and conspicuous waste of the leisure class is demeaning and self-destructive. The contemporary popularity of state and national lotteries reflects this emulative scramble. It is illusory to suppose that access otherwise invidiously denied can be overcome with gaming luck!

Those in the leisure class who are made to feel worthy and superior on invidious grounds also lead underdeveloped and parasitic lives! Their contributions to the substantive generation of the sources of economic growth and development are marginal at best. Their instincts of workmanship are diverted to wasteful and frivolous pursuits; they resolve into an effort "to excel others in pecuniary achievement. Relative success, tested by an invidious pecuniary comparison with other men, becomes the conventional end of action" (Veblen 1899, 33).

In sum, where the use of invidious distinctions destroys the capacity to create and sustain community, the continuity of the community itself will be perpetually at risk. A theory of social change, to be credible, must acknowledge and address this threat to the continuity and efficiency of the social and economic process.

Some illustrations: The invidious use of ancestry in this century has no equal: Veblen, early on, speaks of the "intellectual pre-eminence of Jews" in Europe and contended that persons of "Jewish extraction count for more than their proportionate share in the intellectual life of western civilization." (Veblen, 1915, 223–4). In the Holocaust, perpetrated by Nazi officials between 1939 and 1945, some 6 million Jews were sent to their deaths in concentration camps. Without even approaching the massive, unprecedented horrors of personal and family tragedies experienced, the economic costs alone were monumental. On the assumption that 1 to 2 million were adult intellectuals, well-trained technicians, skilled professionals, seasoned managers, and the like, Western Europe lost a whole multicultural generation of able thinkers and managers in consequence of the predacious genocide grounded solely in the invidious use of a racial-cultural characterization.

The invidious uses of gender and race also generate major social impediments: Affirmative Action programs (measures to correct for prior long-term and extensive discrimination) were introduced in the US in the 1960s to address the problem of discrimination. These programs were designed to open access to jobs, contracts, positions, and higher education to women and racial minorities from which they had long been partially or wholly excluded. As official policy, they were supported politically and intellectually (Livingston 1979). Affirmative Action policies were implemented through quotas, timetables, set-asides, and other measures to increase representation of women and minorities.

That the problems to which Affirmative Action was addressed have not yet been resolved is suggested by the fact that, while women and minorities make up more than 70 percent of the workforce, they hold less than 5 percent of senior management positions in big corporations (Walker 1995, 6). Moreover, median earnings (year round full-time) for men remain roughly half again that of women (*US Department of Commerce* 1994, 431).

Finally, and more directly associated with the leisure class as such, is the invidious use of income and wealth: An invidiously formulated debate over welfare entitlements seems perpetually to be on the political agenda. Those on low incomes who are recipients of public welfare subsidies (e.g., Aid to Dependent Children) are consistently denigrated as a burden that others must bear. Proposals to turn "unearned" welfare into "earned" workfare are legion.

What the denigrators fail to acknowledge, among other things, is that virtually *all members of the community are recipients of public largess* in some significant degree. The subsidies received by the rich, for example, are no more *worthy* than the entitlements received by the poor living at or below the poverty margin, many of whom actually work at the minimum wage. In the federal tax code, for instance, "an enormous array of exclusions, deductions, tax credits, and preferential rates" called "tax expenditures" provide subsidies aggregating hundreds of billions of dollars for those already well off (Peterson 1994, 254–5). Through the receipt of special entitlements and dispensations, and the erosion of progressivity in tax schedules, the economic well-being of upper-income groups are sustained and, from time to time, enhanced.

Similarly, corporate welfare programs in the form of questionable "special spending and tax provisions narrowly targeted to subsidize influential industries" channel billions of dollars in assistance to selected corporate industries each year (Shapiro, 1995, 1). Examples include price-subsidy supports for agricultural commodities, deductions of search and drilling costs for oil and gas industry, low royalties on mining company extractions, and the like (17–27). While all are beneficiaries of one or another subsidy, policy questions remain. Which groups benefit and to what degree? What warrantable public purposes are in fact served by the array of subsidies that obtain? Which ones demonstrably enhance the productivity of the economy and equitably distribute this national product? Invidiously damning subsidies to the poor and ignoring those to the rich masks reality and skirts the needed analytical and normative dialogue.

IN CONCLUSION

The foregoing provides perspective, context, and analytical tools for an interpretative formulation of Veblen's theory of social change. The significance of his contribution in *Leisure Class* is to pose, in a provocative and instructive way, the continuing and profoundly significant questions of: Which direction is forward for an economy? What ought the character of production to be? Whose interests should the economy serve? Where should discretion over policy reside? Which habits of mind and conduct are pertinent to the achievement of economic well-being? Responding afresh to these questions is a research and policy agenda for his followers and for the ages.

NOTE

1 The author wishes to thank Paul D. Bush for most helpful comments on earlier drafts.

REFERENCES

Bush, Paul D. 1988. The theory of institutional change. In Marc R. Tool, ed. *Evolutionary Economics I*. Armonk, N.Y.: M. E. Sharpe.

—— 1994. Social change, theory of. In Geoffrey M. Hodgson, Warren J. Samuels, and Marc R. Tool, eds. *The Elgar Companion to Institutional and Evolutionary Economics L–Z*. Aldershot: Edward Elgar Publishing Ltd.

Dorfman, Joseph 1934. *Thorstein Veblen and His America*. Reprinted 1947. New York: Viking Press.

Goldman, Marshall I. 1995. "Bribonomics" corrodes Russia. *The Manchester Guardian Weekly*. February 26.

Homan, Paul T. 1928. *Contemporary Economic Thought*. New York: Harper and Bros.

Livingston, John C. 1979. *Fair Game? Inequality and Affirmative Action*. San Francisco: W. H. Freeman.

Peterson, Wallace C. 1994. *Silent Depression*. New York: W. W. Norton.

Shapiro, Robert J. 1995. *Cut-and-Invest. A Budget Strategy for the New Economy*. Washington, D.C.: Progressive Policy Institute.

Tool, Marc R. (1979) 1985. *The Discretionary Economy*. Boulder: Westview Press.

—— 1986. *Essays in Social Value Theory*. Armonk, N.Y.: M.E. Sharpe.

—— 1993. The theory of instrumental value. In Marc R. Tool, ed. *Institutional Economics: Theory, Method, Policy*. Boston: Kluwer Academic Publishers.

—— 1995. *Pricing, Valuation and Systems*. Aldershot: Edward Elgar Publishing Ltd.

US Department of Commerce, Bureau of the Census. *Statistical Abstract of the United States 1994*. Washington, D.C.: USGPO.

Vanhecke, Charles, 1995. The Wild West goes east. *The Manchester Guardian Weekly*. June 4.

Veblen, Thorstein B. 1899. *The Theory of the Leisure Class*. Reprinted 1934. New York: The Modern Library.

—— 1904. *The Theory of Business Enterprise*. Reprinted 1932. New York: Charles Scribners.

—— 1914. *The Instinct of Workmanship*. Reprinted 1946. New York: Viking Press.

—— 1915. *Imperial Germany and the Industrial Revolution*. Reprinted 1964. New York: Augustus M. Kelley.

—— 1917. *The Nature of Peace*. Reprinted 1945. New York: Viking Press.

—— 1918. *The Higher Learning in America.* Reprinted 1965. New York: Augustus M. Kelley.

—— 1919. *The Place of Science in Modern Civilization.* Reprinted 1961. New York: Russell and Russell.

—— 1919. The intellectual pre-eminence of Jews in modern Europe. Reprinted 1964. In Leon Ardzrooni, ed. *Essays in Our Changing Order.* New York: Augustus M. Kelley.

Walker, Martin 1995. Grisly experiment on the underclass. *The Manchester Guardian Weekly*, March 26.

INDEX